Briansride

Briansride

A shift worker,
an old bicycle,
and the road to Hong Kong

Brian G. Tripp

Dedicated to my Family,
All of my dear friends,
Everyone who helped so much along the way;
And Diamond Dave.

Table of Contents

1.   the why

In the early afternoon I bought a bunk passage on the Stena Line ferry for the 23:45 sail to Hoek van Holland, near Rotterdam. Knowing I had most of the day to kill, I slowly looped through the streets of Parkeston that were so quiet, one wondered if anyone indeed lived there. Just a few hundred yards from the Harwich Port ferry terminal, I pulled up to Captain Fryatt's pub and knew this would be home for the next 8 hours. Once inside, it was clear that the Captain's was the central meeting place for the local dockworkers; and bored thirsty travelers, awaiting their embark.

The barmaid was kind enough to let me stash the bike in their side yard behind a locked steel gate. Once settled, the local patrons started asking about the trip and before long, I was right at home as the pints flowed and the day wore. I became a guest local yob trading barbs, jokes and insults with the regulars and being let in on all the juicy gossip of their small seaside town. They fed me and beer'd me and shared their smokes, and kept me laughing well into the evening; all the while watching a flow of residents, travelers and transportation workers come and go.

Upon leaving that night, filled with a good meal and a vigorous buzz, they all wished fond farewells. I faded into just another passing traveler who had taken part of their hospitality, moving on to leave them at their bar stools, pondering the daily events and rumors in their little corner of Dear Old Blighty. I pedaled out to the ferry under a strange sensation. It was the mix of lagers and the cold North Sea evening air, the giant ferry lit up against the dark night, and squaring up with the truth that this was it. I was really leaving England and heading for Europe with the apparent plan to cross it and Asia on a tottering pedal bike. The hesitations were soon quashed by the hustle and tempo of the dock compound.

I was quickly guided by uniformed Stena agents into lanes which had me queuing up, dwarfed among the headlight wash of lorries pulling freight trailers, mixed in with autos and scurrying dock agents. I squirmed my way through the heavies and up the ramp into the brightly lit white steel belly of the big ship, while flashing my ready paperwork to all who asked. Once inside, the load masters were shouting out orders as they directed and secured the traffic as quick as possible. Along with a couple of Brit cyclists who were heading for Paris, we were pointed to a side room in the hold that contained several other bikes, where we lashed ours to a rail. I quickly grabbed what I needed from the bags, then headed up to the main deck several flights above. In my Captain Fryatt's stupor, I hadn't paid attention to the color-coded stairwell.

After a short night in the bunk, I took the morning coffee at a window table, staring out at the approaching foggy coastline of Holland, and came to terms with a painful toothache that had now gone beyond a steady dose of aspirin. Descending the wrong stairwell put me at a loss to find the bicycle room among the white metal doors, lining the wall of the parking deck. With the ship emptying out, I finally asked for help from a deck agent who gave me that roll of the eyes reserved for a fool, and pointed out the bicycle hold where I found mine, the only one left. Welcome to Holland.

It was a sunny Spring day and the surreal feeling of fear and doubt from over two months ago on the journey's first day outside of a pizza parlor, just 35 miles from my California home, came rushing back. Pedaling out of the ferry's hold and down the ramp, the Dutch docks filled the view. I deliberately watched as the front tire rolled off the steel ramp and onto the Continent, and remember holding the moment, a pit in the stomach, that this was the first few metres of pavement that would someday end in Hong Kong. The boyhood fantasy of Pacific to Atlantic was now over the shoulder. Atlantic to Pacific? The tremble stemmed from realizing this part had never been seriously thought out, only fleetingly imagined.

Months prior, as the big departure day approached, I was hoping to keep it low key. The moments after awaking before the feet hit the floor, were spent with the thought that this was the last wake up in my own bed for months and months. This morning would be the last few moments with my wife Sheree and youngest son Cody. His brother Shay was off at college, but Sheree's nephew Caillen was visiting from England, and my brother Kenneth made it up from San Diego. It was a very important family moment given the inherent uncertainty of the journey, as well as the concern of a grand hoopla sendoff being wasted on a guy who may only make it to Arizona and decide that this is too hard. My good friends wouldn't hear of it though, and buddies Bob and Todd, Doug, James and Jimmy rode their motorcycles out from the San Francisco area. Another friend, Chris, threw his bike in the back of his truck and drove out with his son Shea, planning to pedal out with me the first few hours, Shea driving the chase truck.

Jimmy presented me with a good luck card signed by many of my workmates, and an envelope with almost $200 in collected donations, mostly in ones, with the running joke that I'd be able to hit every highway strip club between here and Texas. Everyone took a turn at riding my wobbly touring bike up and down the street, and then with video rolling and pictures clicking it was hugs and handshakes all around. A farewell kiss from Sheree and we were off. It was Groundhog Day, February 2nd, 2008.

2

The date of the annual eccentric event in Punxsutawney, Pennsylvania, never crossed my mind while planning the trip. Several times during the ride, people asked about the significance of starting on that day, but to me it was just Saturday morning; given the plot of the Bill Murray film, it would come to be apt. Awake and pack the bike, ride all day. Awake and pack the bike, ride all day. As Chris and I pedaled out of the neighborhood and down the canyon towards the valley floor, my friends zoomed up from behind and took positions all around us. Enclosed in a circle of snapshot shooting motorcyclist, I felt like a slow-moving head of state. Later that evening in town, a friend of Cody's would tell him he had witnessed the sight as he drove up the hill that morning; he didn't know if it was a funeral or an accident. Nah. That was just Dad.

Chris and I pedaled along the back roads heading towards a lunch plan in Gustine, about 30 miles south. The loaded bike amounted to 95 lbs. That, plus an out of shape body, made for a struggle to maintain Chris's casual pace. We must have looked like the Odd Couple with me in khaki pants and a flannel, humping a bike loaded to the gills, while Chris sported skin tight spandex and riding a new carbon fiber road bike. I tried to maintain a normal conversation between gasping for air and trying to fight the wobble, realizing the weight was too much for the frame and wheels. Relaxing my grip would mean a rapid shake of the bars, and taking a look behind would send it heading for the roadside. To tell the truth, this was the first time the bike had been ridden since loading it up, other than a short run up and down the street at home, it wasn't up to the task. The bike was unpredictable and by the time we arrived in Gustine and found Shea, then hit up the small pizza joint, I knew I'd made a terrible oversight; the bike was dangerous.

The girl at the counter had seen us pull up, and Chris let out a laugh when she asked how far we were heading. "I'm done" he says "but he's going to Hong Kong." "No really, where are you going?" She clearly didn't buy the story. As we sat at the table, a feeling began to creep upon me that these last few words between the three of us were the last of my normal life. Your hours, days and years, of circling between the home and the work life. The wife and kids and neighbors, the house and car and life's maintenance routines. The stores you shop, the restaurants we frequent. All the people you see every day at work, always a common bond of tasks and problems and decisions we share. Real friends you see every day and have known for years, that give one a sense of "this is my place."

We said our final goodbyes as Chris and Shea loaded up his bike, they then drove off and out of sight; and the feeling hit me full force. Perhaps the first time the Northern lights are witnessed, or the first few minutes following a bad car accident, surreal is an apt word. Seemingly trapped in a dream state not knowing if the situation is real or imagined. For the most part, people throw the word around loosely, hell I thought I knew what it meant. Standing on the sidewalk outside the Pizza Factory, I looked down on my spindly shaking ride, a twenty-five-year-old bicycle, and no plans but a handful of Google maps. Just the thirty miles to here was an effort. Across America? And Europe? And Asia? My simple-minded naiveté of the time and distance and effort kicked at the gut. Home was just a phone call away, but I couldn't go there, a child's fear gripped at my chest. Seeing Chris and Shea disappear, I couldn't recall ever feeling that truly alone and afraid before. What have I done?

And now, in front of the Hoek van Holland terminal grounds, that eerie trepidation had awoken and had time to take over again. Despite already crossing the States, I was awash in the emotion that all of the effort so far merely amounted in delivering me to here, where the journey truly begins. After a two-month ride across America's southern route, and a jaunty couple of days in the English countryside, the wheels had now rolled onto Eurasia, the expanse before me was the world's largest landmass. The bike and I such a tiny part of it, all poised at the essential moment of the second starting point. Whether I made it all the way or not, whether my final days awaited, this was my fate. A lifetime of two wheels and daydreams brought me to this junction, as the morning fog burned off. The small talk with the nattily dressed custom's officers, the sound of their solid stamp on the passport, I still remember it. It was April the 16th.

The States were now a memory, a stark exhibition run to school me for the real deal. Finding stories online of folks who had crossed the U.S. wasn't hard, so many had done it. Finding the stories of people who had traversed Europe and Asia took a little more searching, and finding tales of those who had strung the two together...well I just couldn't find them. I knew well that people had, some would take years to touch upon every continent and make a life on the road. It's just that when searching for advice and tips of a direct bicycle circumnavigation, in the waning months of 2007, they weren't there.

Two and a half months previous, when that February departure morning arrived, I hadn't the faith. The previous four months had been spent furiously planning and preparing for the journey. It started a year earlier in January 07', while rebuilding an old Honda dirt bike for a Walter Mitty dream of riding it to the tip of South America. By October, I had become overwhelmed with the task, there was so much more to do to complete the motorcycle and arrange the leave from work; and squeeze the money from a tight family budget. The hearsay dangers of traveling alone through Central and South America were balanced with the attractions and challenges, and as the months rolled on, the little time left was adding to the pressure I was trying to escape from.

Everyone answers their own question as to what it's all about. Life was already 2/3rds over and what had I done? Sometime in your early teens you accept you'll never be a quarterback for the Dallas Cowboys. Your twenties' see the Presidency slipping away, and the prospects of retiring as a forty-year-old millionaire start waning in your 30's. What's left is a nice guy who has done the right things, and hopes that when it's over your people will have nice thoughts about you from time to time; in other words, I was just like everyone else. My wife Sheree had seen me lose it and talk too loud on occasion, threatening to go to work and resign and pack it all in to start a new life somewhere else; while caring less and less about the obligations of home. As time went on, and the rants ramped up, the breaking point was in sight, something was going to happen. In her wisdom, she decided to aim it in a direction, bend it before it breaks. She began suggesting I should just take a leave of absence from work and relax, maybe look for another job or take some classes. All I heard was "take some serious time off" and I knew what I had to do. It was either going to plunge me deeper into the well, or cure the way I was looking at midlife.

Instead of chasing another wild sprint that could be accomplished some other time my thoughts began taking a longer view. Why zip down to Tierra del Fuego just to tell yourself that another want is scratched off the list? What is the point of venturing out to so many places on limited time? What was the prey? Like a straight line traveling through every wavering phase of my life since youth, was the conception that "when I retire" or "one of these days" or "if I ever hit the lottery," I would pack a simple bicycle and roam around the world. To slowly get to see and meet the people that shared this tiny rock, the fantasy of having no agenda or timetable, and to languish in warm climes as I followed the seasons around the earth. The bicycle inherently causes you to slow down, no throttle to determine where you'll be the next day; quiet, peaceful pedaling, following the terrain for months on end. No demands or goals, just pedal...another daydream. In October 2007, I threw out all the South American maps and the dirt bike dreams and changed the plan. Why just visit the asylum when you can get lost in its hidden corridors? I know what I'll do, I'm gonna ride my bicycle to Hong Kong.

Rather than a relaxing respite, my "vacations" had a common theme. Cramming an adventure into an event that required months of planning, and daily exertion once underway; usually in the form of a motorcycle ride around a chunk of North America, or a week riding hard in Baja, or racing worn out rental bikes through the Alps on a shoe string budget. I had friends that would take vacations and go lie on a beach somewhere in the Caribbean, or enjoy a quiet week of skiing in the Sierras. In my heart, I knew that stepping back would be the choice of a balanced individual. The free fall intensity of choosing a large adventure and pegging to it a departure date and associated benchmarks, kept me at a fever pace for months. The problems of work and home took a back seat as I escaped in the planning of it, mapping out routes and mileage, living for overtime at work to fund it all. Like a drug or a bottle, the heart knows the adventure is a mask to wear while enjoying the illusion that everything else in life is just fine. Yet unlike anything else I'd ever done, on the morning of departure from home, I was truly unsettled.

The chance of getting hit by a car or beaten for my camera and wallet, or simply disappearing in the nether world of Eastern Europe seemed likely. I'm nobody special who had just bitten off more than he could chew, and everyone, from my relatives to my neighbors to my workmates had been told of this ambitious plan, and now there was no out that would allow me to save face with them ever again. My wife and boys would be happy and relieved if I called it off and the thought of saying goodbye to them had made this dangerous and unnecessary trek feel small and selfish. I felt very small and selfish inside.

But this was it, I've entered Europe. When that pudgy clown pushed away from the Pizza Factory 76 days ago, the only answer was to go as far as you can today, then go as far as you can tomorrow, then string together all these successful days for the next three quarters of a year. The worn advice "be careful what you wish for" was like a screaming flashing red billboard filling the view. I didn't want to leave, I couldn't wait to leave. Get moving. Be the moose.

Clicking into the pedals and heading out on my own, the goodbyes had been said, the money was in place and the time was mine. After the initial hesitation, the brain began to settle down. This was going to be an attempt to ride around the world, an attempt, I couldn't assume that everything was going to work out and mindlessly ride in some trance. To pull this off, it was going to be a challenge every day to stay safe and foresee problems, and avoid bad people and places that could derail the journey; the slightest issue could grow and end it all. Given the heavy load and rough roads ahead, a frame or fork failure was a concern from the first day out. A bad crash or a theft or an illness, none were unreasonable possibilities.

But that first day away from home had me thinking that this whole idea was a crazy crap shoot. It wasn't just a tour to Los Angeles, or San Antonio, or even Orlando, but all the way across the planet to Hong Kong. A true family emergency at home, or simply not being able to maintain the pace needed for the time off granted from work could end it; due to limited funds and time, and patience from the family, this was going to be a one-shot deal. The two thousand dollars already spent on visas and shots, the leave approval from my job and my finances, it all weighed in. Just get through today in one piece, easy. Tomorrow is...well tomorrow is not my concern. Today is all that matters. What could go wrong?

2. and go

Road trip! That's what it felt like the first day or so heading south, like a slow motorcycle ride through the familiar Central Valley. My thoughts were in the disbelief zone, while the physical limits were nagging loudly, keeping the pace very casual the first few days. Friends had asked about my training program leading up to the ride, and I just played it off. Jeez people, what do I need to train for? "I'm going to be riding a bicycle every day for months!" Presently that didn't seem like a cool answer. I imagined people reading the morning newspaper, glancing over a blurb about the inactive guy on the wrong side of forty whose pump pops while taking a crack at some screwball bicycle trip. They mutter "what an idiot," and turn the page.

The first couple of days only amounted to about sixty miles. On the first night, just north of Los Banos, a kind-hearted dairy farmer let me set up camp in his front yard, just as an all-night rain began to fall. The next day was Superbowl Sunday, calling for a short ride to Dos Palos in order to grab a room and watch the game. The sweet little Hindu lady running the half star motel kept insisting that I give her my car's license plate number; so, I did. As I was sitting there celebrating that most hallowed of American holidays with a six pack and a can of Chunky Soup, it struck that I could have called up my son or a buddy, and had them drive an hour to watch the game with me. But it wouldn't have been right. The goodbyes had been said, the journey had begun, and I had to look ahead. The New York Giants, who'd have figured?

The next few days was a tour of the in between towns, places set between the main travel routes of Interstate 5 to the west, and Highway 99 to the east. Firebaugh, Mendota and Kerman. The good Reverend running "Our Lady of the Assumption" in Caruthers gave me his blessing to snooze in the church's side yard, as he worked late into the night. The grounds were being prepared as a polling station for the next day's "Super Tuesday," focusing on the Democratic and Republican Presidential primaries. Then, it was on through Hanford and into Corcoran, where I took a cheap room, only after a worn-out trailer park didn't like my type.

My legs and lungs were like an old neglected car in the backyard, being coaxed back to life. The right knee was clicking and thudding with a dull pain on every stroke. The Brooks leather saddle, the pride of Smethwick, was causing butt blisters already, and the neck was aching from holding it up, to look forward. Experimenting with the weight distribution wasn't helping with the unstable handling issues, coming to wobbly terms with the shaky beast had only one solution: do not take your hands off the bars. I couldn't quell the rapid headshake. Yet despite the problems, the saving grace was thinking about how a real honest to goodness lifelong dream was unfolding. The brain was in overdrive with thoughts of taking photos and feeling the land, feeling the road. Daydreams of really pulling this off pinged through my head, joined by the sensation that the terrain and wind and clouds and the bike were all connected somehow, and playing in the same game. Like being shot out of a cannon you didn't know you were in.

The ride slowly passed through crops and orchards, then into vineyards and dairies. The land was so flat and the mountains so far away, that the day's goal was to just head for the horizon. A daisy chain of mini mart stops; eat a couple of bananas, drink down a chocolate milk, and keep on rolling. Eventually, on the fifth day, the oil derricks of Bakersfield appeared. After a night to the north and a night to the east of that wide congested sprawl, came the first big climb. A thirty-five-mile ride with twenty-five of it climbing to the top of the Tehachapi's over Highway 58, sporting a 3600-foot elevation change. That morning at a highway breakfast diner, when I asked for a large glass of milk, the typecast waitress laughed out loud. She said "What? Are you still a little titty baby?" A nearby table with four truckers chuckled at the remark, I just sat there, silent. They just had no idea what my day was going to be like.

The knee was griping really loud but the mind said suck it up, it can only get worse or go away. I had a small stash of painkillers to break into in case of an emergency, and had considered taking one before the climb, but thought better of it. It would be a sweet reward at the end of the day, when I could kick back with a beer and a bed. For hours, it was a slow deliberate climb up and up as I tried not to think about the heavy load and the wobble, just search for the trance and the perfect gear, and get lost in the iPod. After a lunch in Keene at the halfway point, the road continued climbing, until breaching the mountain top town of Tehachapi. The evening was very cold, and I was glad to find a cheap room. After a couple of beers, I hit the sack early, but then came the trains. They were passing through town at all hours of the night, blaring me awake with their serious whistles. I don't know how people sleep there.

The next morning, the reward came. The twenty or so miles into the Mojave Desert and its namesake town was either an outright downhill, or at least a happy slant. Stopping for a break sent me tumbling onto the pavement of a Mojave gas station, and it hadn't been the first time. Until this trip, I had always used the "toe strap" style pedals, the familiar leather straps that hold the foot centered. For this ride, I decided to jump into the new century with a set of "clipless" pedals and its partner in crime, the cleated shoe. This popular and efficient method uses a "click in–click out" cleat on the bottom of the sole, that firmly attaches itself to a fitting built into the special pedal. A quick side motion

of the foot locked the shoe in or out of the contraption, and when given thought, worked a treat.

When not given any thought, it sometimes left me free falling to the ground while wishing that darn foot would break loose. Mine was a bumpy learning curve. A recurring theme was when I would touch the right–side forward pannier against the street curb, it then catches and pulls the bike hard to the right. The pannier releases and falls off as I go down in the street, never getting the left foot released. Bang, boom. Look around to see who was watching. Standard learning curve, with abrasions.

Today's issue wasn't brain fade. The nut plate of the left shoe's cleat had failed, becoming dislodged from its molded anchor point, which prevented the cleat from turning as I "clicked out." Hence, the cleat, and therefore the shoe, remained locked to the pedal. Fortunately, there was a second nut plate aft of the failed one, that I could attach the cleat to. Unfortunately, this positioned the pedal closer to the foot's arch. Not a big deal in most cases, but this wasn't most cases. With just one week into the journey, my brand new $90 mountain bike shoes were not living up to the task. I tried moving the right cleat to the same setting but the pedaling just didn't seem right, the forward cleat was closer to the ball of the foot and gave the best power position. And from that day forward, the right foot felt good, the left, a bit odd.

After a night of urban camping in a vacant lot alongside a busy road in Palmdale, it was a long day with a short climb over the San Gabriel Mountains. On February 10th I made it into the Los Angeles Basin and headed for my stepbrother Geoff's house in Highland, well after dark, and well after his welcoming party had gone home. The final hours that day were spent wading through the lamp lit suburb streets of San Bernardino, with Geoff occasionally homing me in on the cell phone. Damn it was good to get to his place.

Expecting my arrival hours earlier, his girlfriend Willow and he had planned a nice dinner with their neighbors, Matt and Ruth. The party re-started after my arrival with cold beers, good food and great people. I was liking my chances after putting down a seventy-five-mile day. I recall telling Ruth, that while pedaling through the dark streets tonight, the thought occurred that I had just ridden a bicycle to Los Angeles! This was the furthest I had ever pedaled a bicycle. The monumental contentment washed over me, I knew then I was going to kick it here for a day before riding on to Mom's place, forty miles away.

Geoff took the next day off of work and we spent it doing what brothers do best. Sit in the quiet backyard, drink beer, talk over the family news, and solve all the world's political problems. He and his brothers, Greg, Gary and Glenn came into my world back in the Seventies. I was in my teen's when my folks went their separate ways, and I can't say as I minded. I was young and wild and scrambling a little money here and there, with no one at home to say when too much fun was enough. Poor Mom had a time of it, working as a telephone operator at the State Capitol building while holding the house together and providing for big sister Maureen, little brother Ken and myself. One day she met Jim from nearby South Lake Tahoe, and things began to change.

Jim's wife Helen had passed by way of cancer some years before and these two struck up a good thing, soon afterwards I met the brothers. Six to ten years older than me, and a ton of life experiences between them, Greg and Gary came first. At the time Glenn was serving in the Navy and Geoff and his girlfriend were hitch hiking their way through South America. Before long, Mom and Jim tied the knot and he moved in to our Carson City home. After an initial spate of clashes with Jim, mostly originating from his moving in and me being an unruly party animal fool, I began to see and heed his wisdom. The man lived as an example of how a gentleman should conduct himself, and over the years my respect for him grew. His sons and the three of us became close friends, and when he passed back in 99,' it was like losing my own father. Mom never went looking again, and I still love solving the world's problems with the G brothers and a nice bottle of scotch.

After a day of rest in Highlands, it was a long forty miles to Mom's in Hemet on the very eastern edge of L.A.'s spread. Not a great distance, but I began the day with a "just wanting to get it over with" attitude and then managed to find a couple of unexpected climbs along the way. The lay-off day at Geoff's reminded the legs and lungs that they're not supposed to be working this hard. But once at Mom's, it was all better. Death and taxes and never going hungry at

10

Mom's house are things we can all count on. Tucked away in her tidy double wide mobile home neighborhood, dear Mom had a nice life that was filled with other retired Moms; who had a penchant for card games and going on cruises. Volunteering for this and that and bingo filled her days, and on occasion, her and a few other wild Grandmas' would hit the road for a weekend in Vegas. They were kind enough to spare us the details.

What was to be a day of rest turned into two when the rains came on the departure morning. The visit/eat/visit/eat routine was only broken for a quick trip to Wal-Mart for a haircut and to pick up a cheap gel cover for the bicycle seat, to fight back the rising blisters. The two days were spent just relaxing and watching my legs not move, and fielding a mother's worries. When her copious questions hit upon my first aid kit, she soon donated an unopened bottle of Vicodin's to the stash; the extra's seemed unnecessary at the time. The next day, we packed the bike and gear into Mom's Hyundai sedan and drove the 15 miles north to Interstate 10, my home for the next month. Oh man, what an emotional moment that was, with Mom welling up as I reassembled the bike at a gas station. Like everyone, Mom had no idea when she'd ever see me again, and was quite aware that this trip wasn't going to be as easy as I kept assuring.

Ahead of me was the vast nothing of the southwestern desert and beyond. Towns became scarce after this point and the next real city was Phoenix, 300 miles away. Behind me was everything, as if my real world was there over my shoulder, and everyone in it had come forward to wish me off. A few precious moments that told me I was to be missed. For those few, it was like taking something very dear from them and leaving only an empty promise of return in its place. I tried to imagine sending one of my sons off on this trip, armed with an old bicycle and a pocketful of Google maps. From that perspective, this seemed really stupid.

3. the how

And now it truly began. After a full week of angling south, the front wheel was pointing east. Once I'd said goodbye to Mom, the road and the wind worked with the bike and carried me with little effort for fifty miles, past the artificial luxury oasis of Palm Springs, and onto its working-class neighbor of Indio. Riding I-10 was great, the state laws from California through to Texas allowed bicycles on the Interstate, due to the lack of alternative routes in the wide-open Western deserts. In the planning stage, the idea of planning a bicycle ride on a freeway sounded like the punch line of a joke.

Double-trailer big rigs barreling along doing ninety, mesmerized travelers bored and flashing dreams as they fight to stay awake on the endless straight road. The reality was a revelation. Rather than straddling the few inches of space between the white line and the pavement's edge of a county road or surface street, here there was room. On the smaller roads, the cars and trucks were still humming along at seventy, only a few inches away, whereas Interstate-10 gave me a ten-foot-wide safety lane. Many truckers would go by giving a wide berth, and I'd never have the heart to tell them how much their well-meaning horn blasts would startle me right out of the seat.

The long road ebbed and flowed the next day out to Desert Center. Most of the day was a gradual climb, but not enough to whine about, just enough to ask a positive force of every pedal. With the tunes on and eyeballing the next rise, time passed as my thoughts kept shining on the disbelief of not having to go to work again until almost next winter. Every company mishmash plan or problem, or work-related human issues, gone. Just find the right gear and push. My new life that may, or may not, pan out

Desert Center is everyone's imagined place of a forgotten western Twilight Zone roadside hamlet. A gas station, the post office and a café, the only concerns left. Whatever once was, has appeared to have been blown away by the dusty desert winds, eerie vacant. Walking into the cafe was like taking a step back five decades. A row of old wooden phone booths survived among the paint starved walls. Several of the dining counter stools were just stumps, missing the seats,

it gave the impression that someone started to vandalize the joint and then business continued on as usual. Its silver lining was the busy Mom running the place, she was friendly and chatty, and in  between taking a couple of orders and keeping an eye on her kinetic young son, she outlined the handed down history of the little niche.

Seems this place had been serving patrons around the clock since it opened back in the 1920's. During the War, General George Patton set up a tank training base nearby to simulate the conditions of North Africa, "and he used to sit in that booth right over there for dinner, and used the same phone booth every Friday night to call home." Then came the shocker, Desert Center was one of the cradles of managed health care in America.

Ol' Henry J. Kaiser, the great 20th century industrialist, had contracted with a local doctor back in the 1930's to treat his workers on the Colorado River Aqueduct project. He deducted a nickel each day from their wages for the coverage. It eventually morphed and snowballed into Kaiser Permanente; never judge a book by its cover. This place had some interesting history, and the food was good too. At the end of the evening she ok'd me to crash in the rusty gutted caboose in the side lot. The digs had seen its share of drunken and amorous teenagers judging by the beer cans and spray-painted wisdom's.

Departed the caboose and flowed out onto I-10 like Huck Finn hitting the river, it was February 17th. That day saw fifty vacant miles of desert shrub-land. Not a tree or a building in sight, all the way to a KOA campground on the Colorado River, in the oasis town of Blythe. Early the next morning, I climbed into Arizona over the Dome Rock Mountain range, crossing my first state line and leaving California behind. Rolling down the other side, I could see a far-off dot in the distance behind me. Soon it became Nick, a Rastafarian looking guy who had pedaled out from Minnesota, and spent three months working

construction jobs in California. Knowing there was nothing ahead of us for many miles, we hit a dried-up little market in Quartzsite for some camp food. As we left, I told him to not wait; ride your pace and I'll ride mine.

Thirty-five miles later, on a good rhythm across a cactus and mesa vista, we came to a highway rest area. It was just about sunset, and Nick had already been there awhile. We set up the tents along the back-fence line and started up the dinner of soup, ham and cheese and tortillas. He was about my oldest son's age and a real sharp kid. As we looked out over the desert scrub and the distant craggy-hill skyline, we finished off a couple of the warm beers I had left over from Blythe, and talked about our trips. His plan was to head for Florida and then loop up, back to home. I fashioned a pipe out of an empty beer can and offered him a hit, to smooth off the day, but he declined. He said he had done plenty of it, and decided it wasn't for him. I'd judged the book by its dreadlocks, and I was wrong.

Up and at em' the next day, busted camp early after a breakfast of oatmeal and coffee, and hit it. Nick was going to break north at Phoenix, and as he motored away, I knew that I'd seen the last of him. Putting my head down, I zoned out and went thirty-four miles before pulling into a rest area, that was closed for maintenance. Arizona had the best rest areas I'd ever seen, they were landscaped and clean, and manned with an attendant that kept things nice; he didn't seem to mind my invasion. This was cool, had the whole place to myself, while lunching on the leftover ham and cheese, enjoying my personal patio on the desert. I lingered for an hour, feeling like part of the quiet terrain. Looking out on the travelers rushing by on the highway, I had the thought that no matter where they were going, they would have to come back. I was going all the way around.

Twenty-five miles later, the day was closing in on the outer edges of Phoenix's influence. After a few days out in the desert, the idea of entering and traversing a big city seemed like chaos. Getting closer to the city also limited the camping options, and as the sun was dropping, the easiest thing to do was grab an overpriced room at an exit near Buckeye. Although a budget buster, the soft bed and shower, and a nice dinner, was a treat.

Ten miles along the next morning, came a moment of human grace. Anytime the bike had to be secured, out came the thin, ten-foot-long coated cable. It came out that morning at a Black Bear diner in Avondale. I was going through the motions of looping it through all four panniers and both wheels and a pedal, then locking it to a newspaper stand. A Hispanic couple in their late thirties were leaving the restaurant, and stopped to talk. After hearing my plans, the woman reached into her purse and gifted me a twenty. I quickly began the "that's not necessary" and "you're too kind" speech but she wouldn't hear of it. Her husband said they just wanted to help, and told me to go have a nice breakfast.

Over sausage, two over easy and a short stack, I pondered the moment. Perhaps a professional adventurer would have gone about it differently. While preparing for the trip, a frequent question was "who's sponsoring you?" It was suggested that contacting the bike or tire, or component, or shoe manufacturer was going to yield some aid. Perhaps a well-placed sticker of someone's product or website, or handing out a few flyers for some cause would be worth a few bucks. Notifying the media about this attempt seemed to be everyone's common advice. With just a few months to plan and prepare for the journey, none of that was ever considered.

I had certainly heard of such fund-raising stories, and had always thought they were just a premise to get someone else to pay for your vacation. In all fairness, imagine the solicitation. Picture an overweight shift worker with no bicycle credentials, walking into any corporate office, armed with a loose knitted plan to ride a no-name bicycle across the world to Hong Kong. Then asking for a little cash. The likeliest response would be "security to the lobby!" But still, this woman's act of kindness was important. Besides Jimmy and friend's strip club fund on the departure day, it was the trip's only cash donation. But it was the first of many kind acts, and each one made me feel as though I was doing something that other people only dreamed about. They couldn't break away from their daily lives, but were happy that someone could.

The very first gift of the journey was the time off itself, from my employer. As a large commercial airline, their maintenance facilities in San Francisco are a giant complex of hangars and shops. It had once buzzed 24/7 with three shifts and several thousand mechanics, repairing and maintaining every facet of their fleet of over 300 aircraft. In recent years, they managed to pare down the operations by outsourcing much of the maintenance to Asia and non-union shops, gutting the workforce to a shadow of its former self.

As the operation's manpower was cut close to the bone, letting someone off for the better part of a year was a rare grant. The grounds for such a grant fell along the lines of continuing a work-related education, or to tend an ailing family member, or a long-term personal illness. Those considerations would only put you in the ballpark; the final decision was at a manager's sometimes lengthy discretion. Because of that, all kinds of advice were offered on how to broach the subject with the boss. "Tell him your Mom is really sick", "tell him you're returning to college", "get a doctor to say you're suffering from too much stress." The general consensus was that the honesty tactic would leave open too many easy excuses to shoot it down.

Nah. This was too big and unprecedented and besides, what causes more squirmy fun than telling the truth? I wrote up a one-page synopsis of the journey's route, included were the rough dates for departure and return, how to stretch out my five weeks' vacation, and the request for the required six months or more of no pay; a "leave of absence." At the time, I was working in the engine overhaul shop, doing tear down and build up on motors for the Boeing 757's. I cornered the manager one day over by the hardware bins.

"Hey, check this out, tell me what you think." Steve was a pretty good guy, about my age but with a lot on his shoulders. He had his hands full running the busiest line of engine overhauls that we still worked on. Company motors, customer motors, and Air Force motors used on the C-17 cargo planes. Top brass at corporate in Chicago, and the military, all wanted his time and reports and assurances. The head honchos at the maintenance base were always breathing down his neck, and of course, scores of employees needed his time. And then he's handed this letter, a request that he had certainly never seen the likes of before. He reads through it, taking his time. "Are you really going to do this? Because if you're crazy enough to do it, I'm crazy enough to let you try." Just like that. Bada-bing bada-boom. It was the green flag moment for the whole journey; that one worrisome factor of the trip's planning that was out of my control, was in the bag. Just two crazy guys.

4. Don

The lesson of Phoenix, was to allot pretty much a full day to clear a metropolis. The factors being the stop lights, traffic and pedestrians, and finding a good route through the city. Today's most direct road was across the south side of town, amid a city reflecting the cowboy and Hispanic and Native influences that created it. The newer architecture of the city's center celebrates Mexico's influence, the rest of the south side had that run-down look that older business buildings give off once they're past their prime, and now occupied for a generation by small struggling shops and bars. The streets were a mixture of people going about their work day, a few homeless and disturbed, but only enough to make for an amusing ride on a nice day. A strikingly cool contrast shines down on the neighboring suburb of Tempe. Crossing over the Salt River finds a downtown full of hip little restaurants, bars and shops, all themed in a faux adobe, a conscious tribute to the Native American and Mexican culture. I cruised on through the pleasant oasis campus of Arizona State University, and eventually reached the next burb out, the faceless working-class sprawl of Mesa.

With the pocket still stinging from the $90 room the night before in Buckeye, the cheap Indian motel looked like a bargain. The room in the dark back lot had an entry door latch damaged by a past dispute, and the guests next door were screaming their way through a loud argument, featuring slamming doors and neutral-revving their parked car just outside. While moving the bureau against the door to provide a sense of barricade, I noticed a few roaches. As I showered and cooked up some soup on the camp stove, there were a few more, but after crawling into bed, the heebie jeebies started. Just as I was drifting off, one crawls up my leg. I jumped up and flicked it off into the dark room, turning on the light in time to see a few scurry away. After an inspection I laid down again, and within a few minutes another visitor crawled up the leg, now pinging the creepy meter. Out comes the sleeping bag, rolled it out on top of the bed covers and dozed off in a bug free cocoon.

Rolling into the morning sun of February 21st, I spotted the Mesa library, and

decided to stop in for some internet time. A table was set up outside in the heat, with a couple of women petitioning for some local healthcare cause. I bought them a couple of cold sodas to watch the bike for an hour, while uploading some pics and updating the blog. The rest of the day was an easy 20 miles out to the perimeter town of Apache Junction, where I hit up a local market for some camp food and found the KOA, still proud enough of their dirt to charge $25 to pitch a tent. It would become the going rate across the States, and with a hot shower, laundry room and friendly folks in charge, you couldn't mind. There I met Robert, a young Jehovah's Witness from the Denver area, living out of his truck, and trying to get a window washing business off the ground. Had a nice talk with him that night, and really wished him well. This aspect of the trip would continue, the play of flicking out a deck of cards, picking one up and reading a snapshot of a person's life, and I am just one of their cards. No matter the depths of their character or problems, we pass by each other with a smile and well wishes, as our paths cross for just a moment. Here on the eastern edge of Phoenix's reach, the radio says a rain storm is expected to pass through tonight. Tomorrow brings the Superstition Mountains.

The Superstitions have been of source of folklore long before settlers began showing up here in the mid-19th century. Native Americans told handed down legends of idyllic ancient civilizations and Aztec treasure. Old timers have their lost gold mine and vanishing cowpoke tales. More recent, there's claims it's an active area for UFO and alien sightings. The first sight of these volcanic formed ranges is impressive enough. After riding across days of flat and rolling desert, the Supe's abrupt rise, jutting over 3000 ft., is like staring at a dark brown wall; with giant boulders and tall Saguaro cactus set among the jagged ridges. Last night's promised weather held off until reaching the Hwy. 60 cutoff, where the two-day climb begins.

As the mist turned to drizzle and settled into a steady rain, the wheels were propped up against a sign post, to don the rain gear. Walking away, the bike rolled and fell, the post putting a decent dent in the top frame tube. Damn. First damage done in the eight years I'd owned it. The concern was that with the extra load, how was this going to affect the frame integrity as the trip wore on, with the constant flexing over rough roads? One could worry about a future moment when the frame might crack, or not worry about it, and someday the frame might crack. It still it hurt a little. Wrapped up in a pair of golfer's rain pants and an off-road motorcycle jacket, the bike and I silently pressed on up through the droplets to the little town of Superior.

The plan to leave I-10 and climb the forty miles up over the Superstitions came from offsetting considerations. Road wise, the climb was going to be a twenty-mile savings, by the time the two highways joined again in Lordsburg, New Mexico. However, the Tucson route was flat and wide, which would have been faster, negating the mileage gain. My thoughts were that this was the last respectable climb until I reached the Urals, months later in Russia. Somehow it just felt like cheating if I didn't soldier over them.

The night in Superior was like staging at a mini outdoor drama play. Camping on the front lawn of a resident's only trailer park, I set up the tent and cooked up some canned spaghetti, while being kept company by a little black dog. He eventually wandered off, and before long, all the park's inhabitants were coming and going, helping the fretted owner look for the little guy. Several tenants informed that this little pooch meant the world to the fellow, and they worried what would become of his delicate mental state if the terrier didn't return. Their cold stares conveyed I missed the gravity of the situation, when I volunteered that they shouldn't worry, all scamps usually return to the food bowl after a good night on the town. Then again perhaps trailer dog had mysteriously vanished into the Superstitions... Crisis afoot.

Woke up this morning, the 21st day after leaving Patterson, and crisis averted, the dog came home! The sweetheart retiree lady caretaker of the trailer park packed me a lunch of eggs and fruit, how nice! Like leaving a base camp, I put my head down and focused on the hump ahead. The twenty-miles up to the hilltop town of Miami took most of the day, on the steepest stretch of road I was to encounter during the entire trip. A sign noted a 6% grade, but judging from riding the Sierras, it seemed more than that. The trailer crowd forewarned several times about the quarter mile long uphill "tunnel from hell." As it turned out, the Queen Creek tunnel wasn't so bad after all, no safety margin, but well lit; yet still a bit spooky, knowing cars and trucks cannot see a bicycle too well once in deep. Turned on the small red flashing tail light and pedaled through as quick as possible, to get it over with and to keep the attention-grabbing reflectors on the pedals moving. The Queen Creek reward upon exiting was finding a slightly different view. The rock formations seemed a bit sharper and craggy compared to the land before the entrance. Perhaps a result of tunnels often being short cuts through layers of earth and rather than snaking through the gradual grades, the changes are more distinct and noticeable at the tube's exit.

Coasted through the forgotten streets of Miami and the marginally livelier town of nearby Claypool. A lonely looking copper smelter up on the hill looked abandoned. Since it was a Saturday, I gave it the benefit of the doubt of being closed for the weekend. The mining industries built these places long ago and had gradually walked away, as overseas minerals became the cheaper option, sharing the story of so many other hamlets out West. Late in the day I pedaled through Globe, where it appeared most people, and therefore, the shops and gas stations and a motel or two had gravitated. The top of this mountain could only float one town.

Out of Globe near sunset, and the road started to lean my way again. Rather than finding digs in town, I decided to make it out into the desert as far as the sun would allow. Feeling the light disappear behind me, I started scoping out for a place to ditch the highway and find a good camp site, but eight miles along, the Apache Gold Indian Casino popped up. Like an island on the back side of nowhere, it was a large spread with restaurants, a gas station, RV camping and an air strip. But most important, tent camping for $5, which included the shower. Standing in line at the Chevron station, which doubled as the camping office, it was hard to not notice the crowd. Winnebago retirees in one-piece jump suits, needing a spot with full hook-ups; and glazed Indians, picking up their evening juice. Such completely different groups brought together by the sanctifying alter of a gambling hall. A 30's something Indian was swaying to and fro with his 12 pack, as well as catching up with the other locals in line. Suddenly he turned to me and said "Don! How have you been? Where have you been hiding? I haven't seen you in two years!"

At first, I looked about for a Don, but sure enough, he was talking to me. He continued on about a job we once worked together up north, and how glad he was to see me again. The others in the store began looking on as if I should remember my old Indian buddy, even as I tried to tell this dude my name wasn't Don, and he must be, well, was mistaken. Felt kind of bad for the guy, but assured him I was doing pretty well in any case, and told him "don't be a stranger."

Oatmeal, I don't get it. Some of the best mileage days were after downing four packets of instant Quaker with a cup of tent brewed coffee, busting camp early and hit it. No snacks, no lunch, just head down and riding. What's in that stuff? Such was the next morning's start as I rolled across fifty miles of the San Carlos Apache Indian Reservation. Dotted with an occasional derelict building, some mobile homes and a few small dusty towns that were no more than wide spots in the road, poverty belied the proud Apache Nation that ruled this otherwise beautiful stretch of high desert. That morning the first bicycle traveler I'd seen stopped to talk.

Chris was heading west, starting in Miami, Florida, and heading for Seattle, two places that couldn't be further apart in the U.S. In Miami, Chris was considered "homeless." He was riding across the country on virtually nothing. The thrift store bicycle was kitted with heavy steel baskets front and rear, with a hodge-podge of various belongings. Homemade fabric gear bags clung to the side, with a couple of one-gallon milk jugs, filled with water, all lashed on by rope. He clued me in on how to get free maps and an occasional bowl of soup from the visitor's centers at each state's borders, and had only stayed at two motels so far. Chris was a good guy, and I had to admire his gumption for pedaling across the states by sheer determination, with barely two nickels to rub together. Out here he wasn't homeless, he was "independent."

To contrast, my old ride was a thoughtful mix match of good parts. Back in 2000, I was talking bikes with my workmate Dan, who was a few years older and one of the true "real bicyclists." You see them everywhere, people who dig the mode or yearn for the endorphin rush so much that they squeeze in a ride at any spare moment, riding with their club on the weekend, or in the mornings before work. Arranging their lives in order to pedal the work commute, and centering vacations on a planned tour. Real bicyclists. I have always admired anyone who can discipline themselves to maintain a day to day focus on any pastime. Bicycle riders can bring themselves into and keep a healthy weight and energy level that can't be bought, and I knew I would never be a member.

Hours of bicycle tales and accomplishment and adventure had poured forth from Dan over the years. At the mention of the dream of someday touring obscure countries and their rough roads, Dan said he might have a suitable frame to build such a bike around. It was a lugged chromoly steel road touring design, and though he didn't have the exact history of it, he knew it had been hand built by a small 10-man shop in Japan called Toyo, in the early Eighties. The story goes that one of the popular American bicycle companies had commissioned it as a prototype touring frame, which company was no more than a narrow guess.

He had a spare Campagnolo Chorus group set of gearing and brakes, and a Brooks leather saddle lying around, so after a handshake and $400, the deal was done. Over the years, I'd changed the bars, steering stem and seat post, in the chase for comfort and fit. The touring racks for the panniers had been added, and in the few months leading up to the grand departure, it all came apart for cleaning and greasing. To aid in climbing hills with the heavy load, changes were made to adapt the Campy shifters to a Shimano mountain bike gearing set; and a reliable Phil Wood sealed crank was installed. It all went back together with thread sealer on every screw. Two weeks before the launch, it was ridden for the first time in several years, just to make sure it shifted correctly; a quick ride up and down the street in front of the house. No bags, no equipment, no load, it seemed fine.

In the afternoon I stopped in the reservation burg of Bylas. Planning to grab some camp food for another night in the desert, the lone market closed its doors for a half hour to do the afternoon inventory count, just as I pulled up. To kill time, I wandered over to the town's roadside rest area and watched a group of local Indian boys skateboarding with surprising style off all the bench, stair structures, and railings, in the only place for miles that had enough cement to do it. With all the broken-down lives and communities around them, these kids still found a way to be cool.

After grabbing a can of stew, I was armed for the night. The small gasoline  powered mini stove I'd packed along gave the freedom to keep at it until sunset, no matter where the day ended, home was wherever I could pop up the one-man tent and crouch around the little burner. As the sun dropped over my shoulder and the reservation was left behind, it became clear that the town of Safford was within reach. It had been dark for about a half hour when I rolled in and found a bargain motel, while awash in the serene sense of exhaustion of banging out a seventy-mile day. A long hot shower, the bike's locked away in the room, and I'm slowly walking down 5th street, scoping for a friendly diner. Tomorrow, I'll cross into New Mexico and try to make I-10 at Lordsburg. It would be another long push, and as I melted into the bed that night, the thought that I was handling this trip better than expected crossed my mind, I was getting in better shape. The body wasn't as achy, and sitting on the bike was hurting less, the sore neck, from having to look forward all day had diminished and the right knee felt better. Be fluid, don't push it and let the conditioning slowly come to you. Before drifting off, I knew that tomorrow would be another good try, but pressing for Lordsburg, another 70 miles away, just wasn't that important.

After breakfast, at a fancy looking place called the Manor House, it was off to a cold morning, and miles of small climbs and dips over the transitional rocky terrain, leading towards the flat New Mexico desert. A routine formed, mentally breaking the day up into three twenty-mile traps. It made the effort less daunting, knowing that along with the frequent roadside stops for a swig or a photo, or a piss, every twenty miles or so I'd take a longer break. Sit down in the dirt, have a snack and just look at the land. Today's second break came at the mini mart gas station in the tiny town of Duncan, not far from the state border. Chatted with a very old man who told a tale of the last time he and his buddies climbed the hill just south of town on their bicycles, back in the 1930's. After helping out a woman who was struggling with where to add oil into her husband's pickup truck, I rolled away; and on the town's edge, met Laurent.

Laurent was a charming Frenchman in his late twenties', who had pedaled his well-worn mountain bike all through Northern Mexico, and was on his way north to see the Grand Canyon. He was a minimalist, traveling with no tent, just a sleeping bag and one small pannier, both held on to the rack with a single rope. We talked for some time about our journeys so far, his lack of gear compared to my setup, and his final plans to reach Los Angeles to catch a flight home. Then he told of his previous day encounter with a fellow American he'd stopped to talk to, an old man watering his front lawn in the town of Wilcox. Once the man discovered where Laurent was from, he proceeded to inform him that he hated the French, and that they were all a bunch of cowards. Laurent brushed it off, felt it was just some amusing slice of the States, but I was a little set back at the rudeness. I managed to get out some muttered apology, to the affect that even if a person feels this, why would you say it to someone who's just visiting us on holiday?

Most Americans could count all the French people they've ever met on one hand, yet we've a popular notion to not like them, classy. Mon ami and I had a few laughs at the old boy's expense, and then wished each other luck and moved on. The incident had me wondering what kind of snipes might be coming my way once landing in Europe, given our combative times. Entering New Mexico, the shadows were growing longer, the goal of Lordsburg wasn't going to happen. Out here the land turned into a flat plain, spotted with small brush, cacti, and a 10-foot-tall funny looking half cactus half tree thing. The terrain didn't give any great hiding places to conceal the tent from the highway, plus I'd have to clear a barbed fence line that went on for miles.

It was just past dusk when at last, a dirt road appeared on the right. I waited until there were no cars or trucks on the horizons, and then zipped down it about 200 yards, then headed out into the Chihuahua Desert scrub, angling for a stand of brush that would at least break up the tent's profile from highway view. Within a half hour, it was dark, the tent was up and the canned stew was warming as I veiled the burner's glow with the flannel shirt, caped over my head. Hidden by darkness from anyone that may drive down the rancher's road, and far from the headlight wash of the highway, this was a game played out with equal parts of fun and fear. For tonight and nights to come, I would act this out on public or private property, sometimes hard to tell, the goal to be hidden from both the good and bad people that may stumble upon the little tent. In reality, the worse that would occur is a sharp word from the property owners, but in the darkness one's imagination runs wild. That night, laying in the desert, only the yelping of a couple of coyotes came close, probably having smelled the stew and wondered who's the new guy? I drifted off feeling safe, the word was stealth camping.

Since climbing up the Superstitions in the rain a few days ago, the weather had turned dry but very cold. The days started out layered with the T-shirt, flannel and a heavy shell jacket, with long pants and a beanie pulled over the ears, at midday the layers were peeled off, only to be put back on as evening approached. Considering it was February and around the 4500 ft. elevation level in the high desert, I colored myself lucky not to have been set back by flurries yet.

That morning, pedaling the 17 miles into Lordsburg was no different. Bundled up and silently moving through the morning chill, when the funny looking cactus commanded attention. Perhaps I'd seen this plant before in the California deserts, or maybe had just seen pictures, but here it was everywhere and it was fascinating. It wasn't like cactus, there were no prickly tines, but rather a plant sampler-plate. Growing out of a trunk, covered with wide fronds that stemmed into a couple of large branches, topped with a large round burst of green fronds that looked like aloe. Rising straight out of the frond bunch was a 3-foot-long stem, topped with a vertical growth of white flowers. Suddenly, bolting out from behind one, shot two small wire-haired pig looking critters, frightened as all hell. They lit out at full tilt ahead of me across the desert, until I lost sight of them, it was a sudden wake-up call that shook me out of the morning trance. Ten minutes later, as the road passed over a small viaduct, the wild pigs startled me again, they leapt out from the road beneath, running wide open until out of sight. It gave pause to where I was, what I was doing. The entire earth was mine, not a car or home or human in sight, as I pedaled towards breakfast among the Soaptree Yucca plants and the high speed javelinas. Flora and fauna that couldn't have been stranger if sprung from the pages of Dr. Seuss.

5. snow brush

I lingered in Lordsburg, taking in the idea of being back on Interstate 10. The wide safety lanes and smooth pavement were welcomed, but along with them came the roaring tractor trailer rigs and more people. After a leisurely breakfast, and a few moments to adjust a derailleur cable, the day was getting eaten up. Twenty-one miles later, I pulled into Separ.

Separ consists of a tire repair service, a trinket shop and a giant white tee-pee. I took a mosey around the shop that was full of American Indian kitsch and New Mexico souvenirs, plus a few groceries. They also had a commendable supply of fireworks, the good kind, that were illegal in most states nowadays. After grabbing a drink, I headed back out across the gravel lot, only to be blessed with the journey's first flat tire. Once the rear tube had been replaced, it was nearing dusk. In front of the tire shop was a sun-dried mother and her young boy, they were eyeing me with true caution as I walked over. As politely as possible, I asked the grouchy looking owner if he wouldn't mind if I just propped up a tent over there, behind a couple of abandoned mobile homes for the night. He looked quite annoyed for being pulled away from his career choice, and said quite seriously "I'd just prefer you didn't."

Not sensing the hint, I returned to the Continental Divide Trading Post and posed the same question to the guy behind the counter. He admitted he hadn't the authority to say yes or no, then he mentioned that if someone were to keep a low profile on their way over to the giant tee-pee at the end of the property, they could probably put up there for the night, no problem. Really? Camp inside the tee-pee? I felt like an eight-year-old at the prospect! The plywood tee-pee was a thirty-foot tall weather-beaten structure, it had baited tourist back in the glory days to stop at the Trading Post, and peruse the genuine Indian jewelry, postcards and jackalopes. Now, it was dilapidated and left to rot, with missing chunks of plywood and faded paint. Very cool, very Route 66-ish. The bike was laid down and pushed under the structure, and we were home. A little trash, some beer bottles, and a fire patch said this had been used as shelter more than once. Tonight however, it was mine, and was added to the caboose on the list of strange places to spend the night.

Eleven straight days of riding had gone by since leaving Mom's. The twelfth day was a cold, steady push, across the Great Divide and into Deming, New Mexico. Along the way, the idea of taking a day off to rest the legs, sleep in, and eat a few decent meals started to form. Until now, the desire for progress was driving the plan, every day on the road was something new and I looked forward to it. The mind was still focusing on the trip as a mission. On the sixty-mile trek across that flat, brush covered plain, a light came on. You're not some athletic machine. Just because this recent exercise is making you feel stronger, you can't dismiss years of a no-fitness regimen. The journey isn't about how fast I can pedal around the world and get back to the rat race. Exhale junior, this time it's

different. Yeah, a day off, plus the laundry was due.

Rolled into town and it all clicked, I found a big clean room at the Deming Motel for $30. The guy running the place, John, was an older man full of grace and vibrancy, just meeting and talking to him was a treat. He was excited for me and seemed to understand what a special chance and undertaking this trip was for someone. He also ran the more expensive Grand Motor Inn on the east side of town, and was good enough to give the nod to go down there and use the laundry room. I spent the next day sleeping in, watching the tube and going out to eat a few times, it was a great recharge.

Headed out the following day and made good time, covering the sixty miles toward Las Cruces on generally declining terrain. On the road that day came Byron, a cyclist on a bargain-rack bicycle who had traveled from Oregon to South Carolina, and was now heading back. Once again, a guy who was traveling with no money, just food stamps that he could only use at Wal-Mart and Dollar General. He was camping out every night by necessity, and making it work. I tried to put on like "yeah I'm camping out a lot too" but the truth was my ride was solid equipment compared to his, plus, I had the means to stay inside and get a good meal when needed. I thought I was roughing it. People like Chris in Arizona and now Byron drove home the realization that everyone's limits are defined by their options. And while their social definition was labeled "homeless", something earnest and honorable had driven them to take this ambitious leap.

It transcended the easy assumptions of mental or substance abuse issues, and hit at our common ground for challenge and wanderlust. Some never feel it, others are controlled by it, but for most people it's kept in the background and fed when possible. Keep it inside the framework, don't color outside the lines, wear sensible shoes and please think of others first. We're taught to save and plan for retirement boy, that's when all your dreams will come true. Buried far beneath those accepted ideals is the animal's need to have an experience.

For many, domestic life seems unnatural in its comfort. The security of the work-a-day life becomes a treadmill. The game suffers no spectators, so keep moving or get mowed over. The deeper a person buys into the American lifestyle, the greater the pain of failing. Like juggling chainsaws while standing on a beach ball, a person knows that one mistake and it could all change. A spontaneous affair, the wrong word to the wrong person at work; a long-term injury could trip you up. An illness or a bad investment, an economic snare could do it. Any number of scenarios could see you losing some or all of what's precious to you, and to those that count on you. Keeping your shit together. It's the most crucial, yet unheralded, of life's fabrics.

Never once had I thought that "one of these days, I'm going to visit Las Cruces." Just shy of that fair city, the road skirted south on the country lane of Hwy. 28. Rarely does a perfect moment present itself, and I had just stumbled into one. The ingredients of such an experience are more than visual, and difficult to wholly convey. This setting was as I headed south, knowing that the eyes of Texas were upon me the next morning, marking the one-third point of America. The daily mileage mark had been met, the body was feeling good, and life on the road was washing away the guy who had left home almost four weeks ago; now a bicycle traveler. Ambling down Hwy. 28, a slight decline in the road made every pedal count for more. I was passing through a corridor of pecan trees and warmed by the rays of a setting sun that filtered through miles of orchards like giant fence slats. Small farm homes, with an orange sky behind them, clicked by as I absorbed it all. The thought of stopping and snapping a picture occurred, but I knew a photo was too small to capture this. The brain, the body, and the earth all came together at once and offered a toke of serenity. I still imagine it.

On the advice of a friendly woman, who was just locking up the Post Office for the night in tiny San Miguel, I headed down a side road for about a mile and pitched the tent on the banks of the Rio Grande. For that evening, this famous river of song and story, that goes on to define the border between Texas and Mexico before finally dumping into the Gulf 800 miles later, was all mine. On this last night of February, it was a slow, green, quiet home to a dozen ducks. On the far side, beyond its bush lined sandy banks, a couple of kids were running their dirt bikes up and down the river road and through the orchards. As the day's last light faded away, they headed back to the family farm, and I was left to contemplate the final night of New Mexico. This place was all about real cowboys, stores selling real fireworks and the strange Yucca plant. After tomorrow, I could always say "I once rode a bicycle to Texas."

The next day's start was a pleasant ride along the river. After grabbing a gas station breakfast, my wheels were joined on the road by a few dozen members of an El Paso bicycle club, and their chase vehicles. They were out for a Saturday morning loop ride, and one of the guys pedaled alongside me for some time, asking all about the trip and wishing me good luck. At some point, the road turned into the Republic of Texas without so much as a welcome sign, I just started seeing "Texas" on the roadside markers of Hwy. 20. Then, the tedious process of picking a way through El Paso began.

There's no real clean bicycle shot across El Paso, other than I-10, which was off limits in a big city. Here, the confluence of Mexico's Juarez butts up against the border in a vivid contrast of city planning, as seen from the hills above. The view combines the sister cities of two million people, but the Juarez side looked like a jagged explosion. The tall hotel and banking structures of El Paso's downtown traipse off into the small business buildings, then into the suburbs, all framed in 90-degree streets with the Interstate cutting through it. Then, at a definitive east to west line, begins Juarez. It spreads out left and right and up a small rise like an open fan. The streets turn and bend and wander like vines searching for water, no real downtown, and all the buildings look homemade. The drug import trade has ripped this city to shreds over the past decade, making it one of the most violent places in the world to live; keeping it neck and neck with Caracas, Venezuela, and our own New Orleans.

Later, I stopped for a break and watched across the border as some Mexican kids played basketball on a heaved concrete slab outside a broken looking school. They ran around in laughter, hitting two pointers, oblivious to the mayhem they were growing up in. One world separated from another, by a chain link fence. While riding past the border control point, I expected to see a large sign declaring "Welcome to Mexico, we don't give a shit about anything." Instead, what with all the giant flags flying and hustle and bustle of commerce, it looked like the entrance to Disneyland.

The rest of the day was parsing a route through the city. After a few stops to ask the locals for the best path to the east side, it was clear that few had any idea. What's wrong with saying "I don't know" upfront, rather than telling a long story that ends with "I'm not sure, you should ask someone." Teenagers were a riot, being the most approachable, and having a lot to say. But despite all the guesses, didn't always know how far it was to the next town. A dollop of Americana was served while passing a supermarket parking lot and being yelled at, through a bull horn, by a group of sign waving Jesus fans who were worked up that I didn't stop and contribute some pocket-faith. Only in 'Murica. Once out on the east side of the city, I stopped at a rundown trailer park-come-trailer storage lot to put up the tent. Problem was... not a soul was there. I looked around and called out several times before the creepie's set in, and then headed off to a McDonald's dinner and a trucker's motel. Just as well too, since some spokes and a tube needed tending to.

Along the way and after, the most common question fielded is "how many flats did you get?" Flat tires of course, being the most common memory of a bicycle's ailments. Even after the evening's maintenance chores, I awoke the next morning to a rear flat. Out on the highways, especially the ones with curbing, the tiniest of steel slivers cause more problems than thorns or glass.  My two-cent theory is that, as automotive tires wear and chunk apart, their steel belts take a beating, then fray. The frayed strands break down, after years of traffic and corrosion, into slivers. These small splinters embed their way into the bicycle's tire tread. When repairing a flat, they reveal themselves while running a hand inside the carcass, or not. Sometimes they only raise their heads and puncture the tube after it has been inflated to 90 psi. In that case, the tire would get tossed after a couple of honest attempts to locate the little pricks. How many flats? I should have been counting...

This morning's flat was an extractable sliver, but it delayed the start. Once under way, things went well, with the wind and terrain in my favor. I passed by Fabens and Fort Hancock, paralleling the Mexican border just two miles to the south, before breaking east again across the breath of Texas. At nightfall, after a seventy-mile day, my home was a highway rest area in the Quitman Mountains above Sierra Blanca. Stealthing up above the pull off, the tent was obscured by the cacti and prickle bushes from the truckers below, stopping to rest or a smoke or take a piss break. When I hit the sack, it was a brisk and clear evening, with a mild westerly wind.

About 2 a.m., I awoke with the tent lying on my face. The wind was blowing so hard to the south that the un-staked tent would be gone, if not for my dead weight holding it down. The gusting forces on the rain cover and the aluminum poles were tweaking and flapping them so violently, I feared the cover would break loose and fly away. Upon opening the flap, to see if there was a chance of securing the whole mess, revealed a snowstorm! It was blowing sideways and had already started to stick! I just zipped up the opening and put on the flannel, then crawled deep into the sleeping bag and laid there, hoping that the rain cover held. If it broke loose, I'd be open to the elements, since the tent roof was a mesh material meant for warm nights and star gazing. Huddled in the bag with the tent wrapped around me, I waited out the night and soon fell back to sleep; knowing all problems look better in the daylight.

In the morning the wind was just as strong, but the snow had stopped, leaving traces of white. It was below freezing with a strong whipping wind, and I played hell trying to get the tent packed up without losing any pieces. Weighting everything down with rocks and feet, I managed to methodically secure it all, knowing that losing control of the flapping tent or rain cover for even a second would set them flying off. They would become tangled and shredded and blown away into nether regions of thorny flora that covered the hillside above. With the mid-30's temps and a strong wind from the north, the morning was a cold chore as I rolled into Sierra Blanca for breakfast, wrapped in every warm item I had. Thirty-five miles later came Van Horn, and I decided today was in the books. There was a nice RV park full of friendly pensioners and a hot shower. Warm is good.

Awoke to Texas the next day, knowing I'd made the right decision, and set to brewing up the coffee and oatmeal in the brisk morning air. Busting camp, I noticed the faces behind the motor home and trailer windows. To the droning hum of a half dozen generators, the retirees sat inside enjoying the warmth, and sipping that first cup of the day. They nodded through the glass when noticed, but otherwise stared transfixed at the character outside making his campsite disappear into the bags and racks of a bicycle. Comfortable rolling homes. Tended by older women who "just can't imagine why someone would want to travel like that." Helmed by their husbands, who understood completely.

At the I-10 and I-20 split, a couple of Corpus Christi musicians had their hands full with a broken boat trailer axle and all the wrong parts. Chris the drummer, and his buddy the guitarist, were in pretty good spirits about the whole ordeal, and took time out to chat and take a few pics. The rolling terrain and favorable winds helped all the way to Balmorhea, which was set off the freeway about a mile and a half. I pedaled in, hoping for a motel after a couple of nights in the tent. And as luck would have it, there were two motels. Motel One was closed but the combo lobby and living room TV set played on. Motel Two wanted too much. I went for a nice meal at the local Mexican diner, with a plan to return to Motel Two later and see if they couldn't be talked into a better rate. The clever tactic was that in the late evening hours, they'd rather rent the room out at a discount than to see it go empty. My shrewd negotiating had worked at a few mom and pop places before.

When I returned, they had no vacancy! I rolled through the small town's dimly lit main street looking for a place to sack out, not feeling so clever anymore, and came upon a dingy vacant lot that called itself an RV park. It was about the size of two front yards and finished in a natural dirt motif. Can't recall if the gruff resident manager even asked a fee, he seemed much more interested in returning to his TV program than dealing with bicycle boy. The tent went up and I laid down, with the neighbor's dog barking at me constantly into the night. Another seventy-mile day in the bag.

March 5th never got into the groove. The morning featured two flat tires within an hour of each other, and the rolling terrain wasn't rolling my way. A strong north wind was crossing the road all day, and the cold continued. In another day, things would  begin to change as the infamous Texas hill country approached. But for now, the vast empty stretches of scrub called West Texas ruled to the horizons. The heat, cold, wind, hailstorms and an occasional tornado make this a tough place to live. Somehow, through it all, people loved this land to the point of religious fervor. Park a trailer inside a barbed wire acre and you're the king of all you can see, whether you own it or not.

Head down and against the wind, take a quick toke and turn up the iPod, then pedal it all behind you. Another day heading east, never to turn around. Just keep going until the Atlantic pops into view, then just keep going until the Pacific pops up. Stare down at the gangly overloaded orange machine and watch the pavement slowly go by, and repeat the mantra: No matter how endless and incremental it is, this is the road to China. I only made 50 miles that day to Fort Stockton, can't fathom where I put the tent up. The notes that night had been written by someone very tired.

Coffee and oatmeal'd up and hit the road by 9 a.m. Another cold day had me layering up in long pants and the golfer's rain togs, as over pants to block the wind. A T-shirt, flannel shirt and the enduro shell; a beanie and fingerless bicycle gloves. A striking figure, riding across the high plains, like someone's mother had trussed me up for a cold walk to school. Yes, I know there is modern cycling gear for the four seasons, but my whole act was off the scales; living in the everyday clothes of cargo shorts and T's. And with all of the specialized food and drink products available to the modern fitness buff, I suppose my habitual mid-day break would make some wince. I looked forward to a couple of bananas and a chocolate milk, whenever available in the gas station mini marts, that had become my favorite restaurants of choice.

Today's stop was a lonely Chevron station outside of the Pecos County town of Bakersfield. The older fella running the place was a Southern-by-the-Grace-a'-God Texas good ol' boy with a big white Stetson. He comped me a cup of coffee as we talked about the journey, the current world affairs, and the potential of next season's Cowboys. He and I were of two different Americas, yet his amazement at the scope of my plans cut across our views of life. We shook hands and he wished me sincere luck, which I mentally stashed in an imaginary magic bag of good karma that I was trying to fill up.

Thirty-miles later, the day's goal of Sheffield arrived in the form of a freeway exit. No town to be seen. Sheffield was five miles off the highway, a blink of an eye in the car but a waste of time and energy at my pace. I pushed on a few more miles up a rise and decided to stealth camp behind a small gas station. I had found that asking was almost always a no, so I just quietly found a vacant area out of view and set up. That night was to be very windy and the temps down into the 20's. Learning from Sierra Blanca, I set up the tent in line with the wind and used rocks to weight down the corners, expecting the worse. A seventy-four-mile day ended with a can of warm beans and a rocky bed behind a forgotten gas station. Another day, another dab of the brush.

6. the bridge

The coolest thing about a bicycle ride is that anyone can do it, you'd be hard pressed to find any adult who's forgotten how to ride one, and hence the old adage. The natural approach to telling this tale would be to never let on that anyone could just jump off the couch and start riding a bicycle down the street, until an ocean appears. The years of experience and knowledge have to be polished up. The skill of tuning the ergonomics to fit, the talent to pack only what is needed to save weight; the knack of distributing the load for balanced handling. The ability to swiftly swap tubes and tires and spokes on the roadside. Riding and camping skills, plus navigation and endurance and... oh blow the damned whistle. Everyone's met a pompous windbag somewhere.

Truth is, anyone could jump off the couch and ride their bike down the street, it isn't the realm of a few fit winners in colorful tights. The only true wall that separates couch guy from ride to Hong Kong guy is simple: Deep inside, you have to truly want to do it. Get up off the couch, jump on the bike and ride down the street...and just keep goin'. Unlike playing golf or guitar or motocross or sailing or hundreds of other possibilities, this doesn't take years of practice to feel you're pretty good at it. For any doubters, picture the simplicity of a bicycle: Two wheels, two brakes, two derailleurs and a steering stem; half a dozen or so moving parts. A few hours down at the local shop with a patient mechanic, or watching YouTube, will school you on the basic needs to keep rolling. Flat repair, spoke replacement or breaking a chain, what the two small screws on the derailleurs control. Walk out with the right tools and begin the trial and error phase, you'll do fine. The greatest challenge isn't physical or mechanical skills, when a hill or a flat tire present themselves, the options are pretty obvious. The only real challenge is the mental one. Of course, everyone starts with a positive bent, whether you're the trepid or audacious type, no one expects to fail. And then, it gets tricky.

March 7th rang in the Texas hill country. I would come to deem it bicycle Purgatory, climbing deceptive undulations all day long. These low hills looked a breeze, compared to a real mountain range, but the never-ending rises to false summits zapped my sense of progress. The promised descents that reward the effort never came. Either a mild dip to the next hump, or being held back by the wind, would take away any real chance to coast and rest. Just making sixty miles took until dark, ending at a nice highway rest area ten miles out of Sonora. The tent went up hidden behind an equipment building, on the green grass next to the RV dump station. Another day of I-10, and a day closer to San Antonio, the mental and geographical halfway point across the U.S.

Took breakfast at a small place in Sonora. I always looked forward to rolling into these little cafes after a short morning ride, mentally perusing the menu of eggs, bacon and pancakes, long before knowing which diner I'd be stopping at. They always felt welcoming, the food's usually decent, but it's the people that make it interesting. Truckers and ranchers and local business men were having that first visit or informal meeting of the day. Retiree regulars saying hi to all the locals as they walk in, and the momentary still that occurs when a stranger enters the door. Traditional, homespun, straight forward Americans, who all love to open up and start talking, once the waitress gets the conversation rolling.

After breakfast with Sonora's finest, it was another day of tackling the low oak and brush covered terrain. Despite a solid day's effort against the wind and hills, I just managed a bit over sixty miles, I can't even recall seeing a building. It was dusk when I admitted that the town of Junction was just too far into the evening, night riding was one of the sins to be avoided, to reduce the chance of a trip ending mishap. It had been too many days since the last shower, and a night in a Junction motel would have been nice; but I pulled up short. Following a camping symbol sign, I went five miles further along on an eastbound service route, and came to a dirt road that soon let out onto a beautiful remote RV park. It was set in a green meadow, and hidden by tall trees.

With only a couple of RVs' in view, and what looked like a shower hut, I relaxed. This would be home for the night. A retiree woman came out of a mid-size travel trailer and told me a tent site was $25 for the night. The head silently flashed "that's a little steep for an empty campground," but I knew that the shower was needed. Then, I recalled that there was only $20 left in the wallet, and seven miles to the nearest ATM machine in Junction. She wasn't set up to run the bankcard, but then offered to call her husband on the cell, to see if they could shine the $5 for the night. As soon as she started to explain, he must have cut her short. "Ma husband sez aif you ain't got da money you gohnt haf to leaf." I politely pointed out that it was now dark, and riding into town on a strange country road was just stupid. "Sorry, I caint hep you."

Crap. Now what? Un-relax. Go figure it out, somewhere in these trees I'd have to suss out a hiding spot and hope for the best. Then, on the way back out the dirt road, there stood a fifteen-foot-high enclosed deer stand. Looking around for any sign of why not, I stashed the bike behind a berm created by the campground's garbage burning pit, then grabbed the essentials and headed up the ladder. The floor space was about the size of a one-man tent, and completely covered with a thick carpet of a thousand dead flies. After a quick sweep out, I moved in and managed to cook up some soup. Working the whole time with the flannel shirt draped over the head like a tent, the stoves glow was sheltered from any eyes, while listening intently for any approaching cars. I soon fell asleep, thinking about the caboose, a tee-pee and now this. Dig it.

The usual waitress banter began after taking a seat at the Junction Cafe the next morning, and soon some of the dozen or so customers were paying attention to the tale. An older black fellow stood up and shuffled over to the front counter and laid down a $10 bill, telling the girl that he was buying me breakfast! His name was Abby, and said he just wanted to do something nice. A saintly gesture, given I hadn't showered or shaved for four days, and must of looked a bit rough. It was a sign of good luck, and it erased the previous night's shun. I stood and thanked him several times, then enjoyed everyone's company for breakfast while outlining the journey... between mouthfuls.

That turned out to be the high point of the day. The hills and the headwinds made it one of the toughest humps of the trip. I'm convinced that there's no such thing as a flat road, the terrain either inclines or declines in imperceptible degrees, only perceived through the pedals. Every small crest that day in the Texas hills was met by an onrush of wind, negating the decline and forcing hard pedaling downhill; getting lost in the tunes was the key to keeping the mind off the creeping pace. Come dusk, it was looking like another night in the brush. But, with the day's remaining light, and knowing a hot shower was almost within reach, I pushed on and made Kerrville, just past dark. I found a decent motel and washed off a work weeks' worth of grime, and had a dinner that didn't plop out of a tin can. And ain't it something, the way things work out. I awoke to a heavy storm, that didn't let up all day. It would have made for a crazy night and a cold wet morning in the tent. It also shot the plans to press on to stay at a friend's house in San Antonio. The relentless downpour in Kerrville made any attempt at progress that day a dumb idea.

Rain. When light, it was actually a peaceful riding experience. The earth's smells are heightened, the noises are dampened and then there's the boost of pressing through nature's moods. When heavy, I had to pull in, the road's surface and car's splashing was fraught with peril. The clothes would become soaked, the shoes would take a few days to dry out. The mental game of optimizing the situations I had control over meant a down day here. The motel's front desk girl directed me towards a laundromat and a library, making use of the down time to wash the duds while updating the blog, and upload some pictures.

The sacrifice of losing a rest day in San Antonio, just sixty miles away, really burned. I was still operating in mission mode, concerned that too many down days could affect the schedule. My loss, for I had once spent a grand weekend with Rick and Donna fifteen years earlier. Rick's brother, Ron, was one of my best friends from back in the Air Force days, and we never lost touch. In fact, his place in Orlando was my U.S. end goal. A small group of us, stationed together at a tiny air base in Germany in the early 80's, formed quite a brotherhood. We managed a reunion of sorts ten years later in Orlando. Rick and Donna ran the party logistics, they put on the barbecues for us and made sure the beer mugs never went dry. When they heard of my ride, they immediately offered up their place as a stopover.

It was Tuesday, March 11th, and the Texas hills were behind me. It was a great downhill ride into the San Antonio sunshine, and I just kept rolling towards the city on I-10. With his red and blue lights flashing and a quick shot of the siren, Sgt. Lopez of the Bexar County Sheriff's Department pulled up. At first, he came across with a "what the hell do you think yer doin'?" A reasonable question. Again, open country no problem, when approaching a city, with alternative side roads, you had to get off the interstate. That point of separation was however, in my opinion, a vague area. Sgt. Lopez however, was not a man of vague opinions. "Get off at the next exit, or I'll arrest you." I wanted to tell him "funny, but I was thinking the same thing." All that came out was "yes sir." With the formal introductions out of the way, things lightened up and we began talking about the ride. He told me that there was a group of county sheriff officers that were serious bicyclists, and they'd be checking into my website, to see how the trip was progressing. He turned out being a real nice guy. In the end I snapped a photo, then made quick work of reaching the next off-ramp.

Arriving at Rick and Donna's in NW San Antonio, I was greeted by their teenage son Ryan. Even though we had never met, he treated me like an old family friend, producing a cold beer and pointed towards the shower. Soon Rick came home, and we caught up on the last decade and a half. Rick was a building contractor who had an exceptional amount of vision and talent when it came to damn near any task. The laptop came out and he showed me all the different projects he'd recently worked on, from their beautiful lake side vacation home, to an old one-room school house he uprooted and moved intact to a client's property.

Before long, the happy energy of Donna came home, with some tasty roast beef sandwiches. The beer and conversation flowed, making me feel right at home. Genuine people are a gift. Looking back, I should have stayed on another day; I would come to learn to just let things flow. This was the halfway point across the States, that was reason enough to reward the legs with a spell, plus it may be years again before I get to spend time with the Reeds of San Antone. Unfortunately, the mission called, and I rolled out the next morning.

It took several hours to traverse the spread of San Antonio and find Hwy. 78 east. Leaving the Alamo City meant leaving the American West, and transitioning into the South. Near Marion, a Ford Bronco slowed down alongside, and the driver yells "do you like chocolate?" I wasn't sure what he'd said at first. Finally nodding yes, he frisbee-tossed a giant bar of Hershey's Chocolate across the cab, out the passenger window and across our gap, nailing me with a perfect shot to the chest. The two-handed grab sent the bars and bike swerving off to the right, I damn near lost control of the wobbly wheels as he motored away without a word. Blessed by a chocolate angel.

Later that day, I sat on the side of a gas station, battling on the cell phone with a service manager at an auto dealership from back home. Sheree was having car problems and I wasn't there to fix them, so the shop was running up the repair costs. I had to pick through what was needed and what wasn't. Five weeks gone, and my absence was being felt, the first pang of guilt. Soon, a bicycle racer pulled into the station, he was training for the "Race across America." The six to eight-person teams would pedal 24 hours a day, nonstop, for 3000 miles from San Diego to somewhere in New Jersey. While we took turns being wowed by each other's plans, I truly could not imagine running a race pace for two-hundred miles at a time, then sleeping in a moving motor home until the next stint. A real bicyclist. Found a bargain motel in Sequin, and ended the evening drinking beer outside the room with a group of migrant oil field workers. I learned that Texas still a lot of oil and gas work going on.

A seventy-mile day back on I-10 across the Texas flat lands brought me to Schulenburg, and the manager of an RV park who seemed a bit taken back that a "tenter" was asking for a night. She was hesitant to say yes, but I poured on the charm and was granted a spot on the back side of the park, away from the proper RVer's. Odd hospitality, but the shower was hot. Unaware at the time that the anti-tent thing would raise its head again, I paid little attention later that night to an old boy in a golf cart, who rolled by to shoot the breeze. As I sat on a picnic table, just waiting to hit the sack, he proposed that tenters usually

37

meant motorcyclists. In this part of the country, motorcyclists are usually the Harley Davidson crowd, and the Harley crowd usually played a late loud night. I hid my amusement at the policy's inability to discern a pedal bike from a large motorcycle. I probably nodded in that "makes sense" motion, given I was being tolerated in an East Texas retiree's RV park. Looking back, whoo-boy.

An early start out on the 10 rolled through a couple of very small towns, and mid-sized Sealy, before crossing the Brazos and ending a sixty-five-mile day in Houston's perimeter city of Katy. There, I passed by the Igloo Corporation. From this factory in East Texas, the famous Igloo Ice Chests are strewn along the sides of freeways all across America. By now, I'd seen every conceivable consumer item imaginable. From tools to tie downs, diapers, clothing and shoes. Gas cans, knives, toys, and even golf clubs. Name it, you'll find it on the side of Interstate 10, just go really slow. What struck me about Katy was the feeling of unregulated sprawl. As night fell, I cruised along a main street that seemed from a simpler era; searching for a cheap hotel, to no avail. Out on the east side of town, a collection of the usual national chain eateries and hotels lined the freeway, apparently sucking the life out of Katy proper.

For the hell of it, I pedaled up to the Marriott's Springhill Suites, just as a limousine pulled up. The door opened, unloading a group of party goers all dressed to the nines, in evening gowns and tuxedos. They were a friendly bunch, out for a fun evening. After hearing the story, they invited me to stay the night and have dinner with them. It all sounded like a good time, until the doorman informed me that the place was getting a hundred and fifty bucks for a room. I bid farewell to my smiling, almost new friends, and headed off into the Texas night; in search of some urban stealth camping.

Across the freeway, a truck stop had a line of empty trailers parked out back, making for a good hiding spot. Rolling the last few yards to the end of my day, a riding glove fell off the bars. Lazily circling around to retrieve it, I leaned too far, too slow, and started to pitch. The right shoe didn't unlock from the clip, and I went down hard with the elbow between the ribs and the pavement. I laid there on my back for half a minute, the pain was sharp. Standing up and collecting the bike, and pitching the tent was agony. Why does it hurt so damn much? Did I crack a rib? Popped a pain killer and a half dozen aspirin and drifted off to sleep, hoping no one had seen me set up. The night passed peacefully in my secret spot, and it felt good to get away with another free night. In the morning, the ribs were aching with a cue-ball sized blue welt. Something was wrong, and it would be months later in Russia before I could laugh or cough again without a reminder.

Breakfast was mini mart style at the truck stop's store, and then off to the goal of the day: cross Houston. The American South's largest city fanned out in every direction, but the quickest way across looked to be straight up the middle. Having skirted the eastern edge of the Los Angeles mass, this was to be the biggest metropolis I'd yet to face, and the surface streets were nerve wracking. The heavy traffic brushed past with little room to spare, forcing the wheels to the road's edge, that lay littered with broken glass and assorted trash and drain grates. Cars jolted carelessly out of parking lots and driveways. After so many days in the open desert and prairies, the inherent caution was quite unnerving, until enough was enough. The Road Warrior took over. I sped up, and forced my place in the flow. Soon I was careening up and down off the sidewalks and

motioning to those behind that this spot was mine; staring others down with a pointed finger that said "yeah I AM crossing this intersection on a red." This was feelin' good!

Then the eye of the storm. The tall modern structures of downtown were set back beyond a curving green park, giving them a sense of their own space. While taking a break next to the President George HW Bush statue, a couple of homeless guys, fellow brothers of the street, asked if I was heading for a nearby "cure for cancer" event. "Good for a free meal and ya don't wanna miss that, today their having chicken!" I graciously declined, but before leaving, took a stroll around George's statue. I noticed his quote about "a new world order" concerning the fall of Communism. I'm sure he meant it in a good way.

Houston's freeway exits made for a game of search and gamble while trying to negotiate the frontage roads that followed the interstate. Some access roads worked out, paralleling the highway. Others wouldn't work out, by curving under the freeway to head back the other direction. I suppose that the Republic of Texas was saving the taxpayers' dollars by not building an off ramp and an on ramp in the same place. At one such losing gamble, where I would have to backtrack or lift the bike over a set of railroad tracks and through a swampy meadow, I came upon Mark.

Homeless, sullen and quiet, he didn't seem to be all there inside his shorn, tattooed head. He had a yard sale bicycle with a few clothes tied on the back, and ropes actually securing his wasted rear tire to the rim. My sunny "how are ya's" seemed awkward and out of place for a guy so down on his life. That he had started in Tennessee and was heading somewhere out west was about all that could be coaxed out of him. That, and the apparent miracle that anyone who gave him money would be immune from cancer. I couldn't pass on such a healthcare opportunity, and offered over a couple of bucks, then bid him goodbye. Feeling newly invincible, I humped the bike over the tracks and through the meadow, avoiding the mush as best as possible. Stopped at an RV "resort" off of I-10 near Baytown, if ever a word was used more loosely, only to be told they no longer allowed tenters. Like others, this place was built on the remains of an expired KOA campground, and once again, they were attempting to attract the better clientele of retired RV'ers. Not so much against bicyclists, but tents meant those gregarious motorcyclists; and we all know what trouble they can be...

They did however, point towards another park, not far away, overlooking Lost River Lake. The older fella running the place gave that "no tent" business at first, but after giving him the verbal tap dance of the journey, he warmed up. Soon I was visiting with the whole family, and they allotted a nice spot back by his double wide trailer and work shop. He turned out to be a first-class guy. While doing some laundry that night, he dropped by. He and his wife had been talking, they wanted to give me a ride in the morning over the I-10 bridge, spanning the lake. Extensive hurricane damage repair work was being done on it, and the lanes had been narrowed, plus it was pretty steep. I thanked him for the concern, but pointed out that I was bound to face dangerous areas along the route, I'll be fine. Hell, it's just a bridge, get a steady pace going and damn the cars, they'll make room. Setting up the tent that night, I found the pole for the rain fly missing, it had been left sitting on the back of a flatbed trailer in Katy that morning. I cut a branch to length to make do, then patched up a tube and had a couple of dry oatmeal packets for dinner, washed down with water. The mosquitoes were so thick, I didn't want to cook outside.

The morning breakfast of March 16th was at a mini mart at the I-10 on ramp, where I met Curan. Curan was one cool guy. He was riding a BMX bicycle all around the country, in reverse. He gave me a display of sitting on the bike normally, but pedaling it backwards, He would only look over his shoulder briefly, to stay on course, constantly judging the roadside and the white painted lines to stay straight. A victim of HIV, he was raising awareness for that cause, plus homelessness and medical marijuana. With a banner sign promoting his homepage across the bike's cross bar, he said he was going to keep it up as long as his health allowed. His style was an odd site, but this former BMX racer had his heart and attitude in the right place.

Soon after leaving, I came to that Confounded bridge. Heavy truck and car traffic, just wide enough for two vehicles, and unnaturally steep. It was a temporary structure put up as part of the major repair project. With a wooden railing, only three feet high from the road, it looked dangerous. The RV park owner's offer and worries were now understood. The climb started up slow and steady, but the cars and trucks were just edging by me and honking in anger, as if I had a choice. Neither had any room for clearance. And then it happened. While hugging the foot-high raised curb as close as I dare, the front right bag grabbed the curbing. It quickly tugged the bars to the right, and down I went hard to the left, failing to unclip the shoe in time. Leaping up as quickly as I went down, I picked up and leaned the bike over as far as possible to clear traffic. By the chance of pure luck, I had gone down during a break between vehicles, a second earlier or later and I would have been squashed, lights out. The traffic had no room to swerve, due to the oncoming flow.

Shaken and scared, I wondered how to get over, or back down, the span. I struggled with reattaching the bag, the horns still blaring at me to get out of the way. The only safe option was to get up on the narrow curb, and with bike in the roadway, walk it over the bridge to the other side. From up on the curb, the top of the flimsy rail was now about knee high. While nervously steering the bike, I couldn't help but sneak glances at the water forty-feet below. My only plan was that if the bike was hit I was diving for the curb surface, to avoid getting tossed over the edge. The horns and angry shouts continued from the passing traffic, until a merciful delivery truck driver came to an almost complete stop and proceeded to creep along, keeping everyone behind him until I had cleared the other side.

As he pulled by, I gave him a big wave and thumbs up, only to watch the rest shout and honk as they passed, one guy even flashed the finger for holding up his busy day. I signaled in return, out of habit, but was so relieved to be off the bridge I just didn't care. I sat down and chilled for a few minutes before hitting the road again, and told myself that this was it. For the rest of the journey, when confronted by a tight spot, I would hitch a ride or walk it or do anything to avoid a risky and stupid moment like that again. That day didn't improve, as I hit some seriously strong headwinds and could only muster along all day at about five mph, striving for every push. These flat lands were the continent's transitional zone between the mountains and deserts of the west, and the swamps and marshlands of the southeast. They were saying hello.

Texas! Enter into cactus and high plains with the coyotes howling at night and exit into a land of flat coastal bayous and alligators. I camped out again somewhere west of Beaumont. Thanks to the headwinds, I missed the mileage goal, and tomorrow's calling for rain. But the winds should be with me.

7. the boys

S on Shay and I had talked about hooking up somewhere along the route, before I left the States. He was further along in his college career than little bro Cody, and his schedule was more flexible. It was especially important to me; if we let the opportunity pass by, it would be months before I'd see any immediate family again. With only about two weeks to go, until the U.S. ended in Orlando, he managed to free up a few days. Given my pace, and his schedule, it came down to Lake Charles, Louisiana, as the rendezvous point. And he was bringing Cody with him!

Pushing best I could the past few days to make Lake Charles, I was now passing through marshlands that sprouted massive oil refinery plants, the initial impression was overwhelming. Giant facilities, matrixes of large above-ground pipe systems running in all directions, rising high into the sky. Hundreds of lights, still faint in the early evening sunset, dotted the complexes; giving the appearance of small cities. They were monuments of industrial infrastructure, serving the over 2300 oil platforms that lay scattered about the Gulf of Mexico.

The plants traipsed into a surrounding community that appeared worn out after years of existing only to support them. While taking measure of a menacing looking long and steep truss bridge over the Calcasieu River into Lake Charles, a BMW sedan pulled up. The two forty-ish women and their guy friend in the back were a lively crew, friendly and full of Southern humor. At the wheel was Rita, saying she had stopped because, as an organizer for a local triathlon, she was accustomed to seeing cyclists "a bit more streamlined." Too true.

From time to time I'd try. Heading out now and again for a twelve to twenty-mile ride in the morning during the nicest days, imagining how this routine would become a part of daily life. Soon, the pounds would drop off and the endurance would increase, the hair would grow back and the sex would be better. And someday, maybe someday, I'd be able to fit into a pair of those black Spandex shorts and a Lycra jersey, without looking like Shamu. Every time, after a few weeks, something would come up, or I'd rationalize that my spare time should be spent in a more productive fashion "just for today." Before long the routine was no more, and the bike was hung on the rafters. Until the next epiphany.

The physical rewards were never enough to drive me through any exercise program. The joy I found on a bicycle was cruising along at a personal pace up a canyon or along a lonely road, until the quiet and the cadence would meld into a trance. In times past, while climbing Del Puerto canyon near home, the trance would be abruptly broken by a group of chatty and happy real bicyclist; motoring past at twice my speed. I would ponder on how much the bicycle industry would gain if they'd concentrate their marketing toward the thousands of people who would just like to enjoy a ride; yet were intimidated by the clothing.

Make it alright to wear what you wear to the hardware store, make it cool to throw on a pair of old shorts and tennis shoes and just go. The colorful outfits are the fruits of good research with true benefits, yet the science behind their development is lost on the people just wanting to test the waters. Everyone had ridden and enjoyed bicycles as kids, why shouldn't the masses enjoy them as grown-ups? Remove the stigma of the funny looking clothes and sell more bikes. Soon, the trance would return and my silly bicycle accessory industry killing thoughts would fade away. When the silent rant faded, lovely Rita was still there; smiling her southern charm. When she heard my boys were visiting, she recommended the nearby Isle of Capri Indian Casino.

Arriving, there was no room at the inn. People were piling in for the St. Patrick's Day parties, plus it was a bit pricy. It was now well past sundown; the only option was to cross that scary bridge in the dark. I got talking with the casino's hotel porter, he confirmed that there were no other lodging options on this side of the bridge. He then mentioned his friend was heading over to Lake Charles, and might want to make a buck. Not long after the call was made, his buddy and girlfriend showed up. We threw the bike in the back of his truck, and for a ten spot he cruised over the bridge and dropped me off at a bargain one-star. The boys were on their way from San Francisco and a storm was beginning to blow in, I'd kick it here for a day.

When they landed at the Louis Armstrong International Airport in New Orleans, Shay, 24, and Cody, 19, needed a ride. A requisite for a rental was a credit card, which Shay left at home. With no plastic, and The Code being too young to rent a car, they were in a bind. Not to be denied, they hit up a different agency's counter. Keeping the conversation with the agent bobbin' and weavin' with questions and jokes, they managed to pass off Cody's ATM card with Shay's driver's license, hoping like hell the guy wouldn't notice the different first names. 200 miles later, they pulled up in front of my room in a Dodge minivan. It was four a.m. on March 17th, St. Patrick's Day, and the rain was coming down. Sipping beer at sunrise with my guys, I had really missed them. Just to sit there and hear them laugh and talk about their trip from our home to this little backstreet motel room in Lake Charles was golden.

Home. Patterson California is a small farming community that lies near the center of the state, about 80 miles southeast of San Francisco. To its west, there rises a small inner coastal mountain range called the Diablos. They make up part of the western edge of the giant bowl that contains the vast Central Valley, a sixty by five hundred-mile ancient ocean bed that stretches from Bakersfield to Redding. The other three directions from town are a flat and broad landscape of crops and orchards, dairy's and poultry farms. A square pattern of county roads connects it all, making for miles and miles of predictable surroundings.

It was all a far cry from the towering Sierra's of my youth, or the ideals of where I would set down roots. The common story of following the work brought my young family here in 1990, after getting hired on as a mechanic with a commercial airline's maintenance facility, based in the Bay area. At first, it was a stop gap move, we were focusing on the cheaper home prices and only figured to stay there for a few years. As the wages improved, we'd move closer to work when the prospect arose.

Life went on in the meantime. As the boys grew and Sheree found work, it became clear that, although my daily life was a seventy-mile commute to Oakland, their stories were woven into this small town. It took years for me to truly accept this little farm patch as home. In time, its blend of longtime residents and farmers and Mexican immigrants, all ingrained in the surrounding agricultural life, convinced me of what a nice little city it was. Fairly peaceful, a strong community atmosphere, and a mix of cultures that provided good life lessons for us all. The boy's lives became part of the patchwork.

Within hours, it became apparent that the rain wasn't letting up, and this wasn't much of a place to hang out for the day. New Orleans was calling. Since we all wanted to see it someday, and were all together, the time was now. We piled the bike into the van and hit the road. The early morning drive through Lafayette and down Highway 90, through quiet towns and antebellum estates, oozed with my imagined view of the South. The boys were crashed out on the bench seats, having been up since yesterday morning. I kept rousting them awake to point out some amazing mansion or broken-down shack, straight out of the movies. By the time we pulled into New Orleans, a big chunk of Louisiana had passed by.

Initially, it occurred that I had cheated on the integrity of the bike ride. What if someone found out I hadn't ridden all the way across the state? Now I'd have to spend the rest of my days telling the tale with a clarification, or hoping that the dirty truth would never come to light. A second look decided that this gut concern was silly, since the why of the worry was the Ego. Only the Ego cared at this point. This was no world record attempt, I wasn't being paid to pedal the miles, the journey's mantra was to be fluid. Don't fight for direction, just nudge and flow. Today the trip was flowing into the Big Easy, with my sons asleep in the back of the van. Life was good.

Found a motel on the Northeast side of the city, near where I'd be heading out of town the next day. We drove through neighborhoods ruined by Hurricane Katrina, two and a half years prior. We were surrounded by signs of the wind and flood damage, block after block of homes abandoned and boarded up, some shops were getting back on their feet; many others remained dead and forgotten. Our motel was two complexes, separated by a parking lot. One, a 70's era structure, stood fast while its mate, too damaged to salvage, was replaced by a new building that had just been finished in the past few months. But the party must go on, and the party was to experience a place I'd heard of my whole life but had never seen, the French Quarter.

It was more than a month after the annual Mardi Gras event, and it didn't matter. Walking down Bourbon Street, the beads still lay in the gutters and it seemed every bar had a live band belting out tunes. We scored some brews from a street vendor under the huge sign of "HUGE ASS BEERS" and munched on fried alligator, taking in the feel of a happier New Orleans. That evening we settled in at an outdoor café, with a blues band jamming into the night. The French Quarter, or Vieux Carre' as the locals once called it, juts above much of the area at three feet above sea level. Thus, it avoided the bulk of Katrina's wake, which flooded the city. A couple of bars even weathered the storm and kept

pouring drinks as the town was pounded. They later became gathering points for many survivors, wandering the aftermath, trying to make sense of one of the worst hurricanes in U.S. History.

The next morning, I was heading out and the boys were staying for another day in the city. The shower wouldn't heat up past room temperature. For the price I expected hot, but let it slide, rather than bother the manager this early. Shay thought otherwise, and went to the office. When the Indian owner arrived and checked, he insisted that the water was warm enough, no problem here. Now I had to have some fun. "I certainly understand how you can't be accountable for the problems of a motel you own, hell if the three of us think the water's cold, and you think it's warm, it's probably just us."

We grabbed breakfast and shortly thereafter it was time to go. Shay recorded the departure; his narrative says something like "we're going to the park to hang out and Dad's riding to Hong Kong." A quick visit but a great boost, seeing the boys was priceless, and riding away from them was tough. Deep inside I wondered why this trip seemed so important. Before pedaling off, I said as much; wishing this lark was over, but I have to finish it. What hurt wasn't the time gone from home so far, but how long before I'd see them again, and what lay ahead. Later that day, Cody scored a black tee shirt that read "Drove my

Chevy to the levee but the levee was gone." New Orleans, this place takes it on the chin and keeps playin'.

The Chef Menteur highway led out of town and into a landscape of hurricane apocalypse. Across a vast bayou, the storm's surge was evident by the debris left behind. Plywood sheets, business signs, and abandoned cars left to rot. Far out in a thickly wooded estuary, there was a boat hanging high up in a tree, deposited when the surge retreated. Crossed into Mississippi at Pearlington, a town clearly hit and rocked hard by flood damage; but then came Waveland. Dear God. This place was punched straight in the mouth. Whole blocks of homes and shops leveled to the foundation. The thought of all these people and possessions and homes forever swept away one cold August morning was sobering. Fifty residents died when the eye of Katrina passed through, with a twenty-five-foot sea surge that wiped out half the town. Waveland?

At a convenience store there I met a middle-aged black guy who was a real character. Jobless and living on the streets, he stayed upbeat by riding his bicycle around town; looking for odd work and entertaining folks with his simple card tricks. He fancied himself a magician, and offered to let me in on all of David Copperfield's secrets; that sounded like a lengthy education so I begged off. At the finale of one of his tricks, he presented the 6 of clubs from his worn deck, as a good luck charm. I stuck it in a front pannier's netting, and there it stayed for the rest of the trip.

By now, life on the road was beginning to feel normal, rather than just another vacation. After 2200 miles, the engine was feeling good. I could pedal a good day away on the flats with an absent-minded effort, as if looking down and watching someone else's legs pumping away. The neck and upper back pains, from constantly looking up and forward, were almost gone. Finding, then setting up and busting camp was becoming as secondary as living off the shelves of a convenience store. I was now an independent hobo that just needed a bike and tent and sleeping bag, nothing or no one else.

Yet the truth was, I needed a great deal else. Back home, Sheree was working six days a week at the Post Office, balancing the bills and handling all the large and small crises. Cody had moved back into the house, and was playing the role of go-to guy for any of my website or parts or contacts issues. Sheree's younger brother Glenn, who had just recently retired from the U.S. Air Force, was taking time out from his travels to hang around and help. Still, the stress was building at home as the vacation pay income would soon be ending. The mortgage and insurance and car payments would soon be taking chunks out of our savings. It was all planned out in advance, but the stack of little unexpected costs, like college books or car repairs or gas climbing to $4.00 a gallon, were adding up and taking their toll.

In the spring of 2008, America was catching on that something really wrong was just beginning. The housing market slump had turned into a free fall, due to record home foreclosures. Wall Street's zealous geniuses, the guys who established all the rules, broke those rules, leaving no honest men to steer the helm. At the time, the average Joe had no idea how bad it was going to slam the world's economy, we just knew it was a different kind of economic dip. Millions of good Americans, who had never missed a payment, were starting to lose their jobs and businesses and homes; as I blissfully glided along pretending not to notice. A tragedy never hits home until it's your home. And so, I pressed on in the trance, even as my own home was losing half its value.

The dream trance protected me, as I lived in that happy place folder that was always nearby, and finally opened. The folder had never conjured the reality of an unwieldy overloaded bike, with wheels swaying under the weight, popping spokes. Back in 01' and 03' she served me well on a couple of week-long trips through the Sierras. With a few clothes and some camping gear, plus a few tools, it only required the rear panniers and a handlebar bag. As self-contained as that seemed at the time, it was still a far cry from the load needed to support living on the bike for months on end.

The last few months of preparation for this trek were spent mentally walking through the imagined days ahead. The list of minimums kept growing, ranging from a decent water purifier to a sleeping pad; weather gear and spare chains, extra spokes and the tools needed to tackle any problem. Phone and camera, radio and iPod; batteries and chargers, headphones. A cooking set with a fuel bottle and a good jacket. The menu of "needed" items kept growing, even as I warned myself this wasn't a motorcycle. A simple medical kit, a small tube of grease and tire patches; how many shirts, shorts, and socks were too much? Scanning the internet for advice on the subject wasn't much help.

The stories I found were mostly from folks who hadn't gone that far for that long. A few others had gone on tour for years and told tales long on experiences, yet short on the details, but for one clear gem. Once out of Western Europe, good luck on finding my 700c road bike tires. The mountain bike size 650c, at about 25mm smaller in diameter, wouldn't be a problem. But re-fitting the bike for smaller wheels wasn't practical. Not only would it require a different brake set and possibly shorter crank arms, to avoid pedal strike, but the cool plastic rain fenders I'd just bolted on wouldn't look right. So...add a stack of tires and tubes to the equipment list.

It was soon apparent that the lightweight Campagnolo road wheels on the bike were not going to cut it. A set of stouter spec 700c Mavic wheels, designed for a tandem bike, were ordered. They had a wider rim and stronger spokes. Stouter meant heavier, but the durability was vital. Before leaving home, I dropped them off at my buddy Ron's house, telling him I'd ride the Campy's as far as they'd go. At some point, he could FedEx the new set. Since Arizona, the rear Campy had been suffering a wobble, due to the overload. It required daily truing tweaks, eventually leading to broken spokes. To affect a happy medium, the wheel had to be relaxed and then re-trued, by way of a total spoke adjustment. I'd then run with the rear brake in the "release" position. The front brake is all ya need right? By the Southern U.S., even that wasn't enough, and replacing a broken spoke or two from the supply was getting to be common. Always the rear wheel, cluster side.

And I was getting good at the drill. Off the bike and flip it upside down, a flick of the quick-release hub and the wheel pops off. Whip out the special holding tool for the sprocket and pull the gear cluster. Install the new spoke, and reverse the operation. After a quick trueing, I was on my way. I had it down to minutes. When a relatively rare repair became a daily exercise, it was time to have Ron send the big iron. I was hoping to make Orlando on the original set, but now the safe bet was to have the Mavic's shipped to another friend's house along the way. Just a few days away was my buddy Mike, an ex-coworker who had decided a few years back to throw in the California towel, and head back home. He'd landed a good job working on government aircraft, and his wife Keri had earned a degree in Family Therapy. Along with their young daughter Kiley, they had made a pretty nice life for themselves in Gulf Breeze, on the Florida panhandle coast.

Meanwhile, the bleak reality of living in defiance of nature continued along the Gulf road. Striking was the chilling sight of lonely mailboxes, customized by their owners. Some were artfully done with the family names and house numbers in ornate raised lettering, others were simply hand painted by children with happy flower designs. Just the boxes were now standing on a vacant driveway, their homes gone. A foundation, or a set of pillars standing in the lapping waves, were all that was left. Some residents had rebuilt and others were in the process. But why? Wasn't it going to happen again? Along the way I often asked locals this obvious question. They generally rationalized that the really brutal storms rarely hit the same spot twice, and the lesser attacks were survivable; other than severe roof and window damage. The tradeoff was living your life in an incredibly scenic ocean setting, enjoying the morning coffee with the Gulf waves swishing up to your back porch, I'm still trying to understand.

The decision to bolt with the boys from Lake Charles to New Orleans in the minivan produced a ripple. Mike and family were visiting relatives this week, scheduled to be back home by the time I inched my way into Florida. For today and tomorrow, they were in nearby Gautier, Mississippi; at his brother Jerry's. "Why don't you just drop by here and meet the family?" Silly not to. After a sixty-mile Tour de Devastation, I arrived in Gautier. As I pulled up, Jerry and his wife Jennifer, their son and four daughters, were hustling out the door to attend their youngest daughter's Holy Communion. I quickly shook hands with everyone, headed upstairs for a hurried wash up, changed shirts, and off we went. My head was still spinning as we walked into the formal function. One moment, pedaling across a landscape of unreal loss; the next, standing in an orderly Catholic church filled with the well-dressed faithful. And I, looking dapper as always, in my dusty shorts and sweat stained Daytona Speedway baseball cap.

Mike's folks were there also. Good folks whose lives were upended by Katrina. They lived three-miles inland from the Gulf. A three-foot flood surge, caused by the ocean pushing back on the streams and then retreating, washed through their home. It destroyed their floors and walls, and they were still living in a FEMA trailer on their property. Mike, Jerry, and nephew David had been spending all their weekends replacing all the drywall throughout the house. After the ceremonies, we headed back to a reception of sorts at Jerry's. His wife Jennifer was a bundle of energy, involved in all her children's and the local community's activities. She was the life of the party, and put on a great spread for the evening's get together.

The next day was spent kicking it in Gautier. We visited Mike's parent's home to view the repair progress, and later took Jennifer's Dad's small boat out to buzz through the many fingers of the local river and bayous, and drink a few beers. Jerry let me take the controls and I had the skiff ripping along wide open, until running it aground on a submerged sand bank, learning too late the trick of watching for the changing water tones. Credit Mike, he tried to warn Jerry that back home the standing joke among friends was to never let Brian ride your motorcycle. And now boat...I'll do better next time. After extricating ourselves, we returned the ship safely and headed back to Jerry's, stopping to sample the Southern delicacy of boiled peanuts. They're so popular here, you can find them at every other gas station. A mushy peanut...I don't get it.

That afternoon, we stuffed the disassembled bike into Mike's SUV and said our goodbyes. 110 miles to the peninsula town of Gulf Breeze, I never touched a wheel in Alabama. What stood out along the way was a roadside billboard of an American flag, the size of an Olympic swimming pool. And then there was the young boy, pushing another kid in a homemade go kart, flying a six-foot wide Confederate flag above them. They start em' young down here. In Pensacola, we made a stop at the local airport and picked up Keri's Mom. She had just landed from San Francisco, here for a job interview; hoping to change her life to be closer to the family. After an Irish Pub lunch, it was off to the idyllic setting of Gulf Breeze.

The two days spent at Mike's were absolute bliss. His sister Teresa and her clan lived just down the street, so after a morning of seeing to the bike and fitting the new wheels, we all headed over to one of Gulf Breeze's snow-white beaches. This place was like living in vacation land year-round, the preferred uniform being shorts, sandals and a nice pair of shades. Saturday night was filled with a great bash at a friend's place a few blocks away. It was a surprise birthday party for the host Tony's wife, and there must have been over forty people, plus enough food and booze to float a boat. A DJ and a karaoke machine were set up out back by the pool, and wasn't Tony an impressive crooner. Karaoke was his passion, and the man was truly entertaining, he sang at ease; a professional presence. Mike had been singing in bar bands ever since I'd known him, so he too was in his element. When they pushed me to sing a tune, I swayed off with "why ruin the evening by scaring the cat?" We staggered home sometime in the wee hours.

The next day was Easter Sunday, and the Sabbath morning was spent in the backyard, in sunglasses, nursing a hangover. A way-too-bright Florida sun shone down upon Kiley and her cousins, all happily searching for those hidden candy filled eggs. Later on, we were joined by Mike's brother in-law, for an evening of shooting some pool in the den, and nursing a beer. David wore well a very stressful regional managers position for the Southern breakfast tradition chain of Waffle House, and had some great stories. Visiting an old friend, and

 seeing him doing well, really made me feel good. Such a memorable stay with great people.

Monday came and everyone headed back to work, and I set out to cross my final U.S. state. Most of the day was spent cruising along the blank white beaches, looking out on an aqua blue ocean. Climbing the bridge at Destin, I stopped to talk with a couple angling for redfish. Before long, the three of us were crouched down behind the traffic wall, sharing some of their Florida herb. Mark was temporarily wheelchair bound from a recent car accident, but he and his girl Terri were making the best of it, beating the crowd with a Monday afternoon fishing trip. The people I'd met so far on this picturesque coast were pretty laid back, enjoying the Gulf life. The chaos caused by Katrina was behind me, and

Florida was beginning to look like one long white-sands-beach blue-water resort. I then headed north out of Destin over Choctawatchee Bay towards Freeport to pick up Highway 20, crossing into the state's hinterland, the interior Panhandle. The white sands and blue water resort notion evaporated abruptly.

The next morning, I was sitting on the walkway outside of a Freeport gas stop, enjoying the breakfast java with a pastry and a banana, after a night of stealthing it out in the woods. People would pull up and top off the work truck, or zip in and grab their morning brew, then run off to their busy day. It struck me that I was once one of them, but for now on a different path. A path that had jumped off the carousel and lead to this curb and a mini-mart breakfast, on a workday morning; watching them go around and around. Finish up here and casually pedal into the heart of the Florida jungle, with no idea how the day would unfold. Sitting there, cross legged on the warm curb, sipping a morning cup. I'd never felt so free.

8. bears

Highway 20 cuts through this flat wilderness of sandy soil and wet swamp forest like an arrow. No homes or businesses for hours on end, giving the day a treadmill feel, with no sense of progress. Sixty-miles in, I came to the junction town of Clarksville, where a friendly sheriff ok'd me to camp out at the rest area on the Chipola River. For the following day's effort, the same identical scenery droned on. Staying lost in the tunes and the tokes, and sucking on a rising toothache, took the attention away from the pulsing ribs. Another day of a pencil straight highway, bordered by forest and swamps and palmetto, a slow growing and long living small palm plant that grows weed like throughout the jungle. Miles go by with no services, desert like in its hopelessness if a problem arose. The occasional dirt road cutting into the thicket of trees and vines said that some hearty people lived out there somewhere, secluded in the deep wooded bogs.

Soon after taking the Hwy. 267 cutoff I met Ken, Wendy and Malcolm, the family was bicycling from Whitehorse, Yukon, around the continent, on a bird watching mission inspired by teenager Malcolm. They said their biggest problem so far was locating bicycle mechanics when needed, Wendy joked that I should join them on their way west, so they wouldn't lose any more time to

repairs. After all those miles from the far North, I suspected they were better at it than they gave themselves credit. While imagining the undertaking of such a long journey in support of their son's passion, I also imagined it qualified them as the coolest parents in all of Canada.

The day ended at the crossroads spread of Wakulla Station, at the lone diner of Savannah's Country Buffet. I soon met Len, the classic old timer regular and somewhat master of ceremonies, greeting all the other locals walking in. He was a great guy to have dinner with, full of the area's information and history, having lived around here his whole life. Hearing my story, he confided that someday he'd like to do something crazy like drive down to the Florida Keys before he checks out. It wasn't unusual to find people who had lived their whole lives in a relatively small circle, the older generation's life usually only interrupted by Uncle Sam sending them off to fight somewhere in their younger days. Between Len and the lady that owned the café, I was cleared to put up in the woods behind the restaurant. But, they warned, there was a bothersome black bear that was enjoying the local garbage cans lately. Having spent years camping in the Sierras, I had dealt with the breed before, and had a sense of their nature. I played it off, saying a good yell usually shoo's them away from camp, dog like.

As soon as I had the tent set up in a small sandy patch, doesn't Yogi show up. With a tall stand of brush between us, I gave the mid-sized male a loud shout, and off he went. Then he came back. Another bark and off he went again. Then he came back. I yelled again. The animal was obviously used to humans and this was his scavenging zone. As night fell, I decided he was more of an annoyance than a problem. I climbed inside the tent and began writing in the journal and getting set for bed. As I was talking to my friend Ron in Orlando on the cell, the bear showed up again. He was hanging around outside the tent, breathing with a snort and loitering like a lost dog. I gave it another yell and off he went.

I tried to continue the conversation, but before long I could hear the grunting sound of bear breath, but couldn't tell from what direction. Telling Ron I had to hang up and get rid of this pest for good, I grabbed my only weapon, a slingshot with a folding arm brace called a Wrist Rocket. I climbed out and found the beast twenty feet up in a tree, almost directly above the tent. Scrounging for a dozen or so small rocks in the sandy soil took some time but the bear was patient. In the dark night all I could make out were his eyes shining yellow by the light of my small Petzl headlamp. Standing there in the woods in my boxers and socks, I took aim at the yellow marbles, and let loose.

A dull thud and guttural exhale sounded every time I nailed him, and eventually he began down the trunk. As he did, I just kept plunking him on his descent, knowing that when he touched down, he was either going to be convinced or pissed. Luckily, he hit the ground running and went crashing through the trees in the other direction, he never returned again that night. Walking into the diner the next morning, there was Len and the other regulars.

They all had a good laugh over my breakfast tale of how I took care of the town bear last night. It was good for a funny story, but at the time it didn't seem like a Daniel Boone moment. Had Yogi decided to leave the tree and come my way, I hadn't a plan B.

The endless bush continued thru Newport and Hampton Springs, along Hwy. 98. Somewhere in the middle of the day, I passed up a road profoundly called Hells Half Acre. It was so apt, should have been the name of the entire Panhandle. Made Perry after a fifty-odd mile day and found a decent priced motel room. After dinner, I touched base with my buddy Chuck, another old airline workmate who lived in the small town of Inverness, still a two-day ride to the south. I was looking forward to seeing him and the family and their friends; I had dropped by a few times in recent years while working with a bike team at Daytona, and was always shown a good time. He was working during the week up in Georgia, at a business jet center along with another old mechanic friend, Rich, whom I hadn't seen in 13 years. Rich and I were both motorcycle nuts, part of the original Oakland maintenance crew, and had a common interest of getting tuned up and going to Dead shows together back in the early 90's. Due to the timing of their weekend and my progress being on different schedules, we agreed that I would ride the next day to Chiefland. They would drive up in the truck to meet me, saving me another day of riding.

The ride to Chiefland was a pleasant day, cycling along the "hurricane evacuation route." Public signs and Red Cross billboards warned people of the days left until hurricane season, much like counting down the retail days until Christmas. East of Perry, I stopped at a gas station somewhere in the boundless jungle and met a wonderful couple who traveled around the country setting up promotion booths at concerts and racetracks. Everyone you meet hears about the trek, and every once in a while, there are those struck by it, people who really feel it. Meeting those along the way whom you strike an accord with was so fulfilling, and was always a mental boost. These two women were really appreciative of the adventure and expressed some of my own thoughts, to the sense that I was completing a dream that many people could only hope for. They were happy for me.

Knowing the day was going to end with seeing some old friends, I pressed on. Just before reaching Chiefland, after a sixty-mile day, I crossed the historic Suwannee river of Stephen Foster and Al Jolson fame. Foster's "Old Folks at Home" eventually becoming Florida's state song. My Chiefland staging post was outside a mini mart on the south edge of town, awaiting Chuck and Rich's arrival. After going inside for a cup 'a joe and a pastry, I just sat on the curb outside; knowing I'd have to wait almost an hour or so for them to show.

Soon the barrel shaped woman running the mart, who was nice enough inside, came out and warned that I couldn't loiter outside the store, and had to move on. I explained that I had already arranged with some friends to meet me here, "they'll be here in less than an hour." She didn't give a damn, insisting I leave right then. I agreed, with no intentions to. My assumption was that after

54

she went inside, her attention span would be lost in the TV set hanging from the ceiling. I continued to relax on the curb, and was surprised by her focus, when she appeared a short time later just pissing mad, and really let me have it. Politely bullshitting, I peacefully sugar coated the case that my temporary presence couldn't possibly be a real problem, "hey any of that dee-licious coffee left?"

"You'd better leave before I call the cops" she says and I was all aboard. I imagined the knee slapper that conversation would turn into with an officer. When I said the police would find the situation quite funny, she stormed back inside and I could hear her wincing on the phone, reporting the criminal element "right outside the store." Then, time passed as I waited to see who showed first, the local Gendarmerie, or Chuck. Soon enough, my friends pulled in and up to the pumps. Saying hello's and pulling the bike apart, and suggesting the sooner we leave the better, I blew a kiss to my mini mart friend as we pulled away. On journey's end people would ask me "what was the best country you passed through?" Too many variables to declare a clear winner. But after leaving the States, never again did I run into another campground queen, or a line of aggravated motorists that would rather see you fall off a bridge than to hold them up. Or, a territorial gas station diva.

The hour-long drive down to Inverness would have taken a full day on the bike. It was spent laughing at the gas station lady, and catching up on old times with Rich and Chuck. Once there, along with Chuck's wife Vanessa and her daughter Christine, and Chuck's daughter Courtlin, we went for dinner. For some reason, I ordered alligator, again. Having eaten it on every previous trip to the deep South, I decided after that meal that never again, it just isn't that good.

Saturday March 29th was spent lounging around Chuck's place, the home he had grown up in. That evening, along with his lifelong friend Frank, we hit up a couple of the local watering holes and met a few more Inverness natives. The next morning's revelation was an itchy case of chiggers. The microscopic tick like pest was probably picked up stealthin' out in the jungle. Ain't nuthin free. Like an angel, Vanessa went out and bought some anti-itch cream and special soap to combat the burning and intense itching, mainly on the legs. It seemed to work, and days later in Orlando, the problem would be past. But I still had to put up with Chuck and his non-stop "welcome to Florida" jabs over my red scratchy skin. On Monday, Rich climbed on his Harley and headed back to

Georgia. I took the bicycle's steering head apart to re-grease and tighten the bearings, while Chuck tinkered about on his BMW motorcycle. It was a

welcomed day of doing almost nothing.

On Monday, Frank showed up and we headed out to the Gulf on Homosassa Bay in his boat. It was a great day of cruising and checking out the girls, drinking beer and stopping at a waterside bar for lunch. Boating is a big part of the life down here, and rich or poor, most people muster up enough for a small craft to party, fish, and explore all the scenic waterways. Lifestyles are built around the Gulf waters, with homes and businesses dotting the banks. And the rule of no drinking and boating is a tough one to follow. You're constantly floating into cool looking bars or restaurants that look like a wonderful place to put your feet up and relax; have lunch and a brew, and chat with the other locals. Everyone was enjoying themselves on a nice day in a beautiful setting of blue water; the bikinis and the oak forests coming right to the water's edge.

Once again, my hosts had to head back to work. After grateful goodbyes, I hit the road. The path led south through Floral City, then east past Bushnell and Groveland, coming to Winter Garden after a sixty-five-mile day. The morning ride went through back roads lined with old homes and thick Spanish moss, draping down over the lanes. The terrain was very flat, with the occasional and almost unnoticeable rise that only the pedal would sense. It was a tour of the country life, quietly passing open fields and small towns, and small bodies of water that seemed to go on in every direction.

In Winter Garden there was an RV park, crowded with the squalor of permanent residents, and asking $25 for a tent site. It was early enough, so the search was on for a city park or wooded area to put up. With no luck, I returned to the RV park to find the office closed, a note on the door said to return in the morning after 8 a.m. to pay for the site. I set up, had a shower and hit the sack. In the morning, up and at em' early, busted camp and hit it for the final day of riding in America; pedaling past the closed office to continue my cross-country camping crime spree. Orlando was only thirty miles away, yet with the traffic and stop lights, it was slow going. It was midafternoon before arriving at my good buddy Ron's house on the east side of Orlando, set in a park-like gated community. It was Wednesday April 2nd. By chance, it was two months to the day that I rolled away from Patterson.

Ron was a special friend. Back in the early 80's I was fortunate enough to spend the entire stint of my Air Force enlistment at tiny Hahn Air Base in the Hunsruuck Mountains, of what was then West Germany. It was one of the best times of my life, made so by a colorful group of fellas all bunked at Barracks 310, one of them was Ron. He and his roommate Kerry, along with the two guys next door, Steve and another Ron, moved their four beds into one room and turned the other 2nd floor room into a lounge. Beer and music seemed to flow from the lounge 24/7 as we all worked different shifts. We were all in our early 20's, wrenching on fighter aircraft during the day, and playing hard at night. The place became a hangout for many, although a core group of friends called it home, and my roommate Jim and I were lucky enough to be part of it. It was a time of hard work and laughter, and pulling off capers, and discussing everyone's latest disciplinary action or girlfriends. All in a haze of good German beer, and a cloud of hash. I'd met and fell for my wife Sheree during this time, and she too became one of the gang.

Over time we all went our separate ways, but always managed to stay abreast of everyone's lives. We even pulled off that small reunion, sans Jim, back in the mid 90's, hosted by Rick and Donna, now of San Antonio. All thanks to Ron keeping the clan in touch. Now, twenty-six years after last seeing him, my old roommate Jim made the trip down from his life in Missouri, just for the occasion. Along with Rich, who traveled down from Georgia to Inverness, it was the second time in a week an old friend had made a special trip to see me. Jim and Ron had strung a checkered finish line tape across the bottom of the driveway, but upon my arrival at his cul-de-sac, they weren't ready yet with the homemade signs and the camera. Picture Jim, holding a beer up in the middle of the street, my old buddy I hadn't seen in over two decades, telling me to "go back" and circle for a minute until they were ready for the "spontaneous" videoed moment of arrival. This guy. After all these years apart, he was still cool enough to tell me "not so fast" without even a hello or a handshake. Formalities were for other people, once drinking pals, you always know each other. They filmed it, I broke the tape, and was welcomed by a sign offering "ass patches and Preparation H."

Ron's wife Danielle, and their young son Patrick, put up with the three of us for the next few days, as we concentrated on swilling beer, tending the bar-b-cue, and throwing horse shoes in the backyard. Jim was a football star back in his high school days and had brought his competitive edge to horse shoes, gleefully defeating Ron and I most of the time. Ron had contacted a local newspaper, the East Orlando Sun, who sent a reporter and photographer to come out and do an article on the adventure so far, the trip's only media moment. We broke up the party for one afternoon to hit up a local department store for some shorts, and a bike shop to stock up on tire patches. The shop also donated a cardboard bicycle box. Back at the house, the bike came apart and was fitted into the box, cross bracing the container with a few 2 x 4's and wood

screws, to prevent a crush. The gear and panniers filled a smaller box, and then we headed to FedEx, posting it all off to my mother-in-law's house near Cambridge, England.

On the Saturday we took a touristy air boat ride across the local marshes, just to sip beer in a different setting. Then, come Sunday, Jim had to fly back to his state safety inspector's job in Missouri. The next day, Ron headed back to his Space Shuttle career at nearby Cape Kennedy, and Danielle dropped me off at the Orlando International Airport on her way to work. And that was it. I had crossed America on a bicycle.

It was a lifetime goal for many avid cyclists, yet for me, it was only the prologue for the mysteries that lie ahead. As big an accomplishment as it seemed, I would later look back and realize America was the easy part. Familiar roads and terrain, friends and food. The voices of home being a cell phone call away, knowing where I could get away with free camping, and the ability to freely converse with anyone. I still had twice as far to go across ever changing foreign lands, and cultures and languages. Using my airline benefits, I caught a space-available flight up to Dulles near Washington D.C., and then a connecting 777 business seat to London. I knew the next several days would be spent prepping the bicycle and gear, plus catching up with all of Sheree's side of the family. Bikes and good people, things I knew. The reality wouldn't hit home for another full week. The real story was ahead, and it was about to begin.

9. blighty

After a nice meal and a couple of scotch tumblers, I drifted off to sleep and awoke just before a morning landing at Heathrow Airport. Having made this trip several times in the past to visit Sheree's family, I was soon sitting in the back seat of a coach bus and clearing the hubbub of London, en route to the beautiful city of Cambridge. A local bus ferried me out to the tiny village of Girton, and before long I was hoofing down the quiet street of Woodland Park. Finally, I walked into the side kitchen door of the modest attached brick home, where my mother-in-law Pam had lived her entire life; and where Sheree and her three sisters and two brothers had grown up.

I first started coming to Britain back in the early eighties. Sheree's dad Cleon, who passed in 1987, was an American; and so, the kids had the opportunity to join the U.S. Air Force. Sheree and her brother Trevor were the first to sign up, her and I met while stationed together in Germany. Back then, Trevor was serving at nearby Mildenhall  Air Base, less than twenty miles from Girton. In those days, Pam worked around the corner at a local pub called The George, and Trev was always bringing G.I.'s home to party it up with his local friends. I fell into the mix and needless to say, Pam had grown accustom to waking up in the morning and coming downstairs to a gaggle of snoring farting beer-soaked Americans crashed out on the living room carpet. The woman was a saint, I still love to come here.

The troubles and strife of a modern England seem far away once nestled in Girton on Woodland Park. A bakery, the old church, a couple of pubs and the simple well-tended gardens of the village are always a warm snapshot. I take in the beauty of it all and forget the trials of trying to make a decent life in the spendy U.K. economy. The fare is all comfort food, fried potatoes and sausage, shepherd's pie and Yorkshire pudding, all washed down with a beer and a cigarette for dessert. In the mornings, Pam would always rustle up a plate of fried eggs on buttered toast, I couldn't live here but always loved spending a few days at Pam's. For extra income, and with an empty nest, she began boarding foreign students who attended the Cambridge Academy of English, just a short walk away. She's had young people from all over the world stay with her for several months at a time, it kept her busy and she's made some good friends over the years, some who still stay in contact. This time, she had two teenage girls from Japan who were taking up the extra bedroom, so I just pitched my tent in the backyard. It worked out well, since I could stumble home late after making new friends down at The George or The Crown and not have to wake anyone.

The week was filled with putting the bike back together and visiting family. A couple of afternoons were spent walking around the historic college city of Cambridge, the first institution originating almost 800 years ago. The only must was searching for a decent priced flannel shirt, having left mine hanging on the bedroom door knob in Orlando. After leaving the thrift store, I set upon my favorite mission whenever in any European city: wander around the back streets, off the main routes. Cut left and right down narrow, sometimes cobble-stoned side streets, built centuries before the automobile was ever conceived, and find that one ages-old pub that rarely sees an outsider.

The doorways and ancient ceiling beams require one to duck, the one or two patrons and barkeep stare in surprise as a smiling tourist bounds in like he's been looking for this joint his entire life. Over a beer everyone says hello, while wondering how did you ever find this place? "I didn't know it was here but I knew I'd find it." It is fascinating to sit for a few moments, staring at the walls and the woodwork, and imagining the generations of people that had come and gone through these little rooms. Some of these pubs, with little fanfare, had been serving ales since before the Colonies became all uppity and decided to throw off the Crown. First settled by the Romans in the 1st century, Cambridge is now a busy modern city known for its role in England's tech industry. The center of town still has an overgrown village feel with quaint shops and restaurants, with the small river Cams running through the ancient college grounds. And then there's the farmer's market in the central square, that has been doing business since Medieval times.

On the 11th of April I turned 48. Pam and daughters Sharon, Rhonda and Myra were sweet enough to give me birthday cards, and a little spending money that I was dearly grateful for. Cards had arrived from Sheree and the boys, my Mom too. Trevor and Myra's husband Cliff, took me out for a night of dinner, drinking and darts in Trev's village of Needingworth. A fine sight we

were, traipsing back to his place in the wee hours to sleep off a very happy birthday. For the final evening, Cliff and I went to see nephew Tate play guitar in his death metal rock band at the "Man on the Moon" pub in Cambridge. The club had been around long enough that Sheree and her sisters remember going there for dances back in the 70's. Those walls had heard it all.

Alas, the inevitable morning had come. Leaving Pam's was a tough start. My eyes altered from Pam waving goodbye on the front stoop to the thin orange bike underneath me. It would be home for the next six months, and was now loaded with seven more coiled up Schwalbe heavy duty tires and tubes, that had been sent over a month before. The internal questions arose, why was I doing this? What was the point of it? The dangers that lay ahead were overpowering because they were created by my imagination, I was a little scared but more so, nervous with disbelief. It was springtime, and she would be the last familiar face I would see until late fall. Haltingly, I pushed off. With one final wave to dear Pam, the comfort of Woodland Park disappeared under my wheels.

Cambridge was still waking up when I passed through its center and then off to the southeast, passing through Babraham, Haverhill and Cavendish, before making a slight afternoon detour to catch Lavenham. The uniquely preserved medieval village is noted for its twisted and leaning timber framed buildings, caused by constructing them with green lumber in the 16th century. It is rumored to be the inspiration for the "There Was a Crooked Man" nursery rhyme, and was the home of Jane Taylor when she penned the origins of "Twinkle Twinkle Little Star" here in 1806. It was a cold ride through the East Anglian countryside, with the rain and sunshine taking their turns all day.

Despite the elements, it was a peaceful day of small villages and hedge-lined meadows. Country manors and picturesque cottages dotted the emerald green undulating terrain, like drifting through Frodo's Shire.

Reaching Hadliegh after a fifty-mile day, I found a small pub that had remodeled the old horse stables out back into a tidy row of rooms to let. The owner was a busy young man who wore every hat from baker and bartender, to bookkeeper and bed maker. Over pints together in the late evening, he confided

 that after completing a formal education, the move to buy a pub and making a go of it was a better fit than enduring the office life in London's financial district. As I pedaled out of Hadleigh the next morning for an easy twenty-five-mile ride to the ferry port, a pensioner walking his dog stopped to chat. In time asked if I liked cars. "I like anything with wheels." Following him up the block and into his backyard, he pulls open the door of a single car garage. Tugging away a soft tarp, he unveils a perfectly preserved 1928 right hand drive Model A Ford.

The man had bought it forty-eight years ago, after it had spent its first thirty-two years in New Zealand, and he had kept it in fine kit ever since. He was more than happy to let me climb all over it, once he saw the eyes light up. I sat in the front and toyed the controls, crawled underneath and checked out the steering and drive train. We popped the hood halves and talked on about the simple power plant, that had been at technology's cutting edge back in its day. Then, with the cautious formality of starting a small airplane, he moved a lever here and opened a valve there, then pushed a foot button. It came to life in an instant. After he backed it out into the sunlight, I stood in admiration at a true idling relic of history, as the old man beamed behind the wheel. He was the proud owner of a fine motor car. I must have spent an hour there, marveling at the gem. I believe we could have shot the breeze all day in his English garden, but the coast was calling.

I skirted along the rolling south bank of the Stour River, an inlet of Harwich Harbor that ended in the port village of Parkeston, just west of Harwich. To an American, the most notable lore of Harwich was that it was the shipyard and home port of the Mayflower. It originally set sail from here, and after a series of fits and starts, departed Plymouth on England's southern coast in September of 1620; delivering the Pilgrims to Cape Cod some two months later.

And hence, we come to the foretold lovely inebriated afternoon and evening with the happy regulars in lively Captain Fryatt's Pub. Looking back, it became a farewell party of sorts. Here, I left behind the familiarities of language and family for the uncertainties of the Continent. The lit-up Stena Line Ferry waited patiently as the lorries and caravans, plus saloon cars and several "push bikes", efficiently boarded,  then sailed off into the darkness of the North Sea. And still, despite all the planning and effort to arrive at this point, deep inside there was still a fearful boy with a toothache; asking, "what have I done?"

10. koekela

I did have one last point of contact. In 1979, Mom and step dad Jim, along with little brother Kenneth, moved from Carson City to Poway, just outside of San Diego. Ken became good friends with their new next-door neighbor's daughter, Sereni, and they still stayed in contact over the years. She met her Dutch man, Jeroen, while he was a visiting chef at a large hotel in Palm Springs years back. They had now lived here in Holland with their two children, Dominique and Bryce, in the town of Schiedam, just west of Rotterdam, for over fifteen years. I had caught a glimpse of her once, thirty years ago, but we'd never spoke, only knew her now via the emails we'd exchanged prior to arriving in Holland. When they had heard about my trip, they were happy to offer their place for a stay.

Holland was a bicycle rider's dreamland. Bicycle paths, or fietspads, webbed throughout the country like a miniature highway system, complete with street

signs of directions and distance. My head, geared to the mile standard, was processing the kilometres at every point. A kilometre was a tad over 6/10ths of a mile. It was only 20k's to Schiedam; 6(20) = 120. Drop the 0, hence, about twelve miles to go. The mind was so busy

finding the route and taking in the first few sights of Europe, and dealing with the pulsing tooth, I managed to bury the enormity of this momentous day. Good thing, for in a few days it I would be sidelined by it.

Not knowing the exact route, only the general direction, I followed the signs through Maasland and Vlaardingen. The dated roads crossed over urbanized canals that were lined with small, brightly painted motor boats, parked like little cars in front of attached timber-framed homes and shops, hundreds of years old. It was a bit like riding through one of those 500-piece jigsaw puzzles my Mom would work on at the kitchen table when I was a kid. In Scheidam, I met Jeroen at their 1st floor townhouse, and we immediately hit it off. He was a great guy, and was good enough to take some time off from the two bakeries they owned, while Serini finished up with the daily bookkeeping. After a few hours, I knew this was the best chance to ask for help concerning the toothache, before heading out across the unknown.

In no time, we were in the car and headed over to the family dentist, who took me in for an exam straight away. After an x-ray, the doctor determined that there was not one, but two infected lower molars, and recommended a double root canal. Whoa. Speaking through Jeroen, I explained how that would not do, I was on the move and hadn't the time, or cash, for major dental surgery. Any options Doc? The Doctor looked at me very seriously, and again Jeroen translated: "Have you ever had a reaction to antibiotics?" "Nah I'm good, whatever ya got." He asked the same question again. He was about to prescribe some very serious medicine that might put off the inevitable drill, or not, plus some strong painkillers; and wanted to be clear. The entire visit and prescription only ran about $75, and his solution worked. After a week of being racked by the magic pills, including stomach pains and the trots, the tooth pain went away. I didn't get the teeth fixed for another year.

Despite Kenneth's assurances, Sereni didn't know what to expect. She later let on the worry was I may be an athlete, maintaining a keen physical state through a strict diet regimen. Did she have the right proteins and grains in the house? Would he blend in well with their laid-back Euro lifestyle, or was he one of those hard-nosed Americans that thought foreign was different and different was foreign? When she arrived home that evening with the kids to find Jeroen and the athlete planted at the dining room table, strewn with empty bier bottles and a bong, her mind was set at ease. Obviously, Brian wasn't going to be a problem. When first arriving in Holland, Sereni knew zero Dutch. Over the years of total immersion, it became natural to her, and she would sometimes go months without speaking English. She knew the transformation was complete when she began dreaming in Dutch.

Slept in late. After a lazy morning, I hopped on the unloaded bike and headed to their main bakery. I wanted to see the operation and meet Hans, their business partner, and their four employees. Their main shop wasn't a traditional store front, but rather a unit located in an industrial park. Their primary fare of cakes and pies had gained a high reputation with the area's hotels and finer restaurants. They were on a tight schedule and under a heavy workload, but everyone was pulling together and seemed happy to be working there. It said a great deal about Serini, Jeroen, as well as Hans.

Around midday, the crew stepped outside and we all enjoyed a bier and a buzz break, and when they went back to work, I headed further into town to find a recommended coffee shop. Upon entering the dingy looking place, it was clear that coffee wasn't the attraction. Facing a caged booth where one could make a quick purchase, I chose to go left, entering the shop for a proper cup, while deciding on an order. The regulars sitting at the counter sensed a Yank right away, and invited me to take a seat. Soon I was sipping strong coffee and striking up an acquaintance with everyone as they listened to the story, eventually scratching out the website address so they could all follow the blogs and pictures.

The young woman behind the counter passed over a menu, explaining all the choices on the wall behind her. There were several columns of herb with colorful names like "Purple Skunk", "White Widow", and "Northern Lights"; as well as hashish that came in varieties of black, blonde or red. Faced with so many choices, I just told her to pick out something green and tasty. "Strong, medium or mild?" "Strong is better" I said, as my new friends smiled. It was 25 Euros for 5 grams, and with my sparse consumption, it would suffice until I hit the Ukraine border, where I daren't cross with it. I hung out there for a while, enjoying another cup and everyone's company, and then headed back; stopping at an outdoors store to pick up a map of Germany.

That night's meal was fantastic. Just put two experienced chefs in de keuken, pop a few corks and stand back. Jeroen and Sereni put together a great chicken and mushroom sauce dish in a precision display of kitchen grace. Their neighbors, Rien and NIcollette, joined us for dinner, and we dined and talked into the night on life, politics and religion. The wine dinner and good company erased the rising fears I had when riding off the boat, replaced by a temporary joy of being back in Europe. Everyone's life is as they make it, but the pace here was different than the chaotic feel of the States. Despite everyone having to work just as hard to make a good life in an expensive country, they just knew that taking time out, having a bier in the middle of the day, and spending the evening with friends was what you're supposed to do. I admired their life here.

Rolled out of Schiedam and tried to aim as directly east as possible. Rather than the roads, I chose the pleasant, yet meandering, way of the fietspads. No

car traffic worries, but the little lanes wandered all about, avoiding major roads and following the scenic routes. It took longer, and at times I became lost following the mini road signs, but enjoyed living in a bicycle wonderland. A world where everyone bicycled, and the government made up special cross-town and cross-country roadways just for them. The fietspads easily angled me through Rotterdam and down to the start of the Rhine, where it dumps into the Biesbosch, a vast network of tidal wetlands mixing into the Atlantic. Only did about 40k's that day, to Gorinchem, on the Rhine. Didn't really care about making time, just slowly getting used to the idea of really being back in Europe, and dealing with the antibiotic's queasiness. There was a lot of riding along the tops of lawn covered dykes, that sometimes hold back water, or just act as flood protection for the villages. The perfectly paved trails atop them pass by doll house cottages below, all tidy and decorated with small gardens, their windows adorned with flower boxes.

Early on in World War Two, in 1940, Nijmegan was the first Dutch city to fall to the Germans. Four long years later, it was the site of the most forward bridge across the Waal-Rhine to be captured by the Allies, before their advance was stalled by failing to secure the bridge just north at Arnhem; depicted in the grand 1977 war film, "A Bridge Too Far." The next day ended on the north bank of the river, just to the northwest of Nijmegan, in the small village of Andelst, at the first gasthaus I saw. Asking the barmaid at the Café Rene if there was anywhere in town to stay, she gave it a long thought before hesitantly saying I could stay there, if I didn't mind the unfinished state of the yet to be open guest rooms.

The two brothers who had just recently bought the place, Hans and Rene' were remodeling the gasthaus on the fly. They warned that the only problem was that a rock and blues band would be playing all night, and it was going to be loud. Problem? We marched up four flights to the top floor of the old building, and into a tiny tent shaped room, the converted attic. They helped lug the bike up to the second floor, that was home to the only working shower stall. It also doubled as the washing machine drain, and their dirty clothes hamper. "Just move the laundry if you need to clean up", Hans said. I was beginning to like these guys.

Down below, the place was filling up. I went down for a savory, onion topped schnitzel and a bier, then began talking with the patrons, young and old, who wanted to hear the story. As the night rocked and the band rolled on, the place became packed with dancers and drinkers. I must have spoken with every guy, gal, and musician there; with all the chatter, it felt like I'd met everyone in town. By 1:00 a.m., I crawled upstairs and plonked out, never hearing the continuing jam downstairs.

In the morning, only Rene' and I were awake. After helping him move all the tables and chairs back into place, he whipped up a couple of plates of sausage and eggs. Over breakfast we went over Europe's state of affairs, and the effort of running the new business and its future plans, while watching their cleaning lady pick up after last night's party. When Hans arose, the brothers saw me off at the curb, and if I ever walk back into their happy tavern again, it will be a glorious day.

It was a day of headwinds, bier fog, nausea and bowel effects from the Doctor's strong antibiotics. Having never been affected by such medicine, I figured it must be the water, but then thought better of it. Soon enough, I'd have to start filtering water but this was Holland; they must have their water act together, plus, I'd never been affected in visits past. After crossing the Oude Rijn, a Rhine tributary, I decided to abandon the wandering fietspads and try to make up some k's; and swiftly managed to get turned around and lost on a road that wasn't shown on the home-printed Google maps.

It had seemed like a good idea, at the time. Print out the planned route across Europe, and then just shed the sheets as the days went by, rather than carry a bulky Atlas. It may have been a good motorized plan, but I hadn't taken into account the many smaller roads I'd be following on the bicycle to avoid traffic, much less the fietspads. A good map book is worth its weight. Without a clue, I continued fighting a cold wind eastbound and wound up in the small but busy town of Terborg. I felt like hell. With no cheap digs, the settle was a very nice hotel restaurant called the Roode Leeuw, or Red Lion. Laying on the small bed, a strong gloom descended. The initial rush of getting to Europe had abated, and

I was beat from fighting headwinds all day. The frustration of not making good time on the fietspads, the gut-wrenching antibiotics, and the bier buzz from last night's party, all factored in the decision to stay here a day; and try to get focused again.

The overwhelming unknown of what lay ahead was crawling all over. Dutch was quite different from my few German words, and it was hard talking with some people, especially the older folks. The next morning, I went downstairs to call home for a pep talk. While standing in the dark, oak paneled hallway off the dining room, with guests smiling at me as they passed by, all I heard was frustration and anger from Sheree. By now she was over-stressed by my absence, and the fact that we obviously didn't set aside enough money to cover all the unexpected bills. I'm off doing my mid-life crisis thing, and she's working six days a week at the Post Office; and struggling with the problems of everyday life. She was venting to me in tears on a long-distance phone call, when all I wanted to hear was her voice.

I just wanted to hear her comforting familiar voice. I needed it, needed to know everything was alright and that she was proud that I'd made it this far; but that wasn't coming. It had a sobering effect, and all I could focus on was how extracurricular and unnecessary all this really was. It wasn't right, it wasn't just the spending, but the lost income and separation. Everything is just fine until the money stops coming in and then the shit hits the fan, seen it coming for months, I mean what the fuck? I was angry at her, but I knew I was really angry at myself. Thinking I could pull this much time off, thinking I was someone I wasn't. It didn't matter what anyone outside the circle thought, my selfish trip was hurting us. Fuck.

I stayed in the room most of that day, trying to think of that one great excuse to quit this stupid trip. I'd gone far enough. Whatever relief I was looking for was satisfied, and I was tired of riding that damn bicycle; yet there were still thousands of miles to go. In England, people had said that riding through the Ukraine and Russia on your own was just dumb. "They'll kill you and take your bike" was the common point. I would smile it off and tell them that on a bicycle, detours are not an option. Besides, the visas were already bought, and there's no way to avoid Russia. I began to think that with the right mocked up drama, the Russian danger could be real, the seeds of a good excuse.

Inside, I knew what they were saying had some honest weight. Those two countries had suffered social breakdowns, and corruption was rampant. There was a Wild West image with organized crime now calling the shots, and who knew anything about Kazakhstan? The rest of my route was certainly more dangerous, and if I was done mentally, then continuing would be to fight fate, to fight the flow. I needed one great reason. Someway to somehow save face. Sheree would be relieved. Would the boys understand? The guys back at the hangar would never let me live it down. Just one good alibi.

America was a familiar adventure. I had family in California, and friends along the way in Texas and Florida, points I could always look forward to, a goal to pedal towards. It wasn't unlike many motorcycle trips I'd been on; they're a great experience for anyone who's taken some time off work and gone on a road trip. Rough it a bit here, take it easy there, have fun with friends and see some new things. Arriving in England was a normal thing, I've visited family there many times over the years, so that too was a comfort zone. I knew what to expect, and found it all along the way so far. Now, here I was on the edge of the European continent, talking big about going twice as far as I already had. I had bitten off way more than I could chew, and was now faced with walking the walk. Didn't really know where I was going, or what the terrain was like, couldn't speak the languages to share ideas. The food, the customs, who did I think I was? Regular people don't do something this gigantic.

I'm not some world adventurer or a young college guy with unbounded energy. Just the task of crossing Europe and Asia would be enough for those

types, but I had already crossed America. The sobering emotions that day were fear and shame; I missed the family and now may be entering a position where we would never see each other again. The chance that one could cross the Eurasian continent on a bicycle, alone across thousands of miles, through the vague lands of Poland, Ukraine, Russia and Kazakhstan; and for God's sakes, China, without getting hit or beaten or robbed; or killed, seemed slim. Hitting bottom, I wrote in my journal the thought that the words in this purple note book may be the only thing left someday for my sons to remember their crazy Dad by.

Then, that evening, I sat in the restaurant of the Roode Leeuw, nothing better to do but dawdle over a couple of biers and a slow, delicious, mushroom schnitzel. Staring about at the hand-crafted wood walls, the heavy drapes separating the dining areas, and the dense linen table cloths. In this old Dutch hunting lodge-styled room, the cold water of the moment could not be denied; Christ, look where I'm at. Look where I'm sitting. I pedaled here. It was so old world European, natural, not designed. I felt at home, yet humbled that I could never really understand the traditions that created it, Holland. Dinner and a few biers gave time for reflecting over how I simply cannot be in this position and wish it all away, the trip really was bigger than home or bills or fear. I owed it to everyone who had cheered me along the way to embrace every moment, I owed it to myself. Someday I'll be back making everything better and easier for everyone, but these next few months were mine. The hardest answer is always the truth, and the truth was, that there was no turning back.

To ride sixty-miles today and then do it again...and again...and again for months on end, while methodically walking through every problem that arises. As the months wear on, it's hard to stay focused on the reason this was important, when it doesn't seem important anymore. Little by little, loneliness creeps in, as contact with family and friends fade as you progress east. So many good people to meet, but they're not your people. Writing down everything to someday explain this experience to someone, and yeah, at times searching for a respectable reason to throw in the towel. In the lowest moments, a happy face always arrives asking how far you've traveled, or what's life like in California? A boisterous night of clinking glasses, or taking a long look at a landscape you'll never see again, brings back the sense of purpose. Granting blind faith to this ebb and flow of the will is the hardest task, but if you keep moving everything falls back into place. Good or bad, hard or easy, these are just the labels we apply to our day.

That one great reason didn't exist, that's why I couldn't think of it. It wasn't there. The bike, the cash, the time; me, we were all fine. I went back upstairs to the room, laid on the bed and popped a couple of Vicodins from my medical kit, then drank another beer. Within an hour the warm glow was on, and I saw my position in a whole different light. I was the luckiest guy on earth. I'd gone all-in on this and was in the middle of accomplishing a dream. This was the one chance, it wouldn't be better or easier or financially wiser to do this any other time. I had to do this now or be a failure. Before leaving, I'd told Cody that my entire life would be framed as before and after this journey. I could do it, I was doing it, I just had to continue to keep my shit together. Be the moose. My old friend opium, to the rescue.

I called home again the next morning and did get a better vibe, I needed her to understand that the situation deemed I couldn't help her for months, even though I wanted to. This was a mission that had to end in Hong Kong, anything short of that would make this the biggest folly of my life. Long after it's over, it may take pause for thought to imagine the deep rut I'm in at this point. If ever patted on the back for the courage to cross these lands alone on a bicycle, I'll remind myself of these gut punching doubts. It's a wall any person would face and then decide to muster the inner fire to climb over, or not. Once it's over, a callus forms that has you looking back on the rest of the posturing men of your world. Many of them haven't been in these shoes, they know only what they know. It's easy to be brave, until there's something to be afraid of.

Early the next day, Sunday, April 22nd, outside the Roode Leeuw. I straddled the frame and was ready to roll, knowing that from here on the orange bicycle and I were it. No friends, no contacts and phoning home was a bullet. I was really free, and not just poetically. I had walked through a wall inside the Roode Leeuw. I pushed off, clicked in, and dove into the Continent with the smiling abandon of a skydiver, stepping through the hatch.

11. harvest flies

Crossed into Germany at Oeding, a tiny village on route 525. Since the phasing out of border control points, upon the unification of Germany in 1990, the crossing was barely noticeable. Only a small sign with the black, yellow, and red colors of the German flag, and an abandoned one room customs office, stood sentry. The bike spun along a serene path through woods and lonely meadows, coming by couples and groups out for a Sunday morning walk. At one point, the trail dropped into a village where almost every shop was closed, yet dozens of families, young and old alike, sat about the sidewalks and center square enjoying a post-church ice cream. The entire country had experienced an influx of former East Germans and Poles over the last eighteen years since the Wall fell, and I felt one could still tell who were the lifelong residents, and who were the Eastern newcomers, just by their simpler clothing styles and the cigarettes. Rolling along questioning the imagination; it's been years, how could that be?

Only managed a couple of 80k days after leaving Terborg. Despite being held back by the scenic roads and paths, the clarity now was that they were the experience, simply heading east no longer the goal. In Nottuln, along the 525, I settled on a quiet, nondescript gasthaus ran by an 81-year-old Oma, she had operated this little inn for decades. We hadn't but a few common words between us, my German limited to please and thank you, numbers and directions, but she was very sweet after the initial surprise that a guest had arrived. These little places dotted every hamlet, and flourished for years and years, but were now being set upon by the advent of the modern world.

The room was similar to one's I'd seen in the past, like staying in your grandmother's spare bedroom. The tidiness, the dainty vase on the table, the pretty flower prints hanging on the wall, in which tiny harvest flies had been entombed for years between the pane and the picture. A wardrobe cabinet that was a truly fine piece of furniture, made from glossy lacquered mahogany or stained walnut; it all felt so old and cared for. The included breakfast was usually freshly baked bread with ham or cured raw bacon slices, and a boiled egg, along with a rich cup of black coffee; all for only 30 Euros.

In the morning, I had a long talk with her daughter, a lovely woman in her forties, she told me of growing up in the gasthaus. Along with raising her own family in the village, she was expected to take over the business at some point. The times had changed she said, travelers tended to do business by phone or online, satellite television kept people entertained at home, reducing the number of locals taking drinks and meals here. The sons and daughters that traditionally inherited the keeps chose instead to get an education, and move on to more lucrative ways of life. She predicted the eventual demise of the village taverns, no one was standing in line to take over. The dear old Oma, having heard about my family, gifted a postcard of her gasthaus, telling me to mail it home to let them know I was alright. I keep meaning to.

Steered across northern Germany's country roads towards Munster. Crossing a large city is never the first choice, but it was the most direct path towards the day's goal of Gutersloh. While knowing that the cost of staying in gasthaus's and hotels would drop substantially once entering Poland, the cash burn was on my mind, and the aim was a campground; shown by the symbols on the new German map. The expectation that Europe was full of nice places to camp never panned out, due to routing along the minor roads. Sometimes an hour into the morning's ride I'd pass by one, the timing never just right, one of the drawbacks of not having a throttle to control the pace.

Thankfully, Munster was a quick ride through. The town had been almost completely destroyed in WWII by Allied air raids, due to its military command centers, and was now a university town, greatly comprised of modern buildings. It boasted a very well thought out Dutch-like system of bicycle paths along its tree lined streets. What's that? No, it isn't the namesake of the cheese, that stems from the namesake area in the Alsace region of northern France. I Wiki'd it, that's how.

Turned out, the camping symbol on my new German map also doubled as the mark of a hostel. In Gutersloh there was no campground, and the hostel had recently been remodeled into a modern, high-end hotel. Beautiful place, but thanks anyway. As the day went dark, searching through the phone book at a Chinese fast food cafe revealed a relatively reasonable place. The gasthaus was across the road from the world headquarters of the German appliance maker Meile, and media giant Bertelsmann. When I walked in, the tall blonde boomer aged woman owner was busy and curt, as she scurried back and forth between the bar and kitchen and dining room. I'd arrived at the peak of supper time and the rush was on. I settled into a corner booth with a beer and took in the room. It was a comfortable old traditional gasthaus with ax-hewn ceiling beams and wall posts. A pair of transport drivers in the next booth conversed fluently in German, with thick British accents; I'd never heard that. When the action subsided, she sat down with a coffee and thanked me for waiting.

Her story was familiar. As she helped with a dinner order, she told how her father had bought the inn after the War, recognizing the potential for business, due to the expanding corporations across the street. Along with her brother, she now owns it, knowing her whole life this is how it was going to be. Unlike other gasthaus's, theirs certainly wasn't lacking for customers. In the morning, I followed her brother into the basement where he showed off his hobby of collecting and restoring vintage pre-War Miele bicycles and parts. The household appliances giant hadn't made a bicycle in almost fifty years, but just like the old boy's Model A in Hadleigh, I appreciate old machines. Their quality and state speak for long gone craftsmen, and flash on the different owners over time. The perpetuity of good metal reminds us, we never really own it, we're just its keeper.

Through to Grohnde that day, just south of Hameln or Hamelin of Grimm Brothers lore; another search for a camp, another gasthaus. The next few days will be skirting the northern edge of the Harz Mountains, the pace is slower, following the climbing and dropping terrain into what was once a far corner of West Germany, approaching the former DDR. West and East had erased their border years before, but my mind anticipates the remnants of the Deutsche Demokratische Republik. It's been almost two decades since the fall, there'll be no guard towers or barbed wire, so keep an eye out for subtle changes. The expected rains were holding back, and the scene continued to be forests, and meadows, and small villages; but the sensation simmered that things were about to change. With every turn of the wheel, I was getting further away from the known, and nearer the unknown. When living in Germany in the early 80's, such an incursion wasn't possible, and now I'm pinging to see firsthand the differences in the architecture, or culture, or attitudes.

Spent the night in the small village of Rhuden, at a small gasthaus that epitomized a theme. A kind old man and his dear wife were the last in line, their children had grown up and headed off to other lives. In a few years when their health waned, there would be no one to step up, and the penzion would close for good. When I asked if an outsider may want to buy the business, he just stared and shook his head. The sad truth was that the tendrils of modern life were finally creeping into these tiny hamlets, and changing old ways once thought eternal.

The next day began like the last, a morning of small towns, separated by pastoral farmland meadows and knolls, dotted with patches of forests, but today would be different. Today, I would pass from the state of Lower Saxony into Saxony Anhalt, the former front line of the East. The feeling that a way point was about to be reached was fed by the contrast of how these provincial surroundings served to hide the area's cold horror of post WWII Germany; like a family tension that no one dare bring up. For centuries, these generations had lived a simple life of hard work on the farms, raising family, and worship. In the Spring and Autumn, the planting and harvest festivals would bring the neighbors together, a lifestyle of purpose, earned by sweat and faith. Through it all, they had seen changes in borders and rule and nationalities, in the form of the Saxons and Prussia, Kings and Dukes. Hardships and tragedy, and war, had come and gone many a time, and then came the 1950's.

Just a few kilometres from here, the people of the villages and pastureland's and woods just like these, came to be imprisoned in a vastly different world, all by the nod of the victorious powers. The new rulers saw this new border as a compromise of lines on a map, yet the lives of every man, woman and child suffered the repercussions. After another horrific war spawned by their own leaders, that devastated their land and took millions of their countrymen's lives, they awoke from this dark era to the monster of Joseph Stalin. As he took his bite, they were soon living in a controlled world of appointed leaders, and told where they would live and work and what to believe. The Stasi spied on their actions and speech, and dredged their mail for skeptics. The ill-fated were sent East to brutal labor camps for dissension, real or imagined. The fortunate left everything behind and joined the mass exodus West, to escape the increasing Sovietization.

Along route 6, between the villages of Lochtum and Abbenrode, I crossed over. The thought that "there'll be no guard towers or barbed wire, so keep an eye out for subtle changes" was so naive. There was no gradual, there was no subtle, the changes leapt out like a tiger. True, there were no guard towers or barbed wire, no signs of a former border, no placards or memorials noting the demise of the Iron Curtain; but the layout was unmistakable. While the pre-War vintage village centers were the expected well cared for German structures, the outskirts were quite different. Abandoned factories bore very un-German broken windows and perimeters of overgrown brush. The Russian solution of housing, in the form of tall cement apartment towers, surrounded towns. All in disrepair, and spouting the graffiti of youth angst. They had used rough-finished cement for everything, from fence posts and bridges, to their stark buildings. An old house was finished on two sides using roofing tiles in place of siding, like kids building a fort. Clumsy old  motorcycles smoked by, using tiny two-stroke motors, with over-sized fenders and headlamps, designed only for utility. The dichotomy of two worlds so close together, one that never lost its free market world and one just re-learning it. One that cared, and one that wished it could have.

The gloom was lifted on the roll into Wernigerode. There was a giant medieval palace up on the hillside. This wasn't your basic European castle, it wasn't some deteriorated stone lookout of an ancient Duchy. This thing was huge, and had been kept up. It was straight out of the movies, worthy of a Walt Disney dream; it was the Wernigerode Castle, and it was spectacular. I just stared at it and tried to take in every stone wall, tower and steeple. The camera clicked, but the grandeur of this complex could not be captured. I'd never seen anything like it. The story goes that it had been started back in the 13th century by Saxon nobles. It had seen many keepers, but it had survived, and always been improved.

Outside of Quedlinburg I met Marcel, a thirty-something Dutchman, touring from Holland to the Czech Republic on a recumbent bicycle. In short, a standard bicycle is powered from a vertical position. A recumbent is powered from a horizontal position, and the seat is way more comfortable. He was a member of the Hospitality Club, an international organization that connected travelers online. The deal being, that if you provided a traveler with a meal or a bed, or spare couch, or just sleeping bag space on the floor; the favor could be returned, worldwide. Marcel offered to ask his connection in Quedlinburg if I could join them for the night. As we pulled up to the converted 19th century manor, our bespectacled college age host Ernst rode up on a mountain bike, from a day of studies at the local university. He had no problem with an extra guest, and we headed up to his third-floor apartment, where his buddy and girlfriend were busy in the kitchen cooking up our dinner of sautéed chicken and potatoes.

His flat was a spacious high ceiling main room, with three small side chambers for bed, bath and kitchen. But the coolest feature was the large sun room balcony, overlooking the street. After dinner, we all sat out there, drinking beer and passing a smoke, while I told them the story. In time, his friends left and Marcel bid goodnight, while Ernst and I talked into the night about the day's politics and this region's history. He explained that during the later years of the Soviet era, the people earned very little, but there wasn't much to spend it on. There wasn't a lot of products and building materials on the shelves, and what was there had to come from a state-run factory producing batches of low-quality goods, due to the yearly production quotas. If a truck full of shoes or windshield wipers, or say, roofing tiles, showed up in your area, you had better buy up, whether they were needed right now or not. Bartering must have been an art. Recent years have seen financial input from the E.U., and the formerly oppressed citizens were spending their stake and savings on German and Japanese cars, as well as home projects and small businesses. Yet, as far as he knew, there were no plans to raze the shuttered industrial buildings blighting the land, now forever vacant. In the morning, Marcel left early, trying to stay on schedule to meet his girlfriend in Prague. Ernst rode with me past the centuries old timbered buildings of the town's center, and out a casual 20k's to a man-made lake, filling an old mining pit. We had coffee at a small bar, overlooking the few small boats and fishermen, then found a lone park bench to share a final smoke. Ernst was an easy guy to hang out with.

Headed out and left route 6 at Bernberg, moving away from the Harz region. That night's stay was a penzion in Kothen, in a small room out back, hidden behind an overgrown jungle garden of fronds. I took the meals at the main house's basement, at a table set into a covey dug out of the earthen walls. As my elderly host cooked up breakfast, we spoke in the halting tempo of partial language with his poor English bridging my few German words. I gathered that he would be the final proprietor of the place, but my bright side said there had to be hope for this small inn. It had such a humble, cozy, Middle Earth mood. Hopefully one day, some young couple would fill it with new life.

12. Marty

By now, it was near the end of April, almost three months and 3500 road miles away from Patterson. Still in Central Europe, but now entering the second phase of the trip. Although I couldn't yet see the East, one could sense the slow transition had begun, things were getting interesting. The differences in the homes and towns, and the people's lifestyles, were noticeable; changing regressively just in the last few days. A few farmers were using actual horse power, the villages seemed blander, and the characteristics of their center's buildings were different, such as the use of onion top steeples. I couldn't pretend to know my Baroque from my Rococo from my Renaissance period, but there was certainly something different in the structures of the town squares, a Slavic slant perhaps?

This far away, yet the heat was still on. A pay-phone call home confirmed that the worries of everyday life hadn't changed. Despite the Roode Leeuw epiphany, the trials of home, thousands of miles behind me, relentlessly pushed at the mind's gate, demanding entry. But there was no middle ground now to ponder the house, or car and money issues. It was hard to truly let go, but it wasn't my fight right now, I had to stay positive, and home had to cope without me. The pain of failing by choice would be unbearable. The stress of failure would erase years from my life under the weight of attempting a test so grand, and finding out I really hadn't had what it took to do it, only dream it. A relaxing year off, my ass. I was attempting to ride a bicycle around the world. I still didn't know if this trip was right or wrong, or if I was good or bad person for starting it, but I knew I'd never felt more alone. What was certain, what held no doubt, was the task. Hong Kong will arrive if I make it happen, a little each day. A final note scratched down in the journal for this day was "we're all in, the troubles at home will only be worse if I don't complete this."

The battle of the internal arguments played out while quietly rolling by dandelion fields on beautiful spring days, through farmlands scattered with country dachas and impoverished cottages. Their sparse and worn implements told the tale of a people still struggling to catch up to farming in a competitive world; after living for decades in a controlled economy. I tried to imagine myself in their past; to live in such pastoral surroundings, yet to know that you or yours

79

could never leave, or forge a dream, or try to make a better life. Was it possible that if farming in such a beautiful land was your calling, it wasn't so dismal? As an outsider, I could never know these people's dogmas, or rationales, or their take on the new liberated life. I could only be happy their futures had changed.

Following the small roads, and stopping to chat, kept the pace down to 80k days. The people here were friendly, and loved to talk, even if the communication was arduous. A couple of old timers outside a farm house were helping me with directions, and soon, they pulled up a third chair, and a cold beer. We settled into a long talk about the trip, while going over their dated road map. One was a retired NVA, or East German Army officer, and the other, a farmer and auto mechanic. They were amazed at my story, and we laughed and drank and smoked their stale cigarettes for an hour, before I had to beg off. Just a generation ago, this momentary friendship would have been a crime. My farmer friend was wearing a weather-worn Washington Redskins ball cap, and when I told him my favorite team was their arch rivals, the Cowboys, he was clueless. He had no idea the Skins' were a football team, he just liked the hat. The strong Native profile, the dangling feathers. It was America.

Stopped for a beer and brat outside an imbiss stand in Pratau, and joined a table of old comrades who didn't have a word of English, but were anxious to figure out why I was there. Afterwards, one of the men jumped on his bike and lead the way out of town, to point out the river path to a barge crossing the Elbe. Atop the levy outside of town, I had a great view of the city of Wittenberg on the far bank. It was here in 1517 that Martin Luther ignited the Protestant Reformation, by presumably nailing his "Ninety-Five Theses" to the front door of the All Saint's Castle Church, outlining his issues with the Roman Catholics. The gist is, he felt the Pope was fraudulent in exchanging the repentance of sins for cash, as well as suggesting that the church was building its wealth on the backs of the poor. The gall. The Papacy didn't think much of Martin Luther, but his small action in a tiny village has changed the paths of millions through the centuries. Way to go Marty!

The guys running the tethered barge across the Elbe were a couple of happy characters, who enjoyed running this part of the family's business. They were all questions about my ride on the 200-metre crossing, and wanted me to stay at their gasthaus on the other side, in Elster, and have dinner with them. It sounded like fun, so they called ahead, offering up a buddy deal, and said they'd be there in a few hours. I pedaled all around the village looking for the place, but couldn't find it. Trying to ask the locals for a gasthaus I couldn't pronounce, and hacking up "der zwei herren that run the barge" whose names I didn't know, brought smiling blank shrugs. Finally, I gave up and pushed on, following 187, another 15k's to Schweinitz.

Sitting at a corner table, nursing a basic meat and salad dish. Across the room, a tobacco cloud rose above the gasthaus's sullen young owner, and his three rough cronies; gathered around a large table, grunting over some sort of card game. When I arrived a few hours earlier, he seemed surprised and a bit put out. Trying to haggle him down 10 euros didn't help his attitude. Even then, I had to strike out into the village and find a bank-o-mat to get some cash. What I saw of Schweinitz was a few blocks of dull gray plastered buildings, the shade of a battleship, the impression was tidy, but cold.

After dinner, it was too early to retire, plus I'm a sucker for a social challenge. Striding over to the card table and plonking down on the bench, the dudes didn't flinch, they just glanced at the owner with a "your place, your problem" look. There was a palpable awkwardness, as no one knew what to make of it. This close to the border, they were talking in a Polish/German mix and I hadn't a clue what they were saying, or playing. By their gestures and tones, it seemed they'd been doing this for years. They had a short deck of cards, slightly larger than a poker standard, that used multi colored suits. It seemed like hearts, or spades, but different enough to not know. My host poured a round for everyone, and I asked a slew of slow dumb questions, in the wrong language, trying to figure out the game.

They would take turns sitting out a round, and nurse me along on the rules, which I never understood. Before long, they were asking about the ride, and what was California like. Pretty soon, we were having a good time trying to figure each other out, and it turned into another late night. There was nothing sullen about these guys at all. They saw me as a guest, and we hadn't a common language, they just wanted to play their card game and have a drink. The next morning, the innkeeper's sister and I were the only ones up. Her English wasn't bad, and over breakfast she told me they had taken the place over from their parents. She opens, he closes.

Pushed for the Polish border at Cottbus the next day, but meandered too slowly and pulled up short, at a traditional old German gasthaus near the tiny village of Eichow, on the L49. The weather and the scenery and the friendly people made for a perfect day; I enjoyed to no rush. The new-found commitment to the trip had created a state of mind where the eyes and heart were opened up to the new surroundings, and I felt like an ambassador, or pioneer sent forth to see new lands. On a nice day with a rolling terrain, the ebb's flow was flowing, my head riding a good wave. The capable and pretty Anica, the tall brunette who owned the establishment, told stories about how the inn was her father's pride. When she mentioned that for years, it was a meeting place for visiting East German and Russian officials, my mind conjured images of crisp officer uniforms and gray woolen suits, smoking and carousing on a cold vodka-fueled night in the oaken bar cafe. She was the appointed one to continue the business; wanting something more out of life, but would never think of letting down her parents, or displacing the lifelong help who worked there.

The wheels rolled into Poland at the control free border at Forst, on E-36, and headed for Lubsko. Ran into a couple of boys, needing a wrench to tighten up one of their bicycle cranks. They saw my loaded down ride, and gave a look like I was fibbing when I told them I really hadn't the spanner for their style of crank. I left them there stranded, and rode into an eerie border zone landscape. From the journal: "If the decay of the Soviet era was noticeable in E. Germany, Poland is like oh my God." They had joined the European Union four years earlier, but there was no sign of any Western reconstruction funds being spent. So many beaten buildings and heaving concrete slab structures, left to rot, like toy blocks discarded by some giant child.

Poland's Zloty was still being used at 3 to 1 on the Euro, and I smiled inside, after realizing the good deal at the Hotel Zemse in Lubsko. The proprietor was a nice man who was a ringer for Lech Walesa, the Polish Solidarity hero. That night, he had a group of guests over, and was showing them around the place, figured them for a group of potential buyers. A couple of young men, who joined me for a beer, warned that evening against traveling through Ukraine and Russia, the usual thieves and violence story. My concern was that Ukraine was the next country over, and I was still getting bad vibes, maybe this entering the gauntlet notion was real.

The confident, well-rehearsed spiel on how there was nothing to worry about was laid out. The gut believed it, but for a different reason; as in why worry now? All bets were off, since those countries were my route, come good or bad. Zero language skills, not a lot of trip reports from tourist to go on, and no phone. A new lawlessness in a world still realizing the concept of a free market. Just be more careful, and be nice, I told myself. If someone threatens, then attack first. Don't be a victim. Having been a bit ill from the Dutch antibiotics, I made a point to start filtering water here, as a response to the glaring deteriorating conditions. And yet, the town square across the small street in front of the Zemse was very modern, with the old-world flavor retained. Clothing and electronics stores and an internet cafe were in view, while a turn of the head saw the 15th century Zarska gate tower, still standing guard over what was once the town's retrenchment. The hotel itself had the feel and interior of many places I'd would see in the former East bloc countries, that of being remodeled in the 60's or early 70's, and never updated or repainted.

Yellowing walls, worn staircases and faded pictures of flowers with once again, those tiny dead harvest bugs under the glass.

The next morning started with a rousing breakfast of eggs and cheap meat, while telling my story to the men from the evening's investor group, who were humorously suffering a hangover from their late-night drunk. Their wives slowly made their way down, and as I headed into the first full day of Poland, they all wished me well. The owner joined us, and was ever the smiling happy perfect host, and thanked me for staying. I really liked that guy, he was the first Pole I'd spent any time with, and reminded me of the only well-known Pole I could recall.

At 20k's out, I had to find shelter in Nowogrod Bobrzanski, as an early drizzle turned into a rain storm. It was May 1st, Poland's Labor Day, and the occasion found every village shop closed; until I passed a small butcher shop. I tucked inside and began explaining to a middle-aged Mom and Pop, and Grandma, and a cross-eyed brunette girl of about twenty, that I'm only here til' the downpour passes.  It was the family's business, and soon they were making tea, and Grandma left, quickly returning with pastries. They called a friend who spoke English, and soon a blond girl in her mid-twenties showed up. Jolanta was full of life, and coolly excited that an American was in town. She and her boyfriend had lived in London for a short while, and they were trying to start up an auto parts business here. We all ate, took photos and exchanged info, the hospitality was over the top. The experience of these people, being so glad that a stranger walked into their shop and visited, was the first sense that my presence was special; the further I rode from the Western world, the more people were happy to meet me. "What's it like in California?" "How big is your house?" "How many cars do you own?" "What do Americans think about the Polish people?"

I would now live the next five months answering these basic questions to so many. I would repeat the tale of my path seemingly a thousand times, and be a micro-celebrity everywhere I stopped, like being on a talk show all day long. I wasn't a typical tourist, since the bicycle and the direct course around the world deemed a path of small roads, steering through small villages. Even now as I write this, it's sometimes a struggle to determine exactly which path lead through all the small byways. This somewhat random plan would occasionally make me the first American some people would ever meet, and I would often remind myself that no matter the circumstance, keep smiling and be polite. If I became one of the few Yanks they ever encountered, leave a good impression. Hell, this ambassador gig was tough work, it was 2008, and the U.S. hadn't been winning any Miss Congeniality sashes for the past few years.

As the rain eased and I prepared to leave, my hosts said not to fear Ukraine, there's good and bad everywhere, and most people are good. It made for mixed signals, but I wanted to believe that the closer you get, the more people knew; and knowledge dispels fear. It was good to hear for once. I pedaled along the 290 through small hamlets spaced every 10k's or so, noticing the further I ventured, the less dilapidated things were looking. Border areas usually always look like hell, and just as I'm thinking Poland's a rotten wasteland, a pretty cottage or village square wheels by. It was still a strange scene, the years of poor infrastructure upkeep, and the tall ugly Cold War tenement apartments spotting the land made the place look cold. Couldn't help to feel I was riding through a world that visitors weren't meant to see, and my heart went out to these people, making the best of the futile ruins left them. Like the former East Germany, that which existed before Communism was being restored; the Soviet "improvements", left to neglect.

That which had existed before, and that which was yearned again. After an 85k day, I rode into the thousand-year-old mid-size city of Glogow, and after asking around, found a nice hotel with a hostel price. Sitting at a sidewalk cafe in the busy town center, I wondered how the buildings seemed so fresh, after so many centuries. A table of locals, preparing for the evening's May Day celebration, gave me a brief sad history. After hundreds of years of this area's Polish, Austrian and Prussian rule, the town was, of course, seized by Germany in WW II. By the time Stalin's troops ousted them in a month-long siege, the bulk of the city had been leveled.

After the War, the right to private ownership was taken away, and Glogow's ruined Old Town languished for decades, until the late 80's, and into the reconstruction period. The perfect old-world timbered buildings I sat among were modern replicas of the structures that once stood here in the past, erected by its people, who wanted to remember. They invited me to stay for the party and fireworks, but I decided to bow out. I couldn't take every opportunity to party since being sharp and feeling good on the bicycle the next day was part of the "keeping your act together" task. Also, the money was very tight, and even this early, the concern was how it was going to last to Hong Kong.

Poland! The people are so friendly yet stare at me like I'm from Mars. I'm seeing storks in giant nests living atop abandoned chimneys, and told it's a cherished sign of good luck. There's an inordinate number of girls that look like Courtney Cox's sister. Western television programs are shown, with every character's lines, male or female, translated into Polish by the same guy. Waiting to cross the Oder River near Leszkowice, on another tethered auto barge, I was entertained by a bicycle racing event. The competitors ranged from young kids to elderly ladies, all running whatever they could find. They would line up in rows, and take off down the street and around the corner, out of sight. Twenty minutes later, they'd reappear, mostly winded, but for the youngsters vying for the stage win. With the results in, another mixed age group would line up for their heat. It was clear that bicycles were a way of life for these Poles, and the fun didn't stop as your years marched on.

After a 70k day to Rawicz, finding digs was a tough game. It ended at a sports complex with rooms to let, that were designed to house visiting teams; getting them to let me stay was a trick. With no Polish words in me, and a staff with no need for English, the idea that I wanted a room was lost on them. Despite resorting to putting pressed palms together and laying my head on them, charading sleep, their easiest response was "no." Just as I'm thinking "what's so damn difficult", I'd manage to get a chuckle out of them, which kept negotiations alive. It seemed they didn't want me to stay there; until, they saw the bike. Hey, this funny sounding man needs a room!

The room was a decent price, meaning it was coming in around the $10 mark. It overlooked a well-tended soccer field, and had a nice shower, so I decided to stay here two nights; to rest, and come to grips with the new country. With the advent of Europe, and grasping the changing places and culture, I was waking every morning feeling tired. My crazy dreams were to blame. With all the new sights, and losing the ability to freely communicate, the stress back home, and critical navigating decisions at every crossroads; the senses were overloaded. The subconscious was recording everything the eyes missed, and the sleeping hours were filled with rushing action-packed dreams, as the mind tried to sort it all out; and it was all just beginning.

Not wanting to bother the somewhat cold diner staff, I found evening sanctuary in a cellar bar about a block away; bars are where the happy people hang out. Standing out like a sore thumb in the tiny pub, soon several wanted to hear how I came to be in Rawicz. I spent the next day sleeping in, checking out the downtown and getting in a couple of decent meals. By the second night in the cellar, we were all old friends, the beers flowed and the language was bridged. We promised to always stay in touch. You know.

By the time I'd gone 45k's to Krotoszyn, the steam had run out of the road warrior engine again, and I found myself in that blue funk. But why? Maybe the weakness was born from the foreboding of fear and uncertainties ahead, or bad sleep or socializing every night; or just not giving a shit about the goal, I wasn't sure. Missing home after so many months was always weighing heavy, but I had to be honest with myself. The sum of all the factors equaled up to simply being in over my head. As every day passed, I pedaled further from home and I was burnt out. Great exercise and new sights, and good people and adventure of a lifetime, and on and on and blah blah blah and fuck this. How is this going to end? Hong Kong? It might as well be a hundred thousand miles away. I plainly had to keep the head above this gloom, surrendering would be a slow death, because time or money be damned, I was the only one who could help. But not today. Just one day out from a break day, and I needed to stop; I'll continue the Frodo-to-Mordor act tomorrow. I needed another beer and painkiller boost, knowing, it's a solution only when it works.

In Krotoszyn, there wasn't much, but I was directed to the far side of town; to another sports complex. This one was a modern swimming facility, with an indoor pool and jacuzzis, and sauna. It wasn't cheap, but I needed to hole up, and wanted to update the blog and pics. The charming brunette desk girl on my floor didn't know of an internet cafe nearby, but soon we were talking about the trip and her life in Poland. Agnusia was in her late 20's, and had lived in this area her whole life. She then offered to bring in her laptop the next afternoon, but I hesitated, not wanting to foot for another night. When I mentioned I had no plans to use the pool, she went to work, discounting tonight's room and giving a buddy deal for tomorrow. Another day of not riding started to sound just fine.

Hanging out at the Hotel Wodnik was a nice respite; I stayed in the room most of the day, just leaving a couple of times to eat in their cafeteria. No bar, no meeting people, no sensory input. When Agnusia's evening shift began, I gave her a few hours to get things done, and then we sat at her desk and managed to get the pictures transferred, using her computer. We talked about life in Poland and life in general, late into the night. She had very little English, and many times we had to resort to a Polish/English translator website to get a point across. Mentally, it was a good stay. It had felt like a time-out, and it was calming to have a long talk with a pretty face.

13. ions

Consecutive two-night stays at Rawicz, and now here, had me torn between the guilt of slacking off the schedule too much, and the contentment of a returned focus. Trying to remember to not force a situation, and don't aim the agenda, roll with the present and merely nudge the direction. Climb the hills...and walls. I headed out the next morning, surrounded by Poland. Horse drawn carts with auto tires were everywhere, and elderly gents with their round-brimmed black felt Goral hats pedal by on ancient bicycles. A well-worn old man, pushing a well-worn wheelbarrow, fashioned from an old wardrobe bureau, flashed me a toothless smile. Many guys were walking down the street drinking a beer, and thus pissing wherever the need arose, with the casual regard of blowing one's nose. In the fair size city of Ostrow Weilkopolski, I stopped in at a family owned garage, hoping to borrow some slip joint pliers to check the steering stem's bearing crown. The accommodating owner was a balding fellow in his early 50's, with the grit of a lifelong mechanic; along with his wife, they were happy to help.

While he called up his son in law to interpret, she served up tea and homemade soup as the grand kids and grandpa showed up. Again, I was agog at how nice everyone was. In time, the owner took me to the back of his shop, and pulled the tarp away from his proudest possession: a Harley Davidson. He'd been building it out of mix and match pieces for years. Near as I could tell, it started life as a 1940's side-valve War model, and sported front forks, handlebars, seat and fenders from every era since then, up into the early 90's. He was as pleased and chatty as could be about his baby, once he discovered I had an understanding of the mark, and its various generations. He made the point that Harley's were rare and pricey over here, plus parts were mostly a black-market affair during the Communist era, so he was reduced to cobbling together whatever came his way over the years. His poor son in law had a workout, talking a mile a minute to translate our Polish-English rapido gear-head-geek talk. What a wonderful stop, my friend at Serwis Opon was just a carburetor away from finally getting it started. Inspiration shines bright from those back home, who cannot imagine the breadth of this journey; and it also

88

shines from these wonderful people, who could never imagine my life, back home.

At the start, I looked at the trip like anyone else would. All one can envision is the miles of roads and mountains and weather, the focus is on the countries you're about to see, and the changing terrain. By now, it's shaping into being about the people and their hospitality, the wonderment in acts of selflessness are overwhelming. As the trip rolled along, it's becoming clear that someone pedaling a loaded bicycle through your city or town, or village, held a fascination for so many people. A meal, or a drink and a smoke, or a place to bunk for the night, was always being offered. Their camera phones catching the moment, scratching out my email address several times daily, and talking endlessly about the journey, assured me I was never alone; like being some global common denominator.

Still managed a 100k day, ending in Sieradz on Hwy. 12. A young man with zero English offered a night at his mother's flat, where he lived, or at least that was my understanding. He kept saying something about 6, and throwing out the number 26. I didn't understand if 6 was the distance of the bus ride, or I had to buy a bus ticket for 6 or 26 zloty, or what. I gathered he had been to Germany in the last year for a chess tournament, and then thought perhaps we were going to attend some kind of event that night, that required a ticket. We walked over to a bus terminal, and I knew this was turning into something to walk away from. He was implying I put the bike on the bus, but there wasn't enough space, and I was in no mood to break it down. At last, a guy at the stop clarified that the bus ride was 6 zloty, and the apartment was 26k's away to the north.

Waking up 26k's out of the way wasn't going to fly. It was nice of him to offer, so I handed him the 6 zloty; about two bucks, to cover his bus fare, and said thanks, but no thanks. It stood as a good example of just how incommunicado I was with everyone. He was a bit put out, but the confusion had cost about an hour, and it was now dark. Carrying on, and once again, came upon a soccer field sports complex that rented rooms, a trend was forming. The common point here was that these complexes were designed for team tournaments, and hence young people, hence basic cheap lodging. Goaaalll!

I lay in the room that night thinking that if time and money weren't such factors, I may have packed the bike on the bus. Small decisions can lead the trail of experience off into a different direction. Who knows how that may have altered the trip, through either the people you meet, or the new roads taken. The spirit of the trip was to make it up as it went, and let it come to me, only making definitive decisions to remain somewhat on course; like a pinball bouncing erratically down the ramp, yet inevitably chasing gravity. My head was still on a roller coaster, where the numerous good days couldn't be better, and the few bad days couldn't seem worse. Today was a good day, the first week of May was passing and the world was warming up. People would walk up at stops, or pull up in front of me, just to say hello.

The next day, just outside Piotrkow Trybunalski, there was Christoph; the sharply dressed young buck with perfect English, managing a gas station. A few k's down the road, Michael, the college student in his little white car, pulled over. He'd seen me while heading west in the morning, and stopped on his return trip. He needed to know. Where had this guy started from? How far was he going? At most stops, we'd exchange emails, take photos and jot down the website so that they could follow the trip's progress. Regular visitors dropped in all day. For perspective, imagine riding the fifty miles from San Francisco to San Jose, and being stopped four or five times by strangers that wanted to shake your hand, and see how the journey was fairing so far.

Another 90k push ended the next day in Sulejow, at a woodsy campground with cabins and tent sites along the Pilica River. At the rustic bar/grill/camp office, I met Gregory, a Pole in his late fifties who lived nearby, and spoke English as well as anyone who had lived in New Jersey for eighteen years. Over beers, he told all about his time in the States as an illegal immigrant, working construction and running a small business. Once his marriage broke up, he had to repatriate to Poland, and face the sadness of leaving his son behind. He was astute to world affairs, and expressed his insights on the Bush policies, along with being very distrustful of the Polish government. At first, he was a bit wary of me too, remarking my views were refreshing for an American, and felt I knew too much about politics to be a mechanic. More than once, he asked if I was being truthful about my past with him. His doubts and guarded suspicions served as a reminder of the vastly different worlds we had grown up in.

He was interesting to talk with, but his most intriguing topic was an invention he claimed to have worked on for years. Greg said he had developed a unique mass spectrometer, devices using ionization to charge, then identify organic compounds. He claimed his could detect a much wider range of compounds than the current offerings, that were designed for only specific ranges. We see these devices used widely at airports to identify explosives or drugs, but the technology is primarily utilized worldwide in the Sciences. I had a passing understanding on the subject, but little idea of its current technology, and so was left with taking his word for most of the deeper points. His fear was that the Polish government was going to find out about his invention and swoop it up; and thus, was afraid to mail it with any delivery service, or cross a border with the plans. I offered that I knew people in the States that would understand his ideas, and perhaps guide him toward others who could evaluate them.

Once he was comfortable in his trust, he actually warmed up to the idea of giving me the plans to carry home, before I quickly reminded him, I still had to cross Russia and China. We talked about his different options and the different lengths I'd be willing to go through to help him out. But in the end, his paranoia, real or imagined, won out; and the night closed. He promised to roust me in the morning, to join him for his daily bracing swim in the Pilica. Before leaving, he warned me, with serious concern, of the dangers of crossing Kazakhstan alone. I hadn't heard much about the place, good or bad, and it added to the apprehensions of a land I may be spending a lot of time in. The next morning, Gregory hadn't shown by the time I was packed, and the cold river swim didn't sound like such a good idea anyways. Whether he was on the up and up with his idea, I'll never know, but his certainty and subject depth made me want to believe. I wish him the best.

Tracing a somewhat southeast path through central Poland, the land was a generally flat, yet rolling terrain, and it would be a struggle to differentiate it from the bulk of the trip since leaving the boat in Holland. Wavy green fields and farmland, broken up by patches of mixed oak and conifer forests, still made reaching the 90 to 100k goals an all-day steady, but relaxed, push. The lower gears were not being used as much, and the surprise was how different the bike felt, as fitness improved a little each day. I had come to enjoy the occasional hills and rises that would cause me to concentrate, blanking out all external factors such as wind, heat, traffic and noises. The music plays, time and distance figures are crunched, tasks and problems and all other thoughts are sorted out, never noticing the burning legs and labored breath.

A benign disregard flashes the brain upon seeing the top of the hill, before the sobering relief of achieving a way-point kicks in, and the conquered hill now delivers the downhill reward. Now sit up, and perhaps for the first time in the last half hour, really take a look at the surroundings; stand up and allow the blood to flow back into the butt, and shake the numbness out of the hands. Today, the Dutch treat from Scheidam is gone, and I'll miss it; weed allowed the mind to wander through subject after subject, without having to be directed. The timing was almost right, what with the Ukrainian border just a two-day ride away. It would be the first manned border and customs checkpoint since leaving the docks in Holland, and I needn't bring any trouble.

I'd been on Highway 12 for three days. It was a fairly direct road across Eastern Poland, but dangerous in its lack of a safety margin. The constant flow of large trucks, carrying so many Western goods into product starved Ukraine and Russia, kept the senses awake. The names of Poland's towns I'd passed through were getting hard to remember, since they were spelled and pronounced so differently from what I was accustom to. My brain was trained to the English, French, German and Native American sounding cities of the U.S. and Western Europe, the Polish names just didn't stick. Opoczno, Przysucha, Jablonica, were just a few names on the day's route, and my notes fail me as to where I'd spent that night, somewhere to the west of Radom. Perhaps it was Gmina Wolandw., I can't be sure. It didn't stick.

Like all of the larger cities I rolled through in Poland, Radom's central district's architecture was beautiful. Elaborate Neo-Renaissance buildings lined the streets, plazas were filled with shops, markets and restaurants, and the walkways were filled with people browsing and enjoying the day. Created centuries before the automobile, their layouts centralized every need for the city dweller; something that was lost over time, and is now desired once again. Like all of Poland, the awakening feeling of Radom belies the tragic 20th century history that began with the German invasion. I would prefer to not belabor the point, but it was here my Western senses realized this town shared an all too common story with the rest of Poland, I was taken aback.

Thirty percent of Radom's populace, at the time hovering around 80,000, was rounded up, enslaved and then for the most part, exterminated. Thirty percent, twenty-four thousand. Their non-Jewish neighbors were also executed for attempting the smallest form of help. Later on, everyone suffered decades of Red rule, and yet the people here seemed so happy and carefree. Was it because their eyes were still naïve, while discovering a new world since the Soviet dissolution? More likely that they had grown up and old with a very real connection to unspeakable horrors, and knew either first or second hand what truly bad times were. Today, things are better. Their current

living standards are still catching up to the West, but they enjoy enormous improvements compared to their parent's experiences, or they as children. I will later talk to a twenty-year-old Russian who had never experienced a day of Communist rule, and felt his life was as good as any young person's, anywhere.

Despite the time it took to cross Radom, I still managed to put in a good 90k day to Kurow, crossing the Vistula river at Pulawy. I hit up an ATM the next morning, and found neither of my cards working. Before leaving home, I opened checking accounts at two different banks, splitting my cash between them as a precaution to theft, or if say, one bank sees my card being used in Wheretheheckistan, and locks it. Prior to leaving Florida, I called and had them notate that the accounts would be used in Eastern Europe and beyond. No matter. Both cards were now frozen, according to a Kurow bank manager. I pressed on 35k's to the larger city of Lublin, in hopes of finding a main bank that could straighten things out.

Walked into the nicest, modern looking bank within view, in central Lublin. Multi storied, tall glass walls and polished wood paneling. A security man, in a suit and tie, took one of my cards and conveyed the problem upstairs to the appropriate administrator. This place was fancy, very well appointed, and I was confident their personnel's experience and resources could release my card's access with a well-placed phone call to the card company's agent. Moments later, I was shuffled back into the street with a rough explanation that they couldn't help, and that I would have to contact the companies myself, using the phone number on the cards. "A 1-800 number doesn't work outside the U.S.", says I. "That is correct, have a nice day Mr. Tripp," says the suit. A pickle indeed, I had a 100 zloty note and some smaller bills left, equaling roughly $35, and no way to contact my self-appointed fiscal guardians...Attack!

I managed to get the guys in a computer repair shop to let me use their internet, to find a business number to Big American Bank Inc. They then directed me to a nearby post office, which is the only place to find a pay phone, which can only be operated by a phone card, which can only be purchased from the post office. I accomplished that, only to fumble away the first lot of minutes trying in vain to make a long-distance international call. The routine was different, I didn't know the right country code, or when to punch in the "0+"; and the Polish operator had no idea what I was attempting to say or do. Whoever I called sounded Polish, and it turns out the 30-zloty card was only good for about three minutes.

Back inside the post office, I spent the last of my Zlotys, tripling up on minutes. The dear girl behind the counter came out to help, and thanks to her, the call went through. After being placed on hold, I held my breath, hoping that the Big Bank Inc's Muzak interludes and my final Zlotys coincided. Once on, they were happy to help. Just send them a letter or email requesting the account be freed, or perhaps have my wife call them from a stateside phone to verify account access. Calling home required more time and another card, requiring zlotys I didn't have. "Within 24 hours of receiving your letter, your request will be processed." As the phone minutes marched on, and my heart raced, I knew I had to go for the throat.

"Look dude listen, I am not shitting you, I'm on a solo bicycle ride around the world and stuck in Eastern Poland and down to nothing, I'm calling from a pay phone outside a post office using the last of my cash. I did my part by notifying the bank of the travel plans where the card would be used, and you guys dropped the ball here, not me. I seriously need your help, I simply can't take that bank procedural crap for an answer. If you can't clear this, I am left here totally fucked. Now imagine you're me."

The voice on the other end changed, he'd seen the point. After another hold, he came back on and relented to help, now, not later. While my final minutes counted down, we launched into a slew of verification questions, while having them look up my website on the fly, to prove that I wasn't making all this up. Whew. Card unlocked. Exhale.

After succeeding at a nearby ATM, I bought more minutes to phone home, and left Sheree a message to please call my other bank, to verify and free up that card. After profusely thanking the Polish Post girl for her help, I realized that time and spirit wise, the day was shot. I wandered into Lublin's Old Town, a colorful and classic hilltop walled city of a fairy tale impression, that dated back over twelve centuries. Climbing a stone walled path that straddles the hill's ridge, you pass through an ancient archway and into the fortress village. It then spills out onto a cobblestone promenade, once again, lined with well-kept medieval buildings, filled with modern stores, bars and restaurants, and a farmer's market.

Slowly rolling in on the bike, I could only look around in awe, and wish a friend was with me to share this magic place. Surrounded by shops, I knew this was a chance to search for a map of Ukraine, but was limited by not trusting the bike on the busy street to the flimsy cable and lock. After first securing it inside the back of a beer tent, and checking out a department store with no luck, I moved on to a small travel shop on an alley corner. Looking through the window to see what they had, I was approached by an older man, who offered to watch the bike for me as I went inside. He seemed pretty straight up, so I took him up on the offer and headed inside, but still keeping one eye through the window. After finding a map, the next job was finding somewhere to stay, and asked the man about any cheap places in the city. Not a common word between us, we had made it this far into the conversation using basic nouns and hand motions.

Follow me he implies, casting shades of the chess player kid, going for the bus in Siedrawz. Was he going to show me a cheap hotel? Were we going to his apartment? Numbers I understood, but were they kilometres or Zlotys, or how many minutes to get there? Leaving the walled central section, we walked past the shops and headed towards the University area. I soon gathered that Jack was a retired college instructor, and we were heading for his place. We walked away from the downtown, past large broken-down government buildings, deserted years before and rotting from the outside with peeling paint and overgrown weeds, and every window broken and gone. The interiors looked burnt, and had dangling wires ripped from the walls, raided for every electrical fixture.

At one point, Jack ducked into a small shop for a couple of beers, and I gave thought to ditching him and just finding a place on my own. I didn't know how far away his place was, or why I just accept anyone's offer to stay. Again, I decided not to fight the circumstance, and see where it leads. We sat on a bench in a small  empty children's park, and two policemen were soon upon us. As they walked up, Jack motioned for me to not worry, he'll handle this. They were all business at first, having issue with us drinking in the playground; until examining my passport. They then eased up and became all smiles, as they asked us to please move along.

We arrived at the Maria Curie Sklodowska University, named after the Nobel chemist. Lublin was the home of her grandfather, and this was the central of six major medical and technical universities here. Passing through the campus and out the back, we arrived at his weary tenement building. One number he was tossing about was 4, it was the floor he lived on. This late-sixty-some year-old guy and I heaved the ninety-pound bicycle up six flights, past the cold gray water-stained cement walls and bare steel railings, that resembled the fire escape of an abandoned building. Jack was a widower, and his son was grown and gone. The small, simple flat was furnished on one wall with a dark stained wood hutch with thin glass panes, filled with old crystals and plates. Crowning it was an elaborate four litre brass tea dispenser, a samovar, a common point of pride among many households I would eventually visit. His worn, yet cared for, chairs and small couch had neatly placed lace doily's covering their arms. There was the sense that Jack's dear departed wife had most of the decorator input, and she'd done her best with what was available from the Republic's factories back in the day.

We sat in his narrow kitchen as he heated up a dinner from frozen pyrogies, the stuffed dumpling staple that, under several names, I'll be eating quite regular from here on. He then broke out the smokes and vodka, and for the next few hours at the tiny kitchen table we exchanged our life stories; and I explained the trip so far, through simple words, gestures and drawings. Later on, we visited his neighbors, a nice couple in their thirties. Michael was a farmer from England, who had met Monica a few years back when she left Poland to work a summer job on the farm he and his brother owned. They now had a one-year old son, and Michael was biding his time on a waiting period, in order to be allowed to buy Polish farmland.

He stepped out for beers, and when he returned, explained that since entering the E.U. in 2004, Poland began a twelve-year period whereby foreigners, in most of the country's provinces, could only buy land after registering the potential land with the proper Ministry. They then had to reside in the country and rent the property, while cultivating the land for three consecutive years "without interruption." In some areas, the time period was 7 years. After completing the requirements, the "Minister of Administration" would then approve your purchase request, or issue an objection. It sounded like the policies of some apparatchik holdover, but perhaps existed to protect from well-heeled opportunist rushing in to snap up blocks of inexpensive land, before the real estate prices had time to acclimate to the rest of Europe. Maybe it just takes time to teach an old dog new tricks. Maybe stifling bureaucracy naturally creates greased palms. I don't know, but it was a compelling lesson of an honest man's struggle to comply. I hope it worked.

The next morning, Jack treated me, in a word, to a breakfast of cold oily fish and sour kraut from a jar. Ah, when in Rome. After warm goodbyes, I headed out into my final full day of Poland, and went 70k's to the historic border city of Chelm. Over its 1100-year history Chelm had been bounced back and forth between Russia and Poland, and even spent time in the late 18th century annexed to Austria. Like Radom, Lublin, and many others, almost all the Jewish citizens of Chelm were exterminated in WW II, many at the nearby Sobibor Extermination Camp. I ask your forgiveness for beating a dead horse, but not since visiting Dachau outside Munich in 1982 did the emotional blast have such impact. Black and white photos in a book, or watching a Hollywood epic, cannot match seeing the great people here, and thinking that just a few decades ago, a large portion of them were murdered on a twisted theory that good men, protecting their own slice of power, failed to shout down. It forever cast an extremely unfair pallor on the beautiful people and image of Germany. I'll stop now. Promise. It's just that being here, it's hard not to reflect on it.

Chelm was the last real town before reaching the Ukrainian border, 25k's away. Poland had been a good visit; the decay of the Western border gave way to a pretty country and warm helpful people. It was a good transition zone between the West and East, as the gauntlet was getting tighter. It was May 10th, and tomorrow I would enter Ukraine, a country shadowed by warnings since landing on the continent, for its crime and primitive reputation.

And yet, the original plan was to cross Belarus, just to Ukraine's north. I'd rarely heard of any news or events of the place, so it seemed a bit of an enigma. For some reason, they hadn't appeared to embrace the liberties afforded the other former Soviet bloc countries. It may have been as close as one gets to the

Cold War zeitgeist, and a slow ride through would be quite revealing. The first complication was their thirty-day visa. It was a reasonable time limit, until the demand for a border arrival date was added, a date I couldn't possibly pinpoint. The biggest stumbling block was requiring addresses and lodging dates for all accommodations, how in the world? It was too much to ask of a bicyclist. I wanted to comply, in order to see this mysterious land, and didn't understand why their government was so strict. Hell, Communist China was easier. With a couple of weeks to go before my departure date, I hadn't made any progress on their visa's lodging demands.

Russia and Kazakhstan required "letters of invitation" from an "in country" host in order to issue a visa. China didn't require such a letter, they simply issued visas good for one year, yet required that the holder exit the country every two months. Re-entering started the two-month clock anew, weird right? On paper, Russia's letter of invitation meant a citizen knew who you were, and vouched for you during the visit. In reality it was just another way to pad the process, since the letters cost as much as the visa in some cases. The travel visa agency in San Francisco that was handling all of the trip's documents, was ran by a couple of savvy Russian guys, who were wizards at playing the wink-wink nudge-nudge game of acquiring the letters and visa's needed. They were in cahoots with travel outfits in those countries, and secured an invitation letter for me from people I'd never know. Belarus required this expensive letter as well, but wasn't as apt to play ball. One day Renatas and Kestutis just laid out the low down on Belarus. "They really don't care for tourists." "Why's that?" I asked. "They're assholes." Well, it all makes sense now.

They suggested Ukraine, the country directly south. No visa, no invitation, just show up with a passport and you're good for ninety days. It was a major trip altering choice, and put into play a big question. Do I head north at Kiev in central Ukraine and into Russia, putting me back on my post Belarus route; or continue east through Ukraine and cross just a short section of southern Russia, and then onto the entire expanse of Kazakhstan? The question loomed large at the time, since it would determine the duration, hence cost, of the Russian visa, as well as the start date of the Kazakh document. My Ruski friends solved the issue by suggesting that rather than a normal tourist visa, just pony up a bit more for a business visa; it gave a wider time window. I wondered about the authorities questioning why Brian Bicycle possesses a business person's visa, they just laughed. "Tell them you're researching a book!" What could go wrong?

That was months ago. The frets at the time now seemed small, and the upgraded documents gave the freedom to start the visa's clock whenever I arrived at the borders. Now my opinion was to let it flow, see what happens. The challenge of spanning Kazakhstan west to east was looming in my head as an epic story, an unheard-of adventure, that would be heard from me someday. Still, sober thoughts played large, and I knew that the route decision would be decided at the break point of Kiev, in the dead center of Ukraine.

As I traipsed towards the Ukraine border, the traffic began to slow and back up. At 10k's out, hundreds of big transport trucks began lining the eastbound shoulder nose to tail. Driver's feet hung out cab windows as they snoozed, some sat on their folding chairs or ice coolers. Radios played and small stoves were set up cooking breakfast, it looked like a line of tailgaters waiting for the parking lot to open at an Oakland Raider's game, except it was six miles long. I soon stopped and met Mikola and Anatoly, a Ukrainian and Pole. Two, among the many truck drivers in the far-flung queue, they heard my story and broke out the gas-powered stove, and began to brew coffee. They offered a smoke, and served up stale homemade bread with a lovely cheese, hinting the piquant of truck tires. We talked for an hour over the makeshift brunch, as they filled me in on the border jam. It was a minimum two-day customs delay, and camping out to wait your turn was a given for these cross-country truckers. The demand for Western goods in Ukraine and Russia far outstripped the capabilities of Ukraine's border agents.

Anatoly presented me a bright yellow green safety vest, and told me to never ride without it, as he flicked at his throat with his middle finger, making a thudding snapping sound; explaining this was the Russian gesture for drunkards. He deadpanned that their roadways were dangerous, with drowsy vodka-fueled truckers trying to make up time, and that riding a bicycle along them with no margins was crazy. The vest was my only hope, and his face meant every word. They wished me luck and I rode on, wearing the vest every day from then on.

After riding up to the front of the long line, the crossing process for me was far less troublesome. Passport gets attention, forms are filled out, and the bike and gear are given a glance. Then the grill. Where are you going? How long are you staying? Drugs? Cash? Weapons? The agents, dressed like military officers, stared at my eyes as the answers are reeled off, they beamed when I told them I was shooting for China. Drugs? Fresh out. Cash? During the Lublin ATM debacle, I purposely withdrew just enough to get to the border, to avoid having to change a large sum of Zlotys into Ukraine's currency, the Grivna. On paper, I was broke. Weapons? As friendly as everyone seemed, I doubted they were ready for my black bear-plonking slingshot story. Roll a few metres to another station and the process is repeated, perhaps the first round was the "leaving Poland" routine, and this one's the "entering Ukraine" point. Here, the passport gets a stamp, and I'm instructed that the form with my money information is very important, and will be required in order to exit the country. Oh-you-betcha.

I rolled on, feeling like a kid walking into an amusement park for the first time. The line to leave the country was only about a kilometre. Along with the trucks and trailers, entire families, Mom, Dad, the kids, stood outside their small cars; smoking. Their roofs were lashed with mattresses and furniture, like escaping a storm. Stray dogs, seemingly from the same stray brown bony mongrel lab terrier mix mother, wandered everywhere. So many were standing in and along the roadway, I was relieved to find them docile. After a brief stop at a gas station to get out of a come-and-go rain, I ventured forth, into my sixth country. The bike and I, on the road to Hong Kong.

14. radiator

The initial impression felt like Alaska. Grey skies, cold and rain, with long green stretches between villages. Took cover for a half hour in a bus stop shelter, then moved on to the outskirts of a village and hid beneath the overhang of an old vacant house. A curious horse was tethered in the front yard, its front right leg roped to a stake. As the rain kept coming back, I pondered on how living outside all day for months had become so normal that I didn't judge the day's temperature relative to stepping outside, but rather how hot or cold it was in the open. A moment of earthy contentment, just the rain and the wobbly bike, the horse and I. Sitting there alone on some Ukrainian's porch, the joy warmed me, I'd made it this far. No matter what, that could never be taken away. I was making this happen, and before leaving these borders, I'd have reached the journey's mileage half way point. Before leaving Ukraine, I'd be pedaling towards home, not away from it.

In 1917, as The Great War waned on European soil, the empire of Czar Nicolas II fell, giving rise to the Russian Provisional government which soon fell to the Soviet's Bolsheviks. Soon, the Bolsheviks Red Army was embroiled in the Russian Civil War with the anti-Soviet White Army, as well as Ukraine's Green Army and Black Army, and a contingent of Allied Forces. When the smoke cleared, the Soviet Red Army had prevailed, establishing the U.S.S.R as we knew it. Among the layers of the Civil War's chaotic slaughter and trauma, a young family, Isaac and Anna, and their three kids, including teenager Abraham, fled from the small Ukraine village of Kovel, and eventually landed in Brooklyn. Two decades later, Abraham settled in Dallas. Years later, on November 22nd 1963, the women's clothing designer stood in Dealey Plaza and accidentally inserted himself into history, using a home movie camera to film the passing motorcade of President John F. Kennedy. The "Zapruder Film" is recognized as one of the most infamous clips of all time. Yes folks, that was a long walk; but besides the ghetto horrors and horrific battles shared with all of these Ukrainian villages at the onset of WW II, that's the shiniest story I've found about Kovel, where I spent my first night, 60k's inside the border. Now, let's move on.

I glided in looking for a bank-o-mat but found a small penzion first. The mid-30's redheaded mom running the inn was pretty proud of the place, asking

130 Grivna. At seven to one on the buck, it came out to be about $18, not bad for the remodeled home. But, since becoming accustomed to $10 nights, this bourgeoisie rate was bustin' my chops. Of course, I agreed, I was cold and wet. The nearest bank was 3k's away, and after trying to decipher her Ukrainian directions over a beer, I gave up and she called a taxi. She rattled off the mission to the driver from her stoop, and we were off, for about a block. The gruff cabbie pulled over and demanded some money up front before we went any further. He was pretty insistent, and after figuring out what he was on about, I had to make him understand that the reason I'm in the car is to go get some Grivnas. Get it? Dick. We managed to complete the mission and I let him twist in the wind for any fare until we arrived back at the house, then juked him on the tip. The innkeeper's bright eyed seven-year-old boy was just as happy to have someone to shoot pool with in the downstairs garage-come-billiard room, as his Mom was to pawn him off on me all evening, as she sat with her girlfriend in the empty dining room; watching Ukraine soap operas. Kovel. Now I know why Abraham's dad left. Oh, listen to me.

Headed south down the E85 on a clear morning. The road surface ranged from fair to poor for most of the way, shaking the already overworked front fork and stoking my concerns about it. Not far along, I came upon a round-faced middle-aged woman in a peasant dress and sunbonnet, sitting on the roadside with a few flats of eggs and some fruit for sale. No sign, just hoping someone would pull over. The odd sight was a three-metre-long pole at a 45-degree angle, supported by sticks crossed and lashed in a X. Along the pole were a half dozen tied bundles of leaves, bunched up like large green bouquets. She waved, I smiled and rolled on, wondering what those leaves were for. Continuing on, and before cutting east on a back road that would skirt around the mid-sized city of Luts'k, there were two more of the simple roadside stands, sporting the bundle poles. I had to ask. The woman just smiled while grabbing a set and making a backscratching, or scrubbing motion, with them. That couldn't be, imagine the twigs in the shower drain. I still didn't know.

At a kiosk in a small village I stopped for a snack, and among the interested were two boisterous drunks, who insisted I come have a drink with them. They were happy enough at first, and then became more and more demanding as I kept passing on the offer. The vodka was talking, and just when it looked like trouble, a couple of local men showed up and gave them the boost, apologizing for the idiots. The horse drawn carts were in use all over, but with a twist, the harnessed mare's colt, untethered, would run along with Mom, not leaving her side through the fields, or when crossing the highway. The horse's owners, holding the reins, showed no worry the yearling would run off.

The fields had no fences, cows and horses were restrained by simply tying a short rope between their front ankles, others were tied to a two-metre-long leg rope, staked to the ground; others free. They mowed where they stood, and I suppose the farmer would move the animal occasionally to keep the grass down. It was brilliant, with no fences to erect or maintain, or property lines to dispute.

The most striking sight so far, was the way everyone and everything treated the two-lane highway. Wagons were pulled by horses and cows, pulled by tractors, pulled by roto-tillers with their blades removed. Bicycles and dogs and cows and horses went about their day up and down and across the road, all with zero regard for the trucks and cars zooming by. It was hard to say who gets taught the hard lesson first, the fast traffic or the slow animals.

In the village Kivertsi, I stopped to ask about any cheap digs for the night, and the shop mechanics and hangers on at a single bay tire shop offered up hot  coffee and plenty of advice. A boy that couldn't have been any older than twelve produced a pack, and offered a smoke. They directed me 100 metres up the road to a truck stop, that wanted 50 G for the two-bed room, or 25 G if I didn't mind the possibility of a trucker showing up, and taking the other rack. I took my chances after quickly dividing 25 by 7. After moving in, I found the owner, and asked about somewhere to eat. He was talking with a short squat woman of about fifty, painted up to look thirty. She offered to walk down the street and point out a café, but soon, detoured into a bar, whereby she steps up and orders herself a shot of vodka. Tipping it back, she then gets herself a candy bar and the two of us a beer, all the while grinning at me like it was someone's lucky day. There's no food here and it dawns on me this gal's a high-seniority truck stop whore, and I just bought her a couple of drinks. The only other customers were a table of four guys, who confirmed my hunch. I sat down with Andre', Uri, Volky and Pavel, then shoo'd away my time-worn princess. The break up went well, and after a few rounds, the barmaid was shutting shop. The guys had things to do, but were getting together tonight for a few more drinks, and invited me along.

Relaxed a bit back at the room with some bread, cheese and salami from a small house-turned-market down the street, and about 8 p.m., the crew pulled up. Uri and Andre' had returned with a younger guy and a big course looking dude in a green army jacket. I crawled in the back between the new guys in their old red Lada, the quintessential sedan of the East, based on a 1970's Fiat 124. The five of us were soon bouncing the overloaded car down a rough dirt road, deep into the dark woods. Uri turned around and made the pinched forefinger and pursed lips gesture, the global sign of "we're off to try some Ukrainian weed." We parked in total darkness at a picnic table in a small clearing, and with the headlights on, they began to put together a water pipe of sorts.

They grabbed a short pitcher and a pair of pliers from the trunk, and set to opening up the car's radiator drain, half filling the jug with the hot engine water. A two-litre soda bottle, with the base cut out, was set into it, and a small cone-shaped aluminum bowl was set into the bottle's neck. The bowl was stuffed with herb and fired up, and when burning strong, the bottle was slowly lifted, creating a vacuum, drawing the smoke down into the container. They demonstrated how to pull off the bowl, and close your mouth around the neck and inhale while slowly pushing the bottle down into the water, creating a power hit effect. Wow. The radiator bong was something to be experienced. Once. After a few hits, we hung around the table as they impressed upon me the worldwide superiority of Ukraine's pot. It wasn't actually all that good, but since they were kind enough to share, I politely nodded along. "How is this to California weed, good yes?" "Oh, we got nuthin' compares to Ukraine weed, very good." Oh, I shoulda ran for office. Army jacket guy still hadn't cracked a smile.

Among their own chatter, a decision was being made, and they glanced at me now and then to see if I was following the conversation, which I wasn't. Abruptly, they piled into the car and we took off further into the woods, my limited attempt at asking "where are we going now?" brought only silence. We came out to a road and headed off in a direction that didn't seem right. "Where's this go?" Andre' and Uri up front were talking between themselves, ignoring me. I was sandwiched between the silent army jacket and his mate. Shit. What have I let happen? I've lost control. These guys could be taking me anywhere, and after several turns, I had no idea where we're at; and why aren't they answering? No one knows where I am, everything I have is loosely secured behind a flimsy door in a three-dollar flophouse, and I've committed the cardinal sin of getting into a car with four strangers I just met in a bar. My hand feels the four-inch lock blade in my front right pocket, and I know if this goes down someone's getting cut. The silence goes on. This could be it, I'd been warned by so many.

A long fifteen minutes passed, until we drove into a city area, probably a fringe suburb of Luts'k, and pulled up in front of a store where a crowd was hanging out. Exhale. It's the popular place this time of night to buy beer, that's all we were doing. We all piled out and bought a couple of bottles each, and hung with some of the parking lot club; they all seemed friends. What a goofball I am. My buzzed imagination was working overtime, and my stoned friends had little English, Army jacket had none. It was a good scare lesson to keep the guard up, rolling with the moment could lead to a trek ending mistake. After about a half hour, we drove back to Kivertsi and they dropped me off at the truck stop. After handshakes and goodbyes, the day ended, and I crawled into bed. Had the room all to myself.

My second full day of Ukraine began on the road to Rivne, and the sights of yesterday continued. The horse drawn carts were now as common place as any car, the staked horses and cows and goats controlled the brush. Chickens wandered everywhere, I wondered how the owners could possibly know where they are, or who they belong to. Bicycles were cobbled together like Cuban taxis, with mismatched wheels and pedals and chains, that had been salvaged from a motorcycle or farm equipment. My communication skills score me six fried eggs at breakfast, when I tried to order two. And a lovely retired couple were entertained, watching me do a quick fix on the first flat tire of Europe. Drunks are everywhere. There were several tiny one-man kiosks along the road, away from any town or village, that sold only beer and cigarettes. This may be hard to grasp, but imagine a society where so many men drink all day, that you begin to assign varying degrees of normalcy to it. Again, they just piss anywhere, without the slightest attempt to be covert.

After an 80k day came Rivne. Rolling in, I was caught up by a couple of teenage cyclists out on a training sprint, they were all questions about the loaded touring bike, and offered to take me to a cheap hotel in town. Kosia had a very friendly, yet matter of fact grace about him, and said, in fair English, that he was last year's Ukraine champion bicycle road racer for his age group, and had moved to Rivne for the sole purpose of team  training. They had to slow their pace, and I had to pour on the steam to stay near, as they dashed up and down hills on their carbon race bikes. We zipped in and out of traffic and shot through round-a-bouts, with nary a honk or gesture from the cars and buses, they seemed to accept the bike's presence as normal.

After finding his first choice closed, we eventually ended up in front of a hotel that shared a plaza with Rivne's performing arts theater, in a very modern city center. Young shoppers bustled by, dressed in the latest fashions, sporting large glossy shopping bags from the upscale stores surrounding the square. It was so very different from what I had seen thus far, as modern as any city center, with nary a horse in sight. Kosia negotiated a $10 room, and they helped me lug the bike up six flights to the third floor of the palatial sized classical building. I thanked them for being such a huge help, they were two great kids, and I was lucky to have ran into them. Once settled, I took a look around.

Despite the inspiring facade, the place was a wreck. The room's door had been kicked in and poorly repaired with a wooden plank. The cracked sink only clung to the wall by its piping, cold water only. The second floor's rooms had been leased out as women's clothing shops and hair salons. Next door, was an indoor/outdoor restaurant, filled with trendy clients, yet just one block away from the boulevard revealed dirt streets and busted sidewalks, in front of old decaying apartment structures. Their broken windows revealed rooms with signs of life, occupied by folks probably just glad to have a roof. I found a farmer's market and picked up some bread, meat and fruit, then headed back to the room and wandered up and down the hallway, looking for the promised common shower room.

What I found was a door-less room with a cold-water pipe sticking out of the wall, like a plumber's mistake. I gave up and just heated some water on the camp stove for a wash up. It was like living inside a Burbank movie set's façade, and it couldn't be blamed on my search for bargain digs, this was a nice part of town. From the journal at the day's end: "Remind me to punch Vladimir Lenin's mother right in the mouth."

Every night had chores. Whatever the bike required was seen to, usually cleaning and lubing the chain every other day, and patching up a tube if needed. Mainly, the task was the day's laundry, I was only traveling with three T-shirts, four pairs of socks and boxers, and from start to finish, a proper washing machine only appeared six or seven times. The day or two of dirty clothes would get soaked overnight in the room's sink or tub, with a couple of drops of dish liquid from a three-ounce bottle. The next morning, the rinsed and squeezed rags would be spread out under the bungee cords, on top of the tire pile on the rear rack. It never truly cleaned the spots, but washed out the sweat and top dirt. Many days, it would look like a rolling Chinese laundry, with underwear dangling off the back, and socks stuffed in the netting of the front panniers.

It took a few wrong turns to think a path out of the city the next morning. The general country map I'd bought in Lublin gave me an idea of direction, but finding the proper boulevards in or out of a large urban area was hit and miss. Within a few k's, I was back into the countryside, and the sights and sounds and smells of this new world. A runaway horse-drawn wagon, the animal spooked beyond control, burst past on the right shoulder with a screaming grandmother alone in the seat, grasping for the lost reins as a young man, one hundred metres back, ran shouting. A road crew, tarring cracks in the asphalt, were using a tar hopper, fueled by branches they were cutting from the roadside trees to stoke the fire, as they went along. Twice that day, I rolled through police checkpoints screening for drunks. "Dobra den" or good day, as the officers gather around the bike; pointing and smiling at the tire stack and underwear, and bundles of extra spokes tied to the luggage frames, as they share my passport. "Dak-a-yu" or thank you, as they hand it back. Small motorcycles with misaligned sidecars buzzed everywhere, tracking so poorly their helmet-less riders had to lean hard to keep them straight.

The ever-present packs of stray dogs, the deteriorating conditions, this makeshift world of Ukraine had me worried. The bike seemed like a traveling bazaar, with a sleeping bag and tent, tires and supplies out in the open. These people of little means know a traveler, and that means cash and a passport, and so far, everyone is cool; but the fallout of the drinking issues cannot be denied.

The main stay of their economy seems to be supporting it, they even pop up brewery sponsored beer tents in random fields, so you've no need to drive all the way to the next village for a slurp. I stopped for a snack in a small village market, with a common layout. The 20 by 30-metre room had  an empty cement center floor, and unfinished concrete brick walls, lined with all the goods behind a perimeter of counters and sliding glass door freezers, I assumed to prevent theft. Salted meats and bread, clothes and shoes, household products and vegetables and ice cream; and of course, beer.

I pick out some cheese, a cold drink and a writing pen. When I stepped outside, one of those clapped-out sidehacks came reeling into the dirt and gravel lot, pitching into a dusty U-turn stop. The sidecar, so far seen used as a cargo bin, held a camo-donned young man who leapt out smiling at me, thumbs up, and ran into the store. A moment later, he emerged with a litre box of wine, and without a word, ran up and presented it. Dak-a-yu! Dobra den! He ran back in, bought another box, and jumped into the sidecar, waving as they motored away, third wheel in the air and accelerating, crab fashion, out onto the road. What just happened? Here I am worried about getting ripped off, and some vino-angel grants me a gift out of simple unspoken kindness. Standing at midday, in a dirt parking lot with a box of apple wine under my arm, and half considering to pop it open. The disparaging concerns of the Ukraine's drinking issues? I'm no better than they are.

I've yet to mention a very positive and important feature of Ukraine. The gene pool, the farm food, the water; I don't know, but there are more beautiful women here than any place I've ever seen. So many so, that it takes a stunner to stand out from the crowd. As early evening approached, it was looking like a tent night, with no town near, when I came to a small cafe that existed to serve as a coach stop rest station. Walking in to get the nod to prop up the tent out back, and maybe some dinner, I was met by the girl who was taking orders at the meal counter. She was absolutely stunning. Incredible. Tall, brunette, curvy and dressed in tight black with a face that could put her on any magazine cover. Unfortunately, she was in no mood to take a stab at English, as I tried in vain to order something simple to eat; and even less help with the tent question. As a bus load of customers pulled up outside, she waved me off, quite annoyed.

As the passengers wandered in, a woman with some English began to ask about the loaded bike. Our conversation must have woken some long dormant grade school memory in the beauty, because after the travelers were taken care of, she sat down and began to work with me. She apologized, and managed enough to convey she was initially afraid to attempt English in front of everyone, for fear of stumbling and looking stupid. She warmed up when I assured that her sparse words of English were so much better than my complete ignorance of Ukrainian. Soon, we were slowly conversing, and while we got nowhere with the camp question, I did get a pretty decent sandwich. It was getting late, and everyone's opinion was to just keep going another 20k's to Novohrad Volyns'kyj and find a room; but I knew the dark would catch me first.

The gas station guys across the street were of no help, so it was down to keep truckin' and find a stealth site. No sooner did I pull out from the station, when I saw an old woman coaxing a horse into a low field on my right. I wheeled down the dirt path and began voicing foreign grunts and dobra dens and sign language. She understood, and conveyed there was no problem putting up the tent behind a stand of trees below the roadside, if I didn't mind the animal. There was always anxiousness when searching for a safe hiding spot for the tent. I sleep like a stone, and knew if anyone was to sneak up during the night, I'd never hear them. Crawling into the secluded tent, totally hidden in the tall grass brought the relief of knowing I was somewhat safe for the night, and had made it through another day unscathed.

In the morning, the horse came over for a visit. He watched me pack the tent and pedal up the dirt drive and across the highway, for morning coffee. There was lovely Anna, I had the cook and her laughing at my camping with the horse story, while she slowly translated and he cooked up a round of ham and eggs. It was just the three of us in the small diner sharing breakfast, and for the morning moment, was as easy and enjoyable as having a visit with good friends. The warmth of genuine people. And then I'm off.

A 100k day sent me through Novohrad Volyns'kyi as the meadows, forests and intermittent villages continued on into Zhytomyr, the largest Ukraine city yet. Despite the E-40 being a major route across the country, the rough road surface was rattling the fork, frame, and I. The highway itself didn't look too bad, but the road's edge where I traveled was eroded, and demanded constant awareness to avoid that one big rim-bending divot that would set me back for days; with my 700c wheels rare to none locally, it could be a bigger problem than I cared to worry about. I had taken to riding in the smooth dirt just off the pavement as much as possible to save the bike. At the next chance, I'd email Cody and have him contact buddy Dan to source a spare fork, and be ready to FedEx it on a moment's notice.

Zhytomyr was the province, or oblast, capitol. Its 1100-year existence had seen Slavic, Lithuanian, Polish and Russian rule, it had even been sacked by the Mongols back in the 13th century. In WW II, its population was devastated when it spent three years as SS Commander Heinrich Himmler's Ukrainian headquarters. This world is full of historic cities that I'd never heard of. As I rode into the city center, the streets emanated radially from a large central square, lined with columned government and theater buildings. The first stop was a bicycle shop to replace a couple of mini tire levers I'd lost. The mother and son shop owners only stocked them as a part of a complete tool kit, and understandably wouldn't break the set, despite my animated finagling. When they followed me outside and laid eyes upon the orange mule, their eyes lit up. Mom ducked back into the shop, and as I climbed back on, she reappeared with the plastic levers, refusing any payment. Such class. Dak-a yu Madame!

After asking them and several others about a haunt for the night, it seemed that despite the city's size, the Hotel Zhytomyr was everyone's only answer. The simple, block style Khrushchyovka appearance was set among the many elaborate buildings that once housed the oblast's Soviet ministries, giving it an exclusive image. The lobby's marble columned spaciousness had a large restaurant bar to one side, and an in-house hair salon to the other; the place had obviously been built as an auberge to the dignitaries of days gone by. Vintage austere Soviet ambiance hung in the air as the uniformed clerk's dak-a yu's had been replaced by the Russian thank you of "spassi-ba." World Heavyweight Champion brothers Vitali and Wladimir Klitschko had signed their photo hanging above the front desk, indicating that this was probably the nicest place in town, warranting the 145 grivna, $29, charge.

Crikey. I hate this part but I gotta tell ya. Once past the initial impression, a closer look saw the lobby carpets tattered, bare in spots. The desk help that yammered on and on about something wore uniform shirts with the elbow's worn through, and the walls had been painted over so many times, the thick layers were separating. After finding the elevator out of service, I lugged the ride and bags up to the fourth floor to find someone had beaten the room's door to near death, and the few remaining floor and wall tiles in the bathroom were cracked and chipped. But when I found the bathtub full of hot water, I dropped my inspector attitude and smiled at the staff's welcoming gesture. After moving in, I plopped into the deep hot bath and stared at the rusty tap stains running down the wall; trying to think easy on these folks, who are probably doing their best with what's given.

Bebopping down the stairs and into the lobby to treat myself to the restaurant's fare, I met the bellhop kid. From my wet hair, he knew right away what I'd done. He made clear what the concierge fellow had been yammering on about during check in, that I'd failed to understand. This part of the city was to have its water turned off at 10:00 p.m. for two days, due to some extensive system maintenance. The tubs in all the rooms were being filled as a reserve for use in flushing toilets and doing necessary wash ups. Oh, aren't I a special guest, worthy of a warm bath, drawn by a thoughtful host.

After refilling my porcelain reservoir, I walked into the dining area, to an idle staff that seemed surprised they had a guest. The room made it easy to imagine the halcyon days of Red rule. Located in the center of the oblast's government district, and 10k's from an old, yet still active, bomber base at Ozerne, I pretended to see it playing host to the highest players of the Republic. High ceilings and wood paneled walls, with a band stage framed by long heavy red drapes. Table after table of crystal and silverware were set, as if a large group of Party elite were arriving any minute for a grand meal, followed by a boisterous vodka-charged night, dancing with the Party girls to the live band. I hope it happened that way, my night was less so.

My zero ability to read or speak the lingo, and no pretty waitress to play coy with, awarded me a grizzled piece of meat and oily potatoes, a bowl of borscht, and what I deemed the condiment salad. Borscht is a beetroot soup served with a dollop of sour cream that is a staple of Russian life, and is actually pretty good stuff. Then, picture a nice fresh salad with all the veggie trimmings, and then remove the lettuce, leaving only the condiments; the cucumbers, carrots, onions and a vinegar oil dressing. The well-fed elderly woman serving the room's only guest was just bearing my audacity of entering her establishment. When they hit me up for dinner and a beer, at about half of what the room cost, I knew the Party nomenklatura would soon hear about it, in my next reportski.

Lying in bed the next morning, for too long, had me thinking about last night's experience, and the surprisingly constant culture input. The weeks of speaking in slow enunciated speech, the changing foods; and the stares. It was like watching a grand play with new characters and scenes every few minutes. Taking it all in, paying every precious moment its proper due, I've never experienced this for such an extended time. What's passed has turned out well, but looking forward always comes with caution, feeling ever vulnerable for what awaits, the doubt bubble was rising again, an enemy I can't kill. I was only approaching the trek's halfway mark and the enthusiasm was hard to keep in focus. Leaving Germany was like dropping off a cliff, into the deep dark woods of uncertainty, the gauntlet was a blind tunnel with no end in sight. I wasn't a 14-hour airplane trip from San Francisco, I was four or five months of riding ten-hour days through the unknown to get home. That overwhelming shadow was back, and I knew a day off was calling, the first since Krotoczyn in Poland a week ago. Why I would choose to hole up in an overpriced (!) hotel with no running water didn't make sense, but once the thought takes over, another 100k day wasn't in the cards. There was internet service at the telephone company about four blocks away, and the anonymity of a room in a large hotel, I just needed to be alone.

Spent the day off uploading pictures and updating everyone on the blog to the latest progress. With personal home computer services not widespread, or perhaps not yet available, the basement of the main telephone offices, with its fifty desktop computers, had become a cool hang out spot for the local high school and college crowd; some working and some just kicking it. They helped get me started on the Windows program, no different than the familiar, except every command and drop down is in Russian! It was a process of negotiating from screen to screen by clicking on the choices that should be right about there... got it... no... ok should be the next line... got it. I'll have to start paying closer attention. The fee was about a dollar for one hour and only one hour, to

limit screen time. At my first hour's end, the screen reverted to the desktop, and any unsent pictures were lost. The monitor attendant checked the waiting list, and I was in luck, she granted another hour.

On the way back to the hotel, I came upon a movie theater housed in one of the many old Greek style buildings, worthy of an emperor, showing the latest Indiana Jones film. After a minute, I passed on the flick, knowing I'd never understand a word, but checking out the inside of that picture palace would have been worth the entry. I wondered if they had popcorn? Hit up a market that dealt only in meat, eggs, bread, milk and fruit, all ordered across a counter, like a New York deli, that doesn't make sandwiches. Back at the inn, loaded with groceries, I discovered the room's refrigerator was just another item on the Hotel Zhytomyr's honey-do list. Just smile. After a camping stove sponge bath, I managed to soak some clothes, then pulled the wheels off the bike, to swap out the 25mm wide tires for some wider 37mm's, to combat the choppy roads. Before long, there were new and used tires and tubes and drying t-shirts, socks and boxers, hanging everywhere. It looked like someone had lived here for a month, and so much like mission headquarters, that I decided to stay here tomorrow too. Made up a few doorstop sandwiches, washed down with milk and bananas, then enjoyed an evening of Ukraine television with beer and painkillers. Once again, things are looking up.

The next day it was all coming together. It was the 16th of May, son Shay's 25th birthday, and I headed back to the telephone office for a few more hours of internet, needed to email junior and call home. But, once there, I just couldn't dial the number. It was going to be a buzz killer and I was getting back to good spirits. A jackass step, but the thought of a report on money problems on the home front, a summary on how everyone was getting laid off, and whatever house maintenance project just couldn't wait, was just beyond me. The overriding guilt of not being there for her was balanced by the rationalization that this was the longest we'd been apart, and life was climbing all over her. I knew I was silently missed, but the frustrations were out loud. I emailed instead, starting with a vapid "hi, how is everything back there?" Just quit thinking about it, bury it, soldier on. It's selfish to say "it's all about me" but yeah, right now, at this point of the journey, it was all about me. It had to be, or I wasn't going to make it.

On the way back, I bought a couple of cold cans of Coke, something I rarely drank in the States. Now, at times, it was more desirous than a cold beer, my little moment of America. In the can or plastic bottle, it tastes exactly like a Coke in California or Texas. I could lay on the bed, dial in the Dead on the iPod and close my eyes. Take a long sip and pretend I'm not in the middle of Eastern Europe, the door is locked and Ukraine is outside, not in here. Homesickness was just a word, in the last month it's become an honest emotion. It's an unconscious head game induced by constant uncertainty, and I'm grasping at straws and fighting it with a conscious head game of Coca Cola and running-home-to-mama music, and it's working out.

The next morning, while rolling the packed ride out of the room on fresh tires, a gushing horn blowing sound filled the fourth floor. The water had come back on! I turned around and ran a hot bath, shaved and filled the water bottles. It felt so good, I decided to stop and get a haircut, the first since the Walmart in Hemet. The cutey running the lobby's salon wanted nothing to do with me, or my locks, upon hearing the English; I certainly have an effect on these women. After making her laugh by yanking at a handful of mane, and making funny faces and scissor motions, she was soon clipping and chatting away, as I tried to smile and grunt at all the right pauses, as if I had any idea of what she was saying. Ah, clean and shorn and mentally refreshed. Ready to press on deeper into the East.

With Kiev only 100k's away I had decided that the trail would break north there, bearing east of the Chernobyl disaster zone, and enter Russia, to eventually realign with the post Belarus plans. Going straight through Kiev into

Eastern Ukraine would send me into southern Russia for a week or so, then into the widest expanse of Kazakhstan. Experiencing more of Russia and less of Kazakhstan seemed easier, since short of tearing a page out of a world atlas, I couldn't find a map of Kazakhstan. From what I could see on the full country-size atlas maps, there were only a handful of roads in the entire place, and after crossing a third of the empty land, I'd have to waste progress heading north for a week to continue east. The choice of taking a gradual northeast path across Russia would allow a climb over the Urals, and drop me into the north border of Kazakhstan, and its new capital of Astana. I had it all figured out.

Along the wooded E-40, there were more and more roadside vendors offering bottles of fresh juice, potatoes, milk and eggs; and homemade brooms made from trussed together straw. They all offered the bundled oak leaves, hanging from the same angled poles. Whatever they are, they're popular. No table, no umbrella, just an old man or woman resting in a rusty fold-up chair with a smile on their face, their wares sitting in the dirt; and many times, a motorcycle sidecar rig nearby, the family pickup truck. The economy out here in the rural was so shoot-from-the-hip, that these folks were most likely living the same way their generations had for centuries. Now, once again, able to sell their goods, rather than giving it all up to the State.

The midday break at a roadside diner found an outside table full of young men and a girl, playing a round of the national sport, drinking vodka. As I stepped inside, the girl stood and came in to convey through her stupor and mood that she'd rather be with her friends outside, than dealing with me. No lunch here, I get it. When I stepped out, one of the table boys started mouthing off about something, pissed at my presence, I guess. He was pretty liquored up, but his mates were rolling their eyes at him, so I played along, hoping to diffuse things. When he rose up and stepped towards me, his buddies intervened with an arm around, trying to get him to sit down. It was hard to gauge if he was going any further than just barking, but when one of the guys gave me that "best go before this fool tries again" look, it made sense. I pedaled away saluting them with an obnoxiously happy "dobra den!" Worldwide, one can always find young people drunk on cheap booze in the middle of the day. Here, it's just a lot easier.

Later, I came to a brand-new gas station with the latest pumps, a modern office and paved with virgin concrete. There was a new bathroom hut in the far corner of the property, that I decided to make good use of. Open the door and jeez, wasn't it just a hole in a cement platform, it looked like it was built for a commode, and then someone forgot the throne. People were just shatting and splattering through a round opening. Maybe I can wait. This place, this place formerly known as the Soviet Union. It had highways and cities and airports, it had transport and manufacturing. It had art and music and a thousand-year history. It had astronauts circling the planet in an outer-freakin'-space station, as I stood there, staring at this filthy eight-inch hole. But they didn't have anything resembling rural sewage or even septic systems. Guys, come on.

Had to get that off my chest. Truth is I'd would become so accustom to seeing plumbing limited to cities and large towns, that I'd take to doing any necessary business in the countryside, behind a stand of trees or cornstalks. It was always a surprisingly peaceful experience, and clean. Within the last 80k's to Kiev, the road was getting much better, the new gas stations and restaurants with inns were going up everywhere, the place had a boom going on. I pulled up 20k's short of the city to a new, yet made to look old, hotel that cost too much, had no food and felt like a dorm. The Russian border was a two-or three-day ride north from the outskirts of Kiev, and the plan was to stage here, get an early start and try to cross through the metropolis tomorrow. A gas station down the road had a complete traveler's menu of just-add-hot water noodles, Coca-Cola and of course beer and cigarettes, the national fuels. I had fallen into a routine of eating simply because it was needed, and hadn't really counted on looking forward to a meal for some time. Breakfasts were usually the better bet, where there's always ham and eggs. Dinner changed with the changing cultures.

Heading towards a full day of traffic and overpasses, I rolled past a few billboards that, despite the Cyrillic characters, sported the universal McDonald's "M". The tune of "two all-beef patties special sauce laa dee da" started to roll. Damn, if it's on the way... A hamburger, fries and a Coke would be an Uncle Sam trifecta. When I hit the pivotal intersection to turn left towards Russia, the Golden Arches hadn't appeared; being still a few k's south, going towards the city center. I pondered how dumb it would be to continue out of my way, to have a lunch that I'd eaten a hundred times before, it was Mickey D's for Pete's sake, not some touted steak and seafood house. The lunch and the backtrack would chew up a good part of the day, and I had to clear this metropolis of three million before sunset. The map did however, show three other bridges crossing the Dnieper (nee-per), and one could make the case that this would be my only chance to see a part of Ukraine's largest city. The choice was between the nosh for a familiar lunch, or completing the mission for the day.

I'd be lying if I said I headed further south along Peremohy Avenue because of the architecture. I wanted one of those hamburgers bad. It was a weak and emotional decision, primarily driven by the need of familiarity. And it changed the entire journey from this moment on.

15. turn right

After slowly negotiating a giant freeway cloverleaf, to hit up a bank-o-mat across from the Golden Arches, I settled into lunch. I met an Asian student doing studies at the Kiev Polytechnic Institute, the Ukraine's M.I.T., and the jewel of the city's several major schools. His days were filled with constant study and lab work, but said living in Kiev was nice, there were plenty of pretty girls, and a good night life, when his time allowed. The school schedule was so demanding that the liberating thought of riding off on a bicycle to nowhere never occurred to him, but wanted the website, so to dream about it. We already know what they call a Quarter-Pounder with Cheese in France. You know what they call a Big Mac in Ukraine and Russia? They pronounce it "Big Mak"; c'mon Jules, put the gun down. And for all the desire, it didn't taste as good as I imagined, things rarely do. But that didn't stop me from ordering another. On the way out, another customer started asking about the bike, and soon we were at his car, spreading a Kiev city map out on the hood. He pointed out a shortcut over to the Moskovs'kyi Avenue bridge that wouldn't require backtracking, and would also take me through a part of Kiev's central area, and then donated the map. With a full tummy, my thoughts turned away from the pace and back to the experience. What the hell, when would I ever pedal through Kiev again?

Ukraine's capitol was a grand and picturesque fifteen-hundred-year-old city of boulevards, lined with colorfully painted 19th and early 20th century apartment buildings, rich with classical molding and arching. There were modern business offices mixed with Byzantine churches, in a sea of chestnut trees. The avenue's traffic islands were park like, and centered around monuments. It was also very busy; the sidewalks were full of people, and the traffic heavy. At a red light, a fit looking guy in his forties, carrying a blue binder, started talking in English, asking where I'd started. I gave him a quick run-down of the route so far, and as we crossed the street, continued to talk for a few minutes; then I was off. After several more blocks, that bridge should have

appeared; I found a shaded bench and out came the city map.

The map told the story that this hilly west bank of the Dnieper River was the old town, the original fifth century settlement area, judging from the random, crescent patterned streets, versus the grid style layout on the east side of the bridges. Modern urban street design didn't apply to a city as ancient as Kiev, and trying to find a semi direct route over to my bridge required some planning. Having passed my turn, it now required heading on for a couple of blocks, to cross over the street's center divide. As I slowed for another red light near the city's center, there was that blue binder waving at me. We were both amazed to see each other again in the heart of a giant busy city, teeming with thousands of pedestrians. Gennadi strongly reminded me of Sheree's brother Trevor, in looks and manner, he lived in eastern Ukraine, and was here visiting his parents for a few days while straightening out some paperwork for his son's enrollment in a Kiev university.

Telling the story of my wrong turn segued into his pointing out the many sites to visit while in Kiev. I tossed out that if I ever made it back, I'll be sure to see it all, but time's a wastin' and yada-yada... It was a lame out, and he smiled at my weak excuses, then pointed out that by the time the bridge is crossed, I'd never clear the east side's sprawl before evening. He then offered that I should spend the night at his parents flat on the east side, "tomorrow I'll show you around Kiev, it is a beautiful city." My read on Gennadi was that he was a level guy, and he made a good point. It was Kiev, and road-wise, it was the official half way point between Patterson and Hong Kong. Take a day off and enjoy this place.

At first, we attempted to take the train, the signs indicated no bicycles, but Gennadi shrugged them aside. Of course, as we tried to purchase a ticket, the rules were enforced. We then went out to catch a bus, a few streets over. While waiting for one of the shuttle size buses to come by with the right route number, and not stuffed to the gills, I had time to think this situation over. Had I once again said yes too quick? Should I beg off the offer and continue out of town? Again, I'd hooked up with a total stranger and put my faith and immediate future in his hands. I wanted to be diligent, but couldn't let myself think too hard; hell, at this point, who wasn't a stranger? The right bus came along, full of passengers, but Gennadi jumped on and began directing people to move forward and back, or left and right, to accommodate the tourist and his packed bicycle. The choice was made. Buckle up kids, here we go.

I whipped off the front wheel and scrunched the bike vertically into an aft corner, and off we went, crossing the bridge and looking back on the scenic view

of Kiev's center. Trestle train bridges, columned government buildings and bright white Russian Orthodox churches, with shiny gold onion domes and bell towers, built into the dense wooded hills above the river. Through the hazy rear  window, I saw for the first time the figure of the Mother Motherland, Ukraine's greatest monument to the Great Patriotic War, as WW II is known. Imagine a slightly taller, and not as pretty, Statue of Liberty; holding a giant broadsword and a shield. The girl was stone cold stoic. I'd yet to visit our Lady of New York Harbor, but could not picture something more impressive than this enormous presence; made completely of stainless steel, overlooking the Dnieper as it flowed south towards the Black Sea. Looking forward, the Dnieper's east side was a dull spread of Soviet era apartment and business buildings, with open markets and shop fronts.

Once on the other side, we repeated the awkward drill with the bike, as we took a transfer bus a dozen blocks south. On both buses, the process of paying the fare floored me. Even from the back of the packed coach, the people would pass their money forward through a dozen rider's hands to the driver. He, or his assistant in the passenger seat, would make change and then pass the cash back through all the hands again, to the proper person. Gennadi was surprised at my amazement, and said it was a normal nationwide practice. The honor system prevented any problems, and he'd never heard of anyone getting taken. I bluntly assured him that in America, this system wouldn't last two minutes.

After walking a few more blocks, we came to his parent's apartment building, a replica of all the other ten story apartment buildings in the area, with the bottom floors a collection of food, liquor and clothing shops. We stuffed the bike on-end into the closet size elevator and went up to the 7th floor. Meeting Gennadi's parents was a treat, the two retirees had never met a person from the West. They had lived most of their lives as Soviet citizens in the eastern city of Donets'k, Gennadi's home. His father was a decorated mine worker, who had received many commendation awards over his career in the region's dangerous coal mines. Mother had kept the home and tended the garden, which in times past was a true necessity, to provide food and help make ends meet.

They were genuinely welcoming people, who never showed a hint of being put out by their son bringing home a stranger who couldn't speak their language. Mom was active volunteering for the voting polls of the scandal plagued mayoral race in Kiev, that was soon to take place. The TV news was dominated by the shady actions of the incumbent Leonid Chernovetsky. His rivals were Oleksandr Turchynov, the favorite horse of Ukraine's beautiful blonde halo-braided Prime Minister Yulia Tymoshenko, and the third horse was World Boxing Champion Dr. Vitali Klitschko, who was pulling the pro-West young vote. It was an all-out muck fest to rule the capitol.

After a bite and a quick bath, Gennadi's mother treated my rags to an actual washing machine, while he and I took a walk around the neighborhood, with a beer and a smoke. The apartment buildings were surrounded by playgrounds and parking space for the residents, their weary exteriors made worse by the liberal presence of graffiti. We wound up at a nice tropic themed restaurant on a large man-made lake, whose dining and drinking tables were set upon floating decks. It was a pleasant warm May evening, with Gennadi's avid interest in Western politics and life, mixing with good food and beer, or pivo, in a relaxed setting. It made for a good night, and we drank plenty of pivo with vodka chasers until two a.m., when they closed the doors.

Information booths and banners, posters, rally stages and balloons. Democracy was alive in downtown Kiev, with the mayor's election less than a week away. I'd have loved to known the voter turnout, it appeared the whole city was polarized around the three front runners. We struck out early to get a full day of the city, the highlight being Saint-Sophia Cathedral, the adjacent Mykhalovsky Zlatoverkhy (Saint Michaels) Church and the nearby Kyiv Pechersk Lavra. The Lavra was a monastery, built on a labyrinth of caves dug into the Dnieper River hillside, beginning with an Orthodox monk in the 11th century. We toured through the narrow caves that served as hallowed tombs to dozens of worthy monks. The women on the tour knew to cover their heads and legs with shawls, in deference, before entering; but Gennadi had to do some fast talking, when the priests saw my exposed legs. "Beg your clemency, for he is a Godless American rube." Works every time. One needn't believe to sense the sacrosanct of this Holy grotto, and also sense that its keepers would just as soon have none of these shallow tourists clomping about. Within the Lavra's complex, was the above ground churches of Saint Sophia's and Saint Michaels, the collection of golden domes I'd seen yesterday from the back of bus.

Back at the apartment, Gennadi, his father and I, sat at a table outside the small first floor market, drinking pivo and awaiting word from Mom upstairs that dinner was ready. They passed the time helping me read the Russian words on the beer labels, by now I was getting better at substituting Cyrillic characters to make the meaning of words. Several letters were the same as English, A, E, K, M, O, T. Some were a bit different. Their B is an English V, the C an S, the H is an N; P equals R. Still, others had odd shapes and took some thought. Lower case block style "r" swaps for "G", 6 is an English B, a quasi-block style A is our D sound. Block shaped N is P, reverse drawn N is EE, like in glee. When symbols represented a sound, it became a bit tricky. An open armed 4 was a "ch" as in church. Immersion made it a need, rather than a hobby, but none of it too much to learn in a short time. Pronouncing the results, forget it. My substitute method worked for words that had common western meanings, like tire and beer or market. Also, city names that I knew, like Odessa, Kiev, Donets'k. Many times, I'd slowly decipher a word to find it was Russian, and I'd have no idea. "4ePHiriBCke", as close as I can get with this QWERTY keyboard to "Chernigivske" pivo, the cold bottle in my hot little hand.

My new friend's task in Kiev was to arrange tuition payments for his son Antony, who was one of the leading pupils at his college in Donets'k, and had just been chosen to represent the city at a national student conference here. He'd been accepted at one of Kiev's top universities, yet even with his accolades, there was no scholarship help involved; that system didn't exist here, so his parents and grandparents were kicking in the entire amount. The upside for the grandparents, was that Antony would be staying here with them for a few years, working towards a law degree. Gennadi was heading home in two days, and kept making the case that I should abandon the trek north and continue east towards Donets'k; then, on into the historic city of Volgograd in southern Russia. His wife Natasha and son Antony wanted to meet me, and he wanted to show off his small farm implement business. His family here made me feel comfortable, and I had no doubt his wife and son would also be great people. Despite the temptation, the choice to not cross the breath of Kazakhstan and its criss-crossed route structure had already been made. I was truly torn, this had been a great stay, but there were other great stays awaiting, and the adventure had to roll on. Tomorrow, I gotta hit the road.

With decisions made, a spontaneous going away party of sorts broke out that night, and we drank enough vodka to launch into a full-on philosophy and theory conversation about history, and U.S-Ukraine-Russian politics in two languages. The G man rapping in both tongues to drive home the course and fine points of known, and conceived, fact and opinion; do not ask me how. All three were astute in global politics, a trait I accounted to living somewhere that

had a very recent and real history of tumultuous social events. Or they just had better newscasts. There was the collapse and breakup of the U.S.S.R seventeen years earlier, and all of its inherent teething problems, plus the current tension of Ukraine's political future being torn either East or West, by seemingly equal fervor.

In sweeping generalities, the more westerly regions of the country were leaning towards a European Union/NATO alliance, while the eastern parts were loyal to Mother Russia. To boot, the country's beleaguered underdog West-leaning president, Victor Yushchenko, had married Chicago native Kateryna Chumachenko ten years prior; she was a former Washington D.C. policy wonk for Reagan and Bush, and had been accused of being a C.I.A. agent ever since. To the skeptic's credit, one can never take their eyes off the U.S.'s foreign intelligence capers; to the dynamic Kateryna's credit, she was one quite accomplished smart cookie that bravely weathered all the accusations in stride. Overall, a lot of dirty pool had been played in the country of late, including blatantly overt polling fraud and high-level vote count corruption. To boot, Yushchenko was severely disfigured and damn near killed via dioxin poisoning, after attending a dinner party of important Ukrainian intelligence officials, loyal to then-Prime Minister, Victor Yanukovych, in 2004. The fascinating drama of democracy, moving into a bad neighborhood. I learned a lot that night from those two senior citizens, and of course, paid for it the next morning.

The next day was May 20th. I awoke with my brain lurched up against one side of the noggin, at least that was the initial diagnosis. After a stream of tea cups and several aspirins, breakfast and a couple of smokes, the bike was packed; and the late-start-Irish-flu ride from hell was about to begin. All I had to accomplish today was clear the reaches of the city and push 20k's or so into the countryside, then find somewhere to compose for the night. Just before the last goodbyes, I noticed the rear wheel a touch low in pressure, there was one of those tiny steel-belt tines, just visible in the tread. With all the hospitality, I hadn't even glanced at the bike the last two days. In my vodka fog, it was the last thing I wanted to do. Mom and Dad sat in the living room, and watched me take the bags off, flip the bike and set to replacing the tube, and extracting the culprit. Gennadi, in his own fog, thought it was pure comedy. He said it was a sign that today wasn't the day to leave, "stay here and leave tomorrow." It sure as hell didn't take much coaxing. Hang out and rest, take a hot bath, don't drink; way better idea. I was just another Ukrainian vodka sot.

It was that day, just lounging around the apartment, that I weighed out the plans; and how a trip to Donets'k, 700k's away, would affect them. The answer, quite simply, was huge. Riding for a week or so, and having another nice stay to look forward to, with a familiar face, was enticing. Then, Volgograd would be the next big city, and after that, the never-never land of Kazakhstan. That was the part that held me back. I had little information, no detailed map, and the country's west was just a massive empty space. The first couple of days past the border would be a dirt road, before connecting to a zig-zagged paved route. On the other hand, I was going to have to face the similarly vacant Taklamakan/Gobi Desert before it was all over, and taken day by day, things are never as bad as one imagines. Through years of growing up reading National Geographic, motorcycle and bicycle travel stories, and internet accounts of late, I'd never read of anyone traveling through Kazakhstan by any means; much less on a bicycle.

So far on this ride, I'd continually heeded that playing it safe and bringing it on home was the goal, the mantra. In normal life that's not the usual code, pushing my luck was more like it, and I usually pulled it off. Kazakhstan, it was a challenge just waiting, and how bad could it be? People live there, and fearing its unknown maybe the masking of my own self-doubts. If this was easy, everyone would be doing it, going against better judgment is usually when the fun starts; if ya ain't living on the edge, yer taking up too much space. I was filling my head with all the worn motivators, until finally I believed it. Kazakhstan my ass. Screw Kazakhstan. I'll cross that country border to border and probably tell its tales for the rest of my life. "Hey Gennadi, give me your address..."

There were no flies on Gennadi, he'd no sooner seen my mind change when he started making the argument for traveling home with him tomorrow on the train. The logic was either spend a week on the road, or a week with his family; the time is the same, and I'd have more of a chance to visit and rest. Point taken, but that was a little too much, I couldn't do that. The spirit of the trip was riding this bike around the world, I'd felt I hadn't deliberately cheated yet, and I wasn't about to at the halfway point. There are principles involved here, and if I start rationalizing over taking the easy road, where does it stop? I'd be only cheating myself.

Oh, shut up. Something nice was happening here, and following the flow was one of the mantras too. I wasn't a husband, a dad, a buddy, an employee anymore; I was a bicycle tourist traveling around the globe, scratching by on the good will of people I'd never have the chance to pay back. Gennadi's heart was in the right place, and he made a case that could only be countered by foolish machismo. I'll get on that train tomorrow and experience a Russian rail ride. I'll just be sure to not mention it to anyone, if I ever write a book.

Not wanting to put up with another awkward series of stuffing the loaded bike onto city buses, plus feeling the need to do some honest pedaling, I thanked Dad for the stay and left the apartment, late the next afternoon. I crossed the Dnieper, then motored up the hill into the city, to meet Gennadi and his mother at the train station. The climb, the traffic, and the crowds; wrong turns. Getting bad directions from the locals, in part due to my bad Ukraine, which was just English with a Russian accent, drastically drew down my time margin to make the 19:30 evening train. Finally, two young women, who spoke perfect English, told me what to look for and where to turn to find the station. Arriving in the grand hall terminal lobby with zero minutes to spare, I spotted Gennadi up on the second floor, his eyes and arms said "follow me now!" I wrestled the ride up the staircase to the platforms, where Mom was pleading with the conductor to give her one more minute before leaving.

Gennadi had bumped the conductor a few Grivna, to allow us to store the parted-out bike in the metre-wide smoking foyer in the rear of our car. There were no luggage cars, so whatever you traveled with had to fit under the seat, or on the overhead racks. The no nonsense conductor of a late train glared at me, as I quickly pulled the bike apart on the platform, while passengers stared out the windows at the reason the express hadn't left yet. They watched while Gennadi bolted on and off the car, finding spare room throughout the cabin to stuff a wheel here, a pannier there. And then, whoa, what's this? A foreigner, running up the aisle with an orange bicycle frame, smiling a shit-eatin' dobra den grin to everyone. A hug from Mom and we were off.

A pieced out touring bike and its sunbaked rider in cargo shorts wasn't a normal sight, and before I settled in, the entire car knew it. The sold-out car was about three metres wide, and set up with twenty rows; each of two single seats facing across a tea table on the left of the narrow aisle, and two sets of upper and lower bunks on the right, set cross ways. The lower bunks doubled as couches, to sit six passengers. Murmurs of "Ah-mery-kon" could be heard throughout the car, and a look up and down the aisle saw grinning heads poking out, to check out the new guy. Each car had a hostess, or provodnista, quarters up front, and once underway, our pretty blonde attendant came by with a smile, handing out blankets and pillows to all, while taking tea and beer orders.

The next few hours were filled with meeting my surrounding bunk mates and telling the tale; besides myself and Gennadi, our row consisted of a girl and three young men. They all welcomed me to their country, and had all kinds of questions about California and the N.B.A. When they saw the iPod, their eyes lit up, and then took turns sharing it the rest of the evening, the Red Hot Chile Peppers, a hit. As the night wore on, we'd occasionally join the regulars to burn one out back in the smoking foyer, where the bike frame was lashed to the wall; the walk up the aisle was always a stop and greet with the rest of the passengers. I learned that every citizen must possess an "internal passport" with their personal information and photo, the passport is stamped at departure, and they must retain their train ticket to verify that they're abiding their departure and destination plans, if questioned. One may stay up to ninety days outside their residence area, but beyond that, must register with local officials.

Authoritarian as it appeared, they had come a long way from the "propiska" or migration control rules, enforced until the Glasnost era began to slowly change things in the early 1990's. Today, you must have your passport checked when traveling, or register in a new area when moving. But before Mikhail  Gorbachev initiated reforms, outside of hospital care or education reasons, you could very well be denied, with little grievance, the permission to leave your assigned residence region, by the local Ministry of Foreign Affairs. Still crazy, I know, but the knee jerk response to many observations here must always be tempered with where you are; I couldn't compare their world to mine. What used to be accepted here, isn't anymore, and will only get better; much like the accepted social dogmas in the States fifty years ago are reputed today. All accepted truths, are dependent on time.

In the States, I'd never ridden on a train, but for city metros, and in Europe, only day journeys. The Russian Railways have been a long-established part of life, dating back to the mid-19th century. To these people, it was a transportation staple, and this one was like a moving social hour; I was having a great time. It took eleven hours for the train to pitch and rattle through the darkness, making for a great night's sleep, before pulling into the station in the early morning. Donets'k was another town I'd never heard of, but the city of 1.5 million was considered the production and administrative capitol of Ukraine's coal and steel industry; as well as the teenage home of renowned former Russian Premier Nikita Kruschev. My fellow passengers were nice enough to help bring out the widely distributed wheels and bags to the platform, as I threw the bike back together while bidding them goodbye. We squeezed it onto a metro bus, and headed into the city center.

Gennadi was jammed at mid-bus, when he motioned to me that our stop was next, I wiggled the bike out the door; but he was too far forward to make the exit, before the doors closed again. Jumping on the bike, the chase was on. Humping the pedals to keep up, the bus was pulling away as it maneuvered its way for several blocks. The first few moments off an all-night train, in a completely unknown city, in an unknown world, was spent riding headlong in warrior mode; dodging people and blowing red lights, focused on the dirty red lights of a metro bus. I never grabbed a phone number, no address; losing Gennadi now would be hilarious someday, but not today. Finally, the brake lights came on. We backtracked to his place, another ten-story cement apartment building with a heavy steel front door, worthy of a blast chamber, opening onto a worn steel-rail concrete staircase; hinting the bouquet of urine.

The metre-square elevator, stuffed with the bike standing on end, opened on the eighth floor. The bare concrete landing served three apartment doors; yet once inside Gennadi's, everything changed. Like moving from black and white into color, he and his wife had spent serious money and time making a warm, modern home. The roughly 500 square foot flat had been upgraded with a remodeled living room and bedrooms, the bathroom and hall done in hardwood floors. The ceilings had canned lighting, and there was a wide screen LCD television, the kitchen was the next project. Natasha was instantly likable, and her spare English was enough for us to talk, albeit slow. She'd been expecting us, and was busy planning dinner. Soon afterward, Antony came in from his early classes. Antony was a bright, sharp looking nineteen-year-old, who spoke English like it was his first language; his age and demeanor reminded me of Cody. They made me feel like an old friend whom they hadn't seen in sometime. I knew then, I had made the right choice in coming here.

Over the next few days, I just hung out with them and enjoyed their company. I kept falling back on the good reason that it was the halfway mark, and a long stay had been earned. Mentally, those days became the best of the entire ride, I felt at home. We would spend the days checking out the city and browsing the local open market, something of a permanent swap meet, in search of a decent Russian map and of course, the elusive Kazakhstan map, which never came. What's up with that place? Running errands for Natasha's next great meal would turn into a day of visiting the modern downtown's shops and restaurants, walking the beautiful promenade of flowers and monuments on Pushkin Boulevard, sipping beer and girl watching.

Donets'k had been founded on a small Cossack village, but took off in the 1870's when a Welsh business man by the name of Hughes set up a steel mill; thus, its original iteration of Yuzovka, or "Hughsovka." In the '20s, the name changed to Stalino after you know who, and finally to Donets'k in the '60s, at the behest of hometown boy Kruschev's country wide de-Stalinization effort, to remove the barbarous dictator's name from all Soviet cities. Given its relatively young age, and its rebirth after its near obliteration during German and Italian occupation of the War, the city felt and looked contemporary. One day, we ventured out to a steel mill to order stock for Gennadi's business, in his second car, a '70s era Volga sedan, handed down by his father, that he kept in a storage yard garage. The foundry workers allowed me to check out the forging process, as they poured long beams from the orange liquid iron; while Ukraine coyotes, as I'd taken to calling the ever-present mongrel dogs, wandered in and out of the plant, to no one's bother.

While Gennadi talked business, I walked about, taking in the foundry, which had the feel of a giant unfinished shed. The floors were dirt, and overhead, the structure's trestles were made of reinforced cement, rather than the expected steel I-beams; it looked like a decent shaker would crumble the place. I ended up at the scale platform office, and

the girls there put their weighing and billing aside, and had me walk them through all the trip's pictures on the website. The Volga's engine began missing on the way home, and 2k's from Gennadi's storage garage, Dad's car sputtered to a stop. We suspected a fuel block, and needed a wrench to break loose the metal fuel line at the carburetor. He took off for home, and before returning in his Nissan a half hour later, I'd gained a small crowd. The citizens gathered about the old car, they all wondered how I came to be there, and collectively agreed a wrench was needed. When he returned, I gave the fuel line a quick blow back. That was all it took, and I had the unique honor of driving a real Russian Volga in the Ukraine, as I followed Gennadi back to the garage.

The storage garages were made of brown brick with steel doors, and had open maintenance pits in the floor, some pits were half covered by a spare sheet of plywood, like a tiger trap waiting to happen; others, well, just pay attention. Gennadi had one for the car and household storage, and another for his business stock. He was on the waiting list for a third, to move his welding operation closer to home, from a shop south of the city. His business was fabricating and installing barn cleaners, the chain and scraper mechanisms that sweep the dung away from behind dairy cow stalls. An electric motor pulls the scrapers in a continuous oval track, down one side of a barn and up the other, through a trough formed into the cement floor. It then travels up a ramp and dumps the collection into a bin or truck bed, and begins again. It was a heavy steel way of making a living, and he was doing all right, selling and installing all he and his two welders could produce.

The walk back to the apartment revealed the infrastructure deprivation I'd seen in the country's other cities, once away from the town centers. Open man

holes, their covers gone, vandalized for the scrap metal. And the all too common sight of jagged twisted "L" angle steel bars, sticking out of buckled and broken concrete sidewalk slabs; once holding street signs, but now just waiting to rip someone's leg open. I laughed inside at the notion of a California litigation lawyer magically placed here, and looking around wide eyed, then walking only a few feet and becoming giddy, then delirious, then passing out.

The evenings were spent around the kitchen table, drinking tea and vodka, talking shop and world affairs, while awaiting Natasha's delicious dinner. Gennadi had taken up English as a hobby back in his Army days, and was quite good, given his practical experience consisted of Antony and he bouncing it off one another. He had served near the border in East Germany in the early '80s, and we had fun poking at the idea that around the same era, I was serving in the Air Force in Germany, "protecting" Europe from the imagined onslaught by the Soviets. He was just over the fence, guarding the Motherland from an imagined NATO invasion. The awkward afterthought was that, in a different time not so long ago, this wonderful man and I would have been enemies, how fucked up is that? One night, it was his birthday, and a few friends came by. The vodka poured, the guitar came out, and we tried to follow G man as he belted out one Ukrainian folk song after the other. Another night was spent watching the finals of Eurovision, a hugely popular continent-wide song contest between amateur artists, each representing their own homeland. It was ultimately won by a Russian fella. You'd of thought the country had won the World Cup, judging by the celebrations that followed. Personally, I thought the runner-up Ukrainian gal did better...

One of the most interesting kitchen table moments was when, as one topic lead to another, lead to "why do the American movies always make Russians the bad guy?" I pulled out the obvious, that we had spent decades in a Cold War, and had always been taught that the Soviets were our global enemies, bent on taking over the world, spreading Communism and threatening to nuke us into extinction. "It's no big deal now, I mean after all, Americans were the bad guys in all your films, right?" He just stared back. "No, Americans were rarely cast as villains, we used Germans for that." Oh, come on that can't be, level with me. Natasha came down the hall and into the kitchen, Gennadi asked her "can you remember a movie where the Americans were used as the bad guys?" Natasha thought for a moment then looked at me, and shook her head no. They were being straight up. In fact, the Russian media hadn't impressed upon the masses the imminent threat of the West, to the fever that we were taught to fear the Reds; after all, we had never attacked them. The bulk of information from the West, that made it through their tightly controlled media, was to show our decadent, violent lifestyle; and the failures of Capitalism.

Their stereotype of us was one of an overworked and religion obsessed nation that never took time out for fun and family. Imperialistic, culturally ignorant and overweight, while constantly eating junk. I drew the line, and strongly warned them to not allow Texas to paint the entire nation. To them, we were shallow and brash; to us, they were bullish strong arms who wore cheap black leather jackets and smoked cigarettes all day, stinking of vodka. "Some things seem true" said Natasha. She then added that she had already been surprised by my views and curiosity for their world; never having met an American, she assumed I'd have a narrower take on things. We agreed that all stereotypes have kernels of truth, yet normal people recognize it, and it helps us all become fairer minded. If only they served more vodka at the United Nations.

Then came a big history lesson. He asks "so then, who do think won World War Two?" Are you kidding me? "Everyone knows America saved the world by putting the boot on Hitler's neck, then turned around and showed Japan who's got the big stick. We won. Next question?" Like all easy answers, the devil and his details awaited. I was then schooled on the importance of the Battle of Stalingrad, until then, just one of those battle names from the War. I have to admit here that my knowledge of the War extended to the passages in high school history books that I probably didn't show up for, along with movies and a few books, plus what I'd heard over the years from old timers in the U.S. and U.K.; mostly emphasizing the Allied viewpoint. The stories of the Eastern Front were vague to me. So, in surmise and apologies to those who breathe this history, here's what I learned that evening and later on, spurred to further reading.

The Battle of Stalingrad, now Volgograd, was an arch turning point of WW II, and considered the bloodiest conflict ever in the history of warfare, ever. In 1942, the German Army's southern advance was moving steady against faltering resistance towards the aim of controlling the Volga, the major commerce and supply route into central Russia, and to gain a clear path to the oil rich Caucuses port of Baku, Azerbaijan. The life blood of any Army is oil, and the domestic and Romanian oil field supplies were not able to keep up with the Reich's plans. The oil rich reserves of the Caucasus's, to Stalingrad's south, between the Black and Caspian Seas, were of great strategic importance to Berlin; not only for the Wehrmacht's needs, but also to cut off Russia's energy source, and provide a foothold in the northern Middle East. They had it all figured out.

In short, the massive Army Group South's forces were sent far to the east and then split between the objectives of the Caucasus's and the industrial city of Stalingrad, on the Volga. Beginning in the late summer of '42, the Luftwaffe controlled the air over the Volga, decimating the city and preventing any ship born supplies to its defenders. Then the unexpected fierce pockets of Soviet ground resistance brought the two German Groups back together at Stalingrad, and they successfully fought to a commanding position in the city. Eventually, the elsewise overwhelmed Soviet Army managed to break up the Romanian and Hungarian forces that were guarding the German's western flanks, finally blocking their supply lines, and isolating the invaders inside the city. Many of its residents, trapped by Stalin's strategy to prevent a Red Army surrender, fought alongside the Russian soldiers in a building by building, floor by floor and room to room combat to the death, with captured grounds changing sides by the hour.

Aghast that his largest Army could not break the resolve of the pinned down Soviet's vicious rebuke, Hitler's focus on the vital southern oil fields was lost, in a driven obsession to quash the tenacious guerrillas who had been convinced by Stalin, that to lose the city with his name, was to lose the Motherland. Along with the bitter winter and the dwindling German airborne supply line, frostbite and starvation, massive casualties and disease, their invasion failed. After months of the merciless back and forth effort, the battle finally fell the Russians way, in February 1943; their city completely destroyed. 1.1 million Soviet soldiers, thousands of civilians, 800,000 Axis soldier's dead. Over 90,000 P.O.W.'s, most would never see home again. The troop toll halted the Nazi push east, and the loss of Hitler's premier Divisions hobbled Germany's ability to continue fighting at their previous might on the Western front; and of course, denied them the needed oil supplies. In hindsight, historians would recognize it as the tide-turning battle of the entire War.

But who won the War indeed? The answer depends on how deep you want to look. It's true we couldn't have had the Allied successes after D-Day, without the crushing losses inflicted on the Third Reich by the Russians in their many horrendous sieges and battles. But the Russians would have never chased the Germans home, or cared to liberate Western Europe. It's the most examined conflict in history, and thousands of stories have been told, but most of its accounts of heroism and sacrifice will never be known. The surface sheen shows Russia losing tens of millions of people to the War, and left with the dark shadow of Communism. Europe was left a scorched earth, with many of its cities in ruin; and the legacy of the evil men are capable of. The U.S., its infrastructure unscathed, launched into its greatest period of prosperity, by producing and selling to a demolished world the goods it needed to rebuild.

In the process, the American middle class blossomed, and created a standard of life that even today, we assume always existed.

The ugly layer below the sheen reveals the horrors of Stalin's Russia, with a decade of post war Soviet political and intellectual purges, thousands upon thousands of its citizens arrested and murdered. America's domestic economic surge was soon paired with a military surge, that saw profit in conflicts; the senseless deaths still continue. And then there's the half century long lingering wonder of who's going to be zealous enough to push that first button? Can't think about it. But hey, it pushed us to land on the moon, right? The Marshall plan helped rebuild Europe and Japan into strong modern economies, and the failed experiment of Karl Marx's theories are finally waning. But who won the War? Something so complex has an endless string of points to consider, the answer may depend on where in history's timeline one cuts off the debate. The truth is nobody wins a war, they just have a hand in ending it. Your son isn't coming home. You lost.

A kitchen education that never grew dull, and not once in the six days that I spent in Donets'k did I feel an imposition. They fed me, they entertained me and showed me that a family's love, a purposeful means to support them, and a little on the side to enjoy life is all any human wants; no matter what dirt they stand on. In "Innocents Abroad" Mark Twain put forth that "Travel is fatal to prejudice, bigotry, and narrow-mindedness, and many of our people need it sorely on these accounts. Broad, wholesome, charitable views of men and things cannot be acquired by vegetating in one little corner of the earth all one's lifetime." Nailed it. Sell that stupid boat or motorhome you never use in the side yard, don't buy that brand new car or truck that will lose a quarter of its value the moment they hand you the keys. Take that saved money and venture somewhere far away, and sit in the dirt with someone, rely on their good graces and get to know them. It's rounding.

16. Bettina

Gennadi's mother had arrived from Kiev that morning, and it was a sad moment having to say goodbye to her, Natasha and Tony. Knowing I'd blow most of the day picking my way out of the city, Gennadi insisted on driving me to the edge of Donets'k. The second half of the trip, the ride back home, was now under way. Once clear of the vast city limits, the terrain revealed dozens of coal pits, along with the structures and dwellings that supported them. One-hundred-metre-tall pyramid shaped mounds of coal tailings, called terracones, dotted the land by the hundreds. Many of them had existed for so long that their surfaces supported ground brush and pine trees, making them appear as semi-natural terrain features, like the perfect hills placed on a model train's landscape. In some places, the earth was stripped bare, in others, entire hills were shaved off in the pursuit of the flammable rock. As we talked about the visit and the border, and what Russia would be like, Gennadi just kept driving. "I'll drop you off in Khartsyzsk".

We kept going. "Just passed Torez" then "let me take you to the crossroads in Krasnyi Luch." The little blue Nissan passed through a land of small mining villages and green rolling hills, until reaching Sverdlovsk, the last major town before the Russian border. A hundred miles had passed. Once again, there was that butterfly of guilt that wouldn't flutter strong enough for me to care about the lift. I just kept imagining how long it would have taken to pedal to here, to here, to here; and I was in no hurry to say goodbye to Gennadi, that was coming soon enough. In Sverdlovsk, he went to work helping to find a place for the night. The border town was packed with plenty of truckers and travelers, staging for the customs process, so the hotels were full. The third place we hit was a municipal boarding house, it was a true dive, but cheap, and they had a vacancy. Or, they did, until the old woman running the place saw me and balked. After we left, Gennadi explained that she was of the old guard. She didn't want a foreigner, especially an American, staying there; for the police attention I might bring. Safe bet she hadn't read any Mark Twain.

While searching, we pulled up in front of a small one-man kiosk. Typically, they're selling smokes, vodka, chips and beer; but this one had a twist. Atop the white booth with red trim was the familiar golden arches, a metre-high trademarked "M." Without a word, Gennadi gave me that look, assuring that there weren't any Happy Meals inside, just a clever guy's gimmick in a lawyer free world. He eventually found a small inn that would have me, and as we sat at an outdoor table, I nursed a beer, while Gennadi abstained. Although casual drinking was central to their culture, driving under the influence carried severe penalties, and any trace was a bust, for those who cared. While saying our goodbyes, he offered some advice that, ironically, would have prevented him

and I from meeting in the first place: don't be so friendly. Russians are not to be trusted. Thieves, con men, crooked cops, the usual suspects. So far, I'm either on top of it or just plain lucky, or perhaps there's more good people in the world than bad; probably a little of each. He also told me to not to whistle as much. In Russia, the typically idle habit is considered bad luck, and associated with poor people, "when you whistle, no one makes money". After a handshake and hug, he was off. What a great visit, a great family, a great man. I was on my own again, and back to the task. Tomorrow, I will have ridden a bicycle from my driveway, to the Russian Federation, the largest country in the world.

I had a few Grivnas left, and needed Rubles. A young kid, working at the inn, had me follow him around the corner to meet a money changer, who couldn't have been more perfect for the job. Slick dark hair and stubble, black leather jacket. A cigarette flicked in his lips as he tried to communicate the deal, a street financier straight out of a Guy Ritchie film. I knew the going bank exchange rate, and was pleased to find his fees were slightly better. Negotiating would have been tough on several levels. It was a small amount to start with, and then there was the language barrier. Also, it was a black-market deal, and my presence was being noticed by many up and down the block. As G pointed out, the shorts and flannel shirt, and especially the baseball cap, were flashing lights that I wasn't from around here.

I awoke the next morning, still tired after another night of wild dreams and fireworks. They're sold everywhere here, mostly Roman candles and bottle rockets. Who doesn't love getting liquored up and lighting off a few dozen rounds every night? Nobody here it seems. But these dreams; the face and legs and arms are all on board, yet the subconscious is still struggling all night to catch up. It's caught in the sensation tunnel between the life left behind and the gauntlet's end, and I rise every morning feeling as if I stayed up all night watching a crazy movie. The rest of me however, is rolling peacefully through the green of the final 20k's to Ukraine's edge, approaching the border control point. The small facility on this minor highway has the fence and block style buildings of a prison, or military base's, guard gate. A jazzed adrenal rush passes through me, thinking that in minutes, I'll be in there, country number seven. The Russian visa is checked along with the passport, the money declaration that was issued when I entered Ukraine is completed and turned in, after noting how much cash I'm exiting with. The agents are friendly, asking about the trip and wishing me the best. And that's it, I'm in.

But wait. Off in the

distance is another guard gate. Out comes the papers once again, questions abound. Where are you going? How long are you staying? When and where are you leaving? Fill out this form with your cash amounts and do not lose it. "You have no money, how do you plan to support your travel, who is helping you." Agents have me remove the tire stack and open the panniers, so they can poke around; other agents come to talk and smile and comment. People come out of the offices and stand around as the bags are checked, and the documents are passed from hand to hand. I explain about getting ATM cash as needed, yet only show the one card; never letting on about the trip-long trick of keeping the other card between the right shoe's liner and sole, a Visa credit card kept in the left. Figured the weathered, cleated, stinky, tattered bike shoes would be the last to go, if beaten and robbed.

Again, it seemed the earlier checkpoint was the Ukraine exit, then a buffer zone, and now the Russian entrance. It was similar to entering Ukraine from Poland, except these stations are a kilometre apart, and there wasn't a six-mile-long customs line. The older uniforms are all business, but the younger agents are cool, and if the image of America is a cowboy, then the image of California is a surfer. They knew "Baywatch," and asked about life on the beach and rollerblading; rather than explaining the vast differences in the geography and lifestyles of home, I just stopped short. Yeah, you bet, the beach. Cool waves and warm sand, the West Coast has the sunshine and the girls all get so tanned...old and young smile, everyone gets it.

After a few more well-wishers, the blue book gets stamped and there you go. I'm in Russia, I can't believe it. I'm in Russia. As I ride along, I am deliberately taking in the road and the trees and the fields, taking in the air, astounded. The journey has reached a moment larger than me, the physical has just matched my imagination. We all have our grand illusions of self, yet still know the personal truth, who we really are, what we're capable of. I just reached out and grabbed one of those illusions. A regular guy, Joe Lunch Pail, just pedaled into a shrouded and once forbidden land, on that bicycle hanging from the garage ceiling, collecting dust. I wanted to stop and breathe, I wanted to well up, thinking of everyone I'd ever loved and wanting them to see me here, I wanted to...crap. A wobble, a hard growl felt through the seat, a rear flat. The bubble pops, a spoke is broken too.

Just outside the first village of Gukovo, with the bike upside down and tools out, a young man rode up on an old black bicycle. The cheerful teenager had no English, but I managed to relate the trip, and he managed to point out the road to Volgograd. Climbing a small hill that overlooked a round-a-bout, I saw two policemen parked and chatting, and flashed the thought of stopping and verifying the route with them, but the downhill steam was up. I knew the way, and sailed through the crossing. The countryside rolled along a decent roadway with a positive slant, making the most of every pedal effort. The land was green and clean and remote, as if Russia was welcoming me. Everything, from the amazement of being here to the undulating smooth road and the fresh tire was coming together, I was making good time. An hour and a half later, came a village. Odd, it wasn't on my map.

Oh, sure it was, near the bottom. Shit. I had gone well over 30k's south in the wrong direction. Earlier, I'd taken a compass read and dismissed the indication, blaming the turning road, the rolling land, stupid compass. It made sense now, I'd wasted a big chunk of the day, stupid me. A couple of girls at the village market tried to help, but they resorted to phoning a friend with some English skills. She helped plot a course in the intended direction, but the stumbling between us took forever. The correction required some moderate climbing that slowed progress to a crawl, and added to the frustration of making such a fundamental mistake. I had to head further south, then east, just to start heading north again. The rest of the day's effort, and all of the next, would be to get back on track, due to the rolling land, rolling the wrong way.

Finally, I reached the M4 to head north. As the day was closing in, a nice-looking hotel and restaurant next to a police station appeared. A woman came out and tried to answer the price question, but finding I had no Russian, she gave up and fetched Igor, a smartly dressed man in business attire, who was about my age, but with a serious air. At first, he wanted 2500 rubles ($100) for the night, I told him that was way too much and he dropped the price, to about $50. That's better, that's real nice, but it's still too much; I hadn't hit a bank-o-mat yet, and was dealing with about 250 rubles, from the Sverdlovsk money changer. After he informs me the nearest bank is 12k's away in Shakhty, that seals it, I'm moving on. As I'm thanking him, he motions me to wait. Out comes a money clip, and thumbing through it, pulls out a 1000 ruble note and hands it to me, saying "take this, you are my guest for the night". What? Serious? Igor seemed interesting, certainly gracious, and a wee bit of a shady. I accepted.

Inside, he spoke with the hotel woman, she looked surprised, but accepted "my" 1000 rubles. As Igor's grateful guest, I joined him and his friend Mikhail; a tall, similarly doffed man in his mid-50's or so, and Elsa and Julia, a couple of pretty twenty-somethings. It was an evening of beer, vodka, smokes and dinner, as they plied me with questions about the trip, and American politics. Following the general attitudes of others, they liked America, hated George Bush, and doubted a black man could win the vote. Memorable was Mikhail's remark, that he understood what America was, and right now it wasn't normal. It was striking to hear citizens of a far-off country staying abreast of our politics, knowing I hadn't a clue of theirs.

I soon figured out that the charming and talkative Elsa, and shy Julia, were party girls, and my hosts were Russian businessmen. Their exact business never came up. We enjoyed the vodka in what I'd found was the tradition, shot after shot, chased by slices of cucumbers, never mixed. As the empty bottles were whisked away and new ones appeared, Mikhal told of tomorrow's plans. He was off to Volgograd for a blow-out two-day birthday party for his friend, a Russian senator who was turning 50. It began Friday night and ended whenever. Many notable important people would be attending, and he wanted me to be his guest, offering a ride and a hotel room. Oh God, here we go. A ride to Volgograd? This was nuts, I gotta draw the line. Going with the flow, I could probably friend my way all the way to China, but the ride itself was the sacred point. It was becoming like a lover I had one more chance to step out on, then that's it, it's over. It's just wrong. I had no intentions of cheating a ride to Volgograd.

But the chance to attend an exclusive weekend long party with the over and underworld movers of Russian politics and business? Who's ever heard of, or imagined, such an opportunity? My mind flashed to the campfire stories I'd be pulling up for years under the pine trees, with beer in hand. "Then there's the time I partied all weekend with the senators, mobsters, media and sports stars in Volgograd, they couldn't wait to meet me." It was too amazing to pass up. Screw it, I'm in. I swear, anything but temptation. We bid goodnight around twelve and I retired to a nice room with hot water. Funny how you can watch Russian TV and not understand a word of the news or the crime dramas, but know everything that is going on.

May 30th, Cody's 20th birthday. In the morning, Mikhail and I had breakfast together after he shuffled Elsa out the door as her friend, or boss, picked her up. Soon, his driver showed up in a roomy four door late model Volga sedan, almost the size of a Ford Crown Victoria, and a generation away from Gennadi's Volga that we nursed home a few days ago. The leather interior's backseat was packed with large boxes of something, and the trunk was stuffed with even more, plus suitcases. There was no room for the bike, and Mikhail lit into the driver in anger, the gist was that he had been instructed to allow room for his guest and bicycle. In the driver's defense, it seemed clear that whatever was in those boxes had to make Volgograd. To diffuse things, I stepped up and let my host know this wasn't a problem. "Enjoy the weekend, I'll be fine." "No, you're coming." Mikhail was worked up, his forceful side awoken, there was no diffusing. He then marched next door to the highway patrol substation, and brought out two officers. They were soon looking over and motioning at me, it seemed they understood. He came back and said that his friends were going to free up a car and take me to Volgograd, almost 500k's away. As he was explaining it all, they walked over to say, with apologies, that the car wouldn't be freed up for two hours, does your guest mind waiting?

Who am I dealing with? Who can walk up to a police station and tell the cops you'll be driving my new American friend 300 miles to a hotel in Volgograd? They seemed to revere Mikhail, and I could tell they were now concerned about disappointing him. I then jumped in and stopped it all, saying that "it's too much trouble. It's just not meant to happen, please, thank you so much Mikhail for the offer, but I'm just going to hit the road, it's cool." He impressed on how it was no trouble for them, he would make sure I was comfortable at the hotel until they were ready. I reiterated that I had changed my mind, I really wanted to ride it, but thanks so much for everything. Reluctantly, he shook on it, while apologizing and scratching down a phone number to contact in Volgograd for a place to stay. I pedaled away from the crazy episode, feeling that vapor of guilt lifting, knowing I needed to earn Volgograd. C'est la vie. Damn, when did I get here? It seemed so much had just happened, a full day, beginning with the border crossing, then getting lost and then spending an evening with the mob I mean, businessmen, rather. And what about my campfire story? Dobro pozhalovat' v Rossiyu. Welcome to Russia.

It was a beautiful day as I headed north on M4, a highway as nice as any in the States or Europe. The land was, as always, the rolling hills and fields with interspersed woods. What shouted Russia was the roadside monuments, likely, all erected in the Soviet era. Giant stone alters to the Great Patriotic War. Tank and aircraft sculptures filled the round-a-bout centers, along with smaller homages to the farming life. A huge house sized boulder, how it was moved to this spot I'll never guess, served as a pedestal that dwarfed a restored antique tractor, that sat on top. My take was that the War's sacrifices and hard-earned bounty of the land must never be forgotten, the people must remain ever mindful of the collective that saved them from the Western decadence, and provides their daily bread. Another new trend was the villages, they were located a half to one kilometre off the highway, many only connected by a dirt road. The explanation given for the separation was that the highways were created to express commerce and military in times of need, negotiating a village would only slow things down. Fine logic I suppose, but those dirt roads must be a mess in the early Spring, for the residents who just want to go somewhere for less strategic purposes.

At last, heading east again. I crossed the River Don into the center of Belaya Kalitva, that could have been any European city. The town was built on the strength of its giant aluminum mill, and had airy tree lined streets, free of debris, that made the hotel search an enjoyable ride. When I finally located a place, recommended by a passerby, it was like asking to stay in someone's house, which it was. The woman proprietor who answered the door was hesitant at first, and ran the idea past her old abuela sitting in front of the tube. Their back and forth didn't sound promising, so when they asked the equivalent of $50 for the night, my inner cynic saw it as a ploy to discourage. Or am I just reading too much into it, or always expecting flophouse deals? I just wanted to get behind a door, lay on a bed, take a shower, whatever ya  want lady. The flat, just off their front room, had a roomy living area and bedroom with a kitchenette. After getting to know my hostess, she loosened up. Soon, there was a soft knock at the door, she brought in a tea tray and sat down to hear about the trip, as well as escaping the loud TV her mother was glued to.

I knew this mental see-saw was human nature, to be ever aware of people and their intentions, until everyone turns out nice. The internal voices "my God there's an American at the front door, I'm not so sure he should stay here." "I'm sensing you don't want my business, what's your problem?" After everyone sheaths their swords, communication ensues. "Hey I kind of like this guy." "This woman is a joy." This benevolent hindsight never sits in the front seat, it's only recalled after rehashing the moment, once the door is closed and the guard is let down. The respite in Donets'k was missed, and by now I recognized that every border crossing was accompanied by a pullback, brought on by being overwhelmed by a new land and language; and being so far away. I had to shift back into lone wolf mode, didn't want to. Yearning to escape Russia behind a closed door was a clear message; I needed to camp out somewhere, get into it, and absorb this new place; plus save a few rubles.

In the morning, a $4 phone card at the market had dialing instructions only in Russian, to be expected. After reaching a wrong someone, I bought another, and with a bystander's help, punched in the number. He indicated I couldn't dial international with these cards, go across town to a post office. Finding a combo market and post office on the west side, I repeated the process, blowing $8 before the lady running the store implied the problem wasn't the card; this phone couldn't make an international connection. Go to the central post office. After finally finding the unmarked, second floor office on a small side street, I humped the loaded bike upstairs, and managed through charades to purchase another phone card. With the postal workers help, the phone was ringing, I desperately wanted to wish Sheree and Cody their late happy birthdays. When the line was picked up, a man with a thick English accent answered, gaaw... I got it wrong again... and hung up. We redialed and when he picked up again, I realized it was Glenn, Sheree's brother. He had recently retired from the Air Force and was on his own casual world trek, and staying at the house for a while to help out. Cody wasn't home, Sheree hadn't much news, and Glenn's small talk consisted of household chores. It cost $24 all told, for a few minutes chat, and it didn't fill the hole I thought it would. Face it dude.

Riding was the only answer. The negative energy of the morning was positive energy in the pedals, pushing towards the finish and getting home was the only way out. Wishing myself past Russia, Kazakhstan and China, I became emotional, thinking of the day I'd reach Hong Kong, that magical province on the China Sea. I'll be doing a jig in the street, while pouring a beer all over the bike and myself, I can see it, framed as the greatest moment of my life. After living in that clip for too long, the surrounding world creeps back in. How can I dip into that state? This is really it, the greatness of that day exists in every second. You're riding the M21 through the green countryside of the Rostov Oblast, how could it be better than that right now? Rich, famous, poor, forgotten, no matter your station, how many bastards have experienced the moment I'm in right now? When Hong Kong actually does arrive under these wheels, so too will punching the time clock, don't wish this away whining. I keep forgetting. Due to the telephone morning, the sun was growing dim after 80k's. Just west of Morozovsk, a tractor path, winding around the back side of a pond, appeared on my right. Without hesitation, I glanced for no traffic east or west, then shot off the road and bounced down the track for a couple of minutes; before sliding the bike into the deep grass between a stand of trees. Safe!

In the morning, I was awoken by the sound of a diesel tractor putt-putt-putting along the tree line. When it arrived at my tree break, a voice rang out over the rough idle, then putt-putted away. I have no idea what the farmer yelled, but point taken; I busted camp. Once on the road, breakfast was a Vike and a Doors album. The sun was warm and the groove was on, and the hesitant thoughts of yesterday seemed silly, making it feel like my first real day in Russia. The nice morning soon changed to a noontime light rain, and then heavy rain, with lightning and thunder off in the distance. The wind was blowing my way, so rather than searching for alee, it felt good to just keep pedaling through the bluster. The iPod was set to shuffle and clearing skies slowly crept up from behind, as the storm passed and the blue world returned.

That afternoon, two motorcyclists on BMW 650's zoomed past, and then pulled over to chat. Marcin was from Poland and Bettina from Germany, they started in Bavaria and were heading for Mongolia. Meeting Bettina was memorable, she hailed from  Munich, yet could have been from San Francisco, her English flowed like water. Like a dam breaking, I found myself bursting with blather as we talked back and forth about our journeys and realizing, that for six weeks now, I'd been speaking my tongue v e r y - s l o w l y and carefully enunciating every syllable. The rapid-fire exchange, the gestures, the slang that only comes with a native tongue, cast her light to me as a window to the world, way back there, before the gauntlet. But ah, her first language was German, she was very good. Her profession? Bettina worked in the international business world, as a translator.

As we talked, four riders pulled up on modern Japanese sport bikes, followed by two cars. They were members of the Bike House motorcycle club of Volgograd and Volzhsky, out on a weekend club run. Rene', a wiry handsome guy of thirty or so, was President of the Volzhsky chapter, and spoke good English. He introduced the members, including Telman, President of the Volgograd club, and seemingly, the group's alpha. A stocky man of about fifty, he spoke through

Rene', and was very interested in everyone's tale. We had quite a gathering on the roadside, with eleven people and six motorcycles, two cars and a bicycle. After a group picture, Telman gave me his number and instructed I contact him after hitting Volgograd in a couple of days. When they left, Marcin called it first; he'd noticed an impressive Rolex on Telman's wrist, and noted that any Russian sporting bling like that, was doing well. In all, it was less than an hour's visit, yet as Marcin and Bettina pulled away, I hated to see them go. It had been so long since talking with anyone I could stream thoughts with. Found a $20 room in Surovikino that night and slept hard, tomorrow I'll push to bring Volgograd within a day's ride.

Coffee and oatmeal'd up in the room and hit it. This southern jut of Russia is only about 300k's across, even though my winding route to the Kazakhstan border, to the northeast of Volgograd, will total around 600. Still, the thought of zipping through here and facing that obscure land has me jazzed. After conquering Kazakhstan, comes the belle of the ball, China and all its mysteries. Again, I was dreaming too far ahead, but the mind was pinging all day thinking about it, and the road felt good. Pushing the pedals all that day, through a landscape that was fading from green to brown, I only stopped twice for an ice tea and Snickers break. At just over the 100k mark, came Novyy Rogachik.

While sipping an instant coffee at a gas station, the attendant was working with me on the idea of a cheap night, somewhere nearby. A shuttle bus pulled in, and its riders piled out to use the outhouse on the edge of the station's tarmac. The driver knew the station operator, and soon he was hearing the story. He advised that the last 30 or 40k's into Volgograd's center wouldn't be easy, due to the dense, busy traffic and lousy road surfaces. The message was one of gridlock and cross streets, boulevards jammed with people. It sounded like another typical assault day on another major city. That was for tomorrow, right now all I wanted was to put up somewhere and grab some real food, so when he offered a seat on the bus, he's heading for the central train station anyway, I almost balked. Yeah, the whole "can't take a ride" thing, but the main point was not wanting to reach central Volgograd as the evening approached, seemed too much in my current state. It was about $5 for the lift, versus finding digs here, but the big gamble was getting in touch with Telman. Failing that, the center of a giant unknown city could turn out to be an expensive night.

As the passengers loaded up, there wasn't time to second guess, the wheels and bags came off. There I was, distributing the bike's parts among the seats and aisle. A young Kazak boy, traveling with his mother, was fascinated at the new rider, and the next half hour was spent teaching him ro-sham-bo. Communicating the concept was harder than you'd think. At the same time, the trip's story was being translated through a young woman in the backseat, who would out-loud the tale in Russian as we went along. Entering the city's verge, sure enough, the traffic began to back up, and the squalid roadside deteriorated. The ride became a game of stop and go, which soothed the guilt of catching a lift. Then the famous Volga came into view, and after a few minutes heading north, we pulled up to the enormous train station. If not for the bus shelters and the dirty one-hundred-metre-wide swath of train tracks, it could have passed for a beautiful, yet dusty, parliament building. Stalingrad was under foot.

A young man on the bus was good enough to call Telman's number for me, and explain who had arrived. It all went well, for as the day faded, the Alpha man showed up in a new silver Mercedes E-class. As we shook hands, two beautiful brunettes, whom he'd brought along for their English skills, jumped out and welcomed me to Volgograd. They explained that Telman only lived 2k's away, and I was to pack the ride into the trunk and backseat. One look at the immaculate white leather flashed an image of it, soiled with my rear sprocket mung. Sorry buddy, this car is too nice for that. We threw the bags in the trunk and, unfettered with the extra sixty pounds, chased him back to his place, as a pretty face looked out the rear window, relaying my pace. Like Donets'k, I was once again carelessly bolting through traffic, moments after hitting a giant city.

For a Russian to own a house in the center of a large Russian city, was an expensive ticket, to own one like Telman's, in any city, was quite a statement. I guessed that the two-story red brick house, set behind a matching two and a half metre high wall, to be about five thousand square feet. The wall surrounded an ample yard with gardens and a swimming pool, lending it a real urban fortress feel, complete with an automated-remotely controlled wrought iron gate; letting into the designer tile driveway. It was a beautiful home by anyone's standards. Once inside, I met Telman's wife and their two sons, who greeted me under a crystal chandelier, at the foot of a winding staircase; she was just getting dinner on the table. His eldest son Elbrus, was a calm deliberate natured fourteen-year-old, who seemed mature beyond his years, and had very good English. Twelve-year-old Ramazan was a little wilder, in that smart savvy little brother kind of way. Telman was a busy successful man of Azerbaijan descent, whose family had lived in Volgograd since long before the War. He owned a factory outside the city that produced stylish pavement bricks for roads and sidewalks, as well as a chain of chicken fast food kiosks all over town. Oh, and of course, a popular night club restaurant in the downtown, near the banks of the Volga.

A bank of security monitors hung in the living room with views of the perimeter, along with the driveway's gate control. After dinner, the house tour revealed that the second floor was a complete living area as well, including another kitchen. One room downstairs was dedicated to the Bike House Motorcycle Club, and all things motorcycle; featuring books and posters, art and models and memorabilia. Two large windows had blinds, printed with full scale images of his current ride, the Suzuki Hayabusa 1300, the fastest production motorcycle in the world. The guestroom was the size of a large master bedroom, filled with a king-and-a-half size bed, with an elaborate lacquered headboard. The walls were lined with mahogany cabinets filled with fine crystal, the custom shower was kitted with head to toe water jets, it was heaven. On the outside, I was playing it cool. Inside, I was amazed that such a random path had led to these wonderful hosts, and their incredible home.

17. Telman

Volgograd's history stretches back to the 16th century, and that history almost ended in late 1942, when the city was completely destroyed during the Battle of Stalingrad. After surviving those horrific months of bloodshed, the town's rebirth took hold. After breakfast, Telman and Elbrus took me to the Motherland Calls monument, located on top of the Mamayev Kurgan. The 100-metre tall hill, just north of downtown, was the key high ground during the great siege, changing hands at the height of the battle, sometimes from morning to night; and became the final resting place for tens of thousands of soldiers on both sides. There's a worn-out remark, "is that the hill you wanna die on?" Well, this was one of those hills. The monument itself is a grand structure of a woman in stride, clad in a flowing wind-blown robe, with arms outstretched and holding a 30-metre sword. Climbing the 200 steps to her base, that symbolize the 200 days of the battle, Elbrus told me that when first built in 1967, she was the largest statue in the world, and still remains the largest non-religious one. Again, imagine a woman head to toe, standing just shy of our Statue of Liberty, and its pedestal, combined. Apparently, there's some pretty big Buddhas out there, just edging her out.

A path down the far side of the hill passes the tombstones of the battle's heroic military leaders, leading down to a remarkable giant sculptured fist, holding a torch of eternal flame. It's housed in a large rotunda, whose walls are adorned with the engraved names of several thousand of the over one million Soviet soldiers who perished in the battle, as soft background music plays. We stopped at one general's grave, and Telman proudly pointed out that his grandfather fought alongside the man during the siege, and the two remained friends for years afterward. In the evening, we speed-cruised the city in the Mercedes, as he showed me the streets and plazas and current construction projects using his companies' bricks. We ended up at his night club, and met up with the other members of the Bike House, that I'd met on the road a few days before. Despite having a great dinner at the house, Telman had his chef serve me a delicious boneless chicken breast dish, as he and the members held a business meeting at an outside table. So far, I'd been treated like a visiting dignitary, there was more to see tomorrow, and it promised to be another beautiful day off the saddle.

Spent a good part of the morning with Elbrus and Ramazan at the grievously impressive Battle of Stalingrad Museum, near the banks of the Volga. It was erected adjacent to two of the only ruins left standing amid the city's total destruction: The Old Steam Mill and Pavlov's House. The five-story red brick flour mill was the scene of such fierce fighting during the battle, that for weeks the Germans held some floors, Russians holding others, and from what I'd learned of the horrific fray, it sounded allegory to the entire battle. The remnants of Pavlov's House, named for its defending platoon sergeant, was a simple four-story apartment building. It was scene to such carnage, that in times of lull in the daily battles, Red Army soldiers would go out to kick over the piles of German corpses, so they couldn't be used as cover for the next attack. The museum was a large round building that housed thousands of weapons, uniforms and other artifacts of the day. The dark gravity of seeing a luckless young man's boots, or letter home to Mom, only prepared you to walk up the circular ramp to the second floor.

Emerge into a room over 200 feet wide, whose perimeter is one constant 360 degree sweeping panorama of the battle. Life scale models of tanks and bunkers, downed aircraft, and soldiers were set in diorama upon a snowy frozen urban

damnation that flowed seamlessly into a 40-foot-high circular painting, depicting the rage off into the distance. All from the aspect of Mamayev Kurgan's high ground. Above the Volga, dive bombing Stutkas scream down, while burning buildings and dead bodies and chaotic medical posts fill the senses; as you try to comprehend where to begin looking at the enormous masterpiece. There was no glory, surrounded in hopeless horror; it was a picture of true Hell. As we walked out of the museum, the city took on a different light. There was the remaining wall of Pavlov's, the Old Steam Mill, and the banks of the Volga, all depicted in the panorama; the largest painting in all of Russia. The very ground we stood on, had witnessed what is historically recognized as unquestionably, the very worst of man's ambition. Yet, I'm certain the next time we hear "war is the only answer," it will be muttered by some three-piece asshole, thousands of miles away, who stands to make a buck.

Telman picked us up and we went to a large bookstore, assuring me he could find a map of Kazakhstan. We searched, knowing this was my last chance to find the elusive chart. We had to settle on an atlas, which I would soon tear two pages out of, and leave the rest with them; Kazakhstan, the elusive devil. After dropping Ramazan off at the house, Elbrus and I hit up a local mall where I picked up a decent set of sunglasses, to replace my supermarket bargain rack pair that was down to one arm. Elbrus had become my right-hand man, as translator and guide. He was a good kid, and enjoyed the role his father had assigned him, plus he liked the chance to practice his language skills. Rene', head of the Volzhsky Bike House chapter, and his wonderful girlfriend Lea, collected us in his dated Mercedes, to take us to their clubhouse in Volzhsky, a sizable city, just to the north and across the river from Volgograd. I had once again spaced my tire levers, and he made a quick stop at a bicycle shop so I could run in and pick up a pair. As I met him back at the car, he came walking up with a couple of Cokes he'd picked up at the market next door.

"The blut of Meekee Moss". He handed me a bottle and said it again. The blood of Mickey Mouse. The turn of phrase was simply beautiful, the two most American products ever created, seen through the eyes of a Russian. Perhaps you had to be there, but I'll never forget the expression and Rene's smiling face. There was a lean edginess about the man, he appeared to be Telman's top confidant; and after all, ran a motorcycle club whose members lived a pretty good life, in a land with more than its share of desperation, governed by corruption. Despite his size and friendly face, his eyes conveyed he was clearly capable of anything if crossed; I really liked this guy. Crossing the bridge into Volzhsky, which contained a massive hydroelectric plant, we snaked through the north of town and drove into an abandoned industrial zone. Eventually, we stopped at a small carport, with a few bike projects under it, next to a raised cement platform. It came to light that few souls knew that I was secluded behind a nowhere lot, in a place hidden from the mainstream, in the presence of people who lived well with no jobs. Men like this live by their own laws, governed by loyalty. The law of the jungle works well, until you screw someone, I couldn't be safer.

A rusty steel door opened in the cement, and down a dark flight of stairs we went, to another heavy door, opening into a foyer. Turning left through another iron door, we entered a room the size of a two-car garage, appointed with biker life trappings, guns and a large black bear skin pelt on the wall. The place was a WW II weapons bunker, with thick cement walls and padlocked blast doors at every passage. Rene' impressed that only vetted members were allowed to know the club's location, as he led me through another iron door into his roomy office.

The resources, the street sense and the handle they had on Russian life, there was more than motorcycles going on in this secret den.

We met up with club member Losia at a nice restaurant, where we had an outdoor dinner over a few bottles of, to my surprise, Miller Genuine Draft. Everyone at the table spoke English, and as the beers went by, the talk rolled. When they found out I'd never experienced the traditional Russian sauna, the banya, Losia was on the phone to a friend. As dark fell, we pulled down a narrow dirt road through the trees, overlooking the steep east bank of the Volga. It was clear upon walking through the tall slat fence surrounding the log cabin, that host Igor was an old friend of the Bike House, he had built the place himself along with the banya structure out back. As we were introduced, he offered another MGD, and began to show me the quaint home he was understandably proud of. Losia jumped on his bike to go buy smokes, as we prepared for this centuries-old slice of Russian life. The smooth pine sauna house had a foyer area where you strip down, a cold-water pipe open shower stall, and the small sauna room. A wood fired heater outside the banya heated up the thick steel shelf, which the two-foot pile of rocks was stacked on, behind a short partition. Just as Igor started to tell the story of his daughter that lived outside Chicago, Rene's phone rang. Losia had been hit by a car.

Rene', Lea and Igor took off in the Benz to see to their friend, leaving Elbrus and I to hang out in the small two-story cabin. The place was like an antique store, and the log walls were adorned with the heads of boar and deer, bear, wolf and ram. Igor was a sportsman that had been allowed to leave Russia on several occasions to pursue his big game trips, and knew which door to knock on to speed up the usually lengthy travel approval process. Like the evening air outside, the room was thick with mosquito's that feasted, while I tried to enjoy the magnificent display of the bygone. An antique billiard table, that harkened a western saloon, took up part of the living room. A functioning Victrola style phonograph sat on an old stand, next to a '30s era refrigerator with the compressor system gracefully housed on top; working a champ, judging by the

Milwaukee beer in hand. The clocks, the lights, the tin signs; it was like sitting in an Alaskan cabin of 80 years ago, Igor knew what he liked.

By the time they returned, it was getting late, and the enthusiasm for the banya had waned. Losia had been waiting at a stop sign when he was struck from behind, tossing him into the intersection and breaking his shoulder, sending him to the hospital. Just when it looked like the night was over, Igor's friend Alexander arrived, wanting to get steamed. Now, the banya is back on, and Alex and I paired up; word being the ritual was a two-man job. We stripped down in the sauna's foyer, and then sat, towel covered, in the hot room on a lower bench as Alex poured hot water over the heated rocks. We soon moved to the upper bench, the heat on the far edge of bearable; in a few minutes, it was too much. The steam from the water Alex would splash produced instant heat shots, quickly replaced by the rising dry hot air, that drew the sweat out and away in the hot vapor. In time, my concern was what this must be doing to the blood temperature and the heartbeat, this is how one cooks asparagus. How long can this guy put up with this? He's just human, this has got to be getting to him too.

After a long nine minutes, he stands and motions me out, I feigned that look "what, so soon?" We entered the cold pipe room, and I was directed under the ice-cold stream. Christ, if not for the new experience, I would have passed. The sudden cooling off bit like a prolonged electric shock. After Alex took his turn, it was back into the banya for another heat treatment. Again, time slowed down as the heat took your breath away, the pores opened and talk ceased, and the two of us sat on the top bench silent, leaning on our knees as the steam and hot oven air overtook us. Up and out to the cold stream again. This time, Alex tosses me a bar of soap, and standing naked in the bracing flow, I did a quick head to toe. Once again, back into the room of fire. Once again, after forever, we hit the ice water. This time when we returned to the heat, Alex motioned for me to lay belly down on the top bench, which was hotter than hell. What's this about? Before I could imagine the possibilities, Alex reaches into a wooden box, and pulls out a bundle of steamed leaves.

A bundle of leaves! A bundle of steamed oak leaves! The same bundles I'd seen at the roadside vendor stands since entering Ukraine! He steps up and begins whacking my back with the bundle, up and down the back and legs, and not being easy about it. Then, it was my turn to let him have it; that's why this was a two-man job. Oil in the leaves would surface when steamed, and the thrashing imbued the oil into the skin. Two naked guys beating each other with a tree branch in a little wooden room, heated to 200 degrees; if the guys back at the hangar could see me now! After another rinse, we dressed and stepped out into the cool night air. I'd never felt so good or so clean. It was like the skin was alive and tingled every time I inhaled, as if every pore was inhaling too! What I'd just been through was a mainstay of Russian life, and I now understood why it was so important to them. One could become addicted to the post banya rush. They knew something we didn't.

The next morning was June 4th, I'd been gone four months, and as I lay in the giant guest bed at Telman's, I knew my life had been forever altered. The problems that weighed so heavy, causing my mental snap-or-leave state that prompted the ride, didn't just seem petty, I now knew they were. I had accomplished something, I had seen how I relate to people and problems, unfettered by the need to keep everyone happy; feeling unchained from judgment, mine or others. The interaction with countless strangers, and their response, told me I was a good person. From here on out, and onward through life, as long as the heart beat, everything else was just a game. Whew. Shoulda' had that banya years ago. Today would be the final day of Volgograd's hospitality, I'm ready to move on.

Telman drove the Benz through the debris strewn pot-holed streets, lousy with clueless pedestrians and dogs, as if channeling Schumacher at Monza. Imagine the buses and scooters and drunks and clutter, while the man calmly talks a streak through Elbrus about all thing's town and business; as he utilized the Teutonic acceleration, braking, traction control and suspension engineering to its limits. Skittering through busy intersections, narrowly avoiding bus corners, and honking liberally to clear his way; all in an offhand manner that was crisp and accurate, driving ahead of the car, and never hinting of boast. He was good, and drove like he lived, it was quite a show from the front seat. After one skimming moment I said to Elbrus "maybe your Dad should slow down." Elbrus said nothing.

We zigged out to his factory, and met his staff manning the modest size steel structure, filled with modern German machinery for producing the many styles and colors of paving bricks, that sat stacked and drying in the sun on the three-acre property. His chief engineer and manager, an amiable man in his early 40's, enjoyed answering all of my machine questions in English, as well as being one of the few Kazakhs I'd met, even this far East. We then zagged back through the city, stopping at a couple of his fast food chicken stands, to check up on issues and supply. Telman ran a tight ship, balancing the factory and restaurant, chicken kiosks and family. Although he had been filled in on the Losia incident last night at Igor's, when he picked Elbrus and I up, a visit was in order; and we then shot across the river to the hospital in Volzhsky. It turned out to be an eye opening.

The tiles on the lobby floor of the stone building were chipped and missing, the thick layers of paint on the walls and stairway rails were cracked, and peeling in patches. The one admissions attendant sat behind a small barred window in a tiny office, that offered drinks and candy bars. I imagined the place being built in the '50s, then abandoned for decades and falling into neglect. Then, one day, the staff just showed up and tried to make the best of it. Though I decreed to not stand in judgment of their world, it was hard to shut my eyes to the state of the facility; it was a hospital, and by western standards, it was unreal. A nurse helped Losia down the stairs and outside for a smoke, his shoulder and arm were in a sling. He was in obvious pain, but he said the doctors had done a good job resetting the clavicle, and seeing he had enough pain pills. His mother, who had been visiting him upstairs, came down. They said their goodbyes and she left; it was nice to see this streetwise Russian biker bloke softly assure his small frail mother not to worry, he'd be alright. He then warned me that the person who hit him was a Kazakh. "They don't know how to drive, and you're about to ride a bicycle across their country." Not to worry Losia, I'll be alright.

Not a souvenir guy, but I'd been looking for t-shirts for Shay and Code. Plus, something nice for Sheree and Mom, and maintaining the tradition of putting a smile on my Aunt Juanita's face, by picking up a keepsake spoon for her knick-knack rack. All I'd seen so far was knock-off western garb, with typically misspelled Nike or Abercrombie and Fitch graphics. Telman suggested the answer, a first-class souvenir shop at the "Motherland Calls" monument, atop the Mamayev Kurgan. On the way over, we stopped at the construction site of a recreation and swimming resort on an inlet of the Volga, so he could discuss business with the contractor. Apparently, if you needed a paving brick in southern Russia, you bought it from my gracious host.

The gift shop had everything. T shirts, hats and spoons, lacquered eggs, photos, shot glasses and calendar's; postcards, silverware sets, pens and flags and lighters, all with the monument's image. I settled on a couple of shirts and spoons, a lacquered egg and playing cards, all totaling about $60. When I went to pay, Telman stepped in. No way. I hadn't been able to pay for almost anything since being here, and then insisted that these were for my family, therefore, my dime. But Telman had a way about him. A strong stocky man with presence, about my age but seeming ten years older, a successful business man who knew the game, in an exploitive world. As much as we were together over the last two days, there were times when I knew not to ask certain questions, there was that mystique. When I made it clear I was buying the items, he shrugged me off and turned his back on me, waving me off, as if I didn't exist. The burn dwindled when Elbrus saw the exchange and stepped in. "My father thinks you're a nice boy and wants to pay." Bit of a left-

handed compliment there, but probably just a translation quirk. We left and headed straight for the downtown post office to mail off the goods, and again, Telman footed the bill. This man was beyond good to me. I didn't know how to respond to such generosity, thanking him several times the rest of the day. Telman politely accepted the gratitude, with the grace of someone who couldn't imagine treating a guest any other way.

The next morning, after photos with the family, I said my goodbyes to Telman's wife, high-fived Ramazan and threw the bags in the Benz. I pedaled the unladen bike through the morning streets, and after losing Telman and Elbrus a couple of times, we met at a 40-foot tall Vladmir Lenin statue on the main drag, just north of downtown. As I bid farewell to the man and his son who made my stay in this city so memorable, I realized that in many ways, the last few days were no different than if I'd spent the time in any large western city. Tourist spots, a little history, museums, nice restaurants, it all seemed like a very normal life. Truth was, it was a very normal life by my standards, yet by Russian standards, the people I was the guest of lived better than most in the country. Imagine plucking a true citified downtown dweller from New York, Chicago or San Francisco, and placing them in central Moscow or Volgograd, and negating the cultural differences. Their daily grind of keeping house and getting the kids off to school, making a coffee stop before arriving at the office, lunch and a nice dinner out; really wouldn't change. Of course, there's more to your life than that, there's just much more of the daily grind than anything else. Leave the city limits and things change.

The narrow walking path across the bridge that incorporates the Volga Hydroelectric Station, was separated from the busy roadway by a short cement wall. The path looked to be under constant repair, since it provided access portals to the dam structure underneath. The walkway surface was broken and missing in places, and blocked by air compressors and welding equipment. Twice, it called for heaving the bike up on the units, then crawling over, putting me above the railing, overlooking the churning river over 100 feet below. The obstacles were a small price for the breathtaking view at mid span, with the power of the giant spinning turbines humming under foot, the whole world was the Volga. The two-mile-wide river convulsed and flowed, splitting around a pair of islands on its way south to the Caspian Sea, almost 500 kilometres away. By any measure, the largest river in all of Europe, it drains all of western Russia and connects navigable waterways from here all the way to St. Petersburg, on the Baltic. Surrounded by such immense natural and fabricated force, left me feeling a tiny speck, dumbfounded, that men could build a structure that harnessed it all.

After passing over the shipping locks, the road turned north into the flat tree-spotted floodplains. I remember feeling good about moving again, knowing body and equipment wise, I was as prepared as can be hoped for to face the nebulous challenge of Kazakhstan. A warm faith in self, and faith in the goodwill of whomever was going to play into the story next. Head down, the bike rolled through vast brown stretches of brush, broken up by fields of arboos, the soccer ball size watermelons that are the area's pride. Again, the few villages along the Volga were several k's from the highway, leaving the view barren but for the crow filled pine and oak trees, indicating a night in the tent lay ahead. As dusk drew, I stopped at a roadside diner near the junction of Primorsk, to grab a bite before heading out into the hedges.

Struggling through some chicken-based order, the waitress's husband struck up a conversation. The story comes out, and soon, four guys shooting vodka at the next table join in; next thing, I'm at their table, taking shots. Other locals come and go, all taking turns at buying the half litre bottles, and emptying them shot by shot, a few rounds in and I knew the day was done. They wouldn't allow me to pay for the meal, or any bottles, as we drank and smoked and communicated, in rough translation, into the early evening. At one point, we all went outside as Mucia, one of my new hosts, was going to have it out with a Mongolian truck driver he had been trading loud insults with across the room. The pie-eyed pair squared off on the side of the building as the place emptied out, and everyone grabbed the best seats for what was to be an amateur mess. I stepped in and tried to get them to think of the damage, but their buddies were cheering to let the clearly regular event unfold. With all the discussion, the fire wore off and they both backed down. No one was shaking hands, but the boil was back to a simmer.

The party now turned to three others, zipping their IZH bikes up and down the road out front, the exhilaration of riding motorcycles drunk crosses all borders and cultures! When they gave me the thumbs up, I jumped on and ring-a-ding-dinged south down the vacant highway, it felt so good to have the throttle back in hand after four months away. I ran the 350cc two stroke up through the gears, and on the way back, saw the other two taking the cutoff west towards Primorsk. Pinned and using the entire road, the plan was to set up an arcing apex and pull them in on one final blast, before handing the bike back. As the turn approached, the bike's owner ran out, frantically waving his arms, and I came to a stop just past him. He was indicating pretty strongly I couldn't ride his bike anymore, the whining engine and speed shifts had him concerned. It was a bit thoughtless to put my visceral thrills ahead of respect for the guy's ride. After all, that bike isn't a toy over here, it's how you get to work. But it sure was fun.

As the night wound down, the cafe emptied, and a big car pulled up out front. My friend Umar looked uneasy, and said "mafia." By now I'm getting that mafia in Russia doesn't necessarily mean Paulie Walnuts as we know it, rather, it passes for anyone making their cash on some sort of strong-armed hustle. In walks a large, rough looking guy in his 30's, with dark hair, scruffy stubble and the de rigueur black leather jacket. As he walks in, he stares at me, knowing something's out of place, and sits down shaking hands as Umar makes introductions. As the story is relayed, he glares unblinking at me, like looking at a painting hanging on the wall, not cracking an emotion. It's like some silent interview, and all I can do is occasionally nod and wonder what this monkey's thinking. When the tale finishes, he cracks a smile and reaches out and shakes my hand. "Welcome."

The falling down drunk 2:00 a.m. comedy of trying to set up the tent, in the dark, out back under a stand of birches, had me on my back more than once; debating on how bad could sleeping right here in the grass be? Persevering, I managed to pop it up and crawl inside. Morning arrived with an epiphany, that if I ever make it out of Russia alive, I'll never touch another drop of vodka, it seemed an easy promise. Packing up, I saw that the slanted grassy patch behind the restaurant was littered with rusty iron debris, discarded engine blocks and scrap car parts. Luck was with me last night, as I stumbled and fell several times in the pitch dark. Another near miss. Heading back inside for breakfast, there was the waitress and her husband, again they wouldn't allow me to pay. They sent me off with a half dozen aspirins and a big bottle of water, and waving smiles. Among the rambling thoughts, as I rode along in my addled hung-over stupor, was that there exists in these former Soviet State's a positive coefficient of hospitality. The deeper I venture in, the nicer the people are. I'll always have that night in that little roadhouse.

The scrub, with scattered birch stands and the occasional pines, went by for 80k's. Cattle would wander out on to the road now and again, reminding of the common advice to only travel at night on absolute necessity. For hours, the trees were filled with millions of black birds, their constant cackles would fill every minute, until it faded into white noise. They would launch into great waves of flight, as a single massive dark cloud of motion darting and molding about, like hot oil in an enormous lava lamp, I'd never witnessed so many birds for such a distance. Having been advised by the Volzhsky gang and the cafe crowd of a hotel in Bikova, I headed west 2k's into the town, that was no more than a large village. Nothing stood out, so I stopped at the post office to load up some pics, and was informed by one of the postal clerks, a young man with decent English, that there was no longer a working hotel. Soon the postmaster came in from his dinner break, a balding, stout man in his late 50's. He listened with a grim face, as his employees told the tale of the American, they were all amazed that I'd found their little office. He then confirmed that the inn had been closed for years. Then, in basic English, he says "I will find place."

Then came the balk at the internet bill. What amounted to $17 for an hour's use however, stood up when they produced a chart in Russian of the charges for different upload speeds; the highest they'd set for me, due to uploading the photos, which still failed to completely load. It seemed that the rural post offices had higher rates than the urban ones, how frontier. Following Postmaster Alexander into the warm evening, we walked a couple of blocks away to his two-story apartment building, and stashed the bike into his brick, one-car garage. He made a point of the hefty padlock on the over-sized heavy steel hasp, to assure me the ride was safe. We then went upstairs, and once again, my senses were overwhelmed by how decent these folks can be.

Alexander's son and daughter-in-law, and baby grandson, lived across the hall from Mom and Dad. They were heading off to Volzhsky for three days, and offered me their flat for the night. I couldn't thank two people more; can you imagine if a drifting foreigner blew into your town and without a hitch, you let him have the keys to your place? Words are only words. Words cannot describe the gratitude I wish I could relate to the Russians so far. I went up the street to the general market for a loaf of bread, cheese and milk. Two of the three girls behind the counter were all giggles. The other, with fair English, and I, practiced our international smart ass, bantering comical insults back and forth; I felt right at home.

After returning to the flat, a tiny two room place, consisting of a main room that doubled as the bedroom, and just off that, a narrow kitchen, with a small bathroom. Alexander knocked. He came in with a frying pan of potatoes and sausage his wife had warmed up, as I ate, we talked. The outside world wasn't a complete mystery to him, he was a well-read man. Although the village postmaster had been born and raised and influenced by the Soviet Union, and its new society, he knew a better life existed outside its borders. He was an honest man that would have been a good citizen wherever he'd been born. As I looked out the window at the drab streets, the beat-up dusty tenement buildings, and the rutted dirt lot that connected the housing areas; I couldn't help but to see him as another great person, held back by the disastrous failed social experiment of Communism.

In the morning, he and his wife, and other daughter-in-law, came in with a bowl of Shia, the borscht cabbage meat and onion soup, with a dollop of sour cream, that I was becoming accustom to for breakfast and appetizers. He also presented me with a writing tablet; I'd mentioned the night before that the store didn't have any, and I was running out of pages in the journal. Knowing I may be dropping off the earth in a few days, I made a quick stop at the post office and made a call home to Sheree, to tell her I loved her and that I may be hard

pressed to contact anyone for a while, everything's fine. After goodbyes, I was rolling away once again, from a warm family who hadn't much, but were happy, and happy to share. That's what it's all about, the daily routine of the wife and kids loses its meaning, until it's gone for months.

What feels like an anchor dragging on you is really a stabilizing force that keeps you from drifting. What seems like the desire for fun and freedom is really the desire to accomplish something. To say "I was there" or "I did that" or "I saw that" is really a primal stab at giving your life meaning. It all turns empty unless you have that base to return to, like a fire that needs your tending, in order to keep everyone warm. On the call, her well-traveled brother Glenn said, that after I return, it would only be a few months before I'm ready for another adventure. On the road towards Nikolayevsk, where the trail turns east again, I went over his words, and remember thinking, either he and I are very different, or he has no idea of where I'm at. In body, mind and time, I'd never felt so far from home, and couldn't imagine wanting to ever leave again. If I could just click the ruby red slippers together three times, I'd do it. "But it wasn't a dream. It was a place. And you and you and you...and you were there. But you couldn't have been, could you?"

Alexander promised a hotel in Nikolayevsk. After forging 80k's the day before, with a serious hangover, I decided after a 35k effort to pull in and get right, with a nice room. Pulling into the town square, a large wedding party was just finishing the post ceremony photo shoot. I was soon surrounded by young people, dressed in their Sunday best, taking pictures and giving directions to the hotel, and wondering how I came from California to their town. I'll never know celebrity, but an inkling must be the feeling emoted by everyone I meet, this is nothing short of an ambassadorship. Everyone taking turns standing next to me and having pictures snapped, I'm scribbling out the website address and answering the same questions over and over. I came to enjoy every minute of it, knowing that this window would slowly shut the closer I came to Hong Kong. Above all, I wanted to be as friendly to these wonderful people as their comrades had been to me. Hoping, that years from now, one of these kids would say "I met an American once, riding a bicycle through our village, he was really nice."

But am I? Once the evening's room door shuts, despite my worldly exterior, the inner struggles came back to life, honestly wondering, that maybe I'm just not that chill. Even after the uplifting moment of the square, I settled in and began writing in the journal, the inner nature's ire came unleashed. From the journal, my [sic] verbatim:

"06/07 One hotel. As usual 1940's style building, beat with layers of paint everywhere. Broken down furniture and stairway. Cheap linoleum, rabbit ears TV and a fridge from the late 60's. Less than $20, had to fill in two forms with all info then find out no electricity or hot water until 5 pm (I hope!). And not so fast, hot water only downstairs in lobby in a common shower/bathroom (with a 30 gallon water heater for the whole building). Across the street to another usual bare minimum market. Bananas and a strawberry milk plus a 1/2 ltr of regular milk. Both spoiled I later find out (after returning to the room). Went down the street and bought cereal and another milk and TP. Fucking hotels, hospitals, markets, roads. I'd love to just take one Ruski to America and show them Albertson's, Motel 6. Our engine building facility is cleaner than their hospitals. Watching these stupid young Ruskis glurp down vodka and are so proud of their country, they have no idea how fucked up this place is. I watch their women cringe at their drinking just as any woman would. 4:20 pm! The electricity came on! Oh yeah, no TP in any bathroom on three floors, I checked. I haven't truly relaxed in sometime. Always on guard (amongst such unfamiliar surroundings). The food and the language barrier that has gone on for over a month, the maps all in Russian. Unlike travel by car or motorcycle I can never choose with certainty where I'll be when night falls and every (fucking) key looks like it belongs on the end of Ben Franklin's kite string. I'm stared at every moment even when not with the bike. I'm either dressed funny (no track suit) or I'm the only guy without the ever-present beer in hand. I jot down thoughts in this book wondering if I'll ever make it home alive. One car or truck swerve and it's over. Will these words be the only thing left for Shay and Cody's memory? The closer I get the worse it will be. He almost made it. Can't relax, seem to be fighting fear and home sickness. I'm not a tourist. This is one of the last great adventures for a modern man. I'm 80 k's from Kazakhstan and I can't buy a map. What the fuck? How can such a large country exist with no information? Several times hear the rumors (of cannibalism and wandering wolf packs) of Kazakhstan. Sure we would have heard of that. Oh yes, beds here are never made, the sheets just piled up for you. The Ruski's are so good. This country is fucked up."

In looking back at the journey, I realize that outwardly, I was handling the trip just fine. Looking back on some journal entries, I was struggling with the unknown and uncertainty of it all. The sensation of constantly being adrift in a truly foreign land, with the most unusual yet to come; never having that base to return to and compose your outlook. Dramatically, it was "one of the last great adventures" but all the strife was simply the price to pay for running away from, or enlightening yourself. A Pirsig Chautauqua, hell a traditional Chautauqua, I even had a tent. At the low moments, I would again need to remind myself, that you alone put yourself in this crazy attempt, at great expense and sacrifice for the family. Every day was so eclectic, that the sub conscious was dealing with it as a living dream. A dream to live, and every moment had to be understood.

Yet, the mind is relentlessly bombarded by challenges at all waking hours, and then the brain sorts through it all with those heart pounding, action bursting dreams, that have me waking feeling exhausted. In the past, sensory overload had only been a temporary state of sunshine experiences, now it was an honest condition that was tapping at the red line, as my head tried to quell and comprehend all that was happening. Once again, the ride across America seemed so easy and amateur by now, familiarity is the key, the foundation. Remove it, and the mind is always seeking anchor, as it processes at once basic and extreme information. Good golly Brian, pull yourself together, batten down the hatches, Asia awaits!

The road headed east once again and the land's lush, rolling green meadows and woods, that defined the Continent since landing in Holland seven weeks ago, completed the sudden fade into the sun-dried brown, that began on the approach to Volgograd. Local farmer's sparse attempts to claim back what they could eventually lost out to the arid brush, as the Volga was left further behind. The wind was helping, as if pushing me to the edge of the mysterious Kazakhstan brink. Armed only with a vague map torn from an atlas, the local word was the final 20k's of Russia, and the first 30k's over the border, were dirt roads. It doesn't matter any longer, I'm about to attempt to cross the expanse of Kazakhstan by bicycle, and by now the lack of info is just another challenge. I know I'll deal with it on the fly, and somehow pull it off...someone said I may find a map at the border control.

Horses grazed by the roadside, with the now common sight of their front legs tied above the hooves, with about six inches of rope between them, preventing their free movement. Again, the mare's colts bounding free, but never straying far from mother's side, never a fence, just the animal's own tendencies to keep them restrained. Passed by several cutoffs to tiny hamlets, set off the main road, and rolled through another with the fawning and popular name of Krasn Oktyabr, or Red October. As I approached Palasovka, it had been a 100k day. On the outskirts, there was an older Kazakh couple replacing a flat on their Lada, nary a common word between us, but they figured out the story and smiled for a picture. At the edge of the village, I stopped into another auto repair shop, for some Palasovka info. This tendency came from the thought that the guys were always ready for a break, and they all drove, hence knew the spots and were good on directions. Once again, the gang stopped mid-wrench and boiled up tea, and once again, I accepted a smoke from a boy not much older than twelve. Pedaling towards the only hotel in town, I could see that this little burg, off in the country's southern corner, was another to have been built up in grand fashion by the State, then forgotten.

It wasn't hard to imagine times past when the Soviet machine must have come into these rural communities and spent money like there was no end. Palasovka was a tiny town, yet featured a wide plaza, surrounded by buildings with classic Wall Street like architecture, and a dominating Lenin monument. At some point, and I'm just guessing the mid-'90s, it was all left to slowly fall into disrepair. It was as if a film crew walked away from a set, to be occasionally propped up by the local citizens with a flower bed, or to slap on a coat of paint. Since the collapse, the buildings that once housed a full staff of various local government office workers were either abandoned, or left with a skeleton crew to work in a haunting, mostly empty structure; merely a facade of its intended use.

The hotel was no exception. As in Nikolaevsk, the facility struck me as something required back in the days when government, or military officials on administrative assignments came to town. The staff of one appeared surprised a visitor, much less a foreigner, walked through the double doors. Today's concierge, and only person in the building, was an older woman behind the glass of the register office. She wasn't in the mood to deal with this smilin' Jack, even as I charmed my best "happy to visit your beautiful country" act. She was asking 1500 rubles, or $60, for the night, and refused to come down, even as I politely negotiated; wishing for the language skills to convey that this overdressed village was no St. Petersburg. I shelled out the last of my Russian bills on the room, and some stale bread and a noodle pack from the lobby pantry; knowing that this was probably going to be the last hotel for some time, judging by the map of empty space called Kazakhstan. The towns near any border knew they had the market on travelers, gathering in the last place to grab a room, before the crossing.

After payment, she issued me a one-each electric kettle. Then, off came the heavy rear bags, then heave-ho the bike over the shoulder, up the two flights of concrete stairs with bare steel rails. The room was spacious, with separate bedroom and living rooms, that looked out on the town's central plaza. And so, $60 and no running hot water. Oh, what a surprise. I walk a few blocks away to find a market, and pick up some meat and cheese and milk. Back at the room, and the kettle doesn't work. Down at the front desk, the woman hands me another from behind the shelf in her little office. The cord terminal is almost completely broken off from the base, so I just hand it back with an idiot's thank you, as she stares at me confused. There are fourteen one-litre bottles of water in the room, that implies either "the water doesn't always flow here" or "don't drink the tap water." I break out the camp stove and heat up enough for coffee and noodles, and later, a basin full for a field bath. Then, I follow my routine of plugging in the iPod in an obvious place, so as not to space it out in the morning. Once fed and settled, I looked around this quite comfortable room, and appreciate that this must have been some pretty nice digs back in the day of Soviet supreme rule. I don't let slip the notion that I'm sitting back here, with a beer and a smoke, deep in the heart of Russia; in a hotel room that very few Westerners, if any, have ever relaxed in. As recent as the '90s, the outside world had never seen this part of the secret land behind the curtain, a small remote town in the corner of southern Russia, bumped up against a Kazakhstan border that no one had any reason to come to. I was in deep.

18. spook

W ell, the 6th of June started out normal. The border was just 40k's away, and the goal today was to get about 20k's inside. Knowing what was, or rather, what wasn't, ahead, some internet to upload some pics and let others know my whereabouts seemed important. In the plaza, two women were working flower beds, and broke from their morning task to show me the post office; and as we tried to find common words, up walks their friend Kate. Petite, brunette and friendly young Kate was the local high school English teacher, she offered the use of the school's computers, and asked if I'd meet with her students. We walked about a block north, out of the plaza, and came upon her school. It was set in another imposing Rococo style four story building, surrounded by a tall iron fence, enclosing a dirt lot that had once been a lawn. Grand from the outside, but merely a shell of its intended use; the wide, empty stairwells, hallways and rooms gave the place a cavernous feel. We went up to the second floor amid the stares of teenagers, amazed that their instructor was accompanied by an oddly dressed foreigner. After meeting some of the staff and students, and learning that this was an important final test day, we came to the computer room.

After connecting the camera, the same old problem arose, the pictures just wouldn't complete the upload. We then walked back to the square, picking up my landscaper friends Lidia and Olga and a few others, and marched back into the post office. When it was clear they also didn't have the up-speed, Kate became determined to make it happen. We all followed her across the street to the city's administration building and city hall. By now, I just wanted to get under way, but the Palasovkans were in full-help mode. The team of benefactors had a quick word with someone, and after a thank you goodbye to Kate, I was brought upstairs and whisked into the city manager's office. A tall blonde woman in her late 40's, who was the picture of authority, came in and was bombarded by Lidia and Olga, telling my tale. Looking over the top of her reading glasses, she smiled as we shook hands, then immediately set about giving her office over to me. Her desk, her chair, her computer. She then called in a young Kazakh looking fellow, whom I gathered was their I.T. guy.

158

As he helped with the upload, the staff from the other offices began dropping by. Soon, the furniture was being shifted about to make room for the crowd, and a plate of pastries showed up. Wine and vodka bottles were being opened, candles were lit and a box of chocolates were offered. They all wanted to hear the story, and sat smiling as I reeled off the narrative that I had become accustom to telling, some understanding it, others being translated to; and all the while, the I.T. guy was nursing the picture's upload. I was overwhelmed by how incredible these people were treating me, and when it was over, they gifted me a hat and lapel pin, commemorating 2008 as Palasovka's "year of the baby" or something very close. After group photos and a long farewell to all, I followed Lidia on her bike; first to a bank-o-mat, where I loaded up on the Kazakhstan Tenge (teng-a), and then she showed me the way out of town.

As I rode along towards Savinka, it began sinking in what a burst of joy the morning had been. Another amazing time spent with these wonderful people. In this dimension, almost everyone is nice; in mine, there's a good number of nice people. Why can't my cortex just chill out? Drop the guards, I'm surrounded by great people, the only wet blankets being some of the oldest citizens who were too jaded by the past; and of course, a couple of drunks. As I glided wistfully along, a large blue sign passed by with a message in Russian, Kazakh, some form of Arabic, and finally English; saying something to the effect of "do not pass this point without proper visas and travel documents", the typical border zone alert spiel. I assumed Savinka would be the border control point, since beyond its limits began the 20k dirt road to the Kazakhstan border, and the Google maps showed no structures at the actual line.

Entering the village, I was joined by a young Kazakh boy riding a bicycle, way too big for his little legs. I pointed East, and he motioned me to follow him.

Cool, an escort through the village, let's make quick work of another dusty outpost. After crossing a small bridge over the Torgun River, we stopped to talk to a smiling older gentleman, welcoming me to their burg. As we exchanged niceties, a uniformed border patrol agent appeared, causing the old man to abruptly turn tail. The boy skittered away after the agent barked something to the effect of "get lost." He then turned his attention to me.

Just ahead on my left, was a border patrol office, with three olive-green Army Jeep-style vehicles parked outside, along with a few young armed guards. The middle-aged dark-haired agent was dapper, in pressed army camo, and shaded by an almost too-big-as-to-look-silly military dress hat. Forgetting his manners, he went straight to demanding my documents, which he studied a moment before telling me to pull up outside the office, in which he disappeared with my passport/visa. I turned on the charm with the young soldiers outside, and they were soon smiling through their reserve at my animated mocking of their captain's concerns. We all lit up smokes and things seemed good to go, I was just waiting for the officer to check out my papers and thank me for my patience; you know, these people are all so great. Then the word came that I needed to come inside. Sitting down in the Captain's small office with three desks butted together, I was asked if I minded some questions. It was about 1:30.

Your name and address, where do you work, and when were you born? How did you arrive in Savinka and why are you here? Another officer, a soldier and a local policeman came in, and studied the passport and its visa sticker, they took turns asking similar questions; but the communication was frustrating, so the Captain picks up the phone, "please wait." By now it's clear my day is taking a hit, there's something wrong here, but I keep up the cheerful tourist act, hoping I can get on with the task at hand. A half hour drags by, just staring at the office walls, with an occasional silent "everything's fine, just a few more minutes" nod from the Captain. A plump woman in her late 50's, with a ready smile, walks in and greets me. Her name is lost, but she's the English teacher at the Savinka school, and has been brought in to interpret. The grill starts over with the same questions, and more. "What company are you working for?" They become focused on a tourist story with a business visa. "What business brings you here?" I'm told I must return to Palasovka, this border is for Russian and Kazakh citizens only, not tourists. "A tourist has never come to this village." Obviously, it's not clear to these folks that I'm on a bicycle, routing as direct as I can across Kazakhstan, I can't backtrack or detour north, my schedule isn't that loose. I'm thinking at this point, that surely, they're mistaken. My buddies in Volgograd, the Postmaster in Bikova, the office party in Palasovka this morning, someone would have mentioned something this important.

"You cannot cross Kazakhstan on a bicycle, the roads are piste" she says, meaning unpaved. She was right about that, what looked to be an uncertain number of k's of dirt out of Savinka, and beyond the border, would then connect up to a roadway. The most direct path east would mean a couple of days of dirt. A bit rough, but the straightest shot. "I know, I Google mapped it, the road is my problem." Nothing. It's clear this isn't a suggestion. They excuse me to go stand outside, while their pow-wow continues. Through the office window, phones ring, doors open and close, and soon the Captain emerges with an edict. I am being transferred back to Palasovka, and nodding towards one of the "UAZ" jeeps, he deadpans "please, can you make bicycle in the back?" These bastards aren't joking, they're taking this seriously. To no response, I reiterate that I know the route is hard, I'm up for it, how can you say no?

He's done taking questions and the young soldiers were not smiling anymore, there's something else going on here. It's not just a friendly piece of routing advice or a helpful lift to the next village towards a course correction, the gravity arrives that I'm not crossing into Kazakhstan today, and the inquiries are not over. The bike and gear are broken down and loaded up, two armed soldiers ride up front, and I'm sandwiched in the back between Teacher and another soldier. A few blocks away, we drive down a horrible deeply rutted path through a vacant lot, stopping outside a white-washed wall, another guard station. The driver heads inside, and we quietly sit for 15 minutes, as I ponder what kind of a quagmire this trail must be in the spring. Then, the woman speaks up and assures me everything is going to be fine, and just between us, she knows I can speak Russian. "Why don't you just make it easier and talk directly to them?" I look at her as if she's nuts, this is getting weird.

A different soldier, a young, fresh-faced officer emerges, smiling like he just ate the canary, and takes the wheel. We drive the 20k's back to Palasovka, as he intently studies my passport and its stamps, as everyone chatters away. I don't know what their saying, but the gist tells me the trek has just been halted, or drastically changed; I have those gut butterfly's you get after being caught doing something really wrong, but at the same time knowing that's not the case, I think. On the eastern edge of Palasovka, we pull up to a compound whose white-washed plastered stone walls are topped by concertina wire. The tire shredders are lowered, the candy cane pole gate rises, and a steel wall gate swings open, then closes, as we pass through. Someone expecting trouble?

I'm left in the guard of a group of armed youngsters as my captor's head inside with the passport. I casually reassemble the ride and share the tale with the soldiers who collect around, asking about the trip. A glimmer that the incident is over appears when a smiling soldier appears with the little blue passport, only to politely ask me to come inside, and bring the bike. The room I'm taken to is straight out of a "Law and Order" episode. Dull walls, five steel tables and a dozen chairs, several shaded single bulb lamps hang by their long cords from the ceiling. The station chief is a professional looking soldier in his 30's, and begins the quiz anew, as two of the four armed soldiers begin taking notes; a dusty old man in a dusty gray suit sits down in the corner, as my Teacher continues to smile. For another hour, the questions fly, the bike's bags are pulled off and dumped on the adjacent tables. Your job, your town, your wife. Your parents, your brothers and sisters, what do they do for a living? The mini kits with tire patches and grease, aspirins and band aids are sorted through, a soldier stares at me while he squeezes the sleeping bag, as if feeling for the Walther PPK I must surely be concealing. "Who planned your trip?" "Are you traveling with your money or your wife's?" "Are you in the military?" "Have you ever been in the military?" "Is anyone in your family in the military?" Do my ears deceive me? Have the clouds parted, have the make-believe daydreams of every little boy shined down upon me? These people think I'm a spy!

Stirred, but not shaken, I gladly went along with the Keystone Komrade's grilling, and it wasn't long before my Teacher overtly morphed into an inquisitor. She is asking her own questions, and has warned the station chief to be careful, "he understands Russian", she can tell. Another officer arrives, replacing the station chief. Once again, the trial begins and another hour goes by. "How did you obtain your visa?" "Why do you have a business visa if you are only a tourist?" How much is your bicycle worth?" "Is that Russian gasoline in your camp stove bottle?" I cheerfully reel through all the questions again, trying to keep a happy face, I've nothing to hide, so whatever they want to know, I tell them. They never find the folded slingshot tucked in a bag of tires, or the painkillers mixed in with the diarrhea pills, and my only real concern was that they may confiscate the journal, for it had now become my most important possession. I sure as heck didn't volunteer that I visited Russia for eleven days with a tour group back in 1983. The day was slipping away, and they didn't look tired. After what seemed an eternity, a soldier poked his head in with a message that sent a buzz about the room. The Grand Fromage had arrived.

In walks a plain-clothes, balding bulldog of a man in his late 50's. Dressed in black trousers and a white shirt, he slowly rolled up his sleeves as he stared at me, while hearing the collected intel from Interrogator 2; he was a commanding figure. Could be wrong here, but this guy smelled of FSB, the new KGB. After the briefing was complete, Interrogator 2 departed and Bulldog started in with the same queries, the trick was to continually repeat them until they caught a different answer to the same question. I assured them I hadn't any Russian language skills beyond the please and thank you's, but truth be told, I'd gathered enough key words by now to catch the drift of the conversation, allowing me to readily answer after Teacher's translation, convincing her further that I was faking it. Twice she held up her hand after Bulldog's rapid-fire questions, hoping to catch me blurting out directly to him in the heat of the moment. I was pulling off this "I can't speak Russian" act like someone who couldn't speak Russian, and imagining fiddler Charlie Daniels singing "he may look dumb but that's just a disguise, he's a mastermind in the ways of espionage..."

All of my work history since leaving high school. "What city were you born in?" "Where is your GPS?" My favorite "what is the street address of the hospital you were born in?" They had come to the conclusion that it was impossible to ride a bicycle as far as I had in such a short time, and also kept returning to my Air Force hitch. A soldier remarked that I seemed like a peaceful man, prompting them to ask if I was worried or nervous. I answered no, I hadn't done anything wrong, and this whole thing was going to make a great story. "Wait until my friends at home find out I was detained and interrogated by Russian border security!" They didn't know how to take that, "which friends do you mean?" I added that it seemed unusual that the Russians would treat a foreign guest in this manner. Pulling a diplomatic jewel out of my ass, I said "in fact, before this delay continues, I'd like the U.S. Embassy in Yekaterinburg to be notified of my location" referring to nearest Consulate, still hundreds of kilometres away to the north. And that's when Teacher snapped.

"You are not Russian! You are not Kazakh! Did you not read the signs? You cannot cross at this border, it is PISTE! You are traveling as a tourist on a business visa! Who sponsored your invitation letter? Who issued your visa? An American has never been here! We have never seen a bicycle like this!" The impatient Bulldog and she were now holding a joint interview, I couldn't tell who was asking what. I calmly repeated answers and denials, while the passport-visa was continually being passed around the room to different soldiers; the Embassy remark had lit her up, and those emotions washed around the room. It dawns on me that these guys have been training for years to use these procedures, and one day, here I come pedaling down the road. Francis Gary fuckin' Powers!

Things were heating up, and it crossed my mind that with the snap of a finger, they could toss me in a cell until they'd mulled over my answers, or contacted a higher authority. Then the Bulldog began advancing through the photos on the camera that, along with the iPod and a mini am/fm/shortwave radio, were my only electronic devices. "When is the last time you loaded pictures to your website?" And once again "and your GPS is where? We just need to see it." When he came upon the photos taken this morning of Kate and Lidia and Olga, and the ladies in the administration office, the camera was passed around the room. "Who are these people and how do you know them?" We were now in the same small town, he knew full well who they were, Teacher certainly knew who Kate and the city manager were. "I was looking for a bank-o-mat and asked them for directions, I have no idea who they are", just knowing that the next query was how some pics were taken in the city hall office. Before that occurred to them, Bulldog came across pictures taken in Volgograd with Telman, and the camera is instantly passed over to the old man in the dusty suit, that had been sitting quietly in the corner the entire time. From the silent response and eyebrows, I knew they recognized my wonderful host.

When I'd left the city the other morning, Telman handed me his business card and told me to contact him if I ran into any trouble, I felt this qualified. "How do you know this man?" "He's a friend of mine" and produced the card from my wallet, saying "you're welcome to contact him if you need to verify anything." Bulldog asks through Teacher "does this man have money, is he wealthy?" "I have no idea." "How does this man make his money?" "He's a business man, I think he sells a lot of chicken." With that, the air changed. The interview halted as Bulldog and the old man left the room, I'll be damned, something cracked. Telman you son of a gun, who are you? A short time later, Bulldog returned alone, and motioned for three of the soldiers to leave, and then discussed something with Teacher. She smiled at me, and asked if I would just sign a copy of the report that the soldiers had been scratching out during the interrogation, then I could go. It was over. But. "No, I won't sign it, I haven't any idea what it says."

Here we go again. She didn't have to relate to Bulldog my response, he figured it out. Strong words were said. Teacher begged "you must sign the report, please, and then you are free to go." "I'm not signing anything that I don't understand, and I can't read Russian." The Dog isn't happy. "It is just a report, it is for your protection." "I won't sign it, it could say anything." Dog snaps a demand at her. "You must sign it, then you can leave." "I can't sign something I can't read, no one does that." She turns to inform the Dog, but he's already standing up, raising his voice at the both of us and slams his fist on the table, this was getting real. Teacher is in a tight spot, and I'm now a bit worried, but there's no turning back. "Please it is only what we have discussed in this room, I will read it to you if you like, you trust me don't you?" "Of course, I trust you, (!), but you aren't my lawyer, and I can't put my name on something I don't understand." Bulldog was steaming, staring at me like he was about to rip my head off and venting his anger on Teacher; evidently, "no" was a new word to him. By now, I wasn't so sure about saying no, this may have opened a whole new drama, but signing that paper seemed too risky. Her face was flush and her eyes were beginning to well up, she was becoming visibly upset; she hadn't bargained for being shouted at, or caught between the Dog and I, with neither showing signs of relent. She begs once more "you must sign the report, it is your receipt." "My receipt? That means I get a copy of it?" "No, you cannot have a copy." "Well then what happens if I never sign it, because I'm not, what then?" Teacher and Bulldog pondered the question. "If you do not sign the report, we can't go home." "Well I'm not signing it."

Bulldog nodded to Teacher and they both left the room, leaving a soldier and the bike and its gear spread out over three tables, it was 7:30 pm, I had been detained for six hours. What was next? Were they coming back? During all the questions and accusations and commotion, the suggestion that I must travel north almost 400k's to Saratov, before heading east to reach an allowable Kazakhstan border was put forth. Sometime later, Bulldog said that I wouldn't be allowed at that border either, rather I must travel 36k's south then catch a train over the border to Zhanibek, and begin from there. Next thing, I'm being told the road to Zhanibek doesn't exist, then it does exist, but is impossible to cross. Every time, I pointed out the contradictions, but it went nowhere, just a polite "thanks but we're asking the questions here twerp" smile from Teacher. As I repacked the bike, the young soldier, who had been one of the stenos, said out of the blue "so whatta ya gonna do?"

Stunned, I asked "you have understood everything?" "Of course," as he gestures at the report. Of course. "I'm heading to Zhanibek, on that train over the border." The young man then stood up and came over, becoming stern, and in a soft tone said "they know that's what you're going to do, you will be detained again and this time they'll want money, you should not be in Palasovka tomorrow morning, they may have more questions." He left for a few minutes, leaving me to wonder what was next, sounded like their game was done...for today. It was getting late, and with the soldier's dire advice, heading north was looking like the only option left. When he came back, he said that there was a 21:00 train leaving for Saratov, "you should leave here now, don't be here tomorrow."

By now it was almost 8 pm. Once outside the room, Teacher handed me the passport and said she was glad to have met such a nice man. "Perhaps my students can become your pen pals." Really? You crazy ... "Oh sure, love to hear from them, and thank you for all your help." Wished I could have reeled it off in Russian! After a nod to the soldiers in the yard, I pedaled out the gate, zipping towards town to a train station somewhere. I had no idea where it was, or what to do when I got there, my head was spinning, what had just gone down? Every few streets I'd stop for directions. "Choo choo, you know, choo choo?" I couldn't stop to talk, just lamely beg off the friendly faces and push away, it was past 8:00, and I had the strangest feeling that somewhere, someone was keeping tabs on me.

When I rolled up, a gaggle of teenagers were doing what teenagers do; hanging out on the curb smoking cigarettes. They stared as I rode around the back of the depot and went inside. Trying to buy a ticket to Saratov seemed a simple request, but the woman behind the thick tinted glass wasn't getting it. The bicycle may have thrown her off, and she wasn't game to figure out or help, and the clock was ticking; I needed a teenager. I went out and asked who could help me speak to the ticket office. A girl, as usual, the better students, nodded. I filled her in on my path to here, leaving out the incidents of the day, and then the whole crew followed us over.

Before approaching the window, I asked for a minute to gander the ripped atlas page of Kazakhstan, to see where the big picture led. I hadn't really cared since Kiev, and now, a glance made clear that my border buddies had thrown a serious monkey wrench into the gears. Saratov wasn't going to help, and neither was Samara, five to six hundred k's further north; and by the way, Zhanibek was more like 100k's south, not 36. Two hours ago, the Bulldog was saying I could cross the border east of Saratov, then he said I couldn't. Was he right or wrong? It looked to be about a 300k ride from Saratov to the border, and I'll be go-to-hell if I was going to spend three or four days on the road to find out.

The Samara option meant a similar distance, that eventually would take me to a different crossing, in the same small corner of Kazakhstan, towards Uralsk. The next option was going to Ufa, where I could hump over the Urals and drop into the border south of Chelyabinsk. The whole damn Kazakhstan plan, including my original intents, called for lengthy north-south zigzags and stints of dirt roads, due to the country's baffling lack of routes, in a land twice the span of Texas. I started to explain the problem to the kids, but they just needed to know what ticket I wanted to buy, and quick. The plans of the last three weeks to cross Kazakhstan just had a gaping hole blown in them, I was torn between rolling the dice on the Samara crossing, but what about that Bulldog asshole?

Someone's ignorant authority can't tell me what to do, normally. But this is Russia, and boy oh boy was he pissed off; and then he just vanished. What is he capable of? Does he know I'm at the station? Does he give a damn where I'm at? I'm no spy, they know that now, right? Am I being too paranoid? Why would they want to talk to me again?

"You need to buy a ticket; the train will be here soon." The kids had been telling my tale to others in the station, creating a buzz that caught the attention of the station manager. With basic English, he offered to help with a ticket, and began naming off the possible transfer points. The train was to arrive in less than ten minutes, "how far are you traveling?" The kids were looking at me, the manager was waiting for a response. I stood there bewildered with my stupid black and white Google maps and a torn atlas page, inked with notations and sketched roads, gleaned from Google Earth, my worthless battle plans. North but how far north? Ufa is too far, Saratov and Samara show real roads to the border, but what of Bulldog's wavering info? How did things change so fast? "You must decide, where do you want to go?" Shit. "The train will be here in five minutes." I have no idea, no one knows the border control answers. "We must know..." Fuck. "I need a ticket to Ufa.

19. the Urals

The train clacked along north in the dark. I laid in my bunk, finally able to exhale and examine the tumultuous day, and what it all meant to the ride, and my head. The notion that I'd just lost, after months of being blown by the wind; a Rule popped up and slapped me to its whim. How many could say they'd crossed the breadth of Kazakhstan? One less now. Out there were miles of dirt roads and emptiness; rivers and hills... and certainly hearty, salt of the earth people making a life out there. Back home, I'd spent a few years competing, more honestly, paying my entry fee and participating, in off-road motorcycle events called enduros. Five and six-hour time trials following hell-and-back single-track trails through mountain wilderness terrain, that challenged and exhausted every bean of energy and thought. Three hours in, it wasn't fun anymore, it was simply hard. Yet, the drive to complete the course became more important than life itself.

After hours of climbing hills, rolling down drop offs, fording streams and bouncing off rocks, the battle was over. Back at the van, draped exhausted in a folding chair with a cold beer, you couldn't feel better about yourself. That was the reward, persevering through dusty hot and cold and wet adversity, doing something you loved. Kazakhstan had risen in my mind to be that, times a hundred, and those fuckers stole it from me. It was a border crossing, just not for me. No one I'd met raised a flag; perhaps the "locals only" rule protects an unknown something, perhaps Western Kazakhstan just wasn't ready for visitors yet. No matter, no blame could be cast. The agents did their task. I wasn't ready yet to face the humble truth that in all honesty, it came down to me. Choosing, for God's sake, a dirt road to enter the country. Whatever the reason, I just wanted to sit in silence and wallow in it, but the train experience was all around, and demanded attention.

When the ticket choice was made, the kids kicked into gear with teenage teamwork that I couldn't have been prouder of. The station manager expected the train in moments, and warned that it would only stop for two minutes, "it cannot wait, you must be ready." On the platform, I broke the bike down as the boys began assigning a pannier here and a wheel there, to whoever was traveling as far as Saratov, my point of transfer to Ufa. The folks were glad to help; and a smiling crowd gathered around and phone pictures were snapping, as everyone was filled in on how the Californian came to be in Palasovka. When the Russian Railways cars stopped and the doors opened, on went my couriers, toting my world's possessions, spread about the different coaches. I just knew they'd be fine.

The train's arrangement of enclosed berths, two metres square, had two high bunks and two low, which doubled as seating; a narrow aisle running up the right side of the car. The pretty blonde attendant, Kalena, led the way to my compartment and helped strap the bike frame to a top bunk. As we rolled away, she came back with a  pillow and blanket for my lone bunk mate and I; an elderly bloke, dressed in the traditional everyday woolen suit and tie outfit, common among older Europeans. Our language wall was solid, which didn't matter, since he didn't appear too talkative; as if his peace had been shook and his sleepy time disturbed by the brash arrival of this Western yahoo, who was causing other passengers to drop by to say hi. Later, Kalena poked her head in and he had a word. She returned with two hot teas, served in the prettiest traditional little glasses, nested in steel holders, a lemon wedge and two cubes on the side. When I tried to pay, she nodded no, my buddy had treated. And me writing the guy off. Spassi-ba. Soon it was lights out, and I curled up in the blanket looking back on an eventful day, and wondering what was next, as the train clattered along through the night.

A few hours later we trundled into Saratov, a little after 1:00 a.m., for a 12-hour layover. After thanking and saying farewell to the good folks returning my parts, the bike was reassembled on the empty platform, looking out on a sleeping city. I wandered the lonely terminal, until deciding on which plastic chair to nod off in. The next day was spent catnapping, and trying to remember and write down every detail of yesterday's trial; broken up by taking a ride around the station's surrounding streets to find a bite to eat, and change back the Tenges. The joy of the day was spent people watching. I'd step outside for a smoke and gaze upon the mixed crowd of travelers scurrying through this main hub station, garbed in Eastern and Western clothes, both fashionable and workaday. A funny trend I'd noticed since Ukraine was the men's dress shoes, that came to a pointed toe, seeming an inch or two too long. When the leather aged and took a shrink, the pointed toes would curl up a bit, elf like.

In the afternoon, the Palasovka scene was near repeated as I staged on the platform, awaiting the word to board the train to Ufa, with the bike once again arranged into pieces. Travelers began asking questions and taking snapshots with their phones. Soon were offering to help out by carrying the wheels on, to stash in their compartments. As we boarded, a buzz went up and down the car's narrow aisle, with the energy of everyone repeating the story of the American and his cargo shorts, and baseball hat and bike parts. The car's attendant, again a perky blonde with the similar name of Karina, was filled in and happily showed me to the berth. My new bunk mates were an intelligent looking young man, and a drunken middle-aged soldier, who looked on in wide eyed wonder, at what the hell just barged in.

Nickolai, the electronics trade school student, spoke very good English and became the difference between an interesting ride, and the pensive awkwardness of suffering moody lout Mischa. The career Army sergeant was solidly in the bag, thanks to a half empty 10-litre yellowed transparent plastic fuel can of homemade red wine, parked under his bunk. He would slurp off it between grunts of suspicions and slurred gibberish. Bless him, at least it wasn't vodka. Between fading in and out, he'd blurt out questions through Nickolai, and the more he heard, the more he lightened up; enough so to offer a swig, and filled my empty tea glass with the surprisingly tasty gasoline jug burgundy. Soon, we were all best of friends, as only the friends of a drunk can be. Even as his apprehensions faded, he still mustered to assure me through Nickolai that if I wanted trouble, he would give me a good beating. After yoyo-ing him a bit just to get him a little more riled up, I'd always come back with some form of "Mischa you crazy devil, pour me another cup!" Nickolai was having fun keeping the peace as the diplomatic interpreter, and soon the fuel jug was empty. Before night fell, Mischa was sacked out. Soon it was my turn, and the bunk seats were made up with sheets and pillows, and I enjoyed a long cozy sleep as we rattled the tracks into the night.

At 1:00 a.m., Mischa was awoken as we pulled into Samara, he soldiered out of his stupor and shaking hands, wished me well. Soon after sunrise, Nickolai departed in the small town of Buguruslan. I had to politely decline his offer to stay a few days, knowing, what with everyone's cordiality, I may never make it home. Karina had been the non-stop hostess, coming in on occasion to serve tea, make up the beds and to announce stops. Just before the late morning arrival in Ufa, she came in with a log book and asked if I would write something nice about all of the train's attendants, even though I'd only met her. A flowering review that. And here I was, Ufa.

The last great city leading into the Urals, 750 road miles, and about 400 miles east, of the border guard office in Savinka. The final clackety hours, and the moment of stepping out onto the arrival platform, stung deep. I'd made a mistake, a big one, and it led to the chaotic train decision, wishing for more border information, but the clock was ticking. It was that same gut punch emotion of personal disappointment, usually reserved for being fired, or being declined an important college admission. Closer to the truth, it was that helpless feeling of being told at the door that your scalper ticket is bogus. It helped to remember that months ago in San Francisco, before the Belarus plan fell through, and even before the pivotal McDonald's decision in Kiev, the route through Ufa and climbing up the Urals was part of the plan. Round and round and back on track. Just the thought of climbing the Urals warmed the day and besides, I needed a good workout. Let the journey unfold and roll with it, the trail has now bounced into Ufa.

The station sat on the banks of the river Belaya, and after climbing a steep hill, the city of a million presented itself. Tall buildings, clean streets, tree and grass lined boulevards, it was the nicest city I'd seen since Kiev's west side. A group of boys, skateboarding off the cement obstacles of a bank building's planters and benches stopped me, then started in to dishing out their smart-ass jibes in the most hilarious fashion. Between their wise cracks, they were asking all about the trip, and as luck would have it, their lovely brown eyed English teacher happened by. As the adventure was told, and their young minds twirled up all sorts of questions, the teacher mentioned how great it was to see the kids exercising the language so well. They'd studied it, yet rarely had a chance to use it, much less in the joking string of insults style we were tossing back and forth. Ufa had a fine welcoming committee.

Two of the boys volunteered to show me down the street to a reasonable hotel, and along with the porter, helped with lugging the bike's bags up to the room. Reverting back to their clown act, they took on the role of the hotel's gracious hosts; displaying the clean towels to my satisfaction and sweeping open the curtains, and promoting the view. I assured them I found the accommodations most satisfactory. After settling in and grabbing a hot shower, I headed out to find an internet café, and wasn't one of the little guys sitting in the lobby, reading a magazine. "Internet? Follow me." What a character, I had an appointed personal valet, how convenient.

Internet cafes are good business and this one was no exception. The small room looked out a glass wall onto a bustling city center street, and was filled with students hovering over a couple of dozen terminals. As usual, the Russian Windows prompts were throwing me, and the guy monitoring it all brought another kid over to help out. Sixteen-year-old Arthur was a bright young man with great English, and the resident computer diagnostic. We breezed through uploading a backlog of photos, including a batch that apparently failed to complete the other day at the city manager's office in Palasovka. A native of the region's Bashkir people, and very proud of his city, including its renown as the Muslim center of Russia, he offered a walking tour of Ufa the next day.

June 12th was Russia Day. A somewhat mild national holiday celebrating the country's sovereignty, or reform, from the USSR in the early '90s. Or, as the day's original name put it: Day of the Adoption of the Declaration of the Sovereignty of the Russian Federation. Its first President Boris Yeltsin, an iconic figure heralded and derided for his decisions and actions that helped bring about the historic changes, made the easy suggestion to abbreviate it. A few flags were out and there was to be a big firework show in the evening, but enthusiasm for the holiday reflected the prevailing attitudes of the new Federation. Most people liked their new life, others pined for the old days, I'd imagine split along age lines. For a teenager, Arthur had a very solid hand on his country's politics and the region's history. Early that day, he and one of his friends met me; as we walked along, he filled me in.

Ufa was the capitol city of the Bashkortostan Republic. Roughly, a third of the Russian Federation's districts, or states, are Republics, something of a quasi-sovereign state versus the rest, which are Oblasts, meaning Provinces. Republics enjoy a higher degree of administrative autonomy, usually stemming from their recognition as an ethnic minority's homeland, in this case of course, the Bashkirs. Although Ufa was first established as a fortress in the 16th century under the lead of Ivan the Terrible, the Bashkirs were one of the many offshoots of the Turkic migrations that stretched from the northern Middle East up to Mongolia, founding their stake here long before recorded history. Circled by the confluence of the Belaya and Ufa rivers, the settlement had become an important trading center over the centuries, and was given a population boost when oil was discovered in the region in the 1930's. Soon after that, Stalin hurriedly moved hundreds of factories to the Ural foothills in the early '40s, to escape the German invasion, and prepare the counter offensive. Today, it is one of Russia's largest oil refining points, as well as a significant scientific center. We walked around town for hours that day, as Arthur pointed out the many museums, theaters and universities; as well as his pride, the oldest Mosque in the city.

The square edged, blue toned building wasn't large in cathedral terms, a single minaret domed the main structure, and a lone spire rose above it all. After granting alms to the poor outside the gate, I entered my first mosque, and was surprised at its unassuming interior. Beyond the foyer was a large room of stark white walls around a giant worn carpet, that provided the largely Sunni Islamic faithful a simple place for their daily prayers. It had been standing since 1830, and had weathered the country's on again-off again tolerance of their faith; most recently of course, the Soviet regime's seventy-year outright ban on all forms of religion. The tinge of an intruder's guilt filled me, standing on the room's perimeter, gawking at the faithful in their prayer caps as they humbly kneeled in worship, I suppressed the rude urge to snap a picture. As they finished, and others took their place, several walked over and welcomed me to their house. The brain grappled with the division of Western Christianity's formalities and its florid temples, accomplishing the same ends as this simple building and its patron's quiet devotion. Accepting into or out of any Creed's sanctification, the respect felt in their own house is always compelling.

The thin soled, hand-me-down slipper shoes donated by Telman in Volgograd were appreciated, since my mountain bike shoes were failing fast.

Plus, the pedal-clip fitting in the sole, made long walks sound like a tap dance. The slippers however, were not made for the long cement hike we were on that day. By the time we reached Ufa's highlight statue, the steed mounted image of Salawat Yulayev, on a rise overlooking the Belaya, the blisters were up and popped and painful. Every step hurt. That aside, the Bashkir warrior on the rearing war horse was quite a sight. Salawat led the Bashkortostan region's effort in the late 18th century that joined a national Cossack revolt, the Peasant Insurrection, against the brutal reign of Catherine the Great. The revolt fell short, and Salawat spent his remaining years in a far-away prison; merciful, compared to the Cossack leader Pugachev's fate, who was brought to Moscow, beheaded and quartered. Cathy turned up the heat after that, appointing more local controls across the country to nip similar uprisings in the bud, and the miserable sadness of the Russian people's history continued on.

After arriving back at the hotel, we had made plans to watch the night's fireworks show at a nearby park, but later, Arthur came by and said he couldn't make it. His mom had other plans and he had to stay home. I really need to hang out with an older crowd. Just as well, I was hitting the road tomorrow and an early night was in order. Across the street from the hotel's front door was a

McDonalds, and I swear I looked up and down the road for close options, knowing it was wrong. Like the siren's song, it beckoned me to glide over and relent to the centering experience of a burger, fries and a Coke. Oh, come on don't tell me you wouldn't have been tempted. After ceremoniously dumping the thin slippers in the trash, I hit the rack, but not before enjoying a couple of beers, another painkiller, and the spectacular fireworks show out my room's window.

It took more than an hour to pick my way out of the city and cross its south bridge, then reach the M5 east, to start rolling into the foothills of the Ural Mountain range; the recognized dividing wall between Europe and Asia. It was a beautiful day, the road surface was decent, and the groove came easy, the idea of climbing and coasting for the next several days jazzed the adrenaline. The heart of the journey was all around, and I imagined how as the years flew by, this morning would always be remembered; the day I began climbing these famous mountains, the day I entered the Urals.

Passing a village, two young boys joined me and pedaled alongside for a few k's, until a police car u-turned and scolded them for being on the highway. 70k's of gradual, deliberate pushing, up mild inclines, had me well out of the plains and into lush pine spotted meadows by late afternoon. Stopped on a bridge, studying the tree line for a camp spot, while waiting for the police to clear a truck wreck on the far side of the river Sim. A sweaty, olive skinned man in a brown woolen jacket, rubber boots and a tweed cap covering his greasy black hair walked by. He was heading back towards an almost unnoticed grouping of huts, carrying a simple fishing pole, and staring at me like a Martian had just landed. As I stared back, he hails me over. Sometimes there's a slim form of English, or I can recall a hacked Russian word; between Mikhale and I, there was nothing. He gestured, to know where I was going, and I waved at the trees, plying the camp question. I was drawing pictures of America and Europe in my mini notebook, and he lit up in smiling wonder, once understanding the doodled story. As far as camping, he'd hear none of it. Follow me, he motions.

Village will have to do. What do you call a grouping of cottages and shanties and dirt paths, too small to be deemed a village or hamlet? Such was Mikhale's abode of Tikeevo. Walking to his place down a dirt path, with foot-high grass growing out the center, we passed a couple of square-box hand-fashioned houses with haphazard makeshift add-on's, cobbled from various cast-off construction materials. Shacks created from intermixed collections of plywood, tar paper and logs, pulled from the surrounding woods and leaned against their main structures; as if children building play houses were granted a contractor's license. A thin, ancient, bent over old man cheerfully herded a dozen goats on by, just as we came to Mikhale's front gate. Inside the yard was a dilapidated tin roofed cabin of weathered slats, that looked like a forgotten tool shed. Attached was a thrown together three-sided shelter, that contained what the not-quite 200 square foot homestead could not.

But it wasn't a shack or a shed, or a shanty, or any of those things. It was home to his wife Ula, teenage daughters Anya and Lada, little Margarete and son Andree, who at about six-years-old was the youngest of the clan. Grandpa Uli was a blue eyed, silver haired smiling man in his 70's, and interestingly enough, had a smattering of English; akin to my German, meaning a handful of descriptive words, without the knowledge to link them correctly. The English skills of village neighbor Oslam was relatively good however, and the gregarious Uzbek bull of a man turned out to be a natural comedian and story teller. Uli explained that their 80-metre wide farm extended back in a long narrow plot, dropping out of sight down a gradual hill, amounting to roughly two acres in my guess. He acquired the spot shortly  after private land ownership became possible in the early '90s, through a deal struck through the local farmer's collective. They had the say so on what land would be sold to private ownership or leased, and who it went to. "Peasant farms", the actual term used.

As we sat around a rough, hand hewed table in the yard, smokes were passed around, and we dipped cups into a five-gallon metal milk can of water, lugged from their only source, a nearby well. Before long, Ula was sending the daughters Anya and Lada off to the magazin, or small market, for some groceries and beer. I produced a 500 ruble note, about $20, knowing their hospitality towards me was overtaking their budget. Ula began shaking her head no, but off to the side, Mikhale waved a hand, imploring her to take it; the luxury of beer and feeding a guest was unexpected, plus, he had come home empty handed from the river. I spread on the last of my mosquito repellent, to ward off the thick swarm that seemed to have no effect on my hosts; and as the night rolled, I told my tale. A few villagers dropped by to say hello, Uli was giving me a dose of Russian history, and Oslam told of the pride and struggles of the Uzbek people, along with hilarious stories of his adventures and take on life. Anya and Lada filled me in on their lives at a remote Russian high school, and little laughing Andree ran about in a dervish, enjoying the sudden small party. All the while, a goat wandered in and out of the house, like the family cat.

Ula prepared a simmering pot of potatoes and greens over an open fire, that from this point on through Kazakhstan and western China, would become a normal rural sight. The big cooking, anything requiring more than a small gas or electric burner. was done outside. She finished the broth off by cracking a few eggs on the top of the mix, and that, along with dried fish, pickles and bread, was our feast for the evening. If only I could have recorded the night, somehow capture the moment of falling into the yard of rural Russian farmers and enjoying every minute of their family, their simple friendship and stories, another night I could never replicate or forget. Around midnight, a piss drunk neighbor, who had very recently, like in the last hour or so, been sufficiently beaten to a bloody puff-faced pulp, walked into the yard. This guy looked bad, the atmosphere tensed up as he arrived, and Grandpa Uli gestured to me he was trouble.

Ula, disgusted, went inside as the drunkard related to Mikhale, through his mangled black and blue face and torn lips, of who he had just tangled with. It was obvious Uli thought little of him, and suffered his presence in the yard just enough to keep the peace. Sluggo was eyeballing me from the get go, but after Mikhale told my story, and pointed out the bike, he came over and shook hands. We sat down and shared a smoke, and he muffled on about something I'll never know. Everything was cool, but everyone exhaled when he up and left, like a dark shadow leaving the yard. It signaled the end of the night, and upon entering the home for the first time, I could see it was split into two 3-by-3-metre rooms, the left being a small kitchen with a table, sink and cupboards, no stove. To the right was a room dimly lit by a small, flickering, 10-inch portable black and white TV, framed by bunks and a couple of mattresses, where the entire family of seven slept. The two youngest were asleep on the open floor with a blanket tossed across them, and they set me up on what was probably Mom and Dad's mattress on the floor, they'd given me the best bed they had.

The next morning, I ventured over to the outhouse, a movable shack on wooden skids with no throne, just a hole in the floor and what the... no hole in the ground! Just about an eight-inch space beneath the floor to the dirt. I was stunned enough to put off the job until later, but had to admire the function. It was a small farm, and once there was enough fertilizer to turn into the soil here, they'd move it over there. You're right, it would be crazy in Marin County; but... My eyes keep opening wider to what people have to do to just live, just to make it. One's limits are defined by their needs, so there are no true limits, life can be so much harder than your imagination can muster. Whatever it takes, then in time, that becomes normal.

Soon, an older gent came into the yard and greeted Mikhale and Ula. He was Tikeevo's retired police chief, former mayor, and largest property owner. He had lived here his whole life, and a was real charmer. His English? I don't know how we conversed, but somehow the points were put across, as he and Mikhale and I crawled into his sedan and took a short drive out to his small but pretty dachau, a country cottage not quite the square of a two-car garage, but done up nice. He and his wife lived there, surrounded by some crops, a few pigs and some head of cattle. The grass in his dirt road's center was as tall as the hood, and there and back we bounced along a loose muddy track that would have had the rest of us reaching for the transfer case lever, that didn't exist.

After returning to Mikhale's, we walked down the road, passing another of his properties, a house I gathered was rented out, and wound up at a third, a

half-acre lot full of scattered farm machinery. A minivan-size hut sat in the corner, that from what I could suss, was home to an absent hired hand, who pulled double duty as a guard dog. The quintessence of the tour was when he popped the hood on a Lada, rusting about in the yard, revealing the car's battery to be missing a large chunk of one corner, exposing open cells. "Problem" I pointed out; and with a shrug and a wave, he dismissed it as if it were chipped paint. The three of us climbed in and somehow it cranked over without a hitch, as he smiled over at me. Russia. His name is lost, but he was The Man in Tikeevo; and he let me know, I was the first American to ever visit here.

Around ten, I said goodbye to the family, and within 3k's came to a roadside trucker's café. I grabbed the morning cup and ran into one of the neighbors I'd met the night before. He wished me the best, and as I rolled away, I heard the dreaded pssss of the front tube. The stem had torn, the tube was trash. As I whipped off the wheel to replace it, a crowd of truckers gathered around to watch. As the quick repair went on, the drivers asked about the trip, and passed around my map book of Russia, trying to see how the road led to here. When finished, and the bags went back on, I tore out the few pages I'd need from here to Kazakhstan and gave the rest of the book to one of the guys. He gave his thanks and the crowd said goodbye, but before I rolled away, he came back; he wanted me to sign the book. Huh? He wanted an autograph. No. Really? You want me to sign it? Wow... "Yeah sure, great. Wow... Oh Russia, what magic next? Another first.

The peaceful internal game of climbing again. All your concerns and thoughts abate as you transition into losing yourself in the steady trance, needed to push up a hill. Then the climb's duality of rolling downhill, never pedaling, just allowing the gravity to carry you through the reward as the next climb arrives. The road went up and up then leveled off for a bit, then up and up again, then leveled off again, as if making three giant steps up the mountain. At one pass, a large group of mobile vendors, selling radios and tools, kitchen appliances and clothing lined the roadside in front of a cafe. All around, tents and trucks were grilling up sausages and chicken, pork steaks and kebobs, all offering beer. Everyone was having a good time as tunes blared out from different directions. After I got to talking to a few different truckers and sellers, I just knew that the day could have ended right there, and it would have been another grand afternoon and evening for the ages.

A great atmosphere was on and everyone was so open and happy, almost secondary was the concern that travelers would pull in and a sale would be made, but it must have been working for everyone. I was enjoying the climb and wanted to press on, spurred by the aim of eventually cresting the mountain's true summit, and the psychological goal of entering the geographic border of the Orient. Things were going well and I felt great, the head was on straight and I wasn't wishing the day away, the trip was only to get more fascinating as the stranger lands passed under wheel. There was an internal ebullience going on, and as I pedaled away from the freelance mountain top vendors, I felt like a citizen of the world who was playing tag with the rest of my fellow citizens. Whatever your reserve thoughts, you're probably wrong; we are so alike, we really could all be friends. Just toss in some good beer and barbeque, tunes and a few pretty girls, along with some honest work for a decent life. World peace solved. Next problem?

A long downhill took me into Sim, a beautiful little mountain town that wouldn't have been out of place in the Alps or the Rockies. The road that was cut into the slope on the far side of the valley made it clear that the next morning would start with a long, slow serious climb. A decent hotel with a basic cafe that catered to the winter ski crowd made for an affordable night, and as nice as everyone was, there was still that ever-present initial awkwardness born of the language barrier. Folks are never prepared for an alien walking through the door. In the morning, breakfast was light, as part of the preparation for what was ahead, it's all so mental. The climb is your lot for the day, and accepting that is half the battle, no concern about hitting a kilometre goal or whining inside about facing another hill. Head down, tunes on, and watch your feet go around, Hong Kong ain't coming to me. But as the highway climbs to the sky where winter snows fall deep, things change.

As the road went up, the road surface turned rougher, due to the weather beatings. I had to be wary of potholes that would eat the wheels, especially off here on the edges. The bumpy road caused the left rear pannier to jump off its hooks a couple of times, requiring a stop to re-secure it. The trucks were on the pipe, trying to build their speeds downhill to make a strong run up the next rise, and the two-lane highway was getting tighter. The day toiled on, and whether I was clipping down or crawling up, stress was mounting as the trucks and their wavering trailers would zoom past, just missing the elbow. More than once I pulled aside just to collect my nerves. I began to feel vulnerable on my little bike, at the mercy of the truckers, and hoping they get it right every time, all day long. Blind faith that they're paying attention, and the juiced ones are on autopilot.

Then, downhill, hunched over the bars flat out, I heard a powerful deafening clattering freight train racket coming up from behind, and turned to see two barreling trucks abreast, pulling empty auto carriers with their loose ramps and chains bouncing madly over the rough surface. The towed rigs shook and weaved behind them side by side, filling the entire road as one truck was putting a pass on. The option to brake and quickly pull over in time was lost, since the rear brake was disengaged to combat the truing issues; and as they came upon me, I could feel the road shake. And then, that damned left rear pannier popped off again and slid into the road and under the near truck, as it nipped by inches from my shoulder. The bag caught, it slid along underneath until spit out the back, as I passed it while hard on the front brake, trying to bring the 90-pound bike to a stop.

Gently laying the bike on its side, I slowly walked back up the road to fetch the bag. Cashing in a stack of chits on my saved-up Karma, the pannier missed the tires on its spin under the truck and trailer. The camp stove and its fuel bottle were the only items that would not have survived a pressing, but had the bag been creamed, it would have been tough to make room for the few clothing items and journal binder into the right bag; already full with a cooking kit, some shirts and the jacket. Another bullet passes by. Once stopped, the vulnerability of it all catches up, waver towards wanting to just let go, let the idea that you're going to be caught in this rattling danger zone for another couple of days wash over you. Waver towards any safer option, but what? But it's only a waver. Fuck this road, the mind bites back. I've got every right to use it, and those truckers aren't trying to squeeze my nerves, hell they're up in those cabs at least taking my space into account, the last thing they want to do is smear someone. It's not me versus them, it's us and this goddamned narrow jarring road. But then, they ain't slowin' down any.

Only went 60k's today with 5-12% grades, ending on a high note by flying down into Yuryuzan on a balls-out finale, weathering a late afternoon rain/hale/rain storm with only a front brake, as if nothing could go wrong. Pulled in and slowly cruised around, taking in a quiet Russian mountain town. The same, small homemade homes, and a few state-built apartment buildings. The natural gas lines were all running three metres above the ground, seeming very vulnerable to car bumpers, but also easier to repair. There was that common "once was" feel about the place, and as it turns out, the main business was a refrigerator plant. Needing a bank-o-mat, a pleasant fellow, working in his front yard, sent his young son off on his bicycle to show me the way. Found a lonely motel above an auto repair shop out by the M5 for $16, which was managed by a friendly old lady, living in one of the rooms.

The good soul running the garage was just shutting shop for the night, and was happy to lock the bike up inside. After a grocery hop to the magazin a few hundred metres away, it was another bread and cheese dinner in front of a black and white Russian TV. Nestled in a cozy little room deep in the Urals, shining in the recurring thought that no one knows where I'm at, in a place I'll never be again. This feeling of having disappeared into a tunnel of the unknown began as I entered the former East Germany, I imagined seeing the exit light as the border of Hong Kong province. Of course, the head is blanking a vast chunk of the world's landmass, filled with civilizations, culture, history and beauty. My Western-imprinted mind held it all in a dark room, that heretofore hadn't much honest detail in it about the former Soviet bloc and China. And now, everything was being discovered, a society independently evolved, a parallel dimension. I recognized everything, but everything was a little different.

Fueling a road tar hopper with the roadside's tree branches, modern city's

that hide buckled side streets, filled with twisted steel debris and missing manhole covers, brand new gas stations with brand new outhouses. Nary a guest complaint at a hotel's front desk about no electricity or water. Children smoking, swaths of drunkards, mishmash home construction. A grand scale theatre about a people's post-apocalyptic existence, whereby every structure was built and occupied and thrived, then somehow tragedy caused nationwide strife, destruction and abandonment. The current residents play the role of survivors that moved into and propped up the shells left from the glory days. Someday they'll fix the missing windows, the patchwork roofs, the rusty pipes and heaved and cracked cement; but for now, be glad to have shelter.

Of course, none of that ever happened. The conditions are the results of state-ran allowances for infrastructure repairs, which were either never enough, or sucked up by corruption. A nation of citizens who struggled for basic needs, much less household upkeep, and even then, there were sparse supplies to properly do the job. Today, the free market wave was enabling folks to undertake the needed upkeep, and supplies were becoming more available, but there's decades of work to do. Their distressful history has forged the overall benevolence, the gracious resolve of these people's strong character. That's what I think.

Never knowing at sunrise what the day's significance will be on the journey's heartbeat, was a blessing. The only thought this morning, as I climbed out of Yuryuzan, was wondering which form of highway breakfast would arise first. Since entering into Ukraine from Poland, the local farmer's grandma would often be offering their homegrown wares on the side of the road, often melons but also corn and potatoes, some fruits. Here in the Urals, the local offering was honey, and I'd stopped a couple of times over the last few days to pick up a small jar. Cheap and natural, I'd pour it down my throat, and tell myself it was an energy boost and healthy; but the truth was, it just tasted good. A mountain cafe appeared, and soon, so did a plate of eggs and toast. While relaxing out on the porch before taking off again, I met Alexander.

He lived in Miass, a fair size city on the mountain's eastern side, and put forth the idea of stashing the bike at the café, and come with him to hike the peaks of the Urals. After seeing his bank of pictures of the high mountain lakes and meadows, the offer was momentarily tempting. The freewheelin' thought of "when will I ever stand atop the southern Urals again" began rising, but I fought it back. I couldn't possibly leave the bike, and realistically, could not take up on every cool offer that came my way. Soon after clicking in, the tunes danced, the rhythm followed, and the climbing trance took over. The hiking offer I'd just passed on wasn't my usual cup of tea, but there was a strong pull to stand on the tops of these mountains. A rare chance, and looking back now, it was a prime case of how one decision affects the next moments events. Days later, I'd wish for a second chance at Alexander's offer...

The day went on, rolling up and down; the Urals pulling me in. Some crests were home to small restaurants and bars, others were held by the locals and their honey kiosks, with the popular homemade brooms and banya clusters. In the early afternoon, two motorcyclists pulled over just "to see what a bloody bicyclist was doing way out here." Geoff and Allen were a couple of middle-aged Brits, traveling around the world on a set of Triumph Tigers, and a slim budget. They were nobly heeding the last wishes of Geoff's mother, to travel the world and ultimately deliver her and Dad's ashes to her birthplace; Boonville, California. The crazy irony, their end goal amazed me. Boonville was a tiny town in the deeply forested hills of Mendocino County, just a hundred miles north of San Francisco.

I'd traveled through there many times over the years on motorcycle rides, to run the twisty remote highway that winds through wooded hills and giant redwoods, on its way out to the coast; always making time to stop and sample a pub glass or two from the Anderson Valley Brewery. Poking at their age and finances, they painted the name of their effort on the side of their aluminum panniers "the poor circulation tour." While we enjoyed the synchronicity of two Englishmen and a Yank, meeting on the top of the Urals and having the common link of a tiny town off the beaten path in Northern California, a pair of Land Rovers drove past with a honk and a wave. Allen mentioned "more world travelers." We eventually said goodbye, and off they went. They were going to be sipping a Boont Amber long before I, so I wished them well and ok'd them to start without me. Their book "Ashes to Boonville" tells the tale.

Some hours later, cresting another false summit at the strip mine vista of Bakal, the road became friendly, seeming to roll down more than up. It brought the glimmer that a good chunk of the mountains were behind me, tomorrow I'll conquer the true summit near Zlatoust, then begin the long descent into the plains, and Chelyabinsk. Enjoying a perfect day and a downhill run across a mountain lake bridge, the Zen was broken when I came upon those two Land Rovers, parked on the far side. One was the classic Defender model, reminiscent of all those African safari movies; the other, a Defender pickup with a camper on back. "Hello" says a dark-haired handsome man in his mid-30's, with a strong French accent. "We are having mechanical problems, not sure what". After so many good deeds, it was my turn. Car problems far from home are stressful moments for anyone, car problems thousands of miles from home in the middle of Russia, much more so. If a guy can lend a hand for a quick fix or a diagnosis, then at least they know what they're facing, and it always feels good to help. This shouldn't take long. I then utter the eight words that change the journey for the next two weeks. "Well, I'm a mechanic, I'll take a look."

Demetri and his friend Gille started in Paris. They were on a cross continent adventure to Western Mongolia, with the aim to reach the ideal region on Earth to view the total Solar eclipse on August 1st. Demetri's camper-laden truck's manual transmission had been noisy, then began jumping out of gear, and now wouldn't re-engage. Gille, a balding bespectacled tan faced man in his 50's, had just returned from a truck parts shop 20k's up the road. He picked up a litre of automatic transmission fluid, claiming his mechanic in Paris said that it was the proper juice for the manual gearbox; which didn't sound right. I crawled under Demetri's truck with a cut off plastic jug to catch and save the gear oil, wanting to check for a sparkled hue that would indicate the transmission was making metal. When the drain plug was pulled, his problem became clear; about a cup of thick black burnt oil dripped out, where I was expecting three or four litres. How was this possible? They hadn't drained any oil out, and it couldn't have leaked out through any seal without leaving an obvious mess but... had he really driven over 4000 kilometres from France with essentially no oil in the gearbox? I was baffled.

After fishing out a half dozen bits of needle bearings, the only move left was to fill the tranny and hope for the best. Both Demetri and Gille insisted the ATF was the recommended fluid, but I held doubt. Even so, given the obvious damage, I made the point that a heavier proper hypoid gear oil may be better at this point. During all this, a group of young Russians, who were camping out in the woods near the lake dropped by with a few cold beers, to see what the tourists were up to. They were a great bunch of guys, loud and happy and buzzed.

They offered that if all else failed, we were welcome to join them for an evening of barbecue chicken, more beer, and of course, vodka. I smiled on the best offer I'd heard all day, but the grim expressions across the Frenchmen's faces were of worry, their grand expedition was melting. Gille and I hopped in his truck and headed east to the roadside truck shop, to fetch the correct quantity of gear oil. Along the way, Gille, a retired retail catalog photographer, recounted how they had left Paris and crossed Germany and the Czech Republic, then Poland, through Ukraine and on to Moscow; where they stayed with a friend of Demetri's.

After returning, we serviced up the transmission, then Demetri and I went

for a test drive. The improvement was that he was now finding 1st and 2nd but 3rd and 4th had to be held into place. The top gear of 5th, having the greatest use at highway speeds, was toast. Suffering too long without lubrication, it gave a deep rattling knock, the finishing death knell. Manual transmissions of any stripe, with oil in them, are famously reliable implements, but this one's problems were fatal. It could last a thousand k's, or it could seize up in ten. Certainly, there were large chunks of a deceased gear shaft bearing scattered about inside that, once under way, would be biding their time before getting bounced into the remaining meshing gear clusters. Demetri didn't have to wait for my prognosis, it was clear this transmission wasn't going to see Mongolia. As the day faded on the banks of the Small Satka, there was nothing more anyone could do... so let's see what the Russians are up to!

A short hike through thick tall brush took us to a small clearing in a stand of birch, where the guys had camp set up. After an hour or so of beer, vodka and smokes, the entertainment began when Gille decided he wasn't comfortable leaving his rig near the roadside. After boasting that the marshy terrain was no match for the Rover's capabilities, he commenced to burying the British legend's rear wheels in a rivulet. After a collective turn of heave ho's and rocks under the wheels, Demetri broke out a brand-new portable winch, still sealed in the box. Now picture a group of mildly to very drunk men, taking turns pushing each other out of the way to display their prowess at operating a winch no one had ever seen before. Clouds of mosquitoes feasted on us as we acted on all suggestions, and wondered "where in this tall grass did I set my beer down?" He was eventually yanked out, and as dark settled, we dug in around the barbecue and enjoyed an endless supply of grilled chicken, salad, beer and vodka. The seven locals had been lifelong friends, and in a mix of Russian, French and English, we all told our tales, with the Ruski's taking turns acting offended, as they told hilarious stories about each other. Around midnight one of the boys, these crazy Russians, decided everyone should, in the spirit of global comradeship, jump into the lake. Gil had the sense to beg off, but Demetri and I played along, and stumbled out to the shore. We stripped down with our new buddies, and buck naked, dove into the cold dark water. The Urals had been good to me.

20. shift!

Part of the night's talk turned to how the transmission problem was to be handled. There was a Land Rover dealership in Chelyabinsk, as well as connections for accommodations at a Catholic Church. Both Demetri and Gille admitted that walking into a foreign car dealer for major repairs, on an issue neither of them had any clue about, could get pricey. Demetri proposed that if I would come along to talk to the mechanics, and make sure they didn't get taken for parts and labor, he'd be willing to make it worth my while, plus a place to stay in Chelyabinsk. Ah, they were a couple of good guys in a bind. The spirit of brothers of the road, the beer haze, and a ninety-mile lift, had me nodding yes. From Chelyabinsk, it was only a one- or two-day ride to the Kazakhstan border, where I'd be allowed to cross. Russia would soon be behind me. Besides, how much time could a trip to the Rover dealer, to explain the issue, square up some parts, and guarantee labor charges take? "I can't take your money Demetri, just be glad to help you guys out." At some unknown hour, we tripped and fell our way back through the pitch-dark brush and branches to the trucks. The camper's dining table dropped down to make a bed, and I don't remember my head hitting the pillow, it had been an eventful day.

Another perfect Ural summer morning greeted us, we bid goodbye to our new best friends, and thanked them for a great time. With Gille leading the way, we hit the road, listening to the Rover's tranny thumping loudly in 4th gear; the main topic being how far we'd go before it crapped out for good. With the possible end of the Mongolian trek impending, Demetri still managed a good sense of humor about it. He was an intelligent, easy going thirty-eight-year old businessman and journalist, who loved Paris and photography; and was clicking pics all along the way for a series of adventure articles he was writing about their trip. He'd spent a good part of his childhood in Britain, so his English was as fluid as mine. Despite the imposing cacophony, we laughed most of the way, trading cuts on the French and Americans, both of us poking at the Russians. As the spread of Chelyabinsk loomed on the horizon, he told of how the Catholic Church deal came about. When they stopped in Moscow, Demetri's friend connected them to a church they could stay at, further on, for a small donation.

That church gave recommendations and contacts to another, and so on. They had now daisy-chained that good will all the way to Chelyabinsk, the front yard gate of Siberia. The city of over a million engulfed us.

We stopped and waited as Gille made a contact call. Soon, a young couple showed and gave cross town directions to the Church. As they spoke, the notion arose that being a Catholic in modern Russia was a mild to middling radical position. These two were Catholics in a world dominated by the Russian Orthodox Church, that seemed to have a problem with the spread of the "new" Christianity, seeing it as a challenge. The drift was that the Russian Orthodox had somehow nurtured their hibernating pre-Soviet influences throughout the banished era, using strong KGB affiliations; and they now had a leg up on acceptance, and the inherent power that came with it. Gille told of other Christians he'd met along the way. Their "churches" were no more than apartment flats, where small groups of believers gathered for services, to avoid expenses and the discrimination that came with the public view. See? Now how was I going to find that out if I'd shined on this ride offer, and just kept rolling down the backside of the Urals listening to Lynyrd Skynyrd?

We weaved our way north through heavy traffic, and went past blocks of beautifully restored 19th century office buildings on the edge of the old downtown. Chelyabinsk was another industrial town turned into a large city

during WW II, when Stalin was ensconcing the military to counter the German invasion. It earned the nickname "Tankograd", for its wartime production of the T-34 tank, and went on to become a major producer of missile and nuclear weapon components. Thus, it became off limits to all foreigners until 1992. Crossing the Miass River transformed the modern cityscape into the busy, worn, contemporary part of town, scarred with massive spreads of shuttered factories and foundry buildings of dirty red brick, and elevated steel rails. At a giant busy intersection, an absolute roll of the dice decision led us down the right road. We pulled into the Church grounds, and parked in front of a life size Jesus statue, welcoming us with open arms.

We were greeted by Father Reinhardt, a peaceful faced German man in his late sixties or early seventies. He calmly took account of Demetri's truck troubles, and without pause, offered his facility. There was a four-bay service garage, one, with a lift; the other three, with grease pits. We also met his mechanic Andre, everyone was happy to help. The Father had very good English, as well as French and Russian, with a quiet wise poise, I instantly admired him. As he showed us to our flat above the garage, he agreed to come with us in the morning to the Rover dealer, and help translate. The flat consisted of a tiny kitchen and loft, over a small narrow living room. The floors, walls and ceiling were done in deep varnished wood, giving the place a warm cabin feel; we had been granted the nicest room in the building, reserved for visiting clergy. After cleaning up, we were invited to join him for dinner in his large flat, at the top of the main church.

The Church itself was a new brick building, completed about ten years prior. The bottom floor was two separate naves with high white walls, and honey-toned pews below tall windows, plus a couple of side offices. Half of the large basement was a kitchen, the other half an open room, used as a play and nursery area for the children of the young mothers of faith, that found daytime sanctuary there. Five floors up above, in the spire, was the manse of Father Reinhardt and the compound's other priest, Father Wilhelm. Father Wilhelm was a few years older than Father Reinhardt, both were quite fit and sharp. Over dinner, I had to mention that climbing eight flights several times a day had to take some credit. Their perch looked out on the north section of the city, a mix of apartment buildings and tree tops, stretching off to the distance, blending into the edge of another large industrial spread.

The four of us, Demetri and I in the broken Rover, Gille and Father Reinhardt in the church's Nissan sedan, pulled into the Land Rover dealer the next morning, and went over what we knew so far with the service manager and lead mechanic. Borrowing an extension magnet, I fished out more of the bearing debris. As if discussing a terminal patient, we all danced around the obvious conclusion: this box was a goner. Turns out the ATF fluid was the correct call, but you needed more than half a pint. They wanted to go ahead and put it up on the rack and identify the exact failure, and look into getting a replacement transmission, or worse case, get parts ordered to open it up and do repairs. Until they figured it out, there was no sense talking costs. With a few hours to wait, Father Reinhardt offered to tour us around Chelyabinsk. To our surprise, he soon left the city proper and drove out a dirt road, passing a trace of Russia's nouveau rich: a series of rare custom designed homes under construction. Soon, we stopped in the clearing of a small stand of trees, in front of a weathered, three-metre-high monument. It was finished in white plaster, and topped by a small onion dome, surrounded by unkempt green brush. "In 1937, hundreds of people from Chelyabinsk were brought here and gunned down by the secret police" said the Father. "Why?" I asked. "The Great Purge" he replied.

To say when the Purges truly started is a blurry line to draw, since General Secretary Joseph Stalin's reign of terror began developing soon after the death of the Soviet Union's first Premier, Vladmir Lenin, in 1924. Beginning in earnest in the early 1930's, and peaking in 37' and 38', it targeted the highest level of Russia's and Ukraine's Soviet governments. Nearly every major political leader was arrested and charged officially with conspiring against the State, "tried" in mock show trials, and executed. Their only true crime was that these men, Stalin's Bolshevik peers, threatened his plans for ultimate rule. As the largely baseless murders expanded, more and more leaders and citizens voiced public and private objections to Stalin's policies. Their complaints warranted the act of sabotage, the only charge or excuse needed to effect their arrest, and then elimination, or sentencing to a gulag. It was all carried out by the Soviet secret police, or NKVD, led by the brutal Nikolai Yezhov.

Stalin's mad pretzel logic had created its own perpetual witch hunt of true and false enemies. The farmers that opposed the State's collective agriculture policies, displaced religious figures, national heroes of the Revolution. Just before being drawn into WW II, a majority of the military's highest-ranking officers were all tortured into false confessions, and shot. Throughout it all, innocent citizens were randomly executed by the hundreds, to instill terror; with an overt message to the masses: "imagine what I'd do if you were guilty." Friends, workmates, and spouses were to report anyone expressing discord with Stalin's policies, even children in school were encouraged to report their parent's conversations at home. The practice wound down after 1938, and as the Great Leader was finally satisfied the purge of his political enemies was complete, the evil eye turned upon the NKVD itself. Its own leadership suffered the same fate they had inflicted on so many. Yezhov himself was eventually tried and executed, and his name went on to play the somewhat honest role of scapegoat, for the many unspeakable horrors.

By the Soviets own questionably rosy records, over 1.5 million people had been arrested, almost 700,000 of those were executed, and there's no telling how many died in or en route to labor camps. Behind such a dense curtain, we're left to listen to either Western scholars, attempting to communicate the tragedies based on terrified survivors, and second-hand reports; or to sympathizers, attempting to quell the depth of these inconceivable crimes against humanity, in order to paint Stalin's legacy in a better light. One such inconceivable crime occurred right here in these then-remote woods. Many of the unsuspecting victims were awoken by a hard knock on the door in the middle of the night, and trucked out here to stand in the cold; and be summarily mowed down by machine gun fire. To this day, bullet ridden skulls are occasionally pushed up to the surface, all across this giant country. An unending reminder of the rule of one of the most wicked and powerful men to have ever lived. Russia's story is long, and sad.

Our Chelyabinsk tour was off to a sobering bang, but it turned around when we drove into the downtown district and walked the Promenade. A stretch of several city blocks of restored 19th and early 20th century buildings, that are now occupied with modern restaurants, bars, banks and electronic stores; catering to the new age of prosperity, all closed off to vehicle traffic. An underground mall of upscale shops and a grocery market filled the void under a major boulevard, it then let out onto the wide red brick-paved walkway that was filled with shoppers, and business types, and young people just hanging out with friends, enjoying a cup of coffee or bottle of beer. It was simply one long plaza, lined with shade trees and large bronze sculptures of average people and animals, including camels, a nod to the importance of the beast that served the region in times past. It was a nice place to linger in, and we knew we'd be back for a night at one of its cafes, to kill a few beers and watch the girls walk by. Months later, I would discover that due to their chemical factories and horrific deadly nuclear plant waste disposal practices, and secretive industrial disasters stretching back decades, Chelyabinsk is counted among the most polluted cities in the world. But the downtown is quite lovely!

When we returned to the Rover dealer in the early afternoon, the plot thickened. The fifth gear's mainshaft bearing was gone, as well as the

 mainshaft's forward bearing. While the costs were not Demetri's concern, the issue of parts and time were. It would be one to two weeks before they could have in hand everything needed to repair the box, or six weeks before a new

transmission could arrive from England. Why so long? The factory in Solihull, outside of Birmingham, didn't have seven-year-old gearboxes on the shelf. All the actors in the play, with no sense of urgency, would carry out the process of locating one, ship it to a central location, and load it on a lorry. That lorry would then truck across the Continent, and negotiate the long waits at the border crossings. The days would turn into weeks. The Frenchman was le merde hors de la chance, know what I'm sayin'?

He had bought the truck under the advice of Gille, who had previously ventured into Africa in his Rover, and had great faith in the mark. He had recommended an independent shop in Paris where the purchase, upgrade work and tuning had all been done. Later, Demetri confided that he knew he'd been overcharged for many things on the deal, but since he wasn't mechanically inclined, and busy with all his other investments, he just went along; assuming the truck and camper would be trouble free once underway. And it would have been. This problem was clearly a human error during the transmission servicing, an absent-minded moment that would throw away thousands spent on the journey, and deny him the chance to drive into Mongolia. We left Land Rover of Chelyabinsk fully apprised of the options; the only hope was the off chance that the dealers in Omsk or Moscow may have some of the needed parts in stock. Upon reaching the Church, Demetri fired off an email to the shop in Paris, to tell of the problem, with the slim hope they'd make good by having a spare gearbox, ready to ship out.

While sipping a beer in the Father's top floor living room, mulling over the day's findings, the conversation focused on the truck troubles. But my curiosity had to know; how did two German priests wind up here, on the far side of the Urals, almost 4000k's from home? Reinhart, a former construction worker who became ordained in his late 30's, had been sent here by the Catholic Church of Germany over 15 years ago, tasked with supervising the building of the Church. The location had been scouted by Father Wilhelm, an East German who first came to the area shortly after Glasnost. The land was a former site of some Trud Army barracks, the labor battalion of conscripted German and Polish citizens, both men and women, forced at the outbreak of WW II to work at construction and mining efforts. They suffered conditions and treatment no better than that of war and gulag prisoners, in effect, they were slaves. The site had special meaning to Russian Catholics of German descent. The Fathers, both members of the Focalare, a movement within Roman Catholicism that focused on overcoming tensions and unifying the many sects of the Church, had created a stellar place of worship.

Neither of them arrived here with any language skills; and although a skilled carpenter, Father Reinhardt had never been involved as an overseer on such a large project. They had to deal with the local rules, written and otherwise, of the contractors and politicians, suppliers and the omnipresent underworld; none of whom welcomed the project. Establishing an unpopular Roman Catholic presence, and learning to speak Russian at the same time, it must have been staggering. The property contained offices, billets, kitchen, a carpentry shop; and of course, the garage. The whole operation floated on a tight budget consisting of donations from their own small congregation, and a yearly stipend from a mother church in Germany. They'd done a fine job, and I became increasingly impressed by their character, and the faith that carried them through the innumerable struggles.

Afterwards, Demetri, Gille and I took the metro bus into the downtown and had dinner on the Promenade. Sitting under the awning of a German restaurant in an outdoor booth, the limit of my assistance had to be spelled out. The likelihood of good news on parts wasn't realistic, but if they did come through in the next few days, I'd stick around; remove and open up the tranny, and somehow make it all work. The rationale on my part was that engineers design any manufactured item around standard sized bearings, seals and O-rings, measured in inches or millimetres. If we got into the box and found we were lacking a few needed pieces, I may be able to source them locally with the help of Andre, the church's free-lancing auto mechanic. The dealership wouldn't have such liberty to shoot from the hip; whatever parts they would install would have to be Land Rover approved, hence more time wasted waiting on ordered parts, that may never show. The shade tree mechanic's motto of "when you do something half-ass, do it right" applied here. I was confident in my chances of repairing the gearbox well enough to get Demetri to Mongolia, and back home, and was up for the challenge. Besides, my trip had gone so well to this point, this struck as a moment of payback, I wanted to help. Clink the steins guys, let's hope for good news tomorrow.

The next day, the assumptions became fact. After a morning call to Land Rover, and a reply from the shop in Paris, the reality that no spare parts or gear boxes were available, settled in. The bouncing ball of hope deflated, and we knew it was time to stop fooling ourselves. Demetri's trip was over, and he had no desire to hop in Gille's passenger seat and continue on. The two were irascible towards each other at best, and over the last day I began to understand why they wanted to travel independently from the start. We would service up the transmission with gear oil, send him off west and see how far he gets. Gil would split for Mongolia; and I'd get the orange mule ready and head out early the next morning, towards the Kazakhstan border at Troisk, 150k's away. As we stood in the churchyard's brick driveway and discussed the ending with Father Reinhardt, up walks the mechanic Andre. After hearing the verdict, he has a talk in Russian with the Father, and comes up with just enough of a story to keep the issue alive: he can make a phone call, and perhaps score a transmission on the black market from his "mafia" connections in Astana, Kazakhstan. A whole new saga deemed "the mafia transmission" was about to be written.

Everyone hated the idea of Demetri's trip ending, and wanted to help. Both Father Reinhardt and Wilhelm expressed their trust in Andre. Ilvana, a local girl who helped out at the Church, assured us that Andre does this sort of thing all the time; in Russia, a mechanic had to be resourceful. I wrote down the vehicle identification numbers, or VIN's, along with all the numbers and codes stamped on the gearbox, and handed them to Andre, as he made a call to his contact. As he talked, I would interject questions, "make sure the box numbers are the same series," "give him the VIN's," "make sure it's the same model," "Is there a core exchange amount?" "Give us a total figure." The VIN numbers weren't mentioned, and no other questions were answered. He hung up and said the tranny would be here in two days, his guy didn't need the numbers yet. It didn't sound right, it sounded too good to be true; but this was Russia, and everything moves on a black market that we're not accustomed to. With suspicions considered, Demetri decided to go for it, on the condition I'd stick around. With that, I committed to hang here for four more days. Two to get the tranny, two to get the truck rolling. Lace up yer' boots boys, here we go.

What follows is one of those times we've all had, when you really wanted to do the right thing, and shortly into the task, realize you've chosen the wrong moment to play the nice guy. If it was only a straight forward tranny swap, if it was only a matter of ordering parts and repairing a broken gearbox, then the nice guy applies his knowledge and labor and everyone goes home happy. But this is Chelyabinsk, on the western edge of Siberia. The distribution networks that deliver any product you want within a couple of days, a system Westerners take for granted, hasn't arrived here yet. As such, the black market fills the void, and buying simple car parts turns on the same daring-do that buying a kilo of cocaine in our world would. I have to admit, that despite this situation, despite delaying my quest, this added an intrigue. The dare played into my choice to stay on, and try to pull this one off.

The first day of the saga was June 20th and we eagerly rolled up our sleeves. The truck with the camper wouldn't fit through the garage door, so after jacking up the camper and rolling the truck from under it, and into the garage's second stall, we positioned the hydraulic lift's arms and raised the truck's underbelly to head level. I set to removing the exhaust system and shift pedestal, the drive shaft and starter motor, then the bolts securing the transmission's bell housing to the engine. With only two bolts left, holding up a cross member brace that supported the gearbox, I decided we'd gone far enough. Until the new part arrives, and verified to be correct, there's no sense in pulling it. Nothing

more difficult than trying to re-stab an almost 150-pound transmission's pilot shaft splines without a proper transmission jack, especially if you don't have to. The day passed without an appearance or call from Andre, and although we assumed the deal was underway, I opined aloud that the shop seemed ill equipped tool-wise, for a guy whose made his living as an auto mechanic. My main wonder was how could it happen without the transmission's model number, did we even hear him mention the year of the truck? No one could recall. Clean up the tools and that's that, now we wait.

And wait. Gille, not being possessed of the same intrigue, spent the following day going over his rig and preparing to depart towards Mongolia the next morning. It wasn't a surprise, turns out that he and Demetri were neighbors rather than friends, and their marriage of convenience had been rough from the start. Of course, the reason partnerships are formed for an overland journey of this scale is to have someone and their vehicle to count on if something went awry. With this scenario upon them, they both knew that two type A's sitting in the same cab together for weeks wouldn't have worked. It seemed an immature approach given the degree of the mission, yet very grown up at the same time. One can hope to change reality, these two decided to just accept it.

In the afternoon, Andre appears and assures us the plan is moving along, his contacts can deliver a transmission to the Kazakhstan border for 4000 euros, but the deal requires half down now, about 75,000 rubles, roughly $3100, as good faith. The other half will be paid after it arrives, and I verify it'll work. Demetri was very leery of giving up the cash with no guarantee he'd ever see the transmission, or Andre, or the money, ever again. We walked up the five stories to run the request past Father Reinhardt. "Andre has been working out of our garage for six months and in that time, he's always been honest with us." Father Wilhelm chimed in with his faith, as had Ilvana, who was working in the basement kitchen along with other volunteers. They were preparing for a youth retreat that was to commence the following day, and last through the week. My advice followed the lines of giving Andre the benefit of the doubt, everyone here says he's square, and shady deals were how things got done in Russia. Of course, it wasn't my wallet at risk.

Demetri returned with the ruble wad from a bank just blocks away, and no sooner did he turn the stack over to Andre, when our mechanic friend disappeared. Sometime later, he returned with his car trunk full of roasted chicken and salad, cucumbers, beer and vodka. He had us follow him down a ladder into the garage's number four grease pit, and then through a steel door, into a narrow underground hallway that ran the length of the shop's back wall. He then opened another steel door, and we entered Andre's world. The cement walled room, seven metres long and four-wide, contained tools and oil, filters and spare parts; as well as a work bench, couch and coffee table, plus storage cabinets. It was Andre's lair, he'd obviously spent time making it a home, and a hideout. As we began pouring and digging into the feast, apprehensions began to fade. Andre was a stocky rotund character, just under six feet whose buzz cut and bright blue eyes gave his round face animation. He laughed easy and after a few drinks, was telling funny stories about all his shady friends, in his smattering of English. Gille and I were enjoying ourselves, however Demetri, although clicking off photos with a forced smile, was possessed of a reserve. He knew that all that lay before us, was bought with his money.

The next morning was full of halfhearted well wishes for Gille, as he hopped in his Rover and motored away for his date with the solar eclipse, in western Mongolia. Demetri was a man who had everything in life he could wish for. He was young, well off, and in charge of real estate and media concerns back in France, that enabled him to live how he wanted. And yet, I knew it hurt him to see his neighbor roll out that day. He wasn't a great fan of eclipses, but he was an achiever, and had set out from Paris to achieve Mongolia; and was, for now, denied. When two of Andre's friends dropped by in the early afternoon and asked us to lunch, we certainly had nothing better to do.

We jumped in Andre's car, along with Ilvana, and followed their two friends to an abandoned, trashy looking, heavily wooded park. A long dirt path led to a locked fence, surrounding a tree shrouded lonely café, with outdoor tables scattered about a large dirt yard. After a couple of honks, a young girl came out and unlocked the gate; Demetri and I gave each other  that raised eyebrow "this ain't good" look. Once inside, it seemed like any other cafe, we grabbed a shaded table and let our hosts do the ordering; out comes the cucumbers and vodka, more beer and chicken. Oh, the vodka in the middle of the day, these guys were putting it down like fish, and I matched them shot for shot, while Demetri and Ilvana had the sense to set their own pace. Smokes all around, and veggie and meat plates covering the table, we had the place to ourselves, as the clear bottles of canned heat kept showing up. Russian filled the air as Demetri and I tried to pick out the few words we understood, to stay with the theme of conversation.

Then with their motions and words, we gathered that the discussion had turned to us, and the mafia transmission. Their gestures, glances and grins at given points began to sound suspicious; they took on a cliquish air about them; they kept looking over to us, as if to wonder how much were we understanding. Something seemed wrong, and we plied Ilvana as to what they were talking about. What were they saying? She had a good grasp of English and had helped us translate so much since the start of the deal, but suddenly had begun to act as if she didn't get our questions. We both realized that every time we pressed her with hard questions about the time line, the VIN numbers, or Demetri's money, she would throw a look towards Andre and suddenly feign selective understanding. I slowed to sipping beer, Demetri began ordering water, were we being played? We didn't push the moment by demanding answers, Andre and his two buddies could reasonably posture ignorance, and they truly didn't understand everything we were saying. Besides, everyone was liquored up, never a good time to draw a line in a secluded cafe behind a locked gate. From that moment forward, Demetri and I would begin to parse every moment since the start of the deal. With the scam notions in our heads, created by the ignored questions, I began to look at this whole Chelyabinsk episode in a different light.

As I sat there in the sunshine and stared across the table at the Russians, the patina of these instant friendships began to wear away. I was blowing it. Yeah, Demetri was a good guy in a tight spot, and sure, I could get a ride or a train lift forward to make up for lost time, but what about the Kazakhstan experiences? Its people, its desert mornings and the unpredictable moments that seem to direct this trip. When the lunch bill came, Andre did the math, then asked Demetri and I for what amounted to 80 percent of the tab. When I made him aware that, I too, could do math, he assured us that it was tradition for the guests to pay more upon the first meal together. Ok Andre, as long as we're furthering tradition. What a gem, if this repair hope was going to linger into these mini soap operas and end badly, I wanted to know soon.

But there was no soon. The next morning Andre said he was off to the Kazakhstan border at Troisk. Again, I asked about the VIN numbers and the truck's year, again he shrugged it off, it's ok. We killed time kicking it back at the flat, and joking around with all the children who had arrived for the youth retreat, some of whom were sharing the couple of rooms off our wing's hallway. We lunched with Father Reinhardt at an airy indoor-outdoor restaurant in central Chelyabinsk, located in the middle of an open carnival park, with all of its rides shuttered. It was a welcomed pause from our concerns, sitting at a table overlooking a pond, and listening to the Father's observations of his chosen life.

By now I'd felt comfortable enough with him, and trusted him enough to ask a question that had long hung unanswered. His ease of self, the unassuming faith, I needed to know. "If a person can't bring themselves to truly believe, yet they live a good life, how would the Lord judge them?" Posturing that if a guy who doesn't cheat on, or beat his wife, or terrorize his kids, and tries to keep the home together; always aims to be square with the people in his world, what about him? Wouldn't a good person who's a non-believer trump the devotee that is constantly pulling dubious business deals, and squeezing in some instant gratification, when he figures no one is looking? With thought, he answered in a comforting tone. "Leading a Christian life is more important than believing." A simple question with a simpler answer, but it was good for me to hear him say it. To my ears, it may have as well been spoken by the Pope.

After returning to the church grounds, the day dragged on into dusk. We began a dinner, and sometimes lunch, routine of walking a few blocks away to a buffet style cafeteria that offered basic dishes of chicken and rice and veggies, on the cheap. Afterwards, we'd buy a couple of beers and sit around watching the back streets of Chelyabinsk. The eatery was on the edge of a group of tenement structures that were framed by a mix of transient shops and tables set up; selling everything from cigarettes to cell phones, vegetables to videos. Indian children begged constantly, using a gesture that alternated from holding their chin in their hands in an expression of woe, then flipping their open palms for donations.

Pestering at our heels, and egged on by their mothers who crouched on the curbs, they looked weathered, dusty and hungry. When I made the move of dishing out my pocket change, that was it. Like bees to honey, they wouldn't give up, any time we appeared. Drunks were curled up in the building's entryways, which wasn't unusual. What was new was the sight of homeless women, pissing out in the open, without any regard to the crowds. They would just squat and look benignly uninterested, as the trail of water ran from underneath their hiked up, well-worn saris. Silently amazed, trying not to gawk too long at...this place. Chelyabinsk was in so deep, and we were deep into Chelyabinsk, fascinatingly crazy. People could visit the high points of cities like New York, Moscow or Beijing, and then say they'd seen America or Russia or China. I say not.

Back on the sanctuary of the church grounds, I wandered around to the carpentry shop, housed on the back side of our apartment/garage building. I'd  seen the three carpenters in their light blue coveralls coming and going for the past couple of days, and managed to catch one's eye; and followed him into the shop. It seemed to be an arrangement much like Andre's auto shop; they were allowed to freelance projects of all sorts, as long as they also took care of the churches' building needs. Upon entering, I was shocked at the condition of the place, piles of sawdust, easily knee height, all around the two-room shop. So much so, there were walkways through it, it buried tools and machines and the lower cabinet shelves, stocked with cans of varnish and thinners. The three guys were measuring, cutting, and sanding away, filling the air with fine dust, all with cigarettes dangling out of their mouths. Are you kidding? The place was a ticking time bomb. The slightest spark or ember into any mound of that perfect kindling would not only light off the room like a giant match, the fire would take out the attached flats and garage before anyone could think. Could it have reached this state without someone seeing this disaster's potential? Without any words to share, I jokingly gestured at flicking a cigarette and motioned a whoosh, as a pile goes up in imaginary flames. They just smiled and shrugged like "no problem, that hasn't happened yet."

I was sharing Demetri's skepticism as we climbed up to the Father's rectory that evening. Going over our vodka fueled suspicions from the secret park cafe, Ilvana's choosy translation skills, and the original doubts concerning the truck's particulars, it didn't faze the Father. While admitting that he couldn't unconditionally vouch for Ilvana, he still had faith in Andre. Perhaps we were just overreacting. Demetri was a guy who was accustomed to controlling his fate, and the thought of his cash out in the streets somewhere ate at him. I was tiring of this limbo, and just wanted to restart the journey, and finally break into Kazakhstan. There were no good answers tonight, so the two of us hopped a city bus and headed downtown, to try to get some internet time and hang out with a beer on the Promenade; a somewhat improved experience of people watching than what we witnessed earlier in the day.

Beautiful young women in summer dresses paraded past, sipping from green beer bottles, and couples walked arm in arm, enjoying the evening heat after their dinner and drinks at one of the many restaurants. As it grew later, the club crowds began to show, and the dance music began to hum from the bars. The Promenade was always a relaxed respite, an assuring scene that showed how much Russia had managed to get some things right.

Another morning arrives. It's the seventh day here, and my thin layer of benevolence has worn through, leaving only the responsibility to honor a promise. I keep telling myself it's no big deal, I'm on a bike, several lost days could be caught up with a lift. Either Demetri gives me a ride further east to Omsk in a repaired Land Rover, then I head south into Kazakhstan's northeast corner, or train south from here to Astana, catching a good chunk of the country. It's the idle uncertainty that has us losing perspective. Demetri keeps busy on his laptop with different magazine projects he's working on, and there's plenty of activity outside with the kids, ranging from toddlers to young teenagers; plus, the extra adult volunteers running about to entertain and feed the bunch.

I go out on long walks around the neighborhood, taking in the sights. People heading to work or school, or out shopping, all so similar to any everyday scene, but played out against a mixed backdrop of crumbling structures and new buildings; maintained landscapes, and trash-filled dirt lots. It's like if Western society began to deteriorate, and everyone continued to pretend as if there was nothing wrong. But Russia isn't deteriorating, it's in a transition phase. It's not going to hell, rather, it's emerging from it. Walking around with a cold beer in hand began to seem so right, never a second glimpse from the passing citizens, and it really felt that you were truly traipsing along, not intent on being anywhere.

Back at the church, the fifth day of the "get the transmission in two days" plan dragged on. The phone never rang, and besides a couple of Andre's friends, who showed up to use the garage for a few hours to change out wheel bearings on an old Lada, it was another throw away day. Andre had two cell phones, the sure sign of a hustler, and hadn't been answering either of them from Demetri's phone, or now, his Lada buddies. When they called, his wife acted surprised to find he had a shop at the church; and no, she hadn't seen him either. If that didn't beat all, the screw was turning slowly, and continued to turn into the next day. By that afternoon, we approached Father Reinhardt and laid out our thoughts; essentially, how do you like Andre's act now? Two days since we last heard from him, plus his friends and wife had no idea where he might be. The father started in about a possible illness or accident, but then came around to the chance that he was either in over his head with the black-market boys at the border, or possibly he'd made off with the cash. He had alcohol problems and gambling debts, and perhaps the temptation was too great; Demetri may be out of luck. Alcohol issues were no surprise, he's a Russian man, but only now you're telling us of gambling issues? He goes ahead and calls a police friend of his, who promises to drop by Andre's apartment and "check in".

That night, using Skype, I spoke with Demetri's friend in Moscow. The two of them were very close, she was the one that helped set up their church-to-church daisy chain, that brought them here in the first place. The French woman had been kept abreast of our developments throughout the deal, and had made it clear that her help was at the ready. She was a player in the Russian capitol's media and political games for some years now, she knew how the country worked, and struck me as nobody's fool. She knew people who had operatives in Chelyabinsk, who could find Andre and get results. "In Russian business, these disputes are sometimes solved at the point of a gun" she says, in the casual offhanded tone of a French socialite. I told her right off that there's not a chance the guy should get killed over this, it's a transmission, not a child ransom. "No Brian, we don't want to kill him, just make him very afraid." Again, I've lapsed into forgetting where we're at, and her words reminded of the matrix below this surface, it is so very intriguing.

And didn't the police visit stir up the mud. The next morning, the ninth day after arriving in Chelyabinsk, our beloved Andre shows up, red-faced-furious for having a police officer show up at his door and alarming his wife, so the story goes. We put forth he has a lot of gumption to be upset; "you've been gone for two or three days, what the fuck is going on here?" "The transmission is time, is coming, is border tonight, nine" he says, pointing at his watch. "Is it going to be the right one?" "I will see it, I will see." The line in the sand is again moved further out. Our minds had filled the void of information with mayhem and worst-case wonders, but when the cherub faced palooka is standing there with a bungling explanation, the glimmer of hope flickers on; at least the hope that the money wasn't completely lost.

Another day of limbo living at the church. Joke with the kids, chat up the mothers, take turns at beer runs to the kiosk across the street; wander over to the dive cafe for lunch. Another dinner with the Fathers. Nine o'clock comes and goes. No phone call, no answers. That night Demetri and I admit this whole affair had been folly, we decide that by noon tomorrow, we'll just go ahead and start putting the truck back together, fill the gearbox with oil and see what happens. C'est la vie. Oh, that's right brother, you're out three thousand dollars.

The sun comes up one more time, and I roll out of bed as the phone is ringing, it's Andre. He's in Troisk, at the border, the transmission will arrive today.

"When will you be here with it." "One, two, three, four o'clock." The absolute make-break hour of noon is history. We're idiots. No, this is going to work out, it's crazy but that's how shit happens, somehow this is going to work, it'll be a story for the ages. It was the same feeling of sunshine you experience after buying a lotto ticket, this could really happen, you can't win if you don't play. My optimism was lost on Demetri, in his opinion this was a stupid gamble from the start, and it hasn't changed a lick. By four in the afternoon, I'd sobered up, it was the gut check of losing. The church mechanic was waiting at the border for a transmission that would never arrive, maybe he wasn't lying, but someone was. Or maybe the chain of screwballs just couldn't pull it off. Every black-market operation over here is tagged with "mafia." I wish. At least with professionals, the product comes through when there's juice waiting.

We end the tenth day in Chelyabinsk, with dinner and brews on the Promenade. Afterwards we meet Oslam, a Muslim Russian Army officer and his beautiful raven-haired fiancée. The young man and his girl were from North Ossetia, a self-governing republic, deep in the high country of the Caucasus. Raised a farm boy, he had attained a law degree and was stationed here, studying to become a judge. He was as sharp witted and funny as anyone I'd ever met, and he fervently loved his woman, the mountains of his homeland, and his beer; but Allah was above them all, with no room for debate. It seemed a walking dichotomy, but somehow in this crazy corner of the world, he fit right in. Dusk turned to dark as we took turns buying rounds at a street kiosk, and talked over everything from Russia and George Bush, to U2 and celebrity boxing. For a few laughing hours, we stopped thinking of why we were still here, before taking a roundabout taxi cab ride back to our church, on the wrong side of the river Miass.

I awoke to the sound of pebbles, rapping the front window of the flat. Groping across the floor in my boxers, it was 6:00 am. Down below, out in front of the garage, was Andre. He hadn't a key to get into the building, but was

199

waving his hands and looking full of news. Throwing on a shirt and shorts, I plodded out the door, tossing out "I think the transmission is here" just as Demetri was coming to. Once I hit the morning air, and saw his long face and his little car, he didn't have to explain; but he did. He'd met the part at the border. It was from a brand-new Land Rover Discovery, not even a Defender, not even the right God damned car. My eyes stared at the bozo that wasted my week, the brain howled. "VIN numbers-part numbers-model year-model car-VIN numbers-part numbers-model year. Model car at least, you goon dumb ass." My voice said "well, I guess we should have written down some numbers, huh?"

Demetri had come down, heard the last of the report, and just stood in silence as Andre produced from his jacket pocket 600 euros, and a promise to get the rest in a few days. And lo and behold, a new fifth gear needle bearing. A fuck all fifth gear needle bearing; what I'd a done for that a week ago. I guess he tried. To save some face, he mounted an enthusiasm, said we could open the tranny, you and me, we could replace the bad bearing, we could have it done in two days. That can of worms' idea never even settled on us, no possibility. Without a word this game was over, we've simply been here way too long. Andre apologized and drove away, it was the last time I saw him.

The early start gave way to a long day spent putting the truck back together, and by nightfall the camper was being secured. Not much was said, there wasn't much left to say that hadn't already been brought up somewhere along the line, it was pretty much all business. The Fathers promised Demetri they'd do what they could to get his balance collected and sent on to Paris, but we all knew the likelihood of that. That night, at dinner at the top of the church, things lightened up a little. Everyone tried to shrug off the episode as a lesson, and I suppose the best light we could shine on it was that despite it all, this too was an experience. It may have not have been a bicycle experience, a Mongolian trek experience, it certainly wasn't a successful experience, but personally, it would be something I'd never forget. Living in and learning about a city in a region, that until the early 90's, was closed to all foreigners, visa in hand or not. Dealing with the wannabe street player auto mechanic and his cadre of working schmuck shady friends, the mysteries of Ilvana, the colorful life of the Promenade, and vodka afternoons. Most of all, the hospitality and benevolence of Fathers Reinhardt and Wilhelm. What great guys, what nice people.

On the thirteenth morning of Chelyabinsk, I loaded the bike and bags into the bed of a small transport truck, cluttered with the buckets, garden tools, and fertilizer bags of Sergei, the church's handyman gardener. He offered to give me a lift across town to the train station, where I'd catch a ride south to Kazakhstan's new capital of Astana. Father Reinhardt had said farewell earlier, before heading out on an errand; and as I threw in the last pannier, I turned, and there stood Father Wilhelm. After shaking goodbye, I offered him a small donation, probably just enough to cover the extra food costs they had incurred for our stay, and he was thankful. Both Fathers, through it all, had managed to stay above all the drama, our daily travails there didn't weigh on them. They always seemed happy we were there, and that they could help out. I was truly glad to be moving on, glad that the eastern progress was about to recommence, but even now I look back on the impression these two men left on me, they had an inner peace which wasn't theirs to speak of, it was for others to feel. Amen.

The ticket to Astana. Again, the ethical shadow came about. I'd spent almost two weeks in Chelyabinsk, two weeks of not sleeping in the Kazakhstan dirt, or shacking up with some new best friends for the night. The time, and exposure and involvement lost was the chief personal concern throughout the stay. I'd easily lost a thousand k's, and Astana was a thousand k's away road wise, about 700 as the crow flies. The train could give me back the time, but not the experience, and it wasn't lost on me what I was doing. I cheated myself out of riding and knowing a massive chunk of Kazakhstan. Before the Defender debacle, before the my-fault-their fault events with the Russian border guards three weeks ago, the vision was to somehow cross the breath of this unfamiliar land. An epic challenge within this great venture. Now, I was skirting in, just beyond its halfway point.

Illvana jumped in the truck's cab along with Demetri, as I bounced about the bed on the ride to the city's huge main train station, to see me off. She came to the rescue when the ticket window girl and I had reached a communication impasse. Ticket lady was insisting I buy a fare for the bicycle too; not getting that the bike would be broken down, and spread throughout the cabin. Once that was resolved, the final moments of this improbable fortnight were spent with hugs and handshakes, like the ending of a summer camp filled with bizarre events. The promises to stay in touch were thrown around, but we all knew the chapter was ending. Ironically, these two represented the Yin and Yang of my time in Chelyabinsk. Illvana symbolizing the doubts and Demetri the hope. She would drift back into the blur of the city's milieu, and he would strike out for Paris the next morning, with my earnest prayers. The better part of his gearbox's forward bearing was in a plastic bag, back at the garage. Bless him, he told me months later the tranny made it as far as western Ukraine, before finally bowing out.

My time came and I carried the ride up the stairs to the platform where the disassembling routine began. Bags clipped off, bike inverted, and with a flick of the brake release and axle levers, the wheels removed. Again, good folks saw the Westerner and his obvious plan, and came forward to help carry the pieces on board, and say hello. Settling into the lower bunk couch, I made the immediate acquaintances, as the murmurs of "Amerikanski" and "velocipeeda" echoed about the cabin. Facing backwards as the train pulled away from station, the cityscape, and soon the sight of Chelyabinsk, faded away forever. A few hours later, we stopped for the document checks at the Kazakhstan border. The dead serious big-hatted border guards jacked up a few folks, but my inspection went off without a hitch. Exhale. And that was that. What was to be a short stay in Russia, and a month in Kazakhstan was looking to be just the opposite. Chely' was a lesson, a well-intentioned detour, a couple of weeks I'll never forget. The next time someone needs a good mechanic, I'll refer them to my brother Kenneth, in Escondido.

21. glow

Astana was all a clatter. Outside the main train station, city sounds filled the background, as the front wheel rolled into the boulevard traffic. Before traveling a klick towards the city center, I had to pull aside and wonder at the chaos. Everyone, every vehicle on the road it would seem, was honking. At first, it's just the din of city traffic, the background sound of drivers alerting others of mistakes and prompting the slow pokes, or a plodding bicycle. But this was different. The streets were echoing with the stressful, blaring dissonance of hundreds of cars and service trucks honking, for no better reason than that others were sharing the road. At a major intersection, where the traffic lights looked to be cycling normally, I gazed for minutes at the sight of a police officer standing in the middle of the junction. He was attempting to meter the automotive flux, while being surrounded on four sides by honking motorist, yelling out their windows at him for their turn. My guess was that local law had given up on its citizens to obey the harmless colored signal lights, and were now forced to go face to face at the busiest crossroads.

Didn't see it coming. When I awoke in the morning light on the train, the scene outside could have fooled me, I may as well have been in Nevada's high desert. Sparse shrub, scattered across wide plains, stretching off to rocky hills. The jubilant Russian Kazakh who manned the bistro car greeted in English, he knew an American was on board, and had been expecting me. As he streamed questions about the trip, he whipped up a plate of eggs and toast, while I sat with a coffee at the warm window and watched the sunrise over Kostanay Oblast. I enjoyed the return of peace after a chaotic fortnight, the failure and drama. The friends and characters and regrets of the last two weeks were behind me, and the thought of riding out of Astana into this scenery filled my head.

After assembling the bike on the arrival platform of the Astana Railway Station, I sat out in front of the terminal on a bench, smoking a cigarette and guessing at, without a map, how to find the eastbound highway out of the city. A young man in his late 20's approached, he was a stocky white fella with brown hair and an air of familiarity about him; and a question on his face. "You're an American?"

He was a Minnesotan, and was employed by the U.S. Agency for International Development, or USAID. His role here was working out in the smaller villages, helping them to modernize their education programs at the elementary school level. Or was he a spy? I didn't care. What he was to me was the first American I'd spoken with in two and a half months since leaving Serini's place back in April. He wasn't the gabby sort, and surprisingly, didn't blink when I told him my tale; he did however, give me good directions to the A343.

As I sauntered through town, there were flags and bright banners and stages set up all about, Astana's lengthy celebration, honoring its ten-year anniversary as the nation's capital, was in full swing. Tonight, in their ongoing festivities, bands would play and fireworks would pop throughout the city. It all seemed very modern and clean.

The city had been founded as Akmola, then Akmolinsk, in the early 19th century, only to be renamed Tselinograd, literally Virgin Lands City, in 1961, in honor of its roll in Nikita Kruschev's vast Virgin Lands agricultural experiment in the 1950's. His well-meaning, yet misguided, and ultimately failed environmental disastrous attempt to increase Russia's grain supply, had brought thousands of young ambitious Soviets to these remote steppes. It forever changed the region's demographics, and hence, its politics. Once Kazakhstan declared its independence in the early 1990's, the city again took the name Akmola for a short time, only to be deemed Astana, meaning "Capital", eight years later when it took over the crown from the southern city of Almaty. I wonder what they'll call it next?

Spent the night in a nice hotel on Astana's outer edge. It ran about 6500 Tenge, trading at about 120 to 1, so just over $50. I'm down to about $1400 in the accounts. China is going to be good to the budget, but I'll need a couple of months to cross it, and the credit card will have to be broken into soon. On the other hand, the next few weeks spent crossing the emptiness of Kazakhstan and China's Taklamakan/Gobi Desert, should have me camping out a lot. It was a case of having to, there's just not many places out there. Striking out east on the A343, under a warm summer morning sun, those new country blues were running wild.

By now, I knew the phases of these blues and how they played out. Phase 1 was the trepidation of the language, the terrain, and culture shock; Kazakhstan was definitely a change from Russia. Phase 2 was the crescendo of the lost in the wood's feelings, culminating in strong thoughts of quitting, until that first good painkiller beer buzz, or lively evening with new friends. Phase 3 was the epiphany, a bright new day, with the luckiest-son-of-a-bitch-on-earth sensation coursing through the blood. Struggling through the Phase 1 mode wasn't imaginary in Kazakhstan. This place wasn't just a new culture, it was a morass of different looking people and stark differences in landscape, the endless meadow of Europe was gone. For the next 4500 kilometres into central China, the outlook was desert.

This region's indigenous people of Turkic-Kazakhs, Mongolians and Uyghurs have the shade and stout features of American Indians, but they were just the start. Before and during the years of Soviet rule, Kazakhstan had been used as a land of good riddance to many ethnic groups that were considered either low caste, enemies of State politics, and or just plain not trusted. The Slavic influences came in several crests, starting with a somewhat homesteading period under the Tsar's rule during the late 1800's. Later, in the 30's and 40's, Joseph Stalin's policies forcibly exiled hundreds of thousands of people of German and Romanian, Polish and Baltic origins to populate Russia's frontier lands. Mass numbers of Turks and Greeks, Tatars and Georgians living in the melting pot of the Caucasus were also exiled, deemed potential foes, as Stalin consolidated his control over the population's psyche.

Entire families were shipped in to settle and populate the land, with strict expectations on their level of farm production, and limitations on their lifestyle and travel. But with the Great Purge in full swing, the upheaval and a life of hard labor was better than a bullet to the head. At the same time, Gulags were being erected throughout the Russian Empire, including Kazakhstan, Siberia and Mongolia. When these horror camps finally ended in the late 1950's and early 60's, it produced another wave of Kazakhstan settlers. The former prisoners stayed on in the area, and along with those Virgin Lands volunteers, it gave white Russia a strong post War presence. Animosities and trouble can always be found if you go looking for them, but surprisingly, Kazakhstan's multicultural populace of different skin, traditions, cuisine and especially religions, have had less clashes than one would assume. Perhaps because of the hard-done roots shared by its people, tough times in a remote land ease the surface tensions; people have had to stick together.

Kazakhstan was a giant crossroads of Eastern Europe and Asia, and the northern reaches of the Middle East. Here, in its north eastern region, the horse culture associated with the Mongolian heritage was strong. I laid down a 100k day, and along the way, Kazakh cowboys worked herds of cattle, and young kids galloped ponies alongside the highway. Yurts, the ancient nomad home of wandering tribesmen, could be seen in the far distance. These round, lattice-framed tents were probably used by men grazing their cattle on the sparse grasses that filled the steppes, and stretched out in every direction. Navomorkovka was only the second settlement seen all day, and approaching the village, the five water bottles were empty, plus some camp food was in order. The local village junior bicycle gang met me as I rolled in, and the kids had me follow them over a dirt field to the local market. The pretty, red-headed mom running the place seemed shocked when I walked in as the boys scrambled to tell her my story. Her blank gawk continued as I shopped a few things, and motioned the need of a place to stay or camp.

She wasn't much help, so after picking up some meat, bread and a noodle packet, and killing a bottle of some very cold beer, it was back on the bike. We criss-crossed the outer points of the village over dirt trails as I followed the boys, searching out a camp spot. After about 2k's, and being turned down twice by skeptical villagers, who didn't know what to think of someone so different camping out on their land; we wound up in a wash, leading down to a wide shallow creek. The tracks of cattle being driven across the creek bed were the only signs of activity, so it looked a safe bet that no one was going to bother me

here. I thanked the guys with a solid hand shake and they beamed, chuffed in that way boys do, when they know they're the cool stranger's only friend in town.

After getting the tent set up, and washing down a slab sandwich dinner with another beer, a herd of fifty or so white and red colored cattle arrived, on their way back home. A few stragglers started up the wash before being shooed back by a cowboy, who saw the small green tent. He stopped, and we fell into the fine-honed single-word waving-hand motion conversation method I seemed to use a lot lately, and shared a smoke. He was a pleasant cowboy chap, and assured that my campsite had seen the last of any returning livestock for the night. Soon, dusk turned to dark, and the evening passed with the iPod silently cranking Pink Floyd through the earbuds, as I stared out the flap at the Kazakh nothingness. It ended as soon as my head hit the folded-up jacket, that had suited as a fine pillow so far.

The rumbling began in a dream. The eyes opened to the morning's dim light, and the rumbling was real, and getting louder. The cattle! They were heading back out, and as I lay on the ground, their stomping hooves seemed headed for the narrow wash. I quickly unzipped the mummy bag and jumped out of the tent, thinking that grabbing the bike and gaining the high ground above the wash was the only move to make. I only managed to gain my feet and pick up the bike before the dust was rising at the top of the wash, there was no time to scramble up the embankment as the lumbering animals approached the crest of the rise. Caught flat footed in my boxers, it was too late. Here they come.

Goats. Just goats. A large herd, perhaps a hundred of them, deftly trucked down the wash, surrounding and prancing around the tent without the slightest intention of trampling anything. As the drove streamed around me, a mounted goat cowboy followed behind, laughing a wide smile at the foolish bicycle man in his underwear. Yeah but I thought...

Breakfast, at the small four table cafe a few k's out of Navomorkovka, was much like the market scene the day before. The woman just stood staring mute, as if Hans Solo had emerged from the Millennium Falcon. She disappeared in the back and her man came out and greeted me. "Hallo, kann ich helfen? Oh damn, German German German; I had to think for a few seconds, and then stumbled out a poor "Ya, essen sie bitte? "Naturlich" he replied, motioning at the tables, then offered "eier, fleisch...ah schinken und kaffee? "Danke." He then stared, sizing me up, grading my German, then smiled. "Nicht Deutsch, English ja?" "Nein, Amerikanische." "Ah, welcome, sit". Feeling like I'd just passed a breakfast exam, I sat at one of the small tables, the two were acting very wary of the stranger in the front room. Soon the wife began to warm up, venturing her English words from lessons long past. Through a nice breakfast, the couple turned out to be alright. Quite curious after all, just a bit taken back at first.

The bright new day attitude was strong that morning, as the pedal rhythm settled in, and I stared out at a second day of riding into a vista of nothing. Again, there was that feeling of peaceful release, knowing that the day's only issue would be "where's the next water?" Without a map, I just relied on the faith that it would somehow appear. As I rested on a small rise in the late morning, a Russian man and his wife pulled over in a Nissan sedan. After asking all about the trip, they said they were headed for their home in Semipalatinsk, some 600k's away, and offered a lift. They advised that the stops on this road were over 100k's apart, nothing else. I expected the offer was coming from these good folks, and was ready. "Thank you so much but I have to ride this, I'll be camping out, I'll be ok" was the rough idea of what was said. As they drove off, I wondered whether I'd regret the decision; accepting a ride in a vacant country of nice people would always be an option, but wrong. This desert was going to change in name only for a few thousand miles, I had to dig in, rather than deny it.

Besides, this land felt so familiar. The brush dotted rolling plains, the small mountain hills, the arid vastness. It seemed so much like parts of Nevada and California, just east of the central Sierras, the high desert. I knew how the road would undulate, I knew how far to the next distant hill range before hitting a crest, it was just missing a few jack rabbits and an occasional coyote. I pretended a Nevada of a parallel universe, I pretended to be home out West; it was a good head game, and gave a confident cadence. And then, some 70k's out, the trek took another turn. Just cresting a rise, a man pulls over in a green, late 90's Honda CR-V. He offered a cold bottle of water and we shared a smoke. With his decent English, he expressed his amazement at the California-to-here story.

Alec, sounding like Aleek, had been visiting with his estranged wife in Astana, whom he still shared a cartography business; and I didn't hesitate to say that if there was one thing Kazakhstan could use, it was a good map maker. He had the dark hair and brown complexion of the region's people, and the easy demeanor of an educated man about him, he was instantly likable. Aleek was also heading for Semipalatinsk, now called Semey, and offered that there was plenty of room for the bike. And he made the same point, that after all, there wasn't much to see between here and there. And what about the water? Again, I politely declined. He strongly re-emphasized the water issue, my "I don't know, I'll be fine" answers probably sounded foolish. He gave me his number and address, and hoped I'd contact him in Semey where he lived with his daughter. She also spoke English, and she'd be thrilled to meet an American and hear the tale. I promised him I would, but knew I probably wouldn't.

As I pedaled on, I thought about the worn joke whereby a devout man is stranded on his roof top, while the town floods. He had ignored the civil sirens and later passes on a rescue skiff, and eventually says no to an air lift, all along claiming he was a believer, and God would save him. When he finally drowns and stands at the Gate, he asks the Lord why he'd been abandoned in his time of dire need. "Dude, I sent you a public warning, a boat ride and a helicopter. What the hell?" Mine was just a case of good people on a warm day, hearing the daunting desert task for the first time. It was appreciated of course, but I've been anticipating the challenge, wouldn't expect anyone to understand. The water? No idea, just know it'll work out.

Just a few k's later, as I rolled up another rise, I see the Honda. There's Aleek leaning up against the fender, sipping water. "Come on, get in, I've talked to a friend in Pavlodar who wants to meet you and have some lunch." Fuck here we go. I didn't know exactly how far away Pavlodar was, but a couple of hundred k's was a starting guess, I felt it coming on. Aleek was a nice guy and he really had a way about him. Again, the grabber was my determined plan, versus giving in to a sweet lift forward, a couple of days closer to home. I knew accepting to Pavlodar meant accepting to Semipalatinsk. I trusted the guy, he was about my age and meant well, so my hesitation hadn't anything to do with him. Left with no good reason but stubborn pride... and then of course there's the water thing... then there's still so much desert still to come, even with a lift... wandering through should-I-shouldn't. I don't know anymore. The wheels came off, the rear hatch opened, and the back of the CR-V swallowed the bike. My new best friend.

Aleek's cartography wasn't of the road map sort, but more of surveying and mapping out sectors used for property lines and official records. He traveled all about the country with his assistant, spending a great deal of time away from home. He handled the field work and his ex-wife managed the publishing and contracting; it sounded like a great business in Kazakhstan's slowly emerging economy, but it was clear his life was one of many long roads. This was the ninth largest country in the world, with only a score of highways to connect its far reaches. As the emptiness passed by, I once again tried to imagine how long it would have taken to get to here, to here, to here. I was cheating, and knew by now that I'd have to be honest about it. People won't understand, but that didn't matter. What mattered is that I was traveling towards the Chinese border, the final country. The final country to cross and I'll be done.

On the outskirts of Pavlodar, despite a planned lunch, Aleek pulled over at a roadside stand that was grilling beef and lamb for shashlik, a kebab-style skewered dish. We sat down with a beer and had a couple of the marinated treats, as Aleek explained he wanted me to experience this traditional Kazakh fare from someone who did it right. Then, it was off to lunch at a restaurant on the south side of Pavlodar, a city of over three million, where we met up with Alim (Aleem) for lunch and vodka. Aleem seemed older than Aleek, but who can tell after a certain point in life, there's no accounting for lifestyles. They were certainly old friends, and they both felt it was important to take me into the city and visit Pavlodar's central Mosque. After a delicious plate of saucy mutton noodles, and thanking Aleem for his hospitality, we did just that. Expecting another pious structure built more for the faithful than the fashionable, I was surprised as we pulled up outside the grounds of the Mashkhur Jusup Central Mosque. It looked like an enormous spaceship had just landed.

It was modern, bright and majestic. Its sand colored smooth stone base was styled in the shape of a giant 200-foot eight-pointed star, the stone walls rose and formed into a circular main entrance room, topped by a hulking fluted turquoise dome, probably mocking the hue of aged copper, and standing well over a hundred feet high. Four minarets towered above it all at four corners, topped by turquoise spires, and the surrounding grounds were a wooded park. It was one of the most impressive building I'd seen in some time, and Aleek was very proud of it; I felt lucky to see it. Would have never even known about it. Again, the journey opened a door and rewarded me for walking through it. But what had I passed? What was waiting for me back there, out there? I'll never know.

The first 100k's south towards Semipalatinsnk, re-named Semey, in 2007, followed a lonely green swath created by the Irtysh River, in a sea of desert. As I looked out the window, I recalled in my planning months ago, thinking how this little strip that stood out on Google Earth would be a good source for water in a dry land, and certainly some good camp spots. I also recalled stories, the notorious history of this corner of the former Soviet Union. We were heading for the city whose name is synonymous with the U.S.S.R.'s nuclear development and testing program.

In a land of westerly winds, the Semipalatinsk Test Site was administered from the formerly secret city of Kurchatov, just 100k's upwind of Semipalatinsk. For four decades, the U.S.S.R. lit off over 400 underground and atmospheric explosions, with its standard disregard for the local populace in full parade. Aleek's take on it was that there had been problems in the past, and a lot of people died both quickly and slowly, but now the testing ban had been in effect for almost twenty years and the health problems were rare. He didn't fear drinking the water, or eating the locally grown meats and produce. Silently, I doubted that there weren't any widespread lingering health issues, but since he lived here and he believed it, I let it lie.

Dry dismal studies on the tragic health effects of radioactivity can and do fill rooms all over the world concerning Kazakhstan, the U.S., Australia, China, India; and of course, Japan. Granted, very early on, scientists worldwide may have been murky on the truly horrid side effects of the military's new toy, but the big players just kept on blasting away, long after the jury had come back; their region's citizens be damned. Especially here. The testing cursed the 50's and 60's generation and those to come, through a variety of cancers and grotesque mutations in many. On and on I know, it's all been said before. Best to just sweep Aleek's and other's denials and wayward beliefs under the rug, where they'll still be radiating well into the future.

The semi-desert steppes of emptiness continued on as the day faded. It was dark when we came upon the lights of Semey, crossing a brightly lit suspension bridge over the Irtysh, that took us to Aleek's side of town. He had bought an apartment in one of the familiar "Khrushchev housing" buildings that I'd come to know and experience since entering Poland. The five to nine-story basic block concrete structures were erected over a thirty-year period, to answer the needs of the progressively urbanized population, and were now privatized.

After the Red collapse, there were a few years of thought and argument put into the policies of relinquishing State ownership and control; of not only land and urban property, but business and intellectual property as well. The Russian Civil Code of 1994 was a significant starting point for the new Russia and its people. It has undergone regular evolution since, to address the changes of their society, such as these emerging independent nations, plus the myriad of needs and demands and political power ploys that I couldn't begin to fathom. Aleek has his own comfortable apartment, that's all that mattered. Once past the standard abandoned building motif foyer and hall, we entered his cheery contemporary flat and was greeted by his beautiful daughter Diana.

Diana was twenty-five with long dark hair and very good English, by the time I'd emerged from the shower she had a load of my laundry going, and was busy with the evening meal. Her first joke was shaking that dirty sweat stained ball cap at me "it's disgusting" she said. Well, yeah. Over the pilaf dinner, the three of us were joined by Roman, Aleek's employee. The thirty-something close-cropped Russian Kazakh was the tech guy of the company, he loved to spend hours on the upkeep of the computers and printers, as well as the sensitive triangulation equipment they used on the job. As the night went by and the stories were told, I relished in the moment of where I was at. Tucked away at a small kitchen table in a generic housing building, in a large city in the far corner of Kazakhstan, a country that I'd have had trouble locating on a map a year ago.

In the middle of it all, Aleek left for about an hour. When he returned, he asked if I would like to head out and visit a friend, and to see the city. Alright then, might as well make the most of my life's lone visit to Semipalatinsk. When we climbed into the Honda, Aleek said something about how he'd dropped off the bicycle. What? The bicycle had been left in the back of the locked car. I'd only taken the two rear panniers inside, and now the rest was gone. He said it was over at his sister's house where it would be safer, but I needed more answers. My questions of just where was his sister's house was useless, I hadn't any idea of where anywhere was. Why couldn't it have been taken inside the apartment? I need to see where it is, my child had been shuffled off to an unknown sitter.

Aleek's response to the very direct questions was that it was wrong to leave it in the car for the few hours that we did, there were thieves about, and to take it inside would bring the eyes of his dicey neighbors. A look around the dwelling's grounds in the low lamp wash showed the same dirty, broken, life debris and zero grounds maintenance that I'd come to expect from these places. I couldn't judge anymore, but according to Aleek, it wasn't a place to trust after dark.

Still, what the hell? Why didn't he mention what he was going to do? There was a weird silence in the car as the brain rolled over this guy's hospitality, his wonderful daughter and astute friend Roman, so far, the perfect host. But the bike was stashed away somewhere in this big city, and I had no idea where it was, and that ate at me no end. Control over what I could control was paramount, and once again, I'd lost the wheel and wasn't at ease with it. I couldn't afford to let it show, playing it cool at the moment; he hadn't shown any other flaws. Maybe he knew what was best, but my thoughts conjured a tomorrow when I'm told the bike has disappeared, and hey we're really sorry and all... Fuck, that was all I could tell myself. But on the outside, I decided to go with it, as if I had another choice.

After a twist and turn drive through the dark streets, we arrived at a narrow one-car-wide slot between yet another pair of cement stack apartment buildings, that led into a central yard. A long silhouette standing in the doorway light of a corner bottom floor apartment gazed at us, with hands shoved in his pockets. Nikolai greeted Aleek, but just stared at me as we met on the stoop. We walked through a short narrow hallway, to enter a dingy small living room. Nikolai was about fifty, and lived here with his grown son; he was tall with salt pepper hair and a lean look of having had a hard-working life. Out came a round of beers, and after some chatter between the two, they settled into a game of backgammon. I just sat there trying to follow the conversation, but it was tough, Nikolai hadn't a word of English. He soon warmed up, just a bit shy towards me given the language barrier. After a bit, they conferred back and forth on some subject, then glanced over towards me.

Nikolai pointed and made the famous pinched fingers to pursed lips international motion of "do you want to get high?" Aleek smiled in relief as I instantly nodded yes; he said he was kind of, but not really sure, if I was ok with it. It was the first buzz since that first night in the Ukraine out in the woods, with the boys and the radiator bong. After a few more beers, we skipped on the city tour and drove back to Aleek's. Another eventful day, that began in the middle of a goat stampede, and ended in a real bed.

The next morning, Aleek was off on local business and Diana left for the office job that she held, along with helping out the family business. The plan was to park in front of their computer with Roman for a few hours to upload photos and update the blog; it was an ordeal that stretched into the afternoon, and looked at times hopeless. The photos would always begin the long slow transfer, and just before completion, the upload would fail. We tried individual pics, we tried reducing their size, nothing worked every time, but eventually we managed to get a decent backlog of photos on to my Photobucket site.

Just the fact that Aleek had internet in his home was a sign of the progress being made toward better service throughout the region, the download-upload speeds would someday follow. Up to this point, I'd only seen the Web in Internet cafes and businesses. Their emerging access was akin to Americans in the early 70's, having only a few TV channels, from 6am to 2am; but made worse here by frequent power black outs. But I fall back on the ease of comparison, it's an ugly habit. This isn't a part of the world that stands the Western light of modern life; it is what it is, and capital-driven progress is coming on a slow train.

Roman stayed for dinner, and afterwards, Aleek and I took off to cruise the town, the first stop was Nicolai's. After getting tuned up, Nick had me follow him up to the roof to show off his hobby of racing pigeons. He'd built a roomy dovecote, filled with eight or ten birds, and from what I could gather, a couple of them were quite accomplished in competition. I'd never met anyone who even talked about the sport, but understood the basic idea of releasing the birds many miles away, and timing their return. It had ancient roots, and was an ideal craft for someone city bound with limited means. Throughout history, great battles and great fortunes had pivoted on the infobahn of homing pigeons, now nobody cared. But I was honored. Nickolai was a hard guy to get to know, and according to Aleek, didn't show his coop of valuable birds to many.

Then, the warm summer night driving tour of Semey began. The city had been renamed just the year before, hoping to distract from the lingering shadow of its nuclear testing history, a deterrent to new business. It had been established as a fortress in the early 18th century, near the grounds of seven ancient Buddhist temple ruins; the seven halls, hence Semipalatinsk. It grew as an important crossroads of Asian trade routes, and due to its remoteness, a place of exile for those free thinkers who publicly disagreed with Russia's Czars in the 1800's. As a result, literary, art and music minded people became concentrated here, which of course affected the city's politics. It grew over the decades into a strong intellectual community, that pushed for Kazakh autonomy with its own political party, the Alash Orda, in the post Bolshevik Revolution days. Alash Orda eventually aligned themselves with Moscow, but their anti-Communist platforms were not forgiven.

During the Great Purges of the 1930's, the city's leaders, along with many of its prominent citizens, were rounded up and executed; closing the spark of another layered story in a sad book. Then, the grand decision to stage above-ground nuclear tests nearby closed the city to all outside visitors. Also, limits were forced on its citizens from moving away, even as they were becoming aware of the health tragedies, through cancer rates and hideous birth defects. The ban lasted until the collapse of the U.S.S.R., driving home once again, that the clouded history of Russia and its provinces are endlessly interesting, but never happy.

We drove through the lit streets' past mosques and palatial office buildings that reflected the region's venerable Muslim history, as well as its place as a once important Soviet city. There were squeaky new modern style office buildings, offset by a large university built in the post war Soviet block-pattern. The main feature was our stop at the "Stronger Than Death" memorial, honoring the many fallen Kazakh victims of the atomic testing years. Aleek said this was Semey's most important memorial. It was a giant dark stone monolith, that must have stood seventy feet high and thirty wide. It had a long cutout within of an atomic mushroom cloud, and the somber statue of a mother, covering her child from harm, at its base. These people were all too aware of what had been done to them, I needed a beer.

22. ponimayu!

We made a quick beer stop at a small magazin, and ended the tour parked on the east side of that well-lit suspension bridge over the Irtysh. It was bright and modern, and gave this city of such mixture and history a touch of the future. People and their hopes are stronger than death, but my outlook on Semey's future was held up by the immeasurable damage wrought by radiation, it wasn't going away anytime in the next few centuries. This city, and its people's resolve, were enlightening.

On the way home, we made the stop at Aleek's sister's house, somewhere on the east side of the river, and picked up the bike. It was out back in a locked shed, and buried under a shelf, with a folding plastic table effectively hiding it. I had really spoiled the script on this one, once again. I had fretted my way up to being quite pointed over the bike's location that first night, throwing in the towel on humanity; but this guy was straight up, he had gone out of his way to secure the bicycle. I tried to be cool, but the defensive instinct is never far away, and he had felt it; and yet so misplaced. I explained as best I could, and apologized for my doubts, he just shrugged.

In the morning, Aleek and Nicolai gave me a lift out of town, and as we gabbed, about 50k's went by. Pull over, the ride has to start. I put the bike together, and we did our handshakes and hugs. The loneliness had abated for a couple of days, as these two had brought me into their lives. It was a meaningful visit all around, and the strangest part of these goodbyes is knowing I'll really never see them again. Good people that will forever remain in this far corner of Asia, as my life stretches out on the M38. East, towards the horizon of China.

But boy, that M38. Kazakhstan's far east butting up against China's expansive western deserts, this was a lonely far corner of the planet. I wanted so much to absorb this, just me and the endless earth's horizon, across legions of a hot desert highway, but now knew that there would always be the opportunity. Someone, something would happen to skirt the miles, but this blowin' with the wind spiel was going to end. One thing was down, there would be no more accepting rides. The lifts so far had made common sense, the stories they led to were priceless, and a vow of no-more was a threat to common sense. It was now a July sun in a very hot part of the world, challenging my guilt to push through it, across a virtually unknown stretch. But common sense never comes home with a crazy tale. The Taklamakan and Gobi is now the great Kazakhstan challenge story I missed out on, and it's my crazy tale to lose.

A car pulls up outside the tiny spot of Novotaubinka, and two guys jump out. They just had to know, "what are you doing out here?" They moved on, but then on the edge of the next village there they were again, smiling and waiting. They then showed me over to their small magazin, where I met the one fella's wife, running the shop. Then, it was next door to the small bar grill, where his mother served the three of us a nice breakfast of fried eggs and bread, raw bacon and coffee. Everyone was wide-eyed as the tale was recounted, and after such a lengthy respite it wasn't a hard decision to pull up for the day in Charsk; just twenty-odd k's from where Aleek and Nicolai dropped me off in the scrub. As per Soviet instructions, the village was over 2k's off the highway. Just outside of town, a dozen young boys were jumping off a low bridge and splashing about in the shallow slow stream of the Char. They saw me coming and surrounded the bike, staring at the machine and rider and talking among themselves, pointing at the gears and luggage. They began a string of questions in Kazakh, with a few trying their rough English, I knew what they wanted to know, "I'm from America." "Amare-eeekaaa" they repeated and the oldest boy stepped forward to get the tale. After quickly outlining the route for them, they asked for a picture around the bicycle; and once again, I followed a group of happy Kazakh boys into a village.

The 3000 Kazakhstan Tenge, or KZT, hotel room came in around $25. It was a basic and tidy, two stories with an exterior of peeling whitewashed plaster covering cinder block walls, with a wooden trellis gable under a corrugated tin roof. The manager, or owner, was a matter of fact woman in her late forty's, and showed me the simple bed/bath/TV room with the reserve of someone selling something they weren't sure of, as if I may balk and look for nicer lodgings. She didn't know me. Later, walking the second story hallway looking for the community toilet, I found that as

decent as the place was, the can was still a double hole outhouse building across the small parking area. Indoor water yes, indoor sewage no.

No troubles. Walking down the vacant street to the local magazin for some off-the-shelf grub, the air suddenly came alive with blowing, swirling, pieces of white copy paper. Hundreds of thousands of the sheets were caught up in a large dust devil that would blow out, then reach and catch the pieces again. As the show danced down the street like a colossal animated cartoon cloud, my mind raced as to how it could be, where it came from. There must have been an entire cargo load or building full of white paper whizzing above the rooftops. I stood in awe until it disappeared out of town; the few people on the street just smiled and walked on, like it had been seen before; I'll never know. After settling into the room with some noodles and a few cool beers, I decided to stay the next day as well. Once again, I fell back on the reason of needing to get the head settled. As if by plan the next morning, it was raining pretty good. The rush ride to Semey, and its friendship-tour days were now behind, chill here in this peaceful small village and get ready to pedal across Eastern Kazakhstan. Feign it's Nevada, without all the single wide mobile homes dotting its plains. Feel what's left of Kazakhstan, I was only a weeks' worth of good riding from the Chinese border.

It struck me while surfing the computer at Aleek's, that when Google Maps was brought up on the screen, it always centered on the U.S. It was now a stroke faster to drag the screen to the west, rather than the east, to center my current location. It meant I was now closer to the end than the start, but also emphasized the vastness of China and the Pacific. Eight countries down, and one real big one to go. How far has it been? It's been so far that a bicyclist is approaching Kazakhstan's Chinese border thinking "I'm almost home!" The yearn to see Sheree and the boys and home was growing stronger as the end became more imaginable, Kazakhstan and soon China. Places so different, places I didn't really belong. Taking stock, everything was still good. The money would just make it, the bike was cool and the homesickness is curable with another cold beer and a couple of painkillers. I was so glad to be right here.

Unexpectedly, the ride down M38 to the crossroads of the M350 just outside Kalbatau wasn't such a lone existence. Soon, after the morning shake off, those first few k's when the morning aches and labored breathing settle into that second wind rhythm, I looked out upon what appeared to be a miniature village. Short, single level one-room desert sand colored brick buildings, with no roofs. Here and there, a dome rose above the rest, all had openings for doors and windows, but had none. It looked like a high school project to practice erecting brick domiciles, perhaps it was the start of a poorly planned and underfunded housing development. About two hundred or more of the structures were jammed into a five or six-acre rectangle, maybe it was some failed old Russian attempt at...oh my.

It was a cemetery. Muslim. Must be Muslim. I couldn't distinguish definitive symbols like the star and crescent, no real minarets, just the few domes. The

Kazakh culture was generally split between Islamic or Russian Orthodox and this site didn't strike Christian. Very simple and respectful, a small home open to the winds and spirits that contained the burial sites, my guess that family members rested within each. It was an arrangement, a style which I'd never seen, or maybe I had and didn't know.

Further on in the midday, a family of Kazakhs were picnicking on the roadside, no rest area or pull off, just parked on the shoulder. They wanted to know the tale, and offered up a drink and slices of watermelon and a smoke. I rambled off the story as pictures were snapped. Perhaps it was a long road trip's lunch stop or a planned day out, I couldn't tell. A pair of Mom and Dads, a Grandma and a kid. They just beamed, so happy to be together. The cemetery villages kept popping up, all a bit different in size and elaboration, but all so captivating and unusual, and serving to stir that this place wasn't Nevada. It's a land of people steeped in customs, ancient and unwavering, that long transcended whichever nation presently claimed it. Despite the landscape, I really didn't know this place at all.

Wild horses. Wild Kazakh horses with their colts grazing by the roadside. Wild, or that was the presumption. The half dozen Kazakhs, a stout native breed that had developed in this region over the last millennia, had no tethers or markings and there wasn't a fence in sight. They looked strong, compared to the gaunt wild ponies outside of Reno. If they were free, or just mondo-free range, was anyone's guess. A few k's short of the spare village of Zhangiztobe,

a long-abandoned Soviet ICBM missile base appeared, its concrete control center and half shell cement missile bunkers blending into the native brush. No proper military base accouterments such as housing or guard gates in view, just the squat tower and dirt hued bunkers, merged  into the desolate brown. I fantasized a scene in a Maryland CIA command post in the black and white buttoned up iron creased days of the late 1950's. A chain smoking agent with rolled up sleeves pours over a sheaf of U2 spy plane high altitude photos, and recognizes an aberration in the desert floor. "Colonel Finley come here, I think we've found more silos!"

80k's had passed that day as I pulled into Zhangiztobe, its center consisted of a few one room buildings selling fruit, another was the general magazin. As I pulled up and leaned the bars against the market's pastel purple wall, dozens of dark eyes were drawn. Little brown children surrounded the bike, mothers stared on smiling and talking among themselves. As though Neil Armstrong had just set a foot on their planet, it would have been hilarious to plant a flag and claim this land in the name of the Great State of California. A crass afterthought, that never occurred at the time. Everyone, once again, was so nice and inquisitive. The kids trailed a line behind my heels between the two stores as I picked up some noodle packets and apples for camp, chattering about every item I perused. Back outside, a crowd had gathered and were snapping pics with their phones, as the stranger filled his water bottles from the well's jug. I knew that if I'd stayed much longer and acquired the inevitable translator, the melons would be sliced and the smokes would be passed around, and soon one of these nice folks would offer up a meal. And a place to stay for the night.

Just knowing that sent a tinge of guilt. Don't be that guy, don't expect that offer, be thankful. A night in the village could also be a night of vodka, and potluck marathon eating, and storytelling. Stronger was the desire to knock out a good day on the road tomorrow, take another good chunk towards closing on the border. Camping just outside the village, in an old cement one room wreckage. There was no roof and partial walls, as if a bomb had exploded years ago, it was my kind of place. The remaining walls blocked the wind and hid the little tent from view. Past dusk, an old white-haired papa shuffled by, wondering what's up. Somehow, without a stitch of English, and with the aid of maps drawn in the dirt, I related the entire from there-to-here story. He left assuring I'd be ok there for the night. It's always nice to have visitors drop by the house.

Nothing but empty panorama stretching south the next morning, so good to set the head down and pedal and get an early rhythm going, knowing it was going to be perfect July day. Life and all its requirements would soon return, this had to be enjoyed. Looking out, far into the infinite brush, I churned on something the old man brought up last night, while expressing his worries of camping out in the open desert. Packs of wolves still wandered these steppes. It was the second wolf warning about Kazakhstan, the first was from the nice ladies in Palasovka, before the border patrol nabbed me. Since their caution also came with a "wild tigers too" tag, I brushed it off.

Hell, I've rarely seen any rabbits out here much less any wild life that could support a family of large carnivores. Oh, but to be torn alive on a dark night on the plains of Eastern Kazakhstan by a clan of fierce grey wolves, it would cast you forever as the cool mythical legend to the great-grandchildren. Fill in your own story kids, he went out swingin'. Turns out, much later, I found this country has one of the largest populations of wolves in the world. Tigers? Well they were forced into extinction around here just in the last century. But yeah, a good story. Skepticism and ignorance, gets me through.

At another Muslim cemetery village, a family waved me over and cheerily heard the "well I left California in February" jabber. Before moving on, the grandma tied a small strip of cotton cloth to the handlebars. Her son explained it was a symbol of hope and good luck, you bet it stayed there. Past the cutoff to Zharma, the road began rising and became more gravel than pavement, and as it climbed over a small series of rocky hills, the desert scrub had changed to a greener tone. At a hilltop near nothing, with no signage or fanfare, stood a giant lonely cement bighorn ram statue atop a pedestal, looking regally across the vista. Further along, on at a crest near the tiny spot of Kriushi, a Chinese business man was taking some clients on a tour in a new Mercedes. He offered up a bottle of cold water, saying I'd enjoy the roads of China. He had a chipper air of young wealth about him, and his English was excellent, in addition to being the first Chinese citizen I'd run into.

He said the country had been pouring mountains of cash into its infrastructure ahead of the Beijing Olympics, set to start in another week; and they knew the highways were the first thing people noticed. In a word, the country was putting on the dog for its world stage, and because of the Games, I'd chanced upon a great time to visit. A couple of hundred metres away, stood a small white and blue trimmed house turned café. Going in to fill up the bottles, I found the folks just taking some fresh potato filled pastries out of the oven and topping them with homemade cream cheese. Ooh lovely. Sat down with the Russian Kazakh family and enjoyed a few of the delights with a cup of coffee, yum. Afterwards the smiling happy Mom, a youthful grandma and a sweating husband, just in from chores, refused my money and wished me the best. I'm out of words to describe how wonderful these people are, it just has to be lived.

Then, after a 100k day, a makeshift truck stop appeared. Not a fueling station, just a concrete gray single story home, with a long porch and a couple of corrals out back. Dad was managing some cattle and horses, along with some goats that roamed freely behind the house. Mom ran the kitchen that brought in all the truck traffic, and three happy young boys ran through it all, chasing each other. Pa motioned it was alright to set the tent up out back, but had concerns of the goats eating the bike's leather seat. After a goulash and macaroni dinner, one of the kids, who had been my constant companion, showed off the yard shower. A high placed large can of water, with a pull string valve. Dad made out that on real hot days the water wasn't too bad; it had only been a couple of days since the last shower in Charsk, but when and where the next? The trick is to just soak down in a cold stream shot, then get all the soaping done at once. Then cringe and pull that valve one more time, and get it over with. I'm such a big girl's blouse when it comes to cold showers, but it's always worth the effort.

The seat survived the night. I packed up and had breakfast with two truckers at the front room's dining table, and then enjoyed a smoke on the porch with them, as the morning sun came up behind us. They said Ayagoz was an easy 65 k's away, and offered a lift. Naw, I'm doing good, thanks. It was another day of nomadic horses and cemetery villages, and a rear flat tire, as the empty plains rolled by. Knowing it was a short k day had me in a relaxed mood, as I wheeled into Ayagoz.

Adjacent to the train depot was a hotel that was a typical relic to old Russia, rather than native of this far Eastern desert. The pallid, pale blue, two level building with white colonial trim hadn't seen a can of paint since it was erected decades ago. The large cement flower garden circles out front had long ago surrendered to the wild vines that crept over their edges, and the parking area out front had full flowering weeds busting through the asphalt. Wasn't certain the place was open for business, but the front door and a few windows were open, so I went in. The cleaning lady stopped sweeping the floor long enough to understand, and booked me a room for about eight dollars. Eight dollars! I'm giving it five stars.

After getting the shorts, socks and tees soaking in the sink, to at least float off the body salt and desert dust, it was down the street to find the town I-net cafe and update the blog, and a few pics. Walking through the front door into a room packed with a young crowd, and at least twenty terminals, a teenage girl pops forward and asks "would you like internet?" As she shows me over to an open screen, a musty old woman steps in front and says "No!" She is pointing me out of the café, to the bewilderment of her teenage assistant, who begins in Kazakh to tell the grande dame that there are open terminals. She is immediately shushed. "No internet, no!" She demands I leave, and on my way

out a young boy is coming in the door. Seeing me, he smiles and says "you want internet?" He grabs my hand and leads back into the room to hear the old bitch bark once again; the little guy turns to me with a look and a shrug, he has no idea what's going on. Wow. With a happy face I assured them it was alright, and winked at Miss Stuffy Pants. Clueless, I had to lay it once again to the older generation's wariness of authority's attention being drawn to a stranger, and by association, them. This path has taken me through many hamlets that simply haven't seen a lot of Western tourist, they're still adjusting. Such a complete mind screw was twisted on these poor folks over such a long time. Father, forgive them, for they do not know...

On the way back to the room with a few beers, a plastered Russian shakes hands and follows along, making plans to drink tonight with his new American friend. The guy's already three sheets. Politely at first, then increasingly firmer and firmer, I try to wave this clown off. When he enters the hotel, I turn, pointing a finger and blare "Nyet! Ponimayu? (understand?)" As I say it, he knocks my hand down, and brings that low angry stare. The standoff lingers. Swing you drunk fuck. The contest finally fades as he shakes his head and leaves. Thank God, that was close. Back in the room, I was kind of shook up, but after a few sips felt pretty good; a little confrontation after all the smiles and unduly nice people gives balance. Just a bad apple, there are certainly a lot fewer public drunkards here than in Russia or Ukraine, haven't missed them.

Spent the evening watching old-time black and white Russian cartoons on a tiny black and white television, and reflecting on the Kazakh adventure; tripping on how the plan to spend a month here and about two weeks in Russia reversed itself, due to situations and rides. True, there's not much here, but I enjoy the days of riding the desert horizons, they're peaceful and it washes you out inside. The next morning, risking that the I-net cafe would be sporting a different docent, I wheeled over, only to find it closed. Let's try the Post Office. The native Kazakh managing the station confirmed the cafe would be closed all day, and then offered to set me up with his admin office computer upstairs; proudly mentioning that it was the only internet connection in town today. Like tapping out a message at the telegraph office in an old West town on the edge of nowhere, I couldn't tie up the connection with picture uploads. But it was nice to jot out a blog, to say "hey everyone I'm still here."

Despite a late start, and being flagged down by folks on the roadside wondering who's that, as well as cars pulling over to chat; and another slow leak rear tire that was needing a pump up every 20k's, I managed to make Taskesken, 100k's away. Heck, one family stopped to talk on their way wherever, and again on the return trip in the afternoon! There was a police checkpoint that was all grim stiff and official, until they inspected the passport and visa. And then, as if someone left the gate open, all the officers in their big hats emerged from the building and began snapping phone photos. Everyone smiled with a mouthful of gold! I was noticing that gold was a popular front row choice here, for both men and women. This is the most desolate place you'll never be alone in.

In the magazin in Taskesken I was making that head-on-the-pillow motion to get some advice on a camp spot, when a local named Nurislam offered a stay with his family, a few blocks away. There were two small white plaster homes on the plot, one for he and his brothers, and the other for Mom and Dad. An outhouse was at the end of the common ground, and a long, open shelter, which housed the outdoor oven; all centered by a hand-pumped well. Mom had a propane burner in the house for a quick tea, but all the large pan and baking tasks were done outside. I'd seen this before up in the Urals but not with such a purposeful structure, it was made of what looked like clay or thick plastered brick. Essentially a half mini-kiln for baking, and half stove top, both with their own fire chamber. His folks were wonderful, very welcoming, and I could feel the luck of having met them.

They were Turkic Kazakhs, Nurislam was about thirty, and an officer with the Kazakhstan Army, piloting supply planes out of a base near Ayagoz. "Would you like to bathe?" Expecting to be shown the bath or water-can shower, I grabbed my little bag and was surprised to follow him a few blocks to a stream, running just outside the village. Stones had been built up to form a metre-plus deep pool, a giant natural tub where his Dad was already enjoying a wash. He said that most homes have a small shower, used mainly by the women, but the men of the village traditionally use the stream. We stripped down and waded in, then dunked under to come to terms with the clear, cold water. It was dusk on a warm summer evening, and a small green meadow surrounded the pool, a beautiful, peaceful setting. So different, open bathing. A natural harmonic of enjoying the back and forth of casually telling the story, while Nurislam translated to his Dad, and all the while soaping up the limbs, having a shave and washing my hair in the creek.

Both homes were adorned with bright floor and wall rugs, and but for the prominent framed prints of Mecca's Kaaba, the décor strongly compared to Southwestern Native American designs. We had a simple dinner of cabbage, mutton and rice, with sweet hot tea, and the mood was lively. Surrounded by a humble home, his parents were a happy pair, and very aware of the world's

events and the players in the American Presidential election season that was under way. It was a great evening. After a good night's sleep in Nurislam's place, I awoke to Mom pulling a warm bread loaf out of the brick oven, and then served up a plate of eggs. They all watched as I swapped out that leaky rear tube with a fresh one, and after a few heartfelt goodbyes, it was back on the road again.

Such a nice stay with such nice people, this whole trip has been so much more about good folks than "wher'd ja go? Wha'd ja see?" It couldn't seem to get much better, but the good people just kept coming.

The 80k-plus ride, pushing along A-356 to Urzhar was a day of strong wind and heat. With the fight and the sun, the water was gone by the time I'd climbed up the hills above the city's plain. A wedding party was at the crest, taking photos and having a pre-ceremony picnic. Soon, I was in the middle of it all. They were in a grand festive mood, and at first offered water, which led to vodka and pastries. The beautiful, dark haired sister of the groom spoke very good English, and gave the group a quick run-down on my progress. And didn't that call for another toast! I'll bet the reception was a hoot.

Where the highway splits into town, a large Volga sedan pulls up with a couple of older well-fed guys and their wives aboard. The driver popped out and jovially inquired as to where I'd come from, he was a happy sort and translated the story to his passengers. The women came out and gave me a bag with cucumbers and a loaf of bread, and one tried to hand over a watermelon! I gratefully explained I couldn't possibly lash on a watermelon. Handing it back, I could see the disappointment in her eyes. The man offered that I must stay at his hotel on the outskirts of town "where Cosmonauts come to rest." Cosmonauts? Well hell yeah! He gave me directions that seemed to wander about in thick Russian-English, but I tried to hang on to the lefts and rights, while imagining just how wonderful his secluded Cosmonaut worthy resort must have been. They drove off and I followed, but after a few k's of pedaling, it dawned on me; I hadn't a clue where I was supposed to turn.

It was approaching dusk, and despite a bag of cucumbers and bread for camp somewhere, with Urzhar and a chance at a hotel were just behind me, I rolled back into town; a kid pointed to the center for a hotel. As I pulled up, the small staff were outside and waiting, as if forewarned, excited that a Westerner had arrived. They brought out a cold beer, and seemed so happy that I'd made it to their little place. It looked like pretty nice digs, with a restaurant and an outdoor dining patio, with a DJ booth already set up. When I rubbed the fingers together, asking for the Tenge, they surprised back with "no charge, you are guest." For real?

I kid you not, they offered a room and dinner in a very matter of fact way, as though they were expecting me. Its location in the center of town wasn't anywhere near the Cosmonaut offer; my senses were swirling as to how and why, I was amazed and grateful. Like a celebrity, the staff escorted me to the room and showed off the two beds, and how to work the TV remote and shower. I assured them it was very nice, and as I wheeled the bike through the door and sat down, a lovely young twenty something Kazakh girl named Sholpan and her ten-year-old sister came through the door. She had excellent English, and because she didn't work for the hotel, it occurred that she had been notified and appointed Urzhar's official translator. That being the case or not, she was great to talk with, as she related the details of the story to the staff, who crowded the room's doorway. We fielded all of their questions.

After a shower and dinner on the patio, she showed up again and kind of broke the ice with all the people arriving for the dance night. The place turned into Urzhar's night club, as the spiffed-up locals happily danced the evening away to the classic rock standards, the young DJ dedicating "Hotel California" to me. After a few beers and turns on the dance floor, the hotel's owner, a native Kazakh man in his mid-fifties', came by and cordially insisted I come with him. In moments, we were tooling up the town's main street in his Mercedes. I couldn't understand what he was saying, he was very much assuring that I would enjoy it, and I could only imagine we were heading to meet someone important, or banya, or girls, or...? It was to be special, but I couldn't have guessed it in a hundred years. He was a friendly fella and was quite excited to show me something. My guesses were way off.

On the edge of town, we pulled into a dirt lot of three yurts, and went inside the biggest one. It was about 10 metres round and dimly lit by a few bulbs hanging from a cross brace. A gracefully aged Kazakh woman, in the traditional ankle length layered skirt, under a rich red heavily embroidered thigh length coat, smiled as my host said a few words. We sat at an old table with a large wooden bowl, and as she pulled the cloth cover away and ladled two cups full, I realized that this was the Kumis I'd read about months before. The lightly fermented mare's milk was a regional custom. It was a special drink, not just for its tradition, but also its tight supply. Commercially it is produced from sugar-fortified cow's milk, but this was the real thing.

Like a good wine, it was to be tasted rather than gulped, and my pal smiled at my every sip. It tasted sour at the start, then settled into a yogurt flavor. The western brain kept thinking of "how long has this raw milk been sitting out?" But its hint of natural alcohol said it's ok, it's self-preserving. My inner Dude flashed upon an ironic White Russian, but the truth was... I wasn't such a big fan of the Kumis. The nomad setting and my host's pride in the drink was the best part, he gave me a true slice of his country's customs. I sincerely thanked him. And yet, like so many experiences on this journey, I couldn't fully cherish its occasion until the journey's retrospect, time ages every moment.

After a couple of cups, we said our goodbyes as he paid the woman. Although here of course, we were in a tent, it occurred to me that ever since entering Poland back in May, I'd never once seen a person use a credit or debit card. Bank cards at the ATM's for notes of course, but at large or small markets, gas stations and restaurants, everyone uses cash. I'd discussed finances with different people; property and car loans were somewhat conventional, but credit cards for daily needs were never seen. Gennadi, back in Ukraine, once said that they do exist and were slowly growing, but why would a person risk getting into debt trouble? As an American with American ways, there was a hallelujah brother and no good answer, all at the same time. No good answer that would stand to reason. Back at the hotel, the dance scene had died down to a core group that hadn't tired. After a few more beers and a couple of whirls, it was looking like tomorrow would be a down day.

In the morning I awoke, wondering what the day would bring. I bet they have a great breakfast planned, probably walk the village and meet more people. Kill the day with a few good meals and kick it here in the room, just relax before striking across the desert, for the final push out of the country. Then I found the restaurant was closed, there wasn't anyone at the front desk either. A walk around saw the patio cleaned spotless, as if nothing had happened there a few hours ago. No guests were about, no staff, not a soul it would seem in the whole place. I was the only one there. Hotel California weird. My magic coach had turned back into a pumpkin and my servants had scurried away. I needed to thank someone, anyone, for the fascinating evening. But there was no one.

And with no adieu, the mule was packed and we rode out of town and into another social butterfly day in the desert. Not 20k's out, a BMW driver stops, and the chatty Kazakh has me follow him into his tiny village of Naualy, to his café. On the way in, another group of a dozen teens, boys and girls, were cooling off by jumping off the low bridge outside of town. They had a hundred questions. The trip, America, my house, how many cars did I own? After a group photo, I finally made the café. My host and I were the only ones at the breakfast table, but soon a few of his friends drop by. We finished off the meal then hung outside, with a round of smokes and vodka. On the road again, I meet Theo and his three friends towing a Lada, with another Lada. Which car needed the most help was hard to say.

Soon, repairs turned the road into thick gravel, as it paralleled a new section of highway being laid. After about 3k's of trying to obey the road work signs, while hopelessly pushing the pedals and steering the heavy bike through the dense pebbles, the fresh asphalt a hundred metres away was calling. Hopping up on the perfect virgin pavement was like flying compared to the gravel, and I figured I'd keep at it until someone yelled at me, but it never happened. 10k's later, it ended back on the old road, and there was Theo and his pals, and the two Ladas. A left front flat on the tow car had them stranded.

When I offered up the bicycle pump, they jumped in and took turns, rapidly pumping up the tire until the rim was off the ground again; off they went.

A family stopped and offered water, and a chance to pack the bike in the back of their Camry and head for a swim in Lake Alakol, just to the south. They would then drop me off in the border town of Bahkty in the morning. It sounded so good, but the no-car ride rule stepped in, plus the border was so close. Just keep riding fool, focus. Just shy of Makanchi, there was the Lada gang again. The flat tire came back, and I actually had the extra water to offer them a needed bottle. They rallied around the bike pump once again and soldiered on, all smiles. Further on, at the edge of town, I pulled into a tire repair hut where my desert friends were having a well-used, but airtight, tire mounted. They were buying the Cokes and smokes and I began with "I hear that Lada sports models are pulled by much faster cars" and "a Lada's engine is measured by how many horses are pulling." They shot back that "American's can't steal Lada's, because there is no automatic transmission." Oh, we were having fun, the translation was a bit slow, but it was great to razz back and forth. Hey, wait. How did our secret national stick shift scandal make it all the way out to here?

Rolling into Makanchi was like rolling into an old West town. Horses and pigs and chickens walked the streets in a traipsing fashion, as if owned by no one. Bicycles rolled by with re-bar for front forks, and horse drawn carts with truck tires were everywhere. I searched out the hotel that was behind the back streets, and set among decrepit concrete structures. There were cement stairways that led to nowhere, others rose to vacant, weed covered platforms. Long-ago abandoned concrete-pillared buildings were just awaiting that one good earthquake to finish them off. There must have been some kind of installation here at one point in time, perhaps military, maybe a factory, hard to say. The hotelier lady wasn't cheery, downright annoyed, and wanted 4000 tenge for the room and 3000 for the shower. I tried to explain, I didn't want the whole banya experience, just a shower. She finally settled on 5000. But then, after inquiring as to where's the nearest bank-o-mat for the cash, she changed tunes again and was back to 7000. I charmed her back to 5k, and took off, only to find the local bank, and their ATM, had closed at 5:00. Returning, it took some dimple flashing sugary sweet talk to let me pay in the morning. She did alright though, the hard-negotiated shower was a chopped off water pipe sticking out of a cement wall, ice cold. When I went to complain she says the cold water was better, healthier for me. Touché! And all this went down with few words in common, she knew what I was getting at, and I knew what she meant.

Later, down in the office to put a few beers on the tab, Miss Cheerful starts scolding me for walking about barefoot. While trying to look as uninterested in her noise as possible, another guest, a middle-aged Kazakh man, there with his wife and young son, came in to pay for the banya. He begins pouring vodka, he then pays for my banya, so he has someone to drink with! Next thing, he's giving orders to the family, telling them in mumbled Russian to go away, he and Brian are going to be drinking all night. Once in the banya, he starts talking big. He'll have the wife bring back more booze, and later on tonight, he's bringing in some girls for us. I'm just gathering all this in spurts best I can, we can't fully understand each other, and the vodka and hot steam are mixing. After the oak leaf bundle-less banya session, which was quite half-ass compared to the Volsky experience, we exit out into the warm night to find Mom and junior still there, sitting in the car. After an intense, pointed, family discussion, whereby Mom dresses down Dad quite sufficiently, my new buddy leaves; in the back seat of the car. And that was that. Vodka! You talk a good game!

In the morning I hit up the ATM for just enough cash to pay the debt and get me to the border, some 60k's away. After settling up, I rode past a group of young guys sopping and mashing up a pile of dirt to just the right muddy consistency, to create a poor man's plaster to coat a new brick shed wall. With some English, they swore by the routine as I questioned how it fared in a hard rain. We all watched as one of the younger boys took the loaded mule on a test ride up and down the street. Soon they invited me to stay for lunch. Walking into the yard, I met Mom and the grandparents and the sisters. It was a big family get together, preparing for a wedding to be held in two days' time. Lunch featured a cow killed "just last night" and as I helped ferry the dishes and plates out of the kitchen to the long outdoor tables, one of the guys explained the sight of farm animals wandering the streets. The distraction was the swarming dark cloud of flies that descended on us, and all the food, as it hit the table. While he spoke, he casually waved his hand across the top of the dishes, parting the sea of flies long enough to scoop a spoonful onto his plate, before they instantly closed back in. Cringing, I coolly followed suit, and loaded up a serving.

The way it worked, was every family paid into a central fund, we'd call it a co-op, and that allowed them a number of chickens, pigs and cows. When it was time to eat, they opened the front door and whichever fowl or swine was wandering by, became theirs to slaughter. Due to the costs and limits, nothing was wasted, what one family couldn't use or store in a timely fashion was offered to another; and the favor was paid back later on. How the co-op kept score on who used what was beyond me, but I had a feeling that in Makanchi, the small village buzz kept the system in check. When I asked about cheaters, he looked at me funny. He didn't know, it just worked; reminding me of the Ukraine bus fare trust. On one hand, it was an innocent working example of true Socialism. On the other hand, it didn't occur to them to label it. It was just a traditional community agreement.

23. green tea

So finally, about 11:00am on July 15[th,] I rolled out of Makanchi and settled into a rhythm to push away the final 60k's of Kazakhstan. It's a good rule of thumb to approach all border crossings in the morning, the chaps in charge are a bit fresher, and it gives time to deal with forms and official stamps. But mainly, it allows time to make distance beyond the centralized authorities before they think of another question or fee; plus, borders are generally seedy areas. Despite the rule, the late afternoon sun shined on my first image of the border buildings. I don't remember a fence line, just a dormitory or office building and terminal; a water tower, and the awning structure covering the two-lane highway. This was it, the Middle Kingdom was before me. The People's Republic of China, the most populous country on Earth, and the only thing between me and home. With papers in order, I rolled into the station. Before even stopping, guards motioned me over to the large long customs terminal. Armed border agents came forward to meet the front wheel at the terminal's entrance, directing me inside as they took the passport away. Likely, seen me coming for miles.

The bike was taken to a side area to the right, just inside the entrance, and without a word, three agents began fiddling with the plastic hasps holding the panniers on. I quickly stepped in to show them the release tabs before they broke something, and as I did, a smiling, uniformed girl guided me back towards a row of plastic chairs. In English, she assured me I mustn't touch the bike repeating "please-how-are-you-please-how-are-you, would you like some tea?" With a clipboard and pen, she starts into the first round of questions as her workmates removed the panniers and began emptying them on a large table. While being served up cold Lipton-like sweet green tea in a plastic bottle, I was flashing back on the interrogators at the Russian-Kazakhstan border and their similar script. How did you get here? How long have you been traveling? Whose money have you been using? How much money are you carrying? The wife, kids, brother and sister. Mom and Dad. Employer? Are you a wealthy man? Have you ever been in the U.S. Military? Would you like another tea?

Soon a higher-ranking man, judging by his age and formal uniform, came in and checked her notes. He then began asking the same questions, plus queried who had made the bicycle? Where will you be staying at night? How many friends do you have in China? Which consulate granted the visa and who is sponsoring you? The camera's stored photos were examined, there was a question of what the small bottle of talcum powder contained. And then they stuck a digital thermometer in my mouth for a temperature reading. Ah, public health care. Would you like some more tea?

The damnedest thing was, this was somehow pleasant. Easy and very polite, like a drawn-out interview one must suffer through for a job you know you're going to be really good at; very un-Savinka-ish. Armed military guards sure, but the prospect of being carted off to a remote, fortified barbed compound, to face a double agent translator and angry interrogators seemed remote. To be fair, that ordeal was due to a dumb-ass trying to cross at a restricted border point, the Russians figured I was up to something; but let's allow dramatic comparisons here. Soon, the Big Kahuna, the Chief Officer of the border station came in, and in perfect English, introduced himself. An older man in an impeccable dress uniform, he expressed amazement at my journey and wished me a happy visit. Would I be attending the Olympics? "Ah, to my great dismay..." Above all, he asked if I had been treated well, and of course, would I like some more tea?

I was instructed to repack the bags and snap them back into place on the bike. After they took turns snapping group photos, the happy smiling inspectors wished me good luck and handed back the stamped passport. It had taken well over two hours, but there ya go, I was in. Walking the bike through the terminal, I'd only gone a dozen metres before hitting another checkpoint, this time with a short sour faced agent hard-eyeballing me in front of a large, airport security size, spectrometer device. Before I could say "I'm the guy that just went through all that over there..." the gruff agent snatched the passport from me and directed that the bags were to come off. A stone's throw away, my green tea friends smiled and turned away, as though Barney Fife and I were the only ones in the building. I robotically detached the bags and watched them all pass through the machine, herking and jerking back and forth as the man carefully examined each red bag with suspicion. My heart sunk like a smack smuggler as he momentarily stared at the clear outline of the still-undiscovered slingshot in the tire bag, but then advanced on without a hitch. His stubby fist slammed another stamp in the book, and I knew to hang the bags back on without so much as a smile or thank you, or my goodness, a cold tea. He was the lone loyal regimented sentry above question, guarding the gates of Kitai from the Western intruder. It's their border, their game, but now I was truly in.

Tacheng, Xinjiang Province, a good-sized city, is just 20k's past the border. As I approached its outskirts, a brown, weathered, happy man on a bicycle joined up. After hearing the words "California" and "hotel", he motioned me to follow. Soon, another rider joined up and got the short story from my partner, then another, and another. The crowd itself caused more to join in. I was so elated, this was so remarkable, it was like the ending of an inspirational movie as I rolled into my first city of China. Surrounded with a posse of close to twenty deputies, all just smiling and pedaling along; imagining the thunder of a glorious U2 anthem.

We stopped outside one place, and several of my boys went in, only to be turned away. No explanation, no matter, just smiles and back on the bikes, to ride closer to the center. And it was all so fascinating. Two and three wheeled bicycles and scooters darting everywhere, colorful banners and signs plastered blocks of buildings, that looked like a perpetual four-story budget strip mall down every road. Glass-fronted stores draped strings of triangle mini flags from the floors above to the trees lining the sidewalks. Large appliance boxes crowded

 the walkways, street vendor carts were pushed along by young boys and ancient men; women in summer dresses strolled about, hidden by parasols.

We stopped out front of another decent looking hotel and my boys ran in, and again, they returned in no time. No rooms they gestured, and off we went. I didn't care, enthralled by the streets of hustle. As if every store's minimal decor meant nothing, just having the empty space to market your wares today meant everything. Any one of the kitchen products or food markets or hair salons or electronics shops could have swapped each other's generic store fronts tomorrow, and it wouldn't have mattered, like vendor space at a flea market. There was a newness to it, as if everyone was awkwardly attempting to emulate a Western image. And of course, like Kazakhstan's cities, all the cars were honking endlessly.

After handshakes and pictures, my helpful group of escorts left me at the front desk of an accepting hotel. The place was nice and the price escapes me, but the Chinese Renminbi, or Yuan, was trading six to the dollar; so, everything seemed a bargain. There is no succinct way to explain the feel of the lobby, but the false front of a movie set came to mind, as if they didn't design it like they wanted, but the way they had been told from on high. Passport info was taken, and no key was issued, there was a 24-hour attendant on every floor to open your room. After a shower, I bopped downstairs to find some dinner, and ran into three Russian-Kazakh freight drivers, who ask me to join them. They regularly crossed the border, and knew the neighborhood. Russian Kazakhs, I knew what this night would be like, and I was up for it. A celebration was in order, for I had just ridden my bicycle to China.

A couple of blocks away, we posted up at the outside table of one of their usual diners and was met by the proprietor, carrying a tray of beers and beer size vodka bottles, and happy to see them all again. What would become a mealtime tradition for the next two months, no matter the time of day, a bowl of watery noodles in a salty vegetable broth hit the table. The dinner bowl was differentiated from the breakfast edition with small bits of chicken. Grigori was a tall, tanned, talkative fellow in his mid-50's who drove the conversations through the night, Viktor was a few years older. His English wasn't as adept, but had no problem keeping up. Yuri was about my age and fluid in English and Chinese, all easygoing veterans of this vast desert route. The trip, our families, and our common routes started the conversation. Then, politics in the U.S., and the troubles with the Russians and Chinese filled the warm night as the beer and the laughs kept coming, fueled by the octane boost of the clear Russian juice. The four of us were on a drunken roll when at some point of the loud warm buzzing table slapping clatter a plan formed, to rise early and rent scooters. My friends were going to take me on the city tour. "You can ride scooter Brian?" "Hell yeah, better than all three of ya" blathered the animated brash braggart, Mr. Vodka.

Next it was off to a telephone center, my buddies wanted me to call home and tell the family I'd made China, their treat. The center was a room full of telephones hanging on the wall, pay an attendant up front for the time and talk away. Somehow, we managed to get through and son Shay answered. I hadn't a clue of what time of day it was in California, and although I hadn't spoken to anyone at home in weeks, the conversation was just a drunken fumble of words. One of those late night stupefied "hey dude guess where I'm at" raves, I guess. Don't really remember much.

Of course, there was no scooter tour the next day. We all hit the sack in the wee hours, and a knock on the trucker's door in the morning found them all nursing hard hangovers. It was just as well, I too was groggy, along with tossing up whatever was in last night's dinner, plus a bout of the trots. After popping a few bismuth or Imodium pills that Gennadi gave me back in Donetsk, I headed out into my second day of China, in search of a market for some fresh basic food. A lovely big-eyed stylist in an empty hair salon beckoned as I passed by her window, and within moments I was in the chair. She clipped away at the mop that hadn't been touched since Zhytomyr, west of Kiev.

Single cylinder diesel three wheeled trucks putt-putting by, three wheeled scooters and bicycles transporting veggies, and bags of flour and rice, filled the streets. Rows of billiard tables, permanently stationed outside and weathered and faded by countless days of rain and sunshine, were full with teenagers shooting pool. Many iron gated alley openings and empty shop fronts were manned by small groups of men, sitting at cheap plastic tables and chairs, smoking the morning away, not appearing too concerned whether someone would stop and buy whatever they had boiling in large pots. There was such

surprising enterprise in every direction, going against what I'd expected to find in the Communist regime; this border town bustle was as alive as any other border city. As I headed back into the hotel with some fruit and just-add-hot-water ramen noodles, I figured the deeper one ventured into the country, the pace would change.

Seconds after entering the room there was a knock at the door. Two policemen smiled a hello and walked in uninvited. One spoke passing English, and inquired if I would like to please sit down and answer some questions. Since they were already in the room, it didn't come across as a choice. He explained that they have to inquire of all foreigners, and began the questions as his partner wrote down the translated answers. Like yesterday's border exam, here we go again. After jotting down the passport and visa info, then came the "who is paying for your trip?" "How much money do you have?" "What is your route?" "Will you be visiting the Olympics?" "Have you enjoyed visiting China?"

Annoying for its unusual nature, but ever so friendly, he even suggested an alternate route to stay off the main highway, silently dismissed. Before leaving, they snapped pictures and thanked me for my time. My pleasure fellas, always happy to help. Not an hour later, the door knocks again and some guy, just some regular smiling middle age man, who had heard an American bicycle tourist was in town, said he just wanted to meet me. After a chat and a photo and jotting down the email address, he departs. Fifteen minutes later, he returns with his buddy. They were such a happy pair; his friend also just wanted a picture and to say hello. I was more grateful than suspicious, and yet taken aback. It was just the start of the days to come.

Clearing the outer city of Tacheng the next morning was a tour of urban renewal, interrupted. A couple of streets were torn up with broken, heaved pavement, bulldozed into metre high humps. The scene was one of major street repair, yet the road was still open without a crew or barriers in sight. The few cars that came by were skirting the trenches, and just managing to clamber and scrape over the mounds, before casually motoring on, as if abiding a speed bump. As in Russia, this didn't appear a litigious world. Once clear of town, I came to a standstill at the first highway sign. Everything, but for the numbers, Chinese; of course. Chinese and oddly enough, Arabic symbols, marching and squiggling across the green signs, with only the arrows recognizable to my Western frequency. My map had the city names in English, and above the letters, in small print, were the tiny Chinese characters. It never occurred that I'd call on them. And so, began the practice of matching the symbols above each word to the corresponding figures on the road signs. Karamay, the next big town down the road, began with a character that looked like a radio with an antenna, walking on two legs. Follow the arrow towards the shuffling radio, and figure there's only 5000 kilometres of good guesses to go.

After being stopped and greeted and asked the story by drivers and motorcyclist several times, I managed to cross over a semi-arable landscape, carved out of the bleak desert, for a mere 60k's before putting on a new rear tire, outside of Emin. Along the way, the road surface became excellent, and ran through irrigated yellow fields of corn and safflower. There was a village whose buildings and homes and thick-walled fences were all made of mud, "from-the---town-of-Bedrock, they're a page right out of his-toh-ree." Outside a market in Emin, a crowd developed, and I was soon surrounded by at least thirty people taking pictures and slicing up watermelon. They served up tea and cigarettes as I told the story. After an hour, I broke free and moved on...for about 200 metres, before another group outside a small diner waved me over.

I couldn't seem to say no, everyone was so nice and they were honestly amazed at my passing by. Before long, two dozen people were gathered around, shaking hands and offering smokes and serving a long leafed hot tea with a marble size nut in the bottom of the beer mug, that I believe was for sweetening. A delicious bowl of chow mein was offered up, and as I finished it, an old man and a studious looking young woman in her early twenties pulled in on a small motorcycle. Ching Lan was the local English teacher, whose friend had phoned that an American bicyclist had arrived. She hurried over on the back of her father's little Honda 125. Their neighbors owned the diner and offered to watch the bicycle, a gut check told me it would be safe, stashed behind the counter. Off I went on the back of her father's scoot, as she followed behind with a friend.

We pulled into their place a few blocks off the highway. Their simple home was a rectangular building, split into three rooms and fronted by a brick walled yard area of about 10 by 15 metres, filled with cornstalks. Mom met me and began slicing watermelon, and then fired up the outdoor kiln oven; again, housed in a separate hut off to one side of the house. Despite a belly full of chow mein, I hadn't the heart to refuse her jiaozi, something of a boiled dumpling dipped in a chili sauce. Afterward, Dad zipped me back to the diner to pick up the bike. Upon returning, I met Ching Lan's brother, a serious-minded lad, about a year younger than Sis. He had just started up a motorcycle repair shop in the village, and the two of us hit it off right away, once he found another mechanic was in the house. The rest of the night was spent on the warm porch telling the tale and listening to this happy family's story, with Mom and Dad getting the translation almost as fast as I could talk, through Ching Lan's rapid-fire skill of dual languages.

One of the three rooms was brother's, where they put me up in his shared bed, although bed doesn't do the raised platform justice. It was four metres wide and three long, filling the room wall to wall, and it would become a common style throughout China's west. No mattress, just a fibre mat and a blanket on a board top, but I slept great that night. Exhaustion, the best sleeping pad. In the morning, I found the toilet hole in the dirt behind the cornstalks. After Mom served up a bowl of noodles and pork, we said our goodbyes, as though they were sending one of their own off into the far unknown. Really wonderful people,

 they didn't feel like just some folks putting a traveler up for the night, I felt welcomed. I had been very lucky to meet them.

The road now undulates under a hot July sky through arid ground, with signs of dried up rows and partitions gouged into the desert for farming. After a couple of small villages, the few patches of melons and grapes faded out, 30k's from Emin, when the desert took back the land. At the bottom of a long decline on the S201, a white Accord pulls over and out pops Fengge, one of the several people who had pulled over to say hi yesterday, on the ride from Tacheng. He's returning to Urumqi, the largest city in western China, and the capital of the Xinjiang province. As I scratched out the website, he told of his bicycle club friends who would be very interested in meeting up and hearing the story. The city is three or four days out for me, and he soon offers that we break the bike down and stuff it into the back seat of the Accord, "we'll be there tonight!"

Despite the heat, the magic of wanting to feel every moment of China's deserts made it easy to say no, I took his number and promised to call once I arrived. There were some pretty vacant lands ahead, but this was it. Geographically, this was the pointy end of the trip, and I wanted to roll it, to feel it; for we were now following part of the northern leg of the legendary Silk Road. Predating western history, scores of travelers had walked these routes for centuries, paving the cultural and social connections between the Far East and Europe.

The conception of trade and imperialism, and the spreading of awareness beyond one's own horizon, all developed centuries before the Greeks or Romans, or the story of Italy's Marco Polo; right along this path skirting above the Taklamakan and Gobi Deserts. In general terms among western populations, there was a vast dearth of information outlining China's lands, their history and development. I felt as though I was about to be served. One could stare out at it through a tour bus window, or study it in an ivy-covered university, but nothing was going to beat sitting in the dirt with the Hans or Uyghur or Mongols and slicing up a melon; and listening.

The road rose from a sandy depression up to a high spot with a village. The route splits south here and the village should be Tiechanggouzhen, but it was a hazard guess, until stopping outside a large, classic pillared building to ask. Out strolls a tall elegant woman of about thirty, greeting hello's in English. Katy confirmed it was T-town, and when I asked about a hotel she was surprised, "here, this is my hotel." I couldn't tell, if there was a sign, I couldn't read it. Sheepish but thankful, I followed her around back to lock the bike in a shed under the three-story inn. We then climbed up the back stairs and through the kitchen, to a wide airy front lobby. She showed me to a modern and clean room on the second floor with a full bath and television, it was a wonderful unexpected find, and it seemed I was the only guest.

Later, after she showed me around the kitchen to pick out ingredients, we had a long talk over dinner. She did her best with pen and paper to school me in the most basic Mandarin, to get by. Hello sounds like "neehow", goodbye is "zaichien", water and food pronounced "schwee" and "sheh-ooh." Yes is "shehga", no is "boo", tea is "cha". And hotel? That's "leeguan", but then "pingqua" seemed popular too. She touched on the common ethnicity of the region, explaining the native Uyghurs versus her dominant Han Chinese, and the quasi Islamic junction of both in the Hui people. And, which explained some confusing clocks, alerted me that all of China, a country comparable in size to the lower 48, was all on Beijing time. That's geographically and administratively analogous to the entire U.S. on D.C. time!

Katy managed the books and cleaned the rooms, her brother managed the maintenance jobs, and they both cooked and catered the guest meals. She had earned a business degree in the East, but returned to her home to make a go of the inn, hoping that the adjacent oil fields between here and Karamay to the southeast would give her steady business. A few days into the great Communist experiment of Red China, and all I've seen is small business hustle and entrepreneurship ruling the day. She was a treat to talk with, and on top of it all, the next day she refused to charge for the room. But I wanted to, I wanted to put up for the great stay and a meal and evening, but she wouldn't take it. "You are a friend, you don't pay." Kool kool Katy.

A hard rain through the night put a fresh face on the sunny morning, as the bike rotated into the desert hills vista of eroded sandstone. The tan to red soft stone sat atop itself in odd shapes, like a crumbled version of southern Utah's Zion, and along with it came the climbing. It was a good measure of the new fitness, and slowed things down to take in the beauty, that turned into a bleak black rock moonscape by midday. It came to a 100k day without a cafe or gas station, and I was thankful for a few clouds keeping the temps down. At a dry riverbed, about 30k's out of the sizable city of Karamay, a group of guys took pics and offered some needed water. They said they'd meet up with me on the edge of town and spend the evening. As the land turned back into sandstone, I was rewarded a long downhill into the city, just as the gift water ran out. As the bike rolled into the wide busy streets, I knew that seeing them again probably wasn't going to happen.

Karamay was a bright city of fresh cement, modern buildings and broad, tree-lined streets. As if someone had recently decided to erect an idyllic planned community on the harsh plains of an alien planet. There was a Disneyland perfection about it, this had to have been by design, rather than evolution. As I sat on a warm spotless sidewalk, dripping light oil on the chain, a well-dressed Uyghur man in his forty's approached and began asking the tale. His flat was a minute away, and the next thing, we're at his kitchen table with cold beers and an offer to stay the night. Turghun was a truck driver whose wife and daughter were away visiting family in the far western city of Kashgar, near the Kyrgyzstan border, just to the southwest. With the family gone, and a surprise visitor from America, he called up a couple of friends to come over for boy's night.

Inside the floor level two-bedroom apartment, the décor had the wife's touch. Light blue carpet and walls, and dainty French style cream furniture, and tea cup hutches with those cabriolet arched legs and lace. When his buds showed, I noticed Turghun locking the front door. Beers all around, and as he told them the story, they began to talk among themselves in Uyghur. It is something of an Arabic tongue I couldn't possibly fathom, but it did explain the road signs. It didn't really matter at the time, what with a 100k day under me and nothing to eat since Katy's this morning, I was hoping they were discussing dinner, but knew that wasn't it. They had me follow them into the main bedroom, that was just as faux antique as the front room, with a low hanging mini chandelier and a flowery bed. When they locked that door, I hesitated. I was visibly leery of the move and Turghun picked up on it, so he filled me in.

We were going to get high. Behind two locked doors, we then crawled over a short partition in front of the bedroom window that faced an alley, the four of sitting cross legged below the ledge. They instructed to hold the low grade schwag in the lungs as long as possible, then exhale out the window. It was like being a teenager again, sneaking a hit at Mom's house, a relaxing surprise which soon led to talk about U.S. pot laws. After I explained that it came down to state laws, some were very lax and some could still demand a little jail time, they dropped the bomb. In China, the penalty for any amount was imprisonment, with years of hard labor or death, which wasn't uncommon, "but tourist ok." Whoa. With that sobering buzz kill, the risk of smoothing off the rough edges didn't seem like such a good idea. Fully understanding

their precautions now, and enjoying their trust and hospitality, it was clear that lighting up in China could be a serious trip killer, an avoidable risk.

While on a long evening walking tour of Karamay, Turghun filled in on the city. The name was Uyghur, for black oil, and it did indeed just begin to sprout up in the 1950's, once petroleum was struck here. For a town of its size, it was one of incredible wealth. There were elaborate parks and business offices and shopping areas. At one square, a giant jumbotron on the side of a building, seeming to exist only to support the screen, was showing one of those "someone thinks they got talent" programs. The warble-ette was belting it out through a system of large remote speakers spaced about the park, while evening crowds strolled about eating ice cream. Everything was clean, a relaxed air, civilized. But there was a thin sheen to this perfect town, evident whenever questions about life in China came up. Turghun would always correct with the emphasis that he and his were Uyghur; "Weegrrr," he would say with zeal. They didn't consider themselves Chinese citizens, rather, an occupied people.

The petroleum industry was controlled by the Han, or what the world considers traditional Chinese. If not for Katy's Chinese primer, and the animosity expressed by Turghun, I'd have never seriously pondered that there was an actual designation, or ethnic title, for the billion Chinese throughout

Asia and the rest of the world. With the discovery of oil in the 50's came control of the zone, via the hasty arrival of thousands of engineers and workers that coincided with the new Communist regime of Mao from 1949 on. It all added up to shoving aside the Uyghurs way of life in a remote region, an affront that they were still not laying down for. It's a story as old as people themselves, lost on the march of time, and only becomes bitter when it happens to your people.

From Karamay, the desert winds blew against me, albeit on an excellent road, over flat terrain. But for an occasional abandoned cinder block structure set way off the highway, or a melon stand, there wasn't a roadside business or home; other than the national gas stations, set at 30, then 20, then 30k's apart. They were nice stops, all red and white and fairly new, staffed by helpful, bright faced young people. Cold drinks and cigarettes, hot water noodles and marinated vacuum-packed chicken's feet, the national snack. After about 100k's, a small cafe looking joint outside of a mud hut village appeared. I stopped to ask about some chow and putting up the tent.

The friendly woman sweeping the stoop was all smiles, and was happy to have me stay. She had to check with the owner though, and as she disappeared inside, two young women stepped out. Another girl came out, and then another, they were all excited and took turns trying to communicate. It soon struck that I'd stumbled upon a genuine Chinese truck stop cathouse. The mind began to dance through the interesting evening ahead, and then the foul faced man in charge stepped into the picture. He began snapping at the girls and waving his arms and motioning me to take off. No one but broom lady made a stand, but it was clear my presence, or business, wasn't welcome here. Too much attention.

From the highway out front of the love shack, I could see a village to the west, and after a 3k ride, came upon a nameless hamlet, where I found a sixty-yuan ($10) room. The front desk was manned by a brother and sister who couldn't have been more than 14 and 12 respectively, both of whom stood dumbfounded when I walked through the front door. There was a voice of a Ma or Grandma barking instructions over the clamor of a loud TV set from another room, as junior made the deal and missy stared on, as though a sun baked apparition in shorts had just vapored into her view. Their perplexity turned to avid interest as they took me to the room, it had an AC unit and a TV, yet it was entirely possible that the toilet and shower had never been cleaned. My glances and questions were lost on them, as foreign noise. All these kids wanted to see was the website and pictures and hear the story, the boy summoned up some slow English and his sis was trying a few words. I wrote out the web address and they took off for the nearest internet café, yelling something back at the hidden voice, and I never saw them again.

Now it was just Ma and me. I brought her up and showed how there wasn't any hot water, she just shrugged and gestured "oh well" and went back downstairs, I passed on the shower. Later, I went out to hit the market for some ramen and found nothing but some crackers amid the empty shelves, as if some natural disaster had just left town. Memorable among the emptiness was four boxes of women's hair color, all the same shade of black. It occurred then that I was going to drop some weight here, the heat and wind and long riding days and a noodle diet was just what I needed, yeah boy. I felt a twinge of narrow guilt inside, thinking how nice a Denny's hamburger would be tonight.

Push. The next morning, the idea of ending the day's ride in a better place put me in a head down trance, just staring at the feet and pedals and taking spirit from the idea that every few metres forward brought me closer to Patterson. There was so much behind but so much ahead, the closing-in-on-the-finish ebullience hadn't kicked in yet, but a good honest day of work was the only path to that threshold. Oh, but there's another melon stand, still strange since this place doesn't come off as prime melon farm land, but it's the crop of choice.

Sun-beaten folks under homemade awnings, or sometimes just umbrellas, would be set up on the side of the highway, many kilometres from anything. They would flag me over and insist I enjoy one of their rugby ball-size yellow melons. It was always such a treat, and more than once I'd devour an entire one myself, it was energy and water and sweetness and filled the spot left empty by the noodles. It was a water intense fruit in a bone-dry dimension, there must be aquifers fed by the mountains to my south. I hadn't seen any canals, and a tree line indicating any sign of water was miles away.

After nine hours of riding, the morning hope of a better place came in a form that represented the life of these people, trying to scratch it out. It captured in a working mode what these folks will do to make it. The derelict, decomposing, three story cement building on the road's right was alive inside its ground level with a kitchen and an open room, with a large long table for feeding groups. Young "Jack" was glad to have me stay there, and showed me the family's house across the road, a single level door-less concrete brick structure that stored hundreds of bags of grain in the front room, as well as a wall-to-wall laundry line. A room off to the left with a lone cot was the cook's quarters that I'd be sharing for the night. After Jack left, I started to unpack the sleeping bag and pad, and soon, I was just staring out the windowless window port with a smoke, taking it all in.

It was like a no man's land. It was an unimagined China. Forethought's of Great Walls and pagodas and jungle temples were tempered by the known deserts ahead, but this place had a post nuclear look. As if Hell passed through here, and then everyone moved back into what was left standing. Since Katy's, and all the way forward until Urumqi, the bicycle needn't shift gears. A desert as flat as still water, speckled with weed-lined, chipped and burnt, cement buildings, with makeshift shade awnings and small motorcycles parked out front. These weren't homes, they were forgotten structures of some past business purpose. Did people own these shells or was there some legal form of squatting going on? Did the Maoist just figure that letting rural peasants occupy

these empty habitats solved a housing problem?

Like being dropped on Mars and left to guess, the strong hunch was that something had been started out here, a movement with big plans and government backing was set in motion, and then faded out, leaving cinder block debris across the land. I didn't know and it didn't matter, it just was, and I was just passing through. Once again, there was the desire to pluck one of these good folks out of here and plop them down in my world. Or the flip side, snap my fingers and place one of my comfortable American friends into this world, without the benefit of slowly transitioning over the course of months as I had. The gaping wide-eyed wonder of their faces could only be imagined. Jack and his Mom and sisters hustled a mini store and a cafe that serviced five busloads of travelers as the night went by. Their home was a grain storage hold, and someone did a lot of trucker's laundry, all this out of two buildings that the wind and rain could blow through. Never a day off, never a thought of golden years, just work until you can't. So many folks I've been the guest of were pillars of fortitude, they had no choice.

Dinner sounded great, chicken chow mein, although here it was pronounced mein jow, same thing. When it arrived, it came with a small empty side bowl to place the bones in, the meat wasn't separated from the bird before being blended in with the noodles. The plucked and purged fowl was laid out on the board and cleaved into about ten portions, head to feet, and cooked to perfection. Every bite had bones, to be carefully parsed through before swallowing. The feet, which are a snack treat here, were set off to the side. Granted, the feet and sinew were expected, but discovering the bright red comb-and-waddle adorned head with its shocked eyes staring up through the delicious brown sweet spicy sauce caused an honest start. I hadn't even seen it there, mixed in with the egg noodles and sprouts. Into the side bowl it goes, but despite that, it was a decent plate of food. It occurred to quit silently whining about the noodle water and just learn how to order something different when the opportunity presents. "Cheerow mein jow", I'll have to remember that.

Oh, and another thing since we're covering meals. Chop sticks. In any Murican' Chinese restaurant, it's a case of "sure what the heck, let's try the sticks, it's part of the experience." A bold limb to climb out on, since there's a set of utensils set off to your right. Here, there is no such thing, forks and knives are for the kitchen. Eating with the sticks is a simple task that must be mastered, ergo, a learning curve. I'd observe others holding the bowl or plate close and deftly working the sticks as an extension of their own fingers, perhaps a second thumb on each hand would make it easier. As the months would pass, I'd only attain the skill of not looking completely foolish while eating in public. Silently, I'd look about a diner or morning noodle hut and think jeez folks, it's been give-or-take 5000 years of groundbreaking ingenuity over here. You've invented parchment and gunpowder, pottery and ink and the compass. The seismometer and rockets, dental fillings and the chain drive and playing cards. And no one here thought of a fork? Of course, they had, they just like their chop sticks. I'm just passing through.

Not long after I sacked out for the night, the chef came home. After lighting some incense, he motioned that I was a guest, and my place was on the cot, not the floor. Gesturing that the cement floor was just fine; please, this is your bed, it's good, I'm fine. But he wouldn't budge. The cot was cleared of his bedding and on went the sleeping bag, he went off to another part of the shelter, and I laid there feeling weird about not paying a dime for the floor space, now a cot. Someday I'd be stumped when people would ask "what was the best place you saw? What was the worst?" I couldn't see any location in that light, I strove to accept where I was for its place. If asked to rate the goodness of people, the answer was becoming clearer. Once rolling off the ferry in Holland, the further East I traveled, the nicer and nicer people became.

It was July 23rd, and the desert highway S201 I'd been on since entering near Tacheng came to an end at the G30/G312 interchange. The G30 being the main east west road between the Xinjiang and the Gansu province to the east, across the melding zone of the Taklamakan and Gobi Deserts. At the junction, there was a large PetroChina fuel station manned, er... womaned, er... girled by a dozen teenagers in orange jumpsuits. They were friendly and chatty but always an eye out for an incoming car or work truck, when they would bolt off in mid-sentence and be ready to pump gas and clean windshields as soon as the car stopped rolling. I sat in the shade with an ice tea for some time, watching their NASCAR pit lane efficiency.

Loosely paralleling the G30 on the lonelier G312, I reached the large town of Changji and found a nice hotel in the center for about $25. It had been three days in the sun, and the room's hot water and a shower and shave, plus the mutton pizza downstairs in the night club restaurant was a centering experience. Afterwards, out in the warm night, I stopped for a beer with a street vendor and his son at their small kiosk. Soon, a crowd of young people gathered.

An hour went by, sipping and smoking and laughing while telling the tale. The kids enjoyed practicing their English slang, and I gave tips on the proper emphasis and interjection of our most popular filthy words. It was such a comfortable evening, just hanging out on the corner, and later, nothing beat the clean sheets and a soft bed.

Like all the former, and now current, Communist countries I'd experienced so far, the city's downtowns are modern and pleasant. Ten-k's out, it's still a hundred years ago.

A good sleep, another shower and a pork n' egg breakfast, plus an easy 40k day to Urumqi, had me in refreshed spirits as I rolled out of Changji in a mid-morning sun. Days like this called for a languishing slow rolling pace, taking in the sunshiny sights, knowing that it was all going to come to me before even one water bottle would empty. The endless desert panorama dovetailed into the hazy vision of the towers of Urumqi's downtown, like the horizon of Oz's Emerald City. Bigger than Houston or Philly, hell, almost the size of Chicago, it was the largest city in the entire western half of the country and supported well over three million people. And no one has ever heard of it.

Born Urabo along the northern Silk Road route several hundred years BC, the Han Dynasty took over the regions rule from migrated Europeans and changed its name to Luntai. It had since seen a layered history of Chinese, then Turk and Mongol, then Chinese rule once again, as the centuries past. Along the way it acquired the Mongolian term for "beautiful pasture", Urumqi. When the Xinjiang frontier formerly came under the Chinese Empire in the 19th century, it was changed again to Dihua, and finally back to Urumqi, once the decades long Chinese Civil War finally settled out in the early 1950's. That moment of bicycling upon a living ancient city over 2500 years old, and known as the farthest city on Earth from any sea, caused an astounding far from home sensation. I wonder if Fengge will answer his phone?

Nearing the center of the city, I pulled up in front of a bodega size market, they're cooking up kebabs and invite me to sit at the sidewalk table and enjoy a couple of sticks. The wonderful merchants stood and smiled as I tested their delicious lamb and pepper delights with a can of sweetened ice tea. They then gladly dialed up Fengge for me. Before long, he pulls up in the white Accord, and we break the bike down and distribute it between the trunk and back seat. I say farewell to my new bodega friends and off we go. Once underway he surprises me with "where do want to stay?" "I thought we were going to your home." Oh no, he explains, my wife and children and parents, there's not enough room. It's not the desert highway story I remember, but hey, slide it. "Well I have no idea then; would you know of a nice low-cost hotel?" He has a friend who runs the desk at a hostel "is that good for you?" Of course, that sounds fine. Around a few blocks we go, and come to a stop. Across the street from the bodega!

We had an odd laugh at the whole affair but no complaints, the Ibex Hotel I'd been glancing at moments before, as I devoured the sidewalk kebabs, was modern basic and clean, it would be home for tomorrow too. Fengge then took off, promising to return the next morning with his friends from the 1+1 bicycle club. After a hot shower, Fengge's buddy at the front desk told of a laundry four blocks away. Deciding to treat my few items to a proper cleaning, I hit the streets. After dropping off the goods, I wandered through an indoor mall, coming face to face with Colonel Sanders. "Ah-say ah-say, I do dee-clay-ah" My opinion of KFC in the states is that the few times I've eaten there, I'm reminded of why I never eat there. Love fried chicken, can't take their version of it. Well shut my mouth.

That place smelled pretty damn good, they didn't offer buckets or pieces, so I ordered up a couple of chicken sandwiches with a soda, and savored every bite. Like the lure of McDonalds in Kiev or a Coca Cola anywhere, with closed eyes I could imagine away the moment and be home. Oh Dorothy, you needn't rare ruby slippers, you needed a chicken burger and a Pepsi. The mall also had a large internet cafe that killed a couple of hours, as I caught up on the news and emailed home. Back at the room, with a couple of beers and a Vike, I ended the day catching up on the Tour de France, watching Spain's Carlos Sastre kick ass up the Alpe d'Huez. Warmly buzzed, marveling at that day's King of the Real Bicyclist.

The Chinese television consisted of multiple CCTV, or Chinese Central, channels that had one English speaking news station, manned by Western and Asian faces that smiled the Party line. Over time, it was clear that any news dulling the Beijing chrome was left out. Commercial breaks were never for products, just promotions for the business environs and tourist attributes of the different provinces, "Visit beautiful Gansu!" The actual programs were heavy with Kung Fu shows set in feudal periods, but hey what do we have to brag about?

On cue at 11:00 am, Fengge arrived with two friends from to the 1+1 bicycle club. The girl of her late 20's was decked out in full bicycle Spandex, and the fella was equipped with a nice camera; he began taking up close detail shots of the mule. We headed out to their friend's bicycle shop in a nice part of downtown, and soon a spread of different noodles and seasoned chicken and beer were brought in. A look around their store saw an upscale Shimano outlet, as modern as anything San Francisco had to offer, with racks of lightweight wheels and glass cases filled with the vaunted Dura-Ace and Ultegra line of derailleur and brake sets. I wondered if the prices were Western or could a guy fly in here and build a gorgeous road bike for a song? The constant flow of members dropping by to say hi never allowed for such questions to be considered aloud, and the hours passed by. The 1+1 club were a group of passionate bicyclists that staged weekly club rides and an annual long tour. Tomorrow's run was an 80k round trip lunch ride to see me off down the road.

After Fengge and friends dropped me off back at the room, I took a walk to burn off the beer buzz, which included picking up the laundry and one more visit to the Colonel. Following the routine, I settled back in at the I-net café. After signing into Gmail, my buddy Doug from the engine shop at work was on the Google Chat. Small things amaze, and to have a chance to back and forth with a friend almost 10,000 miles away was such a treat, someone knew where I was.

24. blow

It's now two days later. Sitting in a hotel room in Turpan, and what a couple of days it's been. Six members of the 1+1 club came by early on July 25th and treated breakfast, then we pedaled out along the wide avenues of Urumqi's business district, stopping along the way to pick up other members, who waited at prearranged corners. Ten bikes in all headed into the brown, low desert hills south of the city, and out onto the flats toward the village of Chaiwopu, past a farm of windmills numbering in the hundreds. Fengge drove ahead in the Accord to arrange lunch, and all along the 40k route, the members would rotate back to have a chat. If I was slowing them down, they didn't seem to mind. As we pulled up to the restaurant, Fengge shuffled us inside to a table set for eleven. The spicy chicken and ...and ...noodles went down well, and hanging with a group of good people who obviously really enjoyed each other was another tiny slice of belonging. Treasuring every minute, I knew that as soon as we said our goodbyes, they'd all head back to the city, and I'd head out alone across the ever-foreboding plains; never to see them again.

Dabancheng came 40k's later, as a small oasis beyond a long salt plain; and along the way was an oh-my moment. Camels. Some with saddles, some with a single rope around their long necks, and others, un-accessorized. It was astounding, looking down upon the old bike, reflecting the thought that we've ridden so far, we're seeing camels. Dabancheng's $14 room details are lost in the memory, to pop up in some future dream. But the next morning's ride will never be forgotten.

Riding south out of the village gave a view of the break in the Tian Shan Mountains, that the road disappeared through. Before it, a half mile wide gravel river bed, with a dozen rivulets wandering through it, created a mini valley of green meadows and trees along the mountains northern edge. Entering the gap was like being sucked into a vacuum. The lone break in the Tian Shans was a strong southbound wind portal, and coupled with the sharply descending road, the bike shot down into the canyon. There was an unfinished new highway being forged across the river to my right, but the roller coaster I was on was the old road. Narrow, bumpy, and littered with potholes. The turns were scattered with gravel at the road's undefined edge, but I didn't care. Deciding to see how fast and far this terrain gift would take me, I hunched over the bars and gave it a whirl.

Eyes far ahead, cluing for divots and sandy corners, hugging the turn's outside edge, then apexing inside using both lanes, the bike zoomed faster and faster. The thought train focused on how much time and space were being covered, and taking in the awe-inspiring barren Mar's-scape rocky canyon surrounding me. The rushing river to my right crashed around house size rocks, in a violent mud colored force that seemed to be measurably carving itself into the canyon. If a vehicle approached up the hill, I don't recall; none passed from behind as the mind raced through, and buried deep, the risks of flying a fully loaded touring bike down a sketchy road in far western nowhere. The bit was chompin', the ears pinned back and the red mist of speed was in the eye as the canyon clipped by like... fuck! Fuck! Fuckin' bag flew off! Faaaaw!

The same old problem that had popped up on occasion since the journey's earliest days had me slowly applying the binders, and bringing the windblown fury to a halt. The front right pannier was almost two hundred metres back up the road, and behind a turn. While it would have been nice to allow a moment for the buzz to wash away, I had to straight off climb back up the hill against the strong gusts to retrieve it. I couldn't wait, lest a clueless motorist came around the bend dragging my tent down the hill, stuck under the chassis.

The mist faded, the bit released, ears flapping normal again, the thrill is gone. When I popped a bag off barreling down the Urals, I secured the hasp with a piece of Velcro wrap that had actually done time in orbit, holding wire bundles together on the Space Shuttle. Not supposed to tell you where that piece came from. It worked like a champ, but it was the only one. I could use plastic ty-wraps on the front latches of course, but the bags were always being removed for some reason, requiring the ty's to be cut, and I only had so many. Whatever inner thoughts obstructed an easy fix, I hadn't done it. And blew one of the most visceral rides imaginable.

Below lay the Taklamakan, known as "the Sea of Death", the eastern sister of the Gobi was the largest and driest desert in China, and known as one of the largest shifting sand deserts in the world. But you would never have guessed it, as the mouth of the canyon spit us out onto its northern plains. A gravel expanse as far as the horizons to the south and east, imagine a dry river bed a hundred miles wide, it was scary in its nothingness. Not a shrub, not a sprout, like landing on a faraway planet. Just a few k's later, the swift advantage of the canyon's tailwind bit back as a vicious crosswind, as the G30 split east towards Turpan.

Wind speed is a hard guess, but if a 50-mph gust can knock a man over, then oh yeah, we were way above that. At first, the head goes down and the body counters hard left, you soak in the acceptance

that this is going to be a bitch for a while, dig deep and do it. It then became harder, even in the lowest gear, to play the balance of steering straight and staying a step ahead of the gusting forces, that pulsed as a car would pass by. The momentary interruption would burble the strong current. It was over 50k's to Turpan, but as the wind increased, it seemed an impossible distance. The body was crouched low to lessen the sail effect that the panniers created, soon the left knee was angled way out to tack the force, then the elbow, anything to keep the bike on the road... then a freight truck or bus would roll by.

Imagine a slow-motion cartoon animation. The crosswind, blowing so strong that the clown is leaning left, the left knee and elbow are pointing out, and the front wheel is pointing to the right, just to angle the bike forward in the fierce wind. No pedaling, just tack-sailing forward. The semi or coach bus passes by, long and tall enough to block the strong wind for about one second, the brain reacts and auto corrects the body to normal, to prevent a fall. The truck blockage passes, releasing a blast that blows the now upright character off the raised road and into a full off-the-bike tumble. As the scene is repeated, I got better at pointing the bike to the right and tucking the wheel into the gravel with the full front brake, just staying on my feet. It worked most of the times, but I still tasted the Taklamakan gravel too many times. Shifting sand desert indeed, I think this damned wind blew it all away.

A little over 20k's out of Turpan, another girl-powered PetroChina gas station appeared, its distinctive red fuel island awning rising above the vacant vista like a shimmering vision of solace. The water bottles could be filled, a cold ice tea and a snack was in order, all awash in the smiling, happy faces of Chinese teenagers. They were all giggling in a group when I wheeled in, until they noticed the state of the beaten, gravel-rashed character rolling to a stop outside the shop. As I walked inside, the air conditioning hit like falling into a pool, highlighting the day's heat.

Inside were comfortable couches and chairs, to relax with your ramen noodles and ice tea. The girls all took turns hearing the loose story, but I was somewhat shell shocked from the day's effort to be too animated. Like a blessing, the wind had slackened a bit before saying farewell to them, as they assured me Turpan was only fifteen minutes away. By car maybe. About an hour later, Turpan appeared, and I already knew I needed a decent room. The morning's canyon exhilaration had given way to a tough introduction of this inhospitable dry hot land. I walked into the lobby of a basic looking hotel, placed along a string of similar looking buildings. White exteriors and tinted windows, the structures were either pre-fab or of a single mind's design. The lobby felt like the one in Tacheng, done to some committee's sanitized standard of white walls and tile. The woman behind the counter understood through my appearance and hand gestures I needed a room, and a price was agreed to and paid. As I began removing the bags to hike the bike upstairs, she came from around the counter and began shaking her finger at me, abruptly pointing toward the front door. She then went back to the counter and came back with the cash, handing it to me and jabbering on, she wanted me to leave now.

What? No. I pointed upstairs, I wanted to stay. I was tired and hot and had dropped the guard for the day, I just wanted to rest. She couldn't explain in any way I'd understand, she just kept on talking and pointing toward the door. What had I done? Fine then, I'll go somewhere else, strange woman. I rode down the street a few hundred metres to another affordable looking place. As soon as I walked in, "no room, no room, go go" said the hand signals, I hadn't even opened my mouth yet. The lady down the street must have called here, they had to be in cahoots, or perhaps there were no rooms? What was this about? I knew I had only been nice to this point, maybe it's the aversion to drawing any attention to them by the local authorities, seen it before. Back up the street again to another hotel, across the road from the first. It seemed ok, I showed the passport and paid the rate. Finally, it felt resolved. Then, as soon as two Uyghur business men walked into the lobby, the desk clerk lady began insisting I leave immediately, and handed the yuans back.

No. Not this time. In English, which was about as much use as speaking Latin backwards, I insisted I had done nothing wrong, I'll be quiet, no problems. I just want to stay here, please, I apologize if I've...whatever. The business men were muttering between themselves but I caught "American" and "Kazakhstan." Then one of them looked at me and said "you had better leave now." A translator! I made the case to him that I'd been turned down thrice today and hadn't done anything wrong, what is this woman's problem? He just shook it off and said "you must leave now" and then turned his back. The conversation was over.

Plenty of desert, so the notion to clear this strange place of frustration and find a home on the range felt like the last option. Passing by a police station, I decided to stop and see if I was missing something. There's a hesitance to mix it up with such a marshaling force as China's National Police Agency of the Ministry of the Interior, but I had every right to be here, I think. The straight approach was worth a shot; but as I walked in the front door and opened my mouth the place came alive. A man came from behind the counter and requested the passport, another officer showed me to a side room and indicated I wait, shutting the door. Through the small glass pane in the door I could see other officers gathering and gawking, what have I done?

About five minutes passed by as I pondered the route and the people I'd talked to, and the places I'd stayed, wondering what transgression was afoot. This is crazy, it had to be something, but I'd couldn't imagine what. Then a young cop walks into the room, he was all smiles, creased uniform, clipboard in hand. In English, he began asking and writing down the usual's. Where have you been-where are you going-when did you arrive? Whose money are you spending-have you stayed in any hotels-are you going to visit the Olympics-what do you do for a living? I politely answered the list then popped the question about the hotel issue. "Oh, you are not allowed" he said, beaming, as if he had given the correct answer. But why not? "You are not allowed" he said again cheerfully, and then furthered that a tourist may only stay at a tourist hotel, which he then offered to guide me to.

But isn't every hotel a tourist hotel...? Then it hit me. In the early 80's I'd visited Russia for a week and a half with a tour group, mandatory at the time was that foreign visitors were only allowed to stay at government approved, or "Intourist", hotels. The idea was to put a shine on the apple. Visitors from outside the Bloc could only stay at upscale hotels, in order to come away with a positive opinion of the Soviet's quality of living standards. That, and the bonus of keeping an eye on visitors, knowing where they were at most times. They even restricted Russian citizens from coming into the hotel bars as guests of the visiting tourist. That practice had faded away now. The new Russia's freedom was more a casual-Friday's control of the populace, whereas China hadn't even considered loosening the tie yet, still all business. It all began to fall into place.

The two turn downs at the first hotels in Tacheng on the first day in country. The modern Ibex in Urumqi was obviously an approved international hostel, the hotel in Changii was a very nice place, ergo at tourist level. The small places, like the forgotten dive in Dabancheng and Katy's place, were in such small villages that perhaps the people didn't care. Maybe the authorities were too spare, the guests too few to be picky, and Katy didn't seem the type to be a fan of the Rules. This was a problem, in that mandated tourist hotels were going to run down the waning budget. I pedaled along following my cop buddy on his police scooter into the town center, through avenues abundantly bordered with trees. It was clear that water wasn't an issue in this oasis, surprising given Turpan's spot in the low desert. As we turned down a tranquil street, fronted by a small green park, I could see the hotel. The obvious reason for the tourist's hotel rule? It was probably the most expensive place in town.

At a 160 yuan, it was more than half again the price of my first choices, but

 the quick math put it at about $26, still a worldwide bargain for the quality of digs. Before handing me off to the concierge, the officer said in so many words that from here on out, just skip the middle man. He advised that every time I pull into a city, go straight to the police station and ask for approved accommodations. And one more thing, "mind if I look inside your bags?" Sure thing pal, you had me at a cold beer and a hot shower.

A beautiful mid-size town, Turpan had existed for over 2000 years. 2000-year-old cities were beginning to trend out here. There were hidden stories here that deserved a few days to take in. The nearby ancient earthen ruins of Gaochang and Jiaohe, the murals of the Bezeklik Buddha grotto caves, all thousands of years old. The region was rich in the vestiges of cities that had risen out of the desert soil, had served rulers and traders along the Silk Road for hundreds of years, and then faded away, back into the sand. Forgotten, like the mythical empires of an old Conan novel. But alas, I was just passing through, like so many visitors through the millennia. And like them, after a thorough day's beating by the sun and wind and gravel, and hotel clerks, my interest in anything but a soft bed after dinner was close to zero.

The 90k's to Shanshan the next day was one long, hot, continual climb. It began on the pebble-desert floor, with a perceptible push in every pedal. Like yesterday, the odd sight of full windshields of freight trucks dotted the gravel desert every so often, attesting to the high winds that sweep across these alluvial plains, tipping the rigs over. Odd, in that the rest of the vehicle was gone, but the windshields were left? As the road stepped up off the desert floor, back towards the Tian Shan's through a beautiful hillscape of tan and red and white layered terra, the heat and the climb had me out of the seat. Weighting each stroke with a full body motion, I wondered, how hot can it get?

These were the Flaming Mountains. Uyghur and Han folklore had them made of slain dragon's blood and angry Monkey Kings. The vivid colors and vertical erosion gullies running up their face made them indeed appear as a dancing flame, which only emphasized the bake. After a 10k climb, a small village appeared on top, and a welcomed gas station came into view. Ah, water. Every sip on a day like this wasn't enough, and even after I filled the gullet and bottles, a nice man pulled up alongside and handed me a frozen bottle. I found room for it. It was an oppressive dry heat, but when the bottles were full, I'd hit the road feeling invincible. The occasional roadside melon stands would appear miles from anywhere, and at one of them, the sun baked vendor flagged me over for a shade break.

He deftly split a melon in quarters with a heavy butcher blade, and I greedily accepted it. He was talkative and pleased I was enjoying his fruit, I couldn't understand him, but caught the gist of his questions, as his Shepard mongrel puppy dog scrambled through my legs and under the bench. The melons were so delicious. Again, the sweet and watery orbs had become a staple of the diet since entering the country, making up for the food I didn't really like and the liquid I couldn't get enough of. When a trucker pulled in with a flatbed trailer, stacked with those giant tires used on mining equipment, the lunch show began. The driver wanted to buy a dozen melons, and the negotiating would have made any car salesman proud. He wanted a good deal on the bulk purchase, and Farmer John was only bending so far. When they agreed on a price, the two began loading the melons into one of the used tires on the bed. I watched silently as the trucker stashed a couple of extras inside a different tire, and soon the farmer figured it out. A challenge, a denial, the volume is turned up. "In this coh-naah we have tha challan-jaa".

The war of words went viral, Farmer John obviously calling the driver a thief, and demanding the stolen fruit back. The driver was aghast at the accusation, going for the "how dare you, l would never" defense. Then the back and forth turned into a shoving match. As the trucker tried to climb into his rig, Farmer yanks him off the truck step and the driver comes around with a lame swing and a miss. John comes in with a solid chest punch, setting the driver off balance and "DOWN GOES FRAZIER!" Melon man then proceeds to jump up on the bed and take back his wares. The puppy and I, at ringside, are

staring on in disbelief the whole time; and of course, I grabbed another chunk of melon. The driver stood up and relented to justice, he knew he was wrong. Next thing the two are all smiles and shaking hands, as if a normal business transaction just took place, maybe it had. He gets in his cab and motors away, waving as if he'll return someday. Farmer returns to me smiling and talking, and gestures if I'd like another melon. Well, yaah.

The day played out with more climbing, the road was a series of steps, never declining, following the Tian Shan foothills. Another village of rammed earth and an Islamic cemetery passed by, both appearing to have risen out of the dirt, rather than built upon it. Camels wandered like range cattle, and up on the hill's ridges stood several long structures. They were erected of dirt colored bricks in a checker board pattern, with openings to allow the winds to pass through, like a course screen. They could be tombs, or storage, and then more and more came into view. But erected right on the ridge's edge? I had no idea. Riding along, I pondered the Celsius-Fahrenheit math, there was some 9/5ths rule of thumb that I'd never learned in school. Since entering China, most of the decent hotels had the day's temperature posted in plastic letters on a small board at the check in desks. 40, 42, 44. Pedal after pedal in the onerous baking heat, it suddenly became clear. 0 to 100 in Celsius is the range from water freezing to boiling. Fahrenheit's range is 32 to 212, exactly 180 degrees. And so, every 10 degrees C equals 18 degrees F, figure 1.8 for the single digits then add back in F's 32.

So, say 42 Celsius. 4(18) = 72. Then, 2(1.8) = 3.6. Now 72 + 3.6 + 32 = Shit! Almost 108 degrees Fahrenheit! My God I'd wished I'd never done that, it's been way over a hundred out here most of the days since the border! Some days over 111. Along with the most insane winds imaginable, this seemed all the crazier. Knowing made it so much worse. Despite the melon breaks and water, the incredible heat had me feeling like an empty bag rolling into Shanshan. Like Turpan, this small city basked among tree lined streets, an oasis that was set against a wisping dune wall of sand at its southern limits that stretched for miles to the east and west. Knowing the hotel rules, my first choice was successful, choosing a decent looking place near the center, rather than looking for the bargain. It almost turned around on me when they wanted a whopping 280 yuan ($46) to stay. I wavered, and began to say my goodbyes, telling them I needed a place for no more than 160. Quickly the rate dropped to 180 and I acquiesced, I wasn't of the mood or strength to keep shopping. When the door opened on the room it was all better, tidy with a shower, a TV and a computer with internet. The view looked over the town and out onto the golden dunes. I decide to stay here for tomorrow too; after Shanshan, there was over 300k's of nothing, not a village or town, until Hami. I would be counting on gas stations and good Samaritans for water and food. Needed to fill up the empty bag.

I was able to have a nice meal downstairs but it was getting to be a game to order, even with a picture of shrimp and pasta on the wall, I had a hard time getting the girl to understand. Soon, the front desk lady came by to help; the trouble turned out that the dear waitress was afraid of not understanding, and goofing the order. When a wonderful plate of spicy mutton and noodles arrived, we were all happy. The next morning, I managed to upload a slew of pics to the website without a hitch, and then ventured out to find an ATM. The card wouldn't work outside the bank. Inside, when it was my turn at the teller window, a sweet young lady was happy to exercise her English.

She pointed out that based on the symbols on the back of my card, this bank's ATM didn't serve those systems, but there was one down the street that would. She actually came around the counter and the two of us proceeded down the street, chatting away for about four blocks to the proper bank, she then waited as I withdrew the money. Walking back to her bank, I tried to imagine a teller doing that for a strange customer in L.A. Along the way, we talked of the trip and how nice Shanshan was. When I expressed surprise that anything could grow out here, she said something about karez. "Underground wells from mountains, so old." After returning to the room, I went online and looked up the word before I forgot it. Karez, oh man you got to hear this.

First developed here around about 200 B.C. and still in use today, these ingenious and ambitious people dug a series of vertical well shafts hundreds of feet deep called "mother shafts", far up in the snow-capped Tian Shan Mountains to the north. They then dug adjoining horizontal tunnels into the base of those mountains, nearby their various settlements, at a very gradual upward slope, to connect with the far away mother shafts. All along the way, they dug adjacent vertical shafts to provide oxygen for the tunnelers, and a way to extract earthen debris. As the high-altitude snows melt, or rains run off, the water is directed into the mother and access shafts. It flows down into the sloped tunnel and out to the plains, arriving at small reservoirs, or tapped into by traditional wells, the whole system working by natural gravity.

I was impressed as all get out by the story. The engineering and enormous man power to dig perfectly vertical shafts, while keeping the underground tunnels, some up to 20k's long, aligned with the mother shaft, and the choice to keep it all underground to reduce evaporation was brilliant. All in ancient times. Multiplied by hundreds, these systems ran across the Tian Shan front from Urumqi and east to Hami. The logistics were unimaginable, it has been referred to as the "underground Great Wall", and it made civilization in this forbidden land possible. The effort changed the direction of history, by providing water to service the caravans, enabling the direction of the Silk Road and its link to early Europe. I then looked up the question of those strange vented brick structures on the hill's ridge lines. They were fruit drying huts, smartly built on the ridge's edge for greatest airflow. Raisins were big around here. No karez, no water. No water, no grapes or melons. No fruit, no strange checker patterned huts and colorful roadside melon-farmer donnybrooks. Everything walked hand in hand.

The sun usually shines on me, even when it doesn't. The next day it didn't, plus the wind wasn't bad. The first day out of Shanshan, after a refreshing day off, was under overcast skies. A few k's out, a white Toyota pickup with a small slide-in camper pulled up. A casual looking middle-aged couple popped out, a young Chinese girl remaining in the cab. Fred and his wife, whose name escapes me dear woman, were a Swiss couple whose life's plan was to work hard for several years at a time, and then take off on another cross-world adventure. They had been through Africa, the States and Canada and were now heading for India through China. An absolutely enjoyable pair who played well off each other, they were full of funny little tales. They were sort of like hippies all grown up, who would have been fun to hang out with. The takeaway from them was the story of Spring, the smiling young Chinese girl who had by now ventured out of the cab. They had drugged and kidnapped her from a border village and were forcing her to...

No just kidding. The Chinese government has a lot of fun with tourist folks who want to drive a personal car, truck or motorcycle into their country. Your planned route, with entry and exit points, must be adhered to. Multiple photos of the vehicle and passengers, and stacks of approved paperwork and fees, are the start; and then there's the hired guide. In this case, Spring. Requiring a prearrangement and assignment by the government, the guide person meets you at the designated border point on the appointment date, and hops in the truck. They must accompany you throughout the trip, and you're responsible for their daily fee, plus their food and lodging.

The official line is that they're there for you. They'll assist as a tour guide and translator, help you with hotel and restaurant services, point out scenic routes, and steer you clear of restricted areas. If you're traveling through on a motorcycle, you must foot for the expenses of a car, as they follow. The job is readily filled by a young person who has good bilingual skills and a yen to travel about, but it's not a stretch to imagine that the youngster is officially debriefed during and after the trip. So please act accordingly. What a nice policy, just don't tell Utah.

It was a mixed day of climbing as the highway followed along the Tian Shan's foothill edges. All traces of karez-fed green belt disappeared around midday, and the vast desert ocean stretched out to the horizon. Twice that day, the sight of toppled freight trucks laying broken in the gravel harkened the carcasses of large beasts. The wind was bearable as it blew south for a while and then blew west, never my way, but at least it wasn't a toppling force today. The rugged Tian Shans to my north were beginning to fade in height but much closer and formidable. Ah, the highlight of the day appeared, a gas station.

Three water bottles were mounted on the bike. One on the seat tube below me, another on the down tube running from the head stock to the crank, and another under that same tube; that bottle just clearing the back of the front tire. Two more were stored in the front right and left panniers, and over time a routine had developed. The primary slot was on the down tube, a natural grab and return. When that emptied, it swapped places with the seat tube bottle; when that emptied, the bottle on the bottom side of the down tube went to the primary spot. Later, I'd stop and exchange the pannier bottles for the empties.

All across the world, traffic passed by seeing the bicycle tourist stopped, straddling his ride, wistfully gazing out into the vistas. Guarded from their view by the rear panniers and the tire stack was a guy just taking a piss. The bottle rotation had almost run its course by the time the shiny red gas station appeared, and that moment of it's-gonna-be-alright arrived. I'd taken to always carry a spare block of dried noodles, but still needed water to go along with it. Fill up the bottles, down a cold ice tea and grab another ramen and a bag of peanuts. We were ready for a night in the desert, then hope to see another gas station tomorrow.

On and off since Urumqi, and solid since Shanshan, a new freeway was being built, that varied from a few metres to a kilometre away. Since there was nothing to stop for, the ride went on until the sun had dropped behind me, stopping at a low viaduct under the new road. A hundred metres from the main route, my home for the night was blocked from the view of traffic, and alee of the breeze. It was a peaceful stealth camp. Foregoing the tent, I laid in the bag in the lonely darkness. Although I hadn't seen any wildlife since entering the country, I could hear something sniffing and pattering about. Was it my imagination or was it the wind? Couldn't have bothered me too much, it had been a long day pedaling against the wind, and I soon fell into a deep sleep.

Steve McQueen once said "I would rather wake up in the middle of nowhere than in any city on earth." The next morning was like that. Just kind of propped up in the sleeping bag, managed to boil some water on the mini gas stove and enjoyed a cup of instant coffee, staring out at the endless rocky emptiness, as the sun brightened the morning sky. Last night's southbound wind was now blowing west, it would be working against me again, but for a few minutes, it seemed this desert was mine. I wanted to carry that notion into the day, and busted camp early enough to still catch a bit of the cool desert air before the sun climbed too high. A few k's away, I came to a collection of buildings that probably has a name but more important, a small magazin.

The older man and woman, who lived in the backroom of the store, stood speechless as I entered with a cheery "neehow", and looked around their mini store that had way more shelves than items to fill them. Let's see, a tub of ramen noodles and another bag of peanuts, my new desert diet that'll make for a fine breakfast, hell it worked well for last night's dinner. Had I wanted a little meat, there was always a vacuum sealed marinated chicken claw, but so far I hadn't been able to break the thought of what chickens walk around in all day to give em' a try. They're quite the snack here, on the scale of our corn chips. The friendly folks were kind enough to boil up some water for my noodles, and breakfast became a pleasant respite, sitting in the dirt leaned up against the building's warm plaster. Rolling out from breakfast was a mental routine, practiced daily. Don't pedal. Then, hardly pedal and coast a bit. Move about on the seat, shake out the shoulders and stretch the back. Let the road decide the right gear, and slowly warm into a cadence. No tapping a Zen satori, just finding the morning bicycle trance, and it often brought a rhythm. And, as the early hours passed, a rhythm was needed.

The land was a panorama of abject desolation. A dry black brown wall of hills to the near north looked out upon absolute nothingness, as far to the south east and west as one could see. Even the American West had nothing this big and wide and featureless. Adding to that, I wasn't familiar to it. Was there a hamlet or a gas station or a road crew just beyond the horizon? The first human to ride across Mars. Trusting that the sun and wind wouldn't claim victory over the five water bottles, I pedaled on in blind faith... and of course then a station would pop up. Or giraffes. That day, larger than life giraffes and horses and cows, dinosaurs and camels, all in the form of cement statues, were spaced out over a

few k's in the swath of nothing. No signs or placards or credits to the artist, just there, like a visual gift to the mesmerized travelers. And the day continued out across the nothing.

Noticeable since crossing the border was a peculiar, always an azure blue, three wheeled pickup truck that chugged along on what I guessed was a single or twin cylinder diesel engine. The two-seater would announce its arrival with a slow paced un-muffled chugga-chugga-chugga sound that carried for miles before passing. In the tingling mind-wandering heat trance, I'd began to imagine the African Queen, puttering down the Ulanga with a gin-soaked captain and a stuff shirt English woman, berating him from behind. "What are you being so mean for Miss? A man takes a drop too much once in a while, it's only human nature." "Nature, Mr. Allnut, is what we are put in this world to rise above." The dream broken every time, by a pair of smiling sweaty workmen, beaming out the tiny cab's open windows.

The wheels pedaled on, knowing there was no town or room or bed, just another night in the culvert under the new freeway. As the sun closed out the day, things were alright. A productive day of covering an undetermined stretch, as I lost track of mileage due to the wildly varying distance numbers posted on road signs, that I couldn't read anyway. I knew the sizable town of Hami was within easy reach for tomorrow, and the August 1st date for the solar eclipse, heralded by my French friends of Chelyabinsk, was just a couple days away. Again, a day in the blank wilderness fades away with nary a creature to be seen. But, as I lay in the darkness, the pitter patter of little feet keeps me awake. The flashlight beam never reveals eyes or outlines, but I can't convince myself the imagination has such clarity. At least they're small feet and there's no growling, I doze off.

The next day, after another instant coffee tin cup sunrise, the long empty road approached Hami, also known as Kumul, depending who's eyes you saw it through, Han's or Uyghur. As the narrow tires struggled through a short dirt stretch of road construction, I looked up as a large white tour bus passed with windows full of white faces looking down on me with benign stares. A wave brought no reaction, as would a coach full of zombies. That beat all, the first western tourist group I'd yet seen, and they just gazed out the windows like it was television set. That's to be expected outside of Palm Springs, but outside Hami? I mean come on, how many bicycle guys riding across the Taklamakan have they seen today?

A package travel company funneling Midwest tourists on a promise to deliver them to the alter of the solar eclipse's sweet spot, bonused with a few side trips to the region's surrounding cultural highlights. "Dumbshits" was the brain murmur of the dehydrated road creature, I don't know why, but that was the moment's thought. Soon after, I came upon the bus pulled over to the side. I caught the glimpse of a wide-bottomed middle-aged blonde woman disappearing over a distant dirt drift, armed with a roll of toilet paper as the entire bus stared on. The poor dear, her biggest audience in years. I kept rolling on, missing the applause.

Hami was a fair-sized city, and not wanting to be bumped around, I rode towards the center and stopped outside a police station. Before dismounting, an officer was quickly at my disposal and invited me inside, motioning to bring the bike. They were pleased to fill out a form with my particulars and wouldn't you know it, an accepting hotel was just next door. I didn't mind the routine a bit, this was how it was done, and I knew I wouldn't be tossed out in the street after settling in. The attending officer was very polite, and showed me to the room, insisting I contact him for any questions or advice of his city. A hot shower washed off a few days of dust before making a dinner walk in the warm evening light. Food was frying and boiling and baking out of numerous store fronts but didn't I fall for another KFC? I know in looking back, I should have tried harder, but the familiarity had a strong appeal, and fate had its way too. As I emerged from another 11 herbs and spices dinner, I was approached by a tall kid from Nashville.

Justin was a graduate student, studying the Chinese language at a university at Chengdu, a Los Angeles sized metropolis in central China. He and his study mate Lian Wan were taking a summer break, as well as putting on an evening English class for young students, here in Wan's home town. It was a joy just to talk to another American, having not done so since the teacher/spy chap outside the train station in Astana a month ago. In no hurry to face the desert again, it was an easy sell when they invited me to stay a day and visit Wan's family home. They also asked if I would stop by their class for a talk with their students tomorrow, after viewing the eclipse.

We met around mid-morning the next day, and headed to the edge of town to visit Wan's family, and their plot that contained a small pig farm. The main half of the house where his mother served tea, was large with high ceilings. And the room's walls were covered with either a wallpaper of, or actual, Pepsi Cola carton sides. Like one  had cut the flat sides of 12 packs out, and neatly adhered them to every inch of the walls and ceiling, I honestly didn't know if it was of fashion or necessity. It reminded of my teenage years, when garage bands would line the walls with empty egg cartons, for the makeshift acoustics.

We soon moved out to the patio and had a wonderful pork and spicy rice lunch. For dessert, Wan's uncle chopped up a few of those yellow rugby ball melons. When I mentioned I'd been living off the graces of roadside melon stands, they told me these delicious sweet fruits were actually called Hami melons. Later, uncle proudly showed off his dozen stalls of giant pigs and wee wee piglets that made the family business. A few of them were so enormous that the wood plank walls of the pens didn't seem up to the task, had Porky decided to leave. Males. Keep them fed and laid and the boots stay under the bed.

We drove around in Wan's car on a neighborhood tour, stopped for some car parts at a friend's shop, and made it back to the town center in the late afternoon. We split up with plans to meet at their English class a few hours later, they had some preparations to tend to, and I wanted to relax for a few hours at the hotel; tomorrow it was back on the road. This next part, well I don't know if I should mention it.

The concern is it might come off wrong, if not posed correctly. The issue is this: Chinese people do not all look the same. I know that sounds like a cosmopolitan absolute, but after being here for a couple of weeks, one does see similarities in wide bands of the population. Perhaps in an ancient time, people from different regions of Asia had a common set of traits? Today I suppose the term is described as minor ethnic groups. As the region's people united over millennia, the traits blended as people moved about. I know I'm on thin ice here. The point is, throughout the two-plus months of traveling through China, I had never seen a man or woman that looked exactly like anyone among the many Asian people I knew from back home around San Francisco. Barring this one incident that afternoon.

Following Justin's direction to the classroom that was about a kilometre away, I was cutting across the grid-pattern city blocks. At one point, after crossing a busy intersection, I entered an open area in front of a market or small mall. The small plaza was filled with vendors selling electronics, candy, women's clothes. Glancing near the back, I saw my buddy Rich. No, I didn't. Rich is a workmate, he lived in Patterson and we often commuted together. The guy in the golf shirt standing behind the vendor table thirty feet away was Rich, dead ringer. When we made eye contact, he even gave me a heads up. My favorite Rich story was one day driving to work, mindlessly cruising with afternoon traffic, passing a Chinese market delivery truck with Cantonese writing all along its length. I innocently said "hey Rich, what's that say?" Rich wakes up from his half slumber in the passenger seat and barks, "how the fuck should I know", and goes back to sleep. Gotta love that guy.

I must have stared at the vendor fella for a full three or four seconds as the brain said "no, look away, that's not Rich it's not." I was stunned, they were virtual twins. I turned my head and marched away. Weird. When I get home, I probably shouldn't say anything to Rich.

Justin and Wan's rented classroom, simply an empty second floor office, was just off a major shopping square. Their students, three boys and a dozen girls, were all in their mid-teens and very excited that another American was visiting them. After introductions, I told them a long version of the story and then answered questions, they mainly wanted to know what my next big adventure was. It was difficult to convince them that this isn't what I do. After this, I'd go back to the day job, paying the bills like everyone else.

They were all very cheerful and receptive, and afterwards many pictures were snapped. Then one of the older girls quietly palmed me a small note, her eyes said it was a secret. At a discreet chance, I unfolded it. In tiny writing it said "life is not easy for anyone of us." I took the note and her look as a reach out. Having some wisps, rumors of their youth's culture, this seemed to quantify a serious point. My interpretation was a want of understanding for the enormous workload of the average Chinese student. Family and school pressures were imprinted on them; to not just compete, but to excel. Twelve-hour school days were not uncommon, and for every winner there's a loser. Suicide was the number one cause of death among China's youth, and the

number one reason for jumping out of a window was school related stress. I was honored that she trusted her thoughts to me, and I wish I had the quick wit to pass a wisdom like "try hard, but only to please yourself," or to at least let her know she was understood. But all that came out was a knowing nod.

Outside in the square, the eclipse was about to happen. Hundreds of people had gathered and there was a festive mood about. Food carts and energy drink stands were set up, everyone had a camera or phone ready; little boys were running through everyone's legs, handing out dark opaque film strips to a lucky few. To the layman, the total solar eclipse was merely an interesting sight, our tiny moon passes in front of the giant sun at just the right angle, as to block it out. I could do the same thing with my thumb but the crowds wouldn't gather. To many around the world, this was a special event. Tourist and scientist alike had traveled from afar to get to the Hami area, perhaps not the most ideal spot in the world, but the largest city near that spot. My French friends from

Chelyabinsk had based their expedition around it, hopefully Gilles made their destination spot somewhere north of here in Mongolia.

When it occurred around 7:00 pm, the sun was still high in the sky. Since all of China was on Beijing time, it seemed late. Had the Party adhered to normal time zone rules, it was actually only 5:00 pm in other countries along the same longitude. The slow-blanking increased to that quelling moment of full blockage, with only a lighted ring around the moon. There was a definite eerie surrounding silence, and a strange twilight hue to the still sky as everyone stood in collective awe. For one queer moment, a couple of dogs barking in the distance was the only sound. And then it passed. A total solar eclipse. I couldn't recall if I'd ever witnessed one, probably not. For a brief moment, a chilling experience, but not one I'd jump on a jet plane for. Mostly, I was thinking about supper.

I bid farewell to the school kids and promised to stay in touch. Always said that, and truly would have, if 'n they'd written. Justin, Wan and I went out to dinner and I thanked them for showing me around Hami, and getting a chance to talk to their class. They would be returning in a few weeks to the Chengdu area, still rebuilding from a massive 8.0 earthquake that struck the area just over two months back. Their university had withstood the shake, but due to primitive and tight budget construction practices, hundreds of thousands of homes and buildings collapsed. Almost 70,000 people perished, and nearly a half-million were left homeless. The numbers they told were staggering. I tried to conjure a single natural disaster of that scale in the States, and outside of a blockbuster action movie, I couldn't imagine.

25. water

The next morning was August 2nd, and I struck out on another ambiguous ride across the Taklamakan, into another day of trusting that the red big top of the PetroChina station would appear in time. The heat came early, and the only way to stand it was to keep moving, for the breeze effect. As the moonscape passed by, I'd try to concentrate on the cadence by counting every other pedal stroke to one thousand, then start over. I reasoned that, after a day of decent meals and a nice bed, I was going to be fine. Hong Kong ain't comin' this way, so pedal then pedal some more. There was only one station that day, and by dusk there was just enough water to boil up for the ramen at my new favorite motel, under the new freeway's culvert crossing.

After just a few k's the next morning, I was so thankful to come upon a highway crew that filled a few bottles for me. Played it cool, but honestly, I had no idea what I'd done without their liquid help. We all sat in the dirt and enjoyed a smoke together, and they tried to put across how far it was to a café, but it just made clear how few and far between everything was out here. As the day rolled, I noticed there had been no roadkill, no nocturnal creatures smeared on the asphalt in recent memory. The bleak nothingness, no snakes or lizards, just a rocky expanse that couldn't be described to any satisfaction. My only friend was the blacktop that, around midday, began to slope my way. We were riding down the backside of a horizon that for a day and a half was all you could see. Near the end of the day, a flat front tire broke up the progress. As I sat cross legged, surrounded by an injured bike and various repair implements, there was a mellow energy that washed through me. A tranquility, that here, yet in the sea of vastness, I held everything needed to fix it and keep moving.

Soon after, I lingered by the roadside in the dusk, waiting for the right time to pick up the heavy load and truck down a short embankment, into the desert dirt. Since there never was much traffic, it wasn't too long a wait. Soon, camp was set up on the lee side of a small rise, out of the highway's view. After boiling up some noodles, I settled into the nightly camp habit of slowly tuning through the tiny Grundig radio shortwave band, trying to catch a snippet of English. There was never a proper program, just either pieces of one or random messages from ham operators from who knows where. Sometimes music, most times someone reading a text in an unknown language; and lots of Morse code would come through. Just to hear voices in the night was comforting in some way, the world I'd left was out there, and I was heading towards it.

It was too hot that night to use the bag, and the short relief of the cool dark hours faded quickly, as soon as the sun began to show. Once again, the day began with the last cup of water in the last bottle, hoping that something would turn up. And again, I was charming my way up to the road crews that were working the new highway. They'd hook me up with water that was boiled clean on a portable solar device that looked like a TV satellite dish, painted a bright silver. The pot was dangled by rods over the convex concentration point, until

hot enough to brew a cup of tea. They only would give up about a litre at a time, since their water supply was meant for the crew's chai breaks, I was thankful for anything.

Four times that day, I managed to beg a litre from the crews spaced along the desert floor, each time it was sucked down as soon as the thank-you's were done. There hadn't been a PetroChina station yet, and didn't sound like there was going to be one, given my pace. With little water and no food, along with the 100-degree heat and fierce wind, I hit the bonk by early afternoon. Bonking is a condition whereupon the energy used to move muscles just goes away. Meals and snacks provide the carbs and sugar to synapse the auto motion of running or pedaling, without much thought. After the on-hand energy is used up, the body begins drawing on its fat reserves. The reserves in the form of fat can't be drawn on efficiently enough to run the machine, and now you've bonked. I felt like a weak battery, filled only with water, no acids or enzymes to create the electrical signal that made the legs move.

Anywhere else the brain would have said it's over, catch a ride to a mini mart, load up on bananas and chocolate milk and find some shade. But here, what? There was nothing, the crux of the challenge of crossing a vast desert as wide as the Western U.S. had arrived. "This was never a vacation" kept clicking in my head, and as such, waving a car down was out of the question. Couldn't be that guy, you'd never get it back. I rested, hunched over the bars, and then pedaled for as far as I could. Sometimes 200 metres, sometime just 100, and then rest again, the legs were gone.

Buildings were appearing in the distance, that was the carrot. Buildings meant people meant water, maybe some food. I'd push along, and then coast to a near stop a few times, then rest again. As they grew closer it looked grim, didn't see any cars or trucks, just mounds of dirt behind some abandoned buildings. There wasn't a soul, as the sun baked on.

People would constantly honk as they go by to say hello, but the dry brain wasn't handling their cheers well, fucking honkers. And please people, quit with the hundreds of beer bottles littering the roadside. And before we address Tibet and human rights, the honking has to stop. Water. The rage is the brain drying out and getting short, knowing it was all on me, I didn't prepare somehow for this heat and distance. Needed a trucker to pull over and get some water, maybe a melon. The heat was winning, the wind was winning, the honkers were winning; and then the road began climbing. Now the anger shifted to the road, why throw a climb now? Thirst dreams of cold ice tea or slushy cola, lying down in a pool of cool water. That fades into wanting just water, and then even hot water. Anything, it didn't matter. Dizzy and tingling were sensations that took up more thoughts while moving forward; wondering if this was dehydration or heat stroke? Quit bitchin', buck up. The darker rocks and a little elevation would mean a creek. Telling lies was ok, that became the next goal, climb the hill. That's where the water is at.

Not a wisp of a drop, but I knew that. The lie brought the wheels closer to the next crest, and if it wasn't for the head wind, it would be a decent coast. Down was better than up as the dead legs pushed forward a few more... what's this? Oh man-oh man-oh man there was the red canopy of a PetroChina station out on the plains ahead! And it wasn't just a gas station, there were buildings and some sort of tollway gates and trucks and cars and people!

Sitting down in the small diner, I tried my best to be the cheery guest and not tear through every glass of water the old woman filled up. Another plate of chicken mein jow, complete with the bones and claws and eyes staring up, but that didn't matter; I loved it. As the day was closing, the old couple in charge were pleased to fill up the five bottles, and I left with a couple of ramen packets. The stop was either the burg of Xingxingxiazhen or just its truck stop, perhaps X-Ville was a nearby village, out of view. In any case, there were no vacancies, or maybe there were no rooms at all, it was never clear. So, another night in the desert beckoned. As the sun dropped, camp was set up, hidden in the wrinkled brown hills to the south. A decent meal, some water and a night's rest were rarely so needed.

Another beautiful desert morning, already getting warm, yet the insane driving wind hadn't awoken yet. On the Grundig last night, I caught a passing frequency long enough to hear an Orwell quote about an autobiography only being trusted if it reveals something disgraceful. Something about a man who gives a stellar account of himself is likely lying. The idea that personally viewed, every life is a series of defeats. It sounded profoundly cynical, especially as I jotted down the daily accounts of a trip so many would never take. True honesty could only be carried out by a perfect person. We all lie to ourselves in some degree, but the quote caused reflection, to grade myself on how I was doing. The conclusion was that this adventure was too blessedly unencumbered, and experiences too amazing, to bother with a cover story. It was all I could do to keep notes. I was trying by George, my days of late just a series of the rider lying to the road, and the road answering back with the truth.

Like knowing a break was needed, the day was kind. Heading for Liuyuan some 85k's away, the aim was a steady pace, while mentally dividing the four litres left to one bottle per 20k's, to avoid yesterday's beating. The plains were as flat as a still water. The temps were down a bit and clouds dotted the sky; and beginning the ride with water, versus begging it off of kind strangers, gave the confidence of control. Knowing what parched felt like, the discipline to resist gulping would rule the day. Deliberate small sips kept the legs going, I was going to pull into Liuyuan intact. Then, like a gift, at 30k's along, came a service station. Oh my, to walk into air conditioning and enjoy an ice tea, a Coke, and a cold bottle of water. Given the desperation of yesterday, how could I ever adequately convey the emotion of feeling empowered, simply by having a couple of bags of peanuts and another ramen bowl packed away?

Water bottles full, the remaining ride to Liuyuan was blessed with a two-kilometre-long cloud, stretching out above. And come and go, it blew along with me for 50k's, all the way in. Just the few degrees of the cloud shade, or the relief from the brightness bouncing off the tarmac, seemed to make the previous day's drama of dying like a raisin out here appear silly. Somewhere along the stretch, three quail appeared, trotting quickly away to nowhere. Fauna exists. And a common soul. A bicycle tourist from Beijing, heading west, stopped to chat. His first question was how was I managing to make any headway against the strong westerlies. I'm sure my answer was along the lines of "or what?"

He was a friendly and fit middle-aged man, and was just a few days into this great wide open, the Tarim Basin, home of the Taklamakan and the western edges of the Gobi. He had climbed over the Qilian Shan mountains, this region's extension of the massive Kunlun range, of which stretches south into the Tibetan Plateaus. The high and low-pressure dance between this immense desert and the surrounding mountain chains create and isolate all these brutal wind forces. He was now being blown west by them, and hence making great time. Next, the wheels caught up to a weathered old man in sandals and a bamboo paddy hat, pushing, not pedaling, a three wheeled bicycle. It was literally loaded to obscurity with at least a couple of hundred pounds of plastic and glass bottles, held in a group of huge burlap bags; each a metre in diameter. He was all smiles, but we could only gesture. He must have supported himself by pedaling and pushing the desert miles, picking up the litter of discarded bottles lining the highway's edge. Smiling, apparently happy as hell, he was

 made of an alloy I could only imagine.

Liuyuan was just a lay-by with a gas station and a couple of shop shacks. A village proper, Liuyuanzhen, existed several k's to the east, but the crossroads of the g215 and my g30 had everything required; water and food for another night of camping. As bad as a shower was needed, and as nice as a bed would be, riding east to a maybe-bed in Liuyuanzhen wasn't worth the detour. After stocking up on liquids and noodles, a sharp tinge on my left arm turned me about as I left the store.

Another woman, for it wasn't the first time in the past few days, was tugging and staring, fascinated at my arm hair. Like a mannequin, I patiently stood, arm arched. The shopkeeper and another woman customer, and my tugger, discussed at length its features, running her fingers through. Then the awkwardness must have been mentioned, as she abruptly pulled back from the spell, apologizing. People here haven't much wispy body hair, and my furry extremities intrigued; she just hadn't seen it before. In a strange way, it was an honor.

No loss on the bed, but it would be another day without a wash. It had been a few days since the last hose-off, and given the extreme temps and effort, things were getting a bit scratchy and le' fumée was rising. Years ago, reading the story of Lewis and Clark's continental expedition, the thought crossed that if I'd been alive and young and in the right spot, I could have risen to that. The walking and paddling, the danger and extreme hardships in the spirit of discovery...but I'd have to have a hot shower at least every three days or forget it. Sorry Captain. Another night in the desert called. Just before shooting off to hide under another viaduct, I came upon a spilled truckload of green peppers, swept off onto the highway's margin. An old man and woman stood by with push brooms, paying me no mind as I judged them. Were they salvaging them? Anywhere else, the peppers would be left to rot and blow away.

The desert morning gift once again. As I jotted down the daily thoughts, the west bound wind slowly picked up. By the time camp was busted, it was a full-on gust. As I wheeled back to the road, a group was picking through and bagging the peppers, bound for dinner. It was August the 5th, a little over six months since leaving my garage. Heading south east and turning into the westerly wind, began perhaps the toughest day of the trip. The force and the passing whoosh of the big trucks constantly overwhelmed the power to control the wobbling handlebars. The wind speed was far beyond any experienced so far. And again, the momentary block, then instant wind rush as the trucks and buses passed, tossed me tumbling into the gravel time and again. The wind and a 90-degree day soon had me sucking down the bottles, and after a squirt to clean out a bleeding right knee, the water was running low. The road signs had figured the next dominion of Anxi at 60k's, but the folks in Liuyuan said 78, China's mileage signs had all seemed to be calculated by opinion so far. The highway offered nothing all day in the way of stations, at one point a trucker offered a few litres from a holding tank under his rig. Another offered up a half empty pint bottle. I took them both. Without water or food, and fighting the wind force, the bonk hit again.

Just trying to rest was made a chore, as holding onto the bike took effort. I took to laying it down and just hanging on during the long gusting moments. I didn't know what was to come of the day, my energy and water were gone. I pushed on against the incredible wind, and the hazards of falling off how many more times, and not knowing how far to the day's end. And the fucking drivers and their happy honking. Baked and blown dry, the mule and I, with little options, kept pushing a little bit more. Then, as if in a vision, off to the right, about a hundred metres out from the road was a pool! It wasn't a pool, it was a holding reservoir, perhaps fed by some aquifer spring or karez, I didn't care. It was about the size of a backyard pool, dug into the desert floor. About a half-k ahead, a dirt trail doubled back to it. As I approached the water's edge a small lizard scampered away, notable as only the second wild creature I'd seen, along with yesterday's quail.

As the wind continued, I carefully weighted down a change of clothes, and positioned the soap and razor. Stripping down, without a thought to the highway traffic, I waded in then dove into the metre-deep pool. What a treat. It was cool at first, then seemed ideal, as staying mostly submerged blocked the winds. After a full soap up and rinse, a long thorough shave, and a good spell of just floating, there was new hope to the day. While using the purifier pump to fill the bottles, the t-shirt tucked in the waist band let loose in the wind. It soared over a nearby wire fence and took off west, tumbling across the desert at speed, like it was trying to escape, it was gone. When I was about to leave, I noticed it still in view, caught on something at least 200 metres out, my chance. Skirting through the fence, I made it out to the shirt, caught on a rock edge. Packing only three shirts, it played an important role in the rotation.

Onward, pedaling into the wind and heat, the oasis-break soon wore off. The fact that there was no substitute for food flooded in. Again, the beating continued from the sun above, and the west bound wind. By late afternoon, the bottles were almost drained. The sheer inability to push on the pedals took its toll, every effort against the force was a trick to maintain the bike's direction and balance. Giving up, then trying again, then giving up, then trying one more time. It was too much. At one point, stopped, just hanging onto the bike, squaring against the gusts and exhausted, some crazy thought came. The idea of relenting to the force, just let it blow me where it wants. Roll out there into the desert unknown, at a furious pace into the horizon.

Reaching back and grabbing the fugitive t-shirt from the tire bungees, I balled it up. In a giddy, goofy, heat-demented moment, I tossed it as high as possible. It sailed far above the desert floor and then bound back to earth, tumbling across the gravel on and on, until it could be seen no more. Free

yourself man, go with the wind and find your way home! It was some relief to give up something to this force that fought me every moment; take it! Perhaps someday, an orphan boy or peasant girl, herding goats in the mountains of Tajikistan, will stumble across the mysterious presence of a Timekeepers Motorcycle Club Wild Boar Enduro t-shirt. A legend will be created around it, as the campfire tales are passed on through the generations. I'm quite certain of it.

Finally, the outskirts of what would be Guazhou Town began to appear, at the sight of a railroad overpass. Beyond it, the structures and strung cables of an electric power station. Out of water, the next best thing was a small shade spot under the overpass, where a couple of freight trucks were parked. Just being out of the 100-plus degree heat calmed me, today would soon be over. The truckers, four of them, were gathered in one double cab, playing a card game.

When I tapped on the door to beg some water, they just gestured to leave them alone, and not too friendly at that. What? Hey don't you know your role? You're supposed to be the over-the-top helpful Chinese guys, and I'm the American tourist who just rode across hell, all I want is... well listen to my inner child. Suck it up, ya can't expect everyone to be fascinated by yer little orange bicycle. Tried them again to see if the actual town of Guazhou was 20 or 2 k's away, they didn't want to clarify that either.

Thankfully, 2k's on came Anxi, now known as Guazhou Town. It wasn't much more than a few shops, but it was Shangri La to me. I sat in front of a $10 hotel, with an ice tea and a Coke, after downing a large bottle of water; a beer search was next. Then I met a young man whose parents ran the local hospital clinic; their ward was just a few doors down. It was merely a pharmacy, a bit shy of a two-car garage with three beds. Dad was a general doctor, Mom was the nurse. They were the nicest of folks, and recommended the nearby restaurant where I ordered noodles and beef, but was served rice and eggs. Soon the truck driver's holding tank water from earlier today began a rumblin', requiring a couple of Ukrainian pepto pills to gel things back up. The hotel room's on-demand water heater played a digital Chinese tune when plugged in, then it bleeped a noise as if it had a desperate message from the Princess, then it sounded like a fire alarm. I just unplugged it, and settled for another cold shower.

The plan the next day was to sleep in, and stay here for a day to compose. In the morning, the restaurant allowed me into the kitchen, where we made up a lunch of goat meat, egg and tomatoes. When I emerged into the bright day, the whole plan took a turn. There's something different...the wind. The wind, it was blowing my way! Abandoning the day off, I ran upstairs and threw the bike gear together. Hopped on and shot down the road, now heading east again. Toll police on the main highway forced me off onto the adjacent rough and narrow old highway, still being used by those not willing to cough up the coin. Once again, just like anywhere, the "safe" roads away from the high-speed traffic were dangerous as hell as I shared the cramped road with large buses and trucks, zooming to their next job. Despite a 1:00 pm start, and the bad roads, the bike covered 80k's with nary a pedal. Blown by the same force I'd fought for days! Camping out in another culvert that night, I thought about how this wind had taken on an enemy dimension. Today it had been caught looking, and I popped it hard. It cannot be beaten, but today I took a little back. Or did it gift me? It must have liked the shirt.

The next spot on the tattered map was Yumenchen, about 50k's from camp. The wind wasn't bad and the day was cooler, plus there was a break in the desertscape, with a few green farm patches trying to scrape go of it. The Qilian Shan mountains were visible to the south, and I knew in a day or so the road would be skirting their northern edge, as the desert began to fade. Couldn't be soon enough. A few k's out, a father and his young daughter stopped to talk, and offered their place for the night. It was so good of them, but I was really looking forward to not being anyone's guest tonight, hoping to just shut a door and rest.

It was just another traveler's hotel with a dormitory feel, and of course no hot water. It amounted to about $12, but it had a bed and a door I could isolate behind. Again, the constant cultural newness of everything I saw or learned or felt was jamming the brain with sensations, coupled with the longing to get home. Closing the door and holding up with the Kung Fu fighting dramas, and the continual morning-til-night build up to the Olympics felt like sanctuary. Every step of the Olympic torch bearing was covered live, then rebroadcast at all hours. There was obviously no notion of a budget, since apparently tens of billions were poured into the Olympic venues. Surely, it was the grandest display of Chinese national pride in most of its people's lifetimes. And tomorrow, August 8th, the opening ceremonies were sure to be watched by every good citizen in the country, and a good chunk of the world.

Alas, I had decided to kick it here for tomorrow, and having made that choice, began asking about for an I-net spot to blog and upload some pics. I was directed to the usual desert-village bleak, cheaply constructed, white washed multi storied building with large broken windows; hedged with windblown trash piles. Inside, banks of desktop computers were lined up in rows, filled with young people doing homework and finding out about the outside world. The connection was good though, and I tried to make quick work of the uploads and emails. Like setting a GPS way point every time the blog was updated, it felt like the outside world was clued to my existence. Hey everyone, I've made it this far and am still heading in the right direction.

After another noodle dinner and a market stop, I made it back to the room with a few beers and a couple of noodle packs, plus some bread and fruit. Late at night, peering out at the gas station on the street below, three large freight trucks pulled up. They were trailering what could only be three large sections of a missile or space launch rocket. The massive white open-ended cylinders were seven or eight metres wide, and they filled the long-bed trailers end to end. The thought of snapping a picture chilled too Bond-ish for me. Drawing the curtains closed, I imagined trying to explain that photo at the next police interview.

Holed up in the room the next day, asylum. Outside that thin door was China and its honking cars and vicious wind, form filling cops and helpful inquisitive photo-happy-arm-hair-pulling people and their fireworks. Oh, don't give these folks a reason for fireworks, they're regularly shooting them off at any hour. And today, with the Olympic torch about to be lit 2000k's away, it's the 4th of July all day long. Behind my door, it was a day of peace and rest, and loading up on fruits, bread and juice. The amazing opening ceremonies of Beijing's Olympiad played out of the 16-inch black and white television. Outside my door, the ceremonies were accompanied by a half hour barrage of fireworks in the streets outside. What had to have been thousands of shrieks and pops, it went off until the sulfur scent filled the room. Damn these people were happy, maybe too much so. They'd been pumped full of state propaganda, for perhaps years, since the IOC selection announcement. By now they were bursting at the seams in national pride. All very harmless for such a beautiful event, but a glimpse of the country's ability to mobilize an idea.

Out on the windy desert the next day, I was caught up from behind by Diego. The school teacher and amateur bicycle racer had left northern Spain over three months ago, with the goal of meeting his girlfriend for the closing ceremonies in Beijing. As a real bicyclist, he had some minor sponsorship from a Spanish media company, and a new Cannondale road bike. To keep the bike unencumbered, he towed a lightweight supply trailer. Wonderful guy, who was glad to stop and talk about his days crossing Eurasia. We set out to stick together, and thanks to yesterday's rest, I hung in there with him for about 20k's, until it was clear Diego was a machine. We parted with the nod that we had to find our own pace, his much better than mine. As he pedaled away, I thought about the thousands of kilometres he had slogged, and the many stories he had banked, just to get to my momentary stretch of road. The quick math had him pushing 150k's a day to make his date, more than half again my good day average. Doubtful he factored in this punishing wind. And yet, I liked to picture his face awash in the lights of that glorious stadium show, his sweetheart at his side, as China brought the house down with the grand finale of their world spectacle. I wished him well as he disappeared into the far empty distance.

And the far empty distance just kept coming. Managing about 90k's, pushing pedal over pedal against the heat and invisible gusting force, the flat land was becoming a bit more dirt than gravel. Patchy spots here and there of green desert brush were appearing, like distant tendril fingers, promising of a green world somewhere beyond the horizons. Another overpass camp site came, not long after filling up the bottles in Dongshaman. Like Yumenchen before it, was an oasis spot in the baking void. Trees and crops and irrigation channels were set into the desert floor, and then ended abruptly at the town limits.

This wind. For God's sake China will you just turn it off for an hour? Busting camp is an ordeal, a game played against a merciless force that surges as the sun rises. Rolling up the tent without losing the rain cover or tent bag, or the hat, or a glove, was an exercise of deliberate moves and method. It was August 10^{th,} and after six hours of fighting the force and the sunshine, I'd only gone 20k's. In need of water and stuck on a fenced-in stretch of new highway, a green spot with a mud house was coming up, maybe beg some water. Off came the bags, to heave the bike over the tall fence. As I was snapping it back together, a guy pulls up in a small service van. Having no idea what my day had been like, he starts into the journey questions. Forcing a smile, I'm just happy to not be pedaling, to rest and relate. He offers a ride into Jiuguan, some 20k's away. A short distance, but I'll never make it today at this rate. I jump on the offer.

The desert ahead is broken by the structures of the coming town, but before that, there's something else. A rammed-earth mud wall stretches to the north and south, the highway cutting right through it. "Is that what I think it is?" My new buddy confirms it and goes on in pride; this is the reason for his city. Before reaching Jiuguan, we come to Jiayuguan, home of Jiayu Pass, the ancient fortress guarding the Hexi Corridor, and the most western of the Ming era's Great Wall of China. The Hexi Corridor is a Northwest/Southeast path of spring oasis's that enabled the route of the Silk Road to reach this point, before entering the desert. Jiayu Pass was built at its narrowest spot between two hill ranges. 600 years ago, the regions beyond this point to the west were considered the edge of their civilization. Beyond it, the realm of barbarians; the Jiayu Pass

Fortress, often the point of exile for many a poor soul. This gracious fellow pulled me from another windblown night in the desert, and delivered me to the foot of the Great Wall. And I'm certain he introduced himself, but his name is lost on me. We stopped for a quick walk around the grounds of the Fort, then he dropped me off at a $27 hotel in downtown Jiuguan. After I had time to clean up, he shows up unexpectedly, bearing peaches and melons. We cross the street for an evening of beer and schnapps and sash leek, it was nice to have a sit-down brew and mutton talk session with a cool local young businessman. He was very proud of his city's Wall and fortress, and enjoyed fielding all my silly Wall questions.

As an important Silk Road point, Jiuguan, and of course the bastion of Jiayu Pass just to the north, had seen trade and troubles for thousands of years. The natural spring, which I'd mistaken for a runoff pond just outside the Fortress, was the center of it all. Humans had been drawn to this small water source since

before recorded time; beyond it to the north lay the great deserts. Located in a plain between a rugged mountain range and the brutal Gobi, to hold Jiuguan was to defend or control the western frontier, and the corridor into central China. It had seen Mongol and Han; Song and Ming Dynasties take their rule. It had been the beaten path of Indian and Tibetan traders of the East. Arabs, Turks and that famous Venetian from the West had passed this way. Transposed with its place in the dawn of written history, turns out those giant rocket sections I'd seen the other night in Yumenchen belonged to the Jiuguan Satellite Launch Center. The oldest of the country's three spaceports, it was located east of here in an area so remote that they named it after this, the nearest city, some 200k's away. The emptiness all around, the vast vacant space I'd been riding across for almost three weeks was a giant void, yet full of history. If one could only take the time to see it.

Devouring the melon for breakfast and packing away the peaches, I hit the road early, hoping to make Linze by tonight. The headwind wasn't as strong as yesterday, but still contentious. It was a new day, with a rested embracing attitude that this land and the wind are as one, it's not going to end. Find a good gear and push it. There was irrigation here from the snow-capped Qilian Shan Mountains to the southwest, and the resulting tree patches dampened the wind force as the terrain rose. Plugging along with the iPod, a Springsteen song came around where he was talking to the crowd about his teen years, troubles with his father and his near Army induction. I'd heard the piece many times, but today it moved me to thoughts of my oldest boy Shay, who'd seen his share of tribulations. I started crying, it just happened. Pedaling along, welling up tears with thoughts of how much I loved him and his brother; and how far away in time and distance they were. Just wish this shit was over, didn't want to be this far from home ever again

Home tonight was going to be the village of Quingshui, and a cheap dormitory style boarding house that didn't have any tourist issues, and no cops knocking on the door. Breakfast in the morning was across the street at the diner, a small cafeteria style place where everyone gets the same bowl of noodles, and shares one of the five or six wooden tables. A policeman chatted with me, quite interested in the trip, happy and pleasant as can be. Then, he found I hadn't reported in with the local heat. Before I could ride off into the day, he had other plans. Politely, but directly, he ordered me back to the dorm room, to wait, while he called for interview back up. It's China, he's a cop, of course I complied. After patiently waiting on the edge of the bed, he finally shows up with a clipboard partner. We went through the dozen or so same old questions, and when they were satisfied, I was "released." To think, I almost scampered through Quingshui without the authorities discovering where my sister worked! The delay bit into a 100k march to Linze, and of course, a strong SSE wind was waiting for me at the edge of town.

About 35k's along, in the village of Xinbaxiang, I'm told Linze is 25k's away. Another local says 90, and still another guessed 70. I jumped on the new freeway and enjoyed a slight decline, while mathing up the discrepancies. When I ask

273

people the "how far" question, perhaps they see the Western face and give the answer in miles? That still doesn't explain the highway signs, many times the numbers just don't add up; they're just plain wrong about how far it is to wherever. Sure, folks can be mistaken, but the highway department? As the pedals continued to turn and turn and turn into the desert with no real notion of exactly where we're at, I began laughing inside. I was hoping that their local space program was at least using a slide rule.

After pushing through a long hard windy day, the sun was dropping over the Qilian Shan's. According to the roadside markers, I'd well surpassed the 100k mark, as I rolled into what turned out to be Linze. Faux. Whatever village it was, the word there was that Linze was still another 15k's down the road. Yeesh, whatever. "Pingua?" Didn't I score a dive house for about $4, cheapest in China yet. Dinner was another episode of a half dozen people trying to figure out what I wanted, ending in a stroll through the kitchen for a bowl of noodles and goat meat. The shower was cold, I just washed my face. The shitter was a hole out back, I just held my nose. The TV was black and white, I just caught a bit of the Olympics and fell into a hard sleep. Feelin' good though, I knew that despite the wind, this desert ordeal was almost over.

And the Silk Road route continued. By midafternoon the next day, the fair-sized city of Zhangye arrived. Fair sized in that China has an official designation system for the areas covered by its administrative levels. Zhangye was known as a Prefecture level city, an administrative seat of sorts, ranking above and encompassing several county seats, or sub-Prefecture level cities. In turn, it ranks below sub Provincial cities, which ultimately rank below a Province level city. In the Gansu Province, Lanzhou is the top Province level city. The confusing part was that the "city" in the title meant both the urban area and the vast rural area it covered. One could be in the Prefecture city, yet many k's away from an actual structure. Something's lost in the translation, but the gist is that starting at the tiniest village, someone answers to someone who answers to someone on up a ladder of hierarchy. Many more steps than our city-county-state system, and it may explain away some of the road sign's mileage discrepancies. As in, "oh yeah, you've ridden far enough. Yer in Linze, but the town is still 15k's that-a-way."

This came about while sussing out the road signage confusions with a small group of college students, over a few beers and watermelon at a sidewalk table outside a cafe in Zhangye. Their routine was pouring each bottle among everyone's small glasses, surprising how fast that made the bottles fly. After a bevy of bottles, they showed me to an I-net cafe to work on some picture uploads; and saying they'd return soon, insisting I spend the night at their nearby dorm. Winging it on the bet the kids would come through on an unusual evening, I passed a few hours on the slow upload speeds, enjoying the afternoon beer buzz. I knew that in any case, the day's forward motion had stopped.

The I-net cafe's owner, wife and teenage daughter soon befriended me and had heard the whole trek story by the time one of the students called them to apologize. Something had come up, and they couldn't return until 9 pm. We all decided it was a bad bet, so I joined the I-net hosts for dinner, and they showed me to a decent hotel. Of course, an hour after taking my room, there's a knock at the door and the police came in. Examine the passport, ask questions, fill out the forms, leave with a thank you and selfies. You know.

It's their rules yet so maddening. It left me thinking that this must be what celebrities endure. What with the constant staring on the streets and in the stores, the so polite yet so disturbing daily police interviews, it's all I can do to not blurt "what the hell are you looking at?" Then the door is locked, the shower comes on and I crawl into bed knowing I cannot say that. I must hold it together for another month or so, and then it's over. And what would an evening of boozing it up with the college kids have wrought? Drinking half the night would have been great, until it was time to hit the pedals in the morning. And if the cops showed up, my old ass presence at a college dorm would cause unwanted attention for everyone. Small snips can make the big ball unwind. Just as well, today was one of little progress, and what with getting so close to exiting the desert, I really wanted to put down some miles.

In the morning the hopeless hankering for a bowl of Honey Nut Cheerios and buttered toast with a dark coffee was strong. The newscast lady on CCTV droned the rote party line, wearing what looked like a Star Trek or maybe Sgt. Pepper's outfit, like a Thunderbird puppet. Although not wanting to walk out that door into China, I was soon seated at another noodle kiosk. I watched, with benign amusement, as the roomful of people slurp at their bowls with those sticks, flashing on chimps sticking a twig down a termite hole. It dawned now, that here in Zhangye, like Jiuquan and Hami and Turpan, there was traditional three stringed shamisen music softly playing all about the central areas in the mornings. Waking and kindling the proletariat to the subtle background music. There must be little speakers spaced all about unnoticed. The Western mind instantly lashed out at its eerie utopian atmosphere, yet on the other hand, it was kind of nice that everyone gets a pleasant gentle start to their day. Jeez, my twisted head was so full of unhinged thoughts, swirling from cultural submersion and exhaustion. Bah, lace up the boot's boys, there was work to do, and it would turn out to be another tough tough day.

Fighting powerful headwinds, and nine hours of riding, only produced 60k's to Shandan. Early in the day, a treat came in the meeting of Damien and Jill, a Canadian couple that started in Shanghai and were heading for London. Jill's first comment drove home the source of the goofy thoughts and weak knees, "how could anyone ride against this wind?" They had hardly touched a pedal in the last day, as they were being blown along by the force. Damian spoke of increasing police interviews as I headed east, fueled by a national Olympic terrorist paranoia. His bright note was that the winds will slack off near Lanzhou, in a few days. The pair were the first North Americans cyclotourists I'd met in all of Eurasia, and the 3rd and 4th N.A.'s I'd met at all on the continent. It was nice to talk. Later, a man on a brand-new Honda 125 stopped to talk, and from what I could gather, he was on the new bike's maiden tour. After doing a little math, I figured the little Red ride ran him just a tad over $1000, way less than a third of what it would have gone for in Modesto. I latched on to the luggage rack and he whisked me along for 3k's, until the left arm couldn't fight the wobbly bike and the head gusts any longer. I waved in thanks for his help as he pulled away into the distance.

After the night in Shandan, August 15th was looking to be another mental and physical drain. The wind had lessened from a harsh force to a strong breeze and the cruel heat had slackened, but a long gradual climb for half the day kept things honest. As the bottles ran out, the road crested to a decline, but this one was different. The long gradual climb was paying back. The downhill rolled and rolled, I don't know how far, 10 or 12k's. The wheels weren't turnin' and burnin', but at least it was downhill, I just relaxed.

Cruising along, I could see patches of green to the south. The road was rising and dropping into another valley as it followed the hills, like skirting the edge of a bowl. The wind eased even more, and although a bit premature, I indulged my hope to wander. Perhaps the moment had arrived. The terrain ahead was changing and there were green hues on the horizon, the spirits took a leap. I had studied the maps and road signs for days, yet never wanted to let the guard down; now I was seeing the grand layout before me. The desert was almost over my shoulder. I had cycled through the Taklamakan and Gobi Deserts. In high Summer. The closest meaning of Taklamakan derives through its native Uyghur's "you can get in, but you can't get out". I was almost out, never again. Rolling through the highway village of Shuiquanzicun, it called for a quiet celebration, a Coke and a smoke. When an ancient boy said it was only 10k's to Yongchang I smiled and thanked him. Inside I was like "save it dude, it's cool. I know it's 30." I was so damned happy.

26. teardrop dragons

Since the Zhangye area, the road follows along the flickering ruins of the Great Wall. In some places, it would run south and east for hundreds of metres, then disappear. Then, a twenty metre chunk would appear, and on and off again, in varying lengths. Plainly, large sections had been deliberately razed, others left alone in a random pattern. Heralded the world over as a historic monument to medieval mankind's ability of engineering and toil, perhaps this heritage is lost on many locals. Perhaps to them this five-metre-high mud wall of loess, the region's fine grit soil, isn't considered an ancient testimony to early history. Perhaps to them, it's just a big pain in the ass.

Roads and access trails have to be routed, grazing livestock must wander, the Wall's purpose of slowing invasions had long ago faded. Given its material, centuries of erosion were the biggest enemy, but clearly, the mark of power equipment was visible in places. Imagine being the fella at the controls of a front loader tasked with scooping into the face of The Great Wall of China. "Yeah, tell the guy in the tie I'm gonna need that in writing." Approaching the outskirts of Yongchang, the Wall vista played into the scene of

another mud neighborhood. The rammed-earth Wall, the villages of rammed-earth huts and their yard partitions, their outdoor kitchens and johnnys; all were of the same dirt construction method and hue tone of the land. Breakfast chickens and lunch goats and dinner pigs wandered the dirt streets, as they had for eons. But the community's paradox to the 2000-year-old Han and Ming Dynasty barrier announces itself in the view from a small rise. Many homes, whose mud footings are rooted in the ancient soil, are topped with straw-covered roofs, and crowned by satellite dishes. Talking into outer space.

Friendly people met me in the midst of Yongchang. At the word "pingua", a collection of opinions led to the tourist approved hotel. A happy couple followed along, they smoothed over the lodging transaction and lugged the panniers upstairs as I carried the bike. In moments after rolling into the small town, I was feet up in a $30 hotel with cold running water. As the night fell, there was no knock on the door, no police report; no drama. Looking across to adjacent buildings, I could see the "solar" powered water heaters, which were merely plumbed tin barrels heating up in the sunshine and cooling by evening. It would figure that between 2 to 4 pm would be an excellent window to get a not-so-cold shower. Otherwise, as I had been informed many times recently, cold showers are healthy!

The 100k's to Wuwei the next day were pleasant, taking in the joy of the road's general decline and mild temperatures, while mentally preparing for the next challenge. After today, the climbs would begin into the foothills, then over the mountains that separated the country's dry northwest from its humid southeast regions. Perhaps sadistically, the climbs become the bicyclist's goal, consciously pretending anticipation, hoping to gain a mental upper hand; and days of climbing lay ahead. At midday a cyclist approached, his story filled my resolve, but only at the expense of his own struggles.

Neil was an Irishman who had begun his journey in New Zealand, and was heading home to the Emerald Isle. After making his way through Australia and southeast Asia and India, and then some headway into China, visa issues had caused him a serious time delay. He was forced to return to India to correct some paperwork. Any major time and distance lost on a bicycle plays on you mentally, all that effort and discomfort wasted, because some bureaucrat needed a stamp. He was down on his spirits, and losing the desire to keep at it. Like Damien and Jill, he asked what I was eating, as if there was a secret dish besides the noodle-chicken-goat routine. My advice was to never be too shy to enter the kitchen and start pointing out veggies and meat, make everyone laugh and you'll do alright. Then, he asked about the great expanse that lay ahead. Despite his depressed state, I could be nothing short of honest; my beaten and wind dried brain still reeling from the trial.

"The good news is, that heading west, the winds are with you much of the time. But when they're not, it may be the most difficult thing you've ever faced." I went on, "the heat and blank distances go on for a couple of weeks, and there will be stretches where you'll simply run out of water and be overcome by weakness." I knew I wasn't selling it well, but the guy had to know. "At any point of true danger, you can always stick out a thumb, but think about this," I said, driving it home, "if you cross the Gobi Desert on a bicycle, you'll join a pretty small crowd. It'll be something to be proud of the rest of your life." Neil's home was Tipperary, and I know what you're thinking. I wanted so bad to crack "it's a long way to there" but just couldn't do it. The poor guy wasn't up for a silly quip that he'd heard too many times. Feeling bad for his misfortune and state of mind, and knowing the vast continent he still had to cross, his task reminded me of how far I'd come. I prayed the winds were with him. A guilty tinge swept by, lifted by the thought that 3000k's away lay the finish line in Hong Kong. Hell, it seemed like just over that next hill by comparison, the next hill being a mountain range that peaks as the Liupans a few days away.

In Wuwei, the hotel cost too much, but the restaurant offered a meat and potato's meal that was ravished. A computer sales store allowed me to update the blog, and the evening ended watching Willy Wonka and the Chocolate Factory, in Mandarin. Knowing in advance that it all pivots on the Everlasting Gobstopper, Wilder's manic Chinese was a joy. Breakfast was taken at a fruit stand, surrounded by onlookers snapping picks and offering melons. It was another amazing moment, I've never been so interesting this early in the day! And then, on the way out of town, came the surprise of Francois. The Frenchman, riding a recumbent, was headed for Shanghai. He told me that a few days earlier near Zhangye, as the 312 ended, he had thumbed a ride and saw me off in the distance. The lone soul riding up on the new, unfinished, highway. I'd learned my lesson of trying to ride at another's pace ala' Beijing-bound Diego, and we soon lost contact.

That day was one of corn fields, bordered with hundreds of thousands of hemp plants. Twin humped Bactrian camels grazing on roadside scrub, and a curious tiny smoke and snack shop. What once started life as a standard sized van, had been blocked up and completely plastered over, leaving only the side opening entrance. It looked like a child had molded it from green clay, but it spoke loudly. A poor man needed a store, so he made one. The road followed the verge of desert and broke east at Gulang on the S308. Caught a room there for three bucks and change, best bargain yet! When the local police came calling, the pleasant man and woman officers had me run through another entertaining interview, and then treated me to dinner downstairs. By now I'd repeated the life and journey details to the police so often that it was becoming a stand-up act. "The Brian Monologues and Blues Review", coming soon to a Gansu village near you. The room's TV was the most memorable point of Gulang. Apparently, all the room's sets were cabled to a multiple splitter. As the desk girl downstairs surfed channels during the evening, my channels changed too! Three bucks!

The desert-to-mountain land transition continued the next day. The

headwinds were balanced by a generally declining road through a world so many, including most Chinese people, will never see. The spotty remains of the Great Wall now and again, the casually wandering camels, all silent reminders that these days are adventures that will never come again. At the top of a small rise, while snapping pics of a well-used abandoned cave-home that was dug out of the exposed dirt face, created when the highway was cut over the pass, a young man called out from across the road. His invitation brought me into his home, another long, two-room rectangle. A quarter of the space was kitchen, the rest of it living room/bedroom. His parents and grandparents and little sister all lived there, and all slept on the same long board platform, raised a metre off the cement floor. Noodles and bread were served up for lunch, this random beautiful family taking the odd stranger in, and so happy to do it. We cheered on the Chinese rowing team on the small screen and sipped tea, as I went through the story. The young man translated the tale to them, and their lives' story back. That dugout cave across the road was once the family home.

The 60k day ended in what I thought was Dajing, yet the people there said I'd already passed Dajing. I was giving up on estimating distances, or places. The legs knew when a rest was needed and shorter days were their voice. But not here, wherever here was, I want to press on to Jintai tomorrow and post up for a day of rest; I needed a shower and a couple of good meals. Found a cheap spot above a motorcycle repair/grain sales shop/motel that served as the family business and home. Across the way, I sat in a restaurant ordering mein jow as the cook's little girl and her friend stared and giggled at the stranger from across the table. To give her something to do, I handed her a 5 yuan note and asked if she'd run across to the store and buy a cold can of ice tea.

When she returned with the tea, I gestured that she keeps the change as thanks. Her father was on her to return the minor amount, but I assured him it was fine, my thanks for her help. He said a few words to her and she left. Dinner was delicious and when it was almost finished, the girl, about seven or eight years old, came back in and presented me a cord necklace of a polished teardrop stone. The father  would only allow her to keep the change if she spent it on a gift! I was amazed, this sort of goodhearted act was beyond my imagination. I thanked her and her family so much. Mom came out from the kitchen, and they both watched as she tied it around my neck. I would wear it for months and months until the cord broke. Today it hangs by the rear view, a wonderful memory.

The next morning, the legs and attitude said no. Another strong wind was fighting against my southern direction towards Jintai. Although this little room, with no water and a yard toilet, wasn't my ideal break spot; it would have to do. After hitting up the market for the day's chow supply, a group of small girls followed me back to the room. They wanted to come in, and had a hundred questions, but after a bit I had to shuffle them out. The American in me always thinking of the pox of a group of kids in some adult stranger's room. Plus, I wanted to rest, not answer questions. They left, promising to return in the afternoon. Yeah that's great kids, whatever. Bye.

Rest days are just that. Eat a bit then just lay on the bed and try to recoup. Eat a bit more, I could use a shower, but that requires running water... knock-knock-knock. The little girls returned. No, you can't come in. They talked me into walking about the village and showing off their hometown. I'm no good at saying no, and soon we were in mid-village at one of the girl's homes, a small one room flat. Mom and Dad are absolutely radiant at my arrival, and soon the watermelon and biscuits are served up; their proud daughter grinning as if she'd found a new puppy. Words cannot convey how wonderful these people are, I am constantly astonished at their hospitality. Reminding myself that this has to be a day of rest, I bid farewell after a while and make it back to the room. I dozed off for a few hours before being awoken by a knock on the door. Those happy, cheerful schoolgirls were bearing gifts.

The four of them want to come in, and I tried to politely beg off as the little misses marched through the door, showing off the small glass animal figurines they had bought. Alright then, for a minute. As they each presented their gifts, I thanked them so much, but couldn't bring myself to be honest. I hadn't the spare bag space to store or protect the little miniatures. No matter, the cherubs beamed. Such a different world to be in. The children and teens and adults, shop owners and policemen and farmers, all so goodhearted. There was an innocence about them that shined brighter than the Western misgivings of their social system. They lived a basic orderly life, uncluttered by the crazy world beyond the horizons of their remote desert world. This town, whatever its name, seemed a happy place.

Dinner was back at the cafe of the polished teardrop. As I re-greeted the family and sat down to a beer, Father reaches into a tank and throws a very large catfish like creature with a long dorsal fin on the cement floor, in the middle of the room, and walks away. I stared on in amazement as the gasping fish flopped around the dining room, the other guests didn't blink an eye. After several minutes, Father returns and smacks it on the noggin a couple of times with the butt end of a cleaver and carries it back to the kitchen. This let everyone know that today's catfish special was fresh, and I await the day Applebee's takes the page. The meal ended in their back-living room, watching the USA vs. Germany basketball game. Surrounded by this cheerful family, I sat thinking about how I have now, like Ukraine and Russia before, become saturated in China. Fully immersed with the salt of the earth people that make up not the surface culture, not the promoted idea, but the real people that belong only here. Behold the dirt in your hands.

Left the room the next morning, wrapped up for the steady rain shower. Stopped for noodles 20k's out at a small café, and gifted the woman behind the counter with a couple of glass figurines. When I asked about a restroom, she pointed to the cornfield across the road. The drizzle carried on, and after ducking into any shelter for every spell of serious downpours, Jingtai was within reach by the afternoon. Suddenly, a couple of smiling oil workers chugged over to the roadside in a small pickup. With no introduction, they began loading the bike into the back and having me climb into the tiny cab, as if to say "it's raining fool." There was virtually zero communication as the two cheery men, in their well-worn 50's and donned in blue Maoist rags, bounced into Jingtai. Without responding to or acknowledging my "pingqua" utterings, they began cruising for a hotel. I'd been hijacked...by nice people.

They searched out a $5 room, the front desk was managed by a helpful and pleasant teenage girl. After thanking my escorts and settling in, she gave directions to a diner where the chicken and noodle blue plate special came with two heads! Sauntered back through an I-net cafe where the uploads wouldn't take, and arrived back at the digs by 7pm. My girl stood in the doorway, the police had been here looking for the American. She said I couldn't stay, she handed back the rate and asked me to pack up right away. Pow. A punch thrown after the guard is dropped hurts the worst. When I came back downstairs, she shut shop and was kind enough to walk me around Jingtai, searching for an acceptable place. Thankfully, the most expensive places were full.

We then ran across one of her friends, a local bicycle club member who was happy to help, and had the answer. I bid goodbye to my hostess and followed the guy down a few side streets to an unadorned rooming house, across from his clubhouse. "No police here" he says. Later, he drops by with two club members and a few beers. As we took in the night, a group of old people gathered in a small park across the way. Twangy, traditional Chinese music began from a tinny set of speakers on tall tripods, soon they started to bob and sway in circles, almost square dance style. Long into the night, long after my friends had said goodbye, with a promise to return at 9am for breakfast and a club ride out of town, the septo and octogenarians happily pranced about in the dual sport of exercise and social get together. I was under the radar, amid the human sunshine of helpful people, and contented elders.

But how far under the radar? I was hidden in a tiny room with a simple board bed and a dim lamp, down a side street in a small town, virtually in the middle of China. My friends and family could only vaguely guess from sparse blog posts that I'd been in the country for a while. Where? Somewhere. But the authorities, oh they could point to your general whereabouts. I may skirt an interview today, but if there isn't a recorded inquiry from the police in say, the next week, they'd soon be asking questions. Oppressive? Sure, taken through the scope of why they do it. Twist it, and it becomes comforting really, if a tourist disappeared.

I hadn't disappeared, but by now had been gone for over six months from the daily route of home and work. The workplace wouldn't lose a step, but by now Sheree had a dose of what my eternal absence would mean, the take on any messages from home was one of frustration. You play a role together in life and leaving for a few weeks isn't too stressful, but being gone for months causes much to go undone; things unravel. By now the income flow had long ceased, and hard-won savings were being spent to support the household, at a rate never guessed at when laying out the original plan. The big things were considered, but the little things that failed to come to mind while doing the math at the kitchen table were killing her.

Never had a mechanic, electrician, plumber or carpenter been called her whole adult life. Now, every problem that arose cost real money. And, aside from whatever deeds Cody or Glenn could handle, she felt she was facing the troubles alone. Though far far away, I could feel all of this, yet it passed below me. Somewhere in the months of freedom, a point of singularity had passed. Outlooks and expectations were truly erased, daily and long-term concerns were deconstructed. We play a game every day, a game Sheree was now playing alone. Like sitting on that mini mart curb sipping morning coffee in the Florida panhandle, observing the busy commuters pump gas and grab a cup and be there by eight, I was off the carousel. Deep down, there's a price to pay for spectating. Are you really not playing, or did you just give up? Is it possible to experience fulfilled losing? Philosophically, I reached over and turned out the light.

Seven of us slurped a noodle breakfast together, after picking up three more members at the clubhouse the next morning. It was a chatty ride, as the new guys were filled in on the adventure. I did my best to enjoy their company, while hanging on to the wobbly bike bars and working the road as it rose and fell into the foothills of the mountain range that divided the country. After we parted, the undulations increased in degree, but the day paid back with an afternoon of ancient mud villages, that seemed to have arisen in earth's Primordial. Pigs wandered the streets like stray dogs, and a changing red rock and tan landscape led to the first views of terraced farmlands, as sun-beaten farmers in coned hats plowed behind donkeys. Just as the entire journey slowly shifted into changing lands, the wheels were now slowly passing into a changing China. The peaks just a few days away will descend from the planet's temperate zone into the tropics.

The bike rolled through Baiyin, and a decent 100k day ended by stealth camping among the abandoned broken walls of pressed earth huts. Could have been sixty years old, could have been a thousand. An early night refreshed the legs for a 120k push the next day, heading south to the village of Guochengyi; along the way the S207 crossed the historic Yellow River. Second in length only to the Yangtze, the east-west Yellow is honored with deep cultural significance, dating back thousands of years to the earliest recorded accounts of Chinese history. It spawned their earliest civilizations, and today is referred to as the

Mother River. On the river's south side lay the town of Jingyuan, where I stopped on the main street to snap a photo of a butcher shop porch, as they hung and dressed out a dozen goats. The shop owner's son came out to talk, and soon the whole family and I were sitting down to a lovely lunch of fresh goat and rice. Another serving of a welcoming, hard-working family, in a town overseen by elaborate grotto temples, built high above into the bleached tan hillsides.

Riding through a valley of the wide cut Zuli River, the afternoon was filled with corn fields and tiny villages, and cave dwellings dotting the hillsides. There was an ancient atmosphere of the place, the sense that if I'd asked anyone how far back this long strip of oasis had been farmed, no one could know. The caves added a touch of mystery. How far back? Before there were houses? In Guochengyi, a crowd gathered as I stopped to buy camp food, three rambunctious drunks pushed forward and slurred out rapid fire questions that I couldn't understand. Two of them became insulting and posturing aggressive, things were getting edgy. Just when I was thinking "alright folks, now's a good time to step in", a young man did.

He scolded the pair, and they began to laugh it all off. One of them ran over to a street cart and bought me three bottles of waters. "See syeh see syeh", I thanked him many times and accepted the bottles. Quickly bidding "zy jin", I made my way down the road, walking with hero boy. As I went through my general route to this point, he told of a cheap hotel not far away. I asked him how far back that people had lived in those river valley caves, and he laughed. "My grandfather lived in them when he was a boy!" Damn. This place is ever bright with surprises. He said even now, when there's planting and harvesting, some people will sleep there, very cool inside on a hot night. We came to a small hotel that put me up for 30y and no interviews, love these small towns.

The night of the squealing pigs. Off the backside of the room was a yard of pig pens, and they went at it until they were tired, well past midnight. Fully rested, they began grunting again a few hours later. In their short respite, they had to suffer my snoring, so we called it even. The day awoke sunny and still, it was going to be another good day to ride. Like the day before, the fertile river valley of mud villages, terrace cut hills and still more farmer's grottos passed by. I must have "neehowed" two hundred times. These rural farmers, who rarely see a Westerner on this unbeaten path, would stop their tasks to greet me at  the roadside. Old sun baked men, clad only in shorts and sandals and crouching on their haunches, were playing some board game in the dirt under a shade tree. Apparently, they had a club in every village. I couldn't get enough of this beautiful slice of earth, tailored for a bicycle ride. As the 100k day ended in Huining, I knew the route would leave the river valleys and the terrain would begin climbing again to the east, into different lands.

And change it did, but not before a wonderful night in Huining. Again, a picture snapping crowd gathered and a young man eager to speak English stepped in to translate the tale. He brought me to his parent's home, where Mom cooked up a noodle dinner and then allowed me to spend some time on the home computer to update the blog and pics. Once again, no notice, just "Mom I found an American and he's hungry" kind of thing and the folks were all smiles. In the morning they saw me off with a breakfast and hugs, like we'd known each other for years. And then the climbing began, ridge after ridge, up highway G312.

All day long, the brown hills were terrace cut, almost as far as the eye could see in any direction. Just imagining the undertaking was overwhelming. How on earth could this be? The task was obviously done long before the benefit of earth moving equipment, the landscape gave the impression of a tipped over stack of tiles. And rare of it being currently farmed. Did they just do it, or was it at some great rulers' behest? Borne out of maximizing the sloped lands agriculture, it sensibly channeled the rain from deck to deck, minimizing drainage loss. But the vista-filling expanse, the wonder of it, was so vast that the day's climbing effort was hardly noticed. I just pedaled and gaped at the thought of what human toil could create. Google Earth it. Mind blowing, like riding through a Yes album cover.

Nearing a crest at day's end the road entered a tunnel. There was no end in sight, just a dark cave without a trace of illumination. The road narrowed into the dust-filled dim. As I watched white headlights emerged from the haze and red lights disappear, I turned on the rear rack's flashing red beacon and donned my camping headlamp. Then I waited, poised for the "ear" moment when there was no hum of an approaching car from behind, and then bolted into the void. Praying for the best. The lungs and eyes were quickly filled with the silty dust that never settled in the dark air. Two narrow lanes, zero roadside safety margin and not one tunnel light. I hugged the cement curb and pedaled flat out.

The entrance's light faded fast, and for hundreds of metres the meager headlamp's glare was the only view. Soon, the darkness was broken by the headlights of an approaching large lorry, illuminating just enough to reveal the swirling dust storm behind him in the truck's wake. Behind him, another set of lights came, and the only thought was that they aren't looking for a bicycle. The damned tunnel turned out to be just over a kilometre long, and thankfully no cars came up from behind until I was almost to the eastern opening. Upon exiting, I pulled over and sat down, swigging water and composing nerves and silently bashed on the engineers who thought that one through. No vents, no lighting. Their probable response would be "yeah that's not a tunnel designed for bicycles, happy boy." Thanks to be done with that.

The reward was a 7k descent into Jingning. The small town had a new feel and look, and the streets were full. I sat on the curb outside of a seed and grain store for a coke and a smoke, the tunnel nerves still lingering. As a crowd gathered and the questions were answered and the selfies were snapped, the couple who owned the store stepped in, and graciously invited me to stay at their home. They were an early 30's pair, and their shop was small, but stacked high with bags of planting grains. Seemed like good folks, so we locked the bike up in the back of the store and jumped into their Camry.

We stopped at what I gathered was a private elementary school, and picked up their son and daughter. The kids stared on, fazed for a few moments, as Mom explained who the weathered stranger in the front seat was. Their racing minds moved on to their day's school story, rapid firing words I'll never know. Their spacious townhouse had polished wooden floors, a modern kitchen, large flat screen and double sliding glass doors, overlooking a park. Friends dropped by with snacks and Mom called in a dinner order, Chinese food. But I bet they don't call it that. Before leaving to pick up the order, they noticed I'd left the travel kit with the bike. When she returned with a couple of big bags of hot supper, she also had a small bag with a toothbrush and paste, a comb and shaving cream. I couldn't thank her enough, how so very hospitable and thoughtful. After the dinner and a hot shower, the whole group settled in with drinks and watched the Olympic basketball finals. The U.S. topped Spain, and then came the closing ceremonies. A typical evening that occurred worldwide that day, could have been anywhere. A perfect evening, with incredibly good people.

After we dropped the kids off at school the next morning, they even treated me to breakfast. Rested and clean, I bid them farewell at the seed store. People like that were like plugging in the charger, their joy in helping out a stranger gave one a second look at humanity. On the surface, everyone here seemed very happy; altruistic. The benevolence experienced since rolling off the ferry in Holland, extended by the poor, middle, and prosperous alike, ramped up as the wheels turned further and further east. Why? Oh, that's a question for scholars that could spur a thesis or two. These societies have suffered the worst oppression in the northern hemisphere, lives controlled by demagogue dictators with brutal rules; written and otherwise. Now, here and in Russia, things are better. But the trials of the previous generation must scar forward, their social awareness is too keen for it not to.

A mechanic's stab? Western Europe and the lands beyond it to the East were deeply affected by strife and wars dating back well before the 20ᵗʰ century, middle and eastern Eurasia eventually living for decades under the failure of communism. Reliance on, and faith in your neighbor was, at times, all a person or a family or a village had to lean on. It shaped a culture over generations. One could argue that this spirit exists elsewhere; but the notion, the act of off-the-cuff inviting a traveling stranger into your home for the evening is one I struggle with. Could I be that guy? We're not wired like that any longer, perhaps we haven't suffered enough. Perhaps that spirit was a casualty of our post-war bountiful times. Maybe it's just me. Sitting in the dirt with these people, the greatest honor of my life.

Climb. Today's effort will see the crest of the Liupan's. I popped a Vike and turned on the iPod, seeking the rhythm trance as the road rippled steadily upward, all morning and afternoon. Leaving Jingning, the signs read 111k's to Pingliang, one k later, another sign said 101. Later on, passing through a village, a sign said Pingliang was 66k's away. Just in view, another sign said 67. The road sign's mileage engineers were probably the same guys that designed the tunnels. The land was now pine trees and thin air. As the peaks grew near, I could tell a serious effort coming soon, the hump over the top.

Resting on the roadside, sipping water and eating a pear. Even up here, there were little villages and settlements and terraced farms, people going by everywhere. Slowly, the passing days had left behind the vast empty panorama of the Gobi and we're now catching the traces of the coming civilization. Back in the saddle and pushing hard, the road rolled around a bend and my heart dropped. The peaks were still above me, yet the road stopped climbing. Just ahead, the pavement disappeared into a tunnel.

On goes the headlamp and red flasher. After waiting for the clear moment, I bolted into the hole, relieved to see a smattering of glowing lamps lining the tube; but no telling the distance. Traffic in both directions was light, and I pushed time-trial like through the dusty gloom. While dodging silt filled potholes and hugging the narrow curb, I had to remain hyper-wary of the cars behind. Then, the lights faded into a long darkness before the yellow haze of more tunnel lights were visible.

It seemed like the longest tunnel on earth. More lights, then again, more darkness. When I finally emerged, it was like a brand-new day. The sun was brighter, the air warmer and the road declined, making for a grateful long ride into a saddle plateau. The hole was almost two and half kilometres long! Not since that temporary bridge in east Texas had the adrenals raced and cringed at such a dangerous stretch. Within these two tunnels, the journey's fate was in the hands of random drivers who had no clue a cyclist was ahead in the dusty dark. With just under 2000k's to go until Hong Kong, the fear of a damaged bike or body came second only to the fear of losing the journals. The mantra of "one wrong move" ending my one shot called out loud. This tunnel shit was stupid.

Oh, but how the world was greener, a valley between peaks. The land noticeably different with lush hillsides and forested mountains off to the south. It was more a worm hole than a tunnel, asserting the desert-tropic divide of the Liupans. After a gradual rise over the saddle's eastern pass, the road breezed through a wide river valley of terraces and flat farmland down into the city of Pingliang. Pingliang plays a role as the Holy Land in the Taoist and Buddhist faiths. Its Kong Tong mountain, just to the west, is a place of pivotal tales and home to wise men and Confucian scholars. As such, the faithful and curious have flocked here over the centuries, the mountain's nearest city. Trade routes came, then farming and mining and rails followed, it swelled to a couple of million people.

Rolling into a big town, knowing that the first stop should be a police station, I gambled the thought away. I'd glided free the last few days and just didn't care. When a street vendor pointed towards a door between shops that led into a lobby, that was good enough. The girl was all springy when she saw me, happy to let out a $16 room. It seemed like a nice little hidden spot, and after wheeling the bike into the small room, I laid down and nodded off. Waking shortly, I debated to unpack and take a shower, maybe get some chow, should take a walk and see a bit of the streets. But laying there, the thought of just going back to sleep seemed way better...

I awoke in the dark and the phone was ringing. The desk girl said "the police are here you must come down I said you cannot stay, you cannot stay." More than an hour had passed snoozing, and as I was tying my shoes, the door knocked. Two officers stood there with the girl, who was handing the cash back. They pulled the same skit, one reeling the questions, the other jotting answers as I sat on the bed. The desk girl's act, to cover her butt, was that she had told me to leave, and had been ignored. The thought of explaining anything to them would only serve to expose her to some form of reprimand, and I'd still have to leave. I focused instead on making the case of complying with the cop questions, perhaps schmooz them into letting me stay. But why bother? I'd already been refunded. Don't give them a reason.

Politely, they demanded I follow the patrol car through the neon streets.  They led to a wonderful tourist hotel, charging double the rate, and then stood by as I checked in. Their presence caused the clerk to do a diligent yes-man show of information gathering, "we're nothing if not compliant" he may well have said. Then one of the policemen helped the clerk lug my gear up to the room. Everyone smiled, chummed at what must be the American's pleasure at such a better room. A TV with Kung Fu dramas and propaganda commercials! An extra bed! A ceiling fan! "Thank you, China, fuck you very much!" Ah bless em, I had it coming. Obey and comply, why is that so hard? Was I a western rebel dog? Nah. More like, I'll never see another $5 room the rest of my life; and to a dirt camper, they're just fine.

After a dumpling and chili sauce breakfast, I was chompin' at the bit. It was less than 200k's to Xi'an, and a planned stop to see the Terra Cotta Warriors. From start to finish, the only solid tourist plans were to visit the Warriors, and also to see the Three Gorges Dam, still a way's off. Most of the day's ride had a gentle decline, through a wide glacial valley of farmland, another beautiful day surrounded by the terraces and trees. How long could it have taken to create this stepped terrain? The last few days were filled with terraced farmland in every view, surrounded by the work of ancients. Hundreds, perhaps a couple thousand years of incredible earth moving and arranging, all done by hand. No words could describe the labor that created and maintained this functional beauty. I babble on it again, at the risk of overemphasis. It is a wonder of mankind's presence. Brilliant.

In the afternoon, trancing up a 10k climb, the thoughts are broken by Humphrey and Katherine, again. The slow chug-chug of the African Queen approaching from behind. Another three wheeled diesel twin mini truck coughing uphill at about 10kph. As it passes, I reach out and clamped onto the bed, and away we go. Bogey and Hepburn are dead ringers for a pair of old men donned in Commy blues, and no one's passing the gin back, but I don't mind. The good spirited old boys done dragged me all the way to the top before parting ways, what a break. On top it leveled out, and the road was lined with willow trees stretching out of sight; yet still, the frequent villages and

working farmlands made a shot at a stealth camp slim. The route of G312 had taken me out of a glacial valley, up a hump, and onto a high plain, like climbing a giant staircase. In all, a good day that put 120k's behind the rear wheel by quittin' time, at a wide spot in the road named Changwu.

The combination lock, the bicycle components and arm hair all got the once over as I stopped to figure out a stay, amid the wondrous stares of old people. The incessant honking had returned to the foreground too, as the populations increased from the lone desert days. I'd bought the theory of a society recent to a car culture, but now I'd seen another angle too. Pedestrians and bicyclists, people pulling or pushing carts, they rarely looked before crossing the street. It could stem to the same theory, people not accustom to fast moving vehicles. But wouldn't survival instinct correct the habit? Still, with the masses honking at anything and everything, how would anyone know they were honking at you? Rolling the dice again, I followed the crowd's advice of cheap digs and found a $3.50 bin guang. It wasn't a big town, maybe I'd pull it off.

It worked. A favorite dish of goat and spices with noodles and a cold beer from a noodle house a block from the room was sorely needed. After another wash basin bath, I hit the hay with no interviews; can't make Xian tomorrow but another 100k day will pull it within easy reach, the legs are starting to talk.

They were not up for the next morning's early start, after the last few days of climbing, a day off was needed; but not here. Like yesterday, the terraces and farms and pines continued with a slight decline in the pedals. It's the heart of China, the artistry of the balcony-stepped-rice paddies was set into the mountainous background, like a child's imaginary fairy tale land. The road rose and fell as it began crossing ridges, heading southward towards Xian; demanding and rewarding the lungs and legs in succession. It was a tough 110k day, pulling the loaded bike and bod over mountains that played a good game. But the worst of it came in the form of two long tunnels, a kilometre each.

The first one, about 50k's out, was unexpected. The terrain didn't seem to call out for a hole; it was dusty of course, but at least it had a few lights. 15K's later, came the scariest bore I hope to ever see. The road rose up along a ridge line, then humped over the top, and there it was. The tarmac disappeared into a narrow dark gray hole, emitting dust without a spec of light. There was no telling how long it was, it did have a slight down slope, but it just looked wrong. To the highway department's credit, there was a symbol sign indicating that no pedestrians or bicycles were allowed. But miles and miles into a winding two-lane mountain road, what was the alternative? Every fairy tale land has a dragon, the bastards all live in caves.

27. Qin

With the Petzl on the noggin and tail light flashing red, I rolled in, and was blinded immediately. The hole so dark and the dust so thick that the headlamp was useless, and the fouled eyes were stinging. The road was strewn with potholes, only visible from the oncoming headlights. And then the craziest narrow-two-lane-tunnel fear came to be: some oncoming idiot bus driver pulled out, he was making a pass on a freight truck, there was no space left!

Four yellow lights filled the haze, no spare margin but for a one-foot-high curb lining the wall, too narrow to ride on. I jumped up on it and sandwiched myself between the bike and the wall, leaning back hard. The pair of lane-filling monsters closed in, pushing a force of rushing, dusty wind ahead of them like a giant piston, they whooshed by, clearing the bike by inches and trailing a vortex of swirling grit; holy shit that was crazy close! Scared and nervous, I stayed up on the curb, pushing the bike along in the road and walking it the rest of the way. Just get out of this long cave alive, and don't ever play this barefoot mumbly-peg again. The slim ledge surface was layered in tomb dust, no footprints in the silt filth, no one had walked this way in a long time.

A 7k downhill welcomed me back into the sunshine. The little village-ettes and roadside service huts all had wide cement aprons where, for a few yuan, a trucker could wash off the grime from the last two tunnels; and they were busy. The mule and I were covered in gray powder. A boy with a hose motioned me over, and as I went for the water, his Mom ran out and scolded him. This spot was for truck business only! The dragon's tunnel had breached the last pass before the long descent into the Guanzhong Basin. At its center, the noted eastern starting point of the ancient Silk Road, the historic metropolis of Xi'an. It also marked the end to three weeks of pedaling the Gansu Province; we were now within 60k's of Xi'an, the Shaanxi Province's capital city. Calling it a day at some crossroads hamlet, I settled into another $3 hotel, with no police interviews, and featuring a cold and cold running shower. Watching it wash the dark dust down the drain was worth the shivering cringe.

August the 28th dawned with an easy 60k ride into farmed flat lands, clicking of cicadas, toward Xi'an. Negotiating towards the city center, I'm adopted by a young man on an electric bicycle, excited to tell me his cousin is an English teacher. Soon, I'm on the horn with the guy, and between the two, they lead me through the streets. A forty-foot wall appeared, surrounding central Xi'an. We ran its perimeter and circled a large roundabout before entering an arched opening, leading to the inner city. Humanity and shops spilling on the sidewalks, vegetable fruit stands and crowds and alleyways, all packed with trinkets and clothing stands and shoppers and bikes and people everywhere. It was all begging curiosity, but hanging within sight of the battery bike, zipping left and right, gave no moment.

Turning right onto a main thoroughfare, I was set back. The view was filled by a giant pagoda tower, well over one-hundred feet high, and surrounded by a tall brick base, centered in the boulevard's roundabout. Intricate in design and color, I slowed down and stared in awe at one of the most beautiful buildings I'd ever seen. I would later learn it was the Xi'an Bell Tower, and has stood since the 14th century. As I wheeled along, my electric guide waited smiling. "This

way" he shouts, and a minute later we pulled up in front of the Shuyuan International Youth Hostel.

If ever there was an embassy for homesick Westerners, this was the place. A virtual sanctuary, running about $23 a day. Pizza and beer and hamburgers, laundry and internet and Family Guy DVD's. They had a welcoming central bar and lounge, where travelers from all over the world could relax with a rich coffee and tell stories. This would be the staging spot for the next few days, to compose for the final push, plus take a bus tour. Forty k's east of downtown, the Terracotta Warriors Army experience awaited. With the wonderful hosts and guests and offerings, I could truly drop the guard for the first time in months. A shrine of familiarity.

English and Europeans, South Americans and Australians, a New Zealander and some Americans. Ranging from young to old, they'd all spent some time at the Beijing Olympics, that had just ended days before. When they found out how

294

I had arrived, the story floodgates burst open and the brews flowed. Friends were made as everyone took turns telling their own tales of travel magic. Most of their Xi'an tourist plans centered around the Muslim Quarter, with its unique shopping alleys and the bird and flower markets hidden within. But, the common must for all was visiting the Warriors.

The following day's first stop on the Terracotta bus ride was to some factory, miles away from the archaeological site, offering official souvenirs. I wandered about until a marble Terracotta Army chess set caught my eye. I then set to haggling the price for two sets, with shipping, for Shay and Cody. As the sales chief and I bartered to and fro, the rest of the tour group headed for the bus. I set my final price as did he. When I walked away from the deal he came back with an offer, which I then whittled at some more. Before long, my tour mates were complaining, and the bus driver was warning me that they must leave now. The salesman was using this pressure to close the deal, but I wouldn't relent, it was now game on.

Setting the bar one more time and being rejected, I once again motioned "no thanks, thank you" and headed for the steps. As the substantial sale was about to drive off, he came out with one more price drop and we shook hands. Now the idling coach, full of tourists, started making noise. I had to go inside the factory and sort out the sale and shipping addresses. I didn't blame anyone for being pissed, but I'd never see this place again, and the address details had to be solid. And besides, the Warriors had been at attention now for over 2000 years, they weren't marching off anytime today. I kept that fact to myself as I sheepishly climbed up the bus steps before bursting into "thank you's" to the good folks, for not driving off without me.

The discovery of, and museum itself, has had countless articles written across the internet and print, as well as documentaries and world exhibits. It is well considered one of the most significant archaeological discoveries of the 20th century. The coolest bit is that only a small percentage of the 3rd century B.C.'s First Emperor Qin's army and chariots, servants and courtesans, have been realized. Much remains unearthed as researchers are still deciding on how to undertake the daunting task without compromising the un-oxidized state in which the relics exist. On arrival, the visitor is faced with two enormous aircraft hangar style buildings that were erected over the top of the discovery's vaults.

Once inside, the size of the buildings is impressively cavernous. The largest is a couple of football fields long and half as wide, its deep sub level corridors are filled with hundreds and hundreds of standing life size soldiers; the same

light brown tan hue of all the rammed earth mud villages and Great Wall remnants I had been seeing for weeks. You'd have to search hard to see replications, for almost every figure had a different face or uniform or stance, all mixed in with horses and chariots, as if marching into battle. A walkway followed the perimeter of the pit, giving appreciation to the manpower it must have taken just to delicately unearth this peerless wonder. The adjacent second vault was less than half the size, yet just as amazing. Again, a collection of warriors, chariots and horses, but the smaller grouping made the battle arrangements comprehensible.

Emperor Qin's and his army quelled and unified a half dozen earlier divided states to become known as China's first emperor, and established the Xi'an area as its first capital, beginning a string of Emperors and dynasties for two millennia. To accompany him in the beyond, he created the Terracotta Army, over an estimated period of four decades. It was then hidden by layers of wood and matting, then covered by earth. When the project was completed, hundreds of laborers were buried alive with it, to keep it secret; and thousands more killed. And there it lay, hidden for almost 2200 years. The myth was lost in time until 1974 when a dirt-poor farmer named Yang Zhifa and his brothers were digging a well, and hit upon a chunk of clay soldier.

"Well the first thing ya know ol' Jed's a millionaire, the kin folk said Jed move away from there..." wasn't the case. The man knew this might amount to something and brought it to a local museum, whereby within a couple of years archaeologist from all over the world piled in to expose one of the most massive and interesting historic finds of all time. Yang was shoved aside without a great deal of compensation for his discovery. He even had to endure the scowls of his neighbors, as the Chinese government made them all relocate in order to establish the site.

Decades later, the seventy-five-year-old man now sat behind a desk in the visitor's center, signing books for a pittance. Our group had been warned by our guide, as had others, "don't attempt to talk to him, he's just there to sign book purchases." I was honored just to see him, the guy that started this entire wonderful discovery, in the flesh. A scientific phenomenon that brought China tens of millions of tourist and research dollars every year. I stepped forward and extended my hand, he leaned forward and accepted it. "Good job old boy" I said, to the gasp of others, as they scurried into the theater room.

The next day was just a kick around, spent in the labyrinth of small streets and alleyways of the Muslim Quarter; they were filled with market stalls selling everything from shoes to booze. Paintings and grains, jewelry and kebabs; Terracotta souvenirs and straw hats. Buddha carvings and brassieres, fresh butchered meat and wrought iron art and baskets of odd spices. The endless corridors of goods stretched on and on. Women were wrapped in scarves, the men wore the white kufi skull caps, all busy cooking and serving, selling and hustling; a true bazaar. And yet, at the nucleus of this neighborhood of shadowy corridors, filled with the bustling bartering Muslim Chinese commerce, and quite literally in the center of this great walled city, rests the ancient and nationally renowned Xi'an Grand Mosque. Within its 1300-year-old grounds, its peaceful gardens are an olly-olly-oxen-free zone from the bustle of humanity around it.

Meanwhile, the months of living in a single pair of mountain bike shoes had rewarded a spreading foot rash that seemed to leap frog up the limbs whenever scratched. Needing an ointment to combat the spread of cracking skin, I asked around for a drugstore or pharmacy in the Quarter. The advice led me to the door of a shop that seemed to exist out of time. Inside the plain wooden door, hidden behind vendor stalls and leaning pallets, was a small dim room. It was filled deck to ceiling with old wooden shelves stuffed with small glass bottles. The floor was lined with large fiber bags, all filled with herb dust and tree bark and twigs. Much of it was unmarked, the rest was labeled with a handwritten script. None of it made any sense to me, and clearly there was no Tinactin about. Hell, there wasn't anything that didn't look like it required a chanting spell from the old woman sitting behind a corner desk, casting a stare. I was fascinated. It was a natural remedy pharmacy. The narrow aisles had tea leaves and powders, there were bottles of dried flowers and roots and berries. There were tiny dried seahorses and beetles, cloves and oils. Double-double toil and trouble fire burn and cauldron bubble this was the store! Laugh now but it all has to be real. The place, the tradition, the results, all this was here for a reason. We just don't get it, they do.

A long walk for sights and pictures of the central city, atop the Xi'an City Wall, was another must before the day ended. Originating in the 7th century, it was enlarged to its present state by the 14th century's Ming Dynasty. The wall is an almost fourteen-kilometre-long giant square perimeter around the old city. On top, it's as wide as a two-lane road and completely surrounded by a wide moat, lined with trees. Then as now, the only way into the old city was through four drawbridge gates, one per side. They were manned by massive elaborate guard towers, and protected along its entire route by smaller turrets; all within bow shot of each other. In eons past, it was a virtually impenetrable stronghold.

My path to Hong Kong would never cross the classic sections of China's Great Wall to the north of Beijing, as seen in all the vacation ads. But, the grandeur of  Xi'an's Wall was another challenge of comprehension. Just like the boundless terrace layered hillsides of recent days, and the creation of massive clay armies, complete with armament and transport, the labor and engineering that was required to construct this mega fortress overwhelms the imagination. The Chinese people's history long predates Western enlightenment and its conventions. With little to no influences from the West it had, over the many centuries, created an industrious world unique to their beliefs and visions. This country is as close to a parallel planet as one shall ever behold.

As I returned to the hostel for a final night, some friends had left, and new faces had arrived. It had been a busy couple of days here. It was nice to breathe an easy evening with a cheeseburger and a beer, and listen to another newcomer group whoop it up, telling travel stories among themselves. Afterward, the fresh laundry and gear were packed away in preparation for an early departure out the east gate. The road struck through Lantian a few hours out, where in the mid 1960's paleontologists spaded up the remains of a couple of one-million-year-old women; yet still named the discovery "Lantian Man." Girls always gotta work twice as hard. They had lived in the shadow of the Qinling Mountains that rose sharply before me. As the day led on, the rested legs knew this was the last honest to goodness mountain range to push over before the journey's end, and the head was enjoying the climb.

The same G312 route that led into Xi'an led out. It continued up the Qinling face, climbing up and following a top-of-the-world ridge line before descending into a tight river valley, filled with what seemed to be one long, cramped, village. Three tunnels went by that were short enough to not rattle the nerves, and every so often the narrow road would pass under what looked like a temple gate. Word was these mountains were home to many Daoist and Buddhist shrines, perhaps the gabled arches honored their presence or marked a sacred route. So much here has meaning and deserves time. Pedal on.

After the final and longest tunnel, the day was fading as I pulled into a truck wash and tried to ask the man in charge about a spot to spend the night. He came through large, and had me follow him to his home next door where I met Mom and Jr., and Grandpa. They were happy to help, and showed me to a flat spot in their front yard. I became a dinner guest and afterwards, my host brought forth a bottle of some clear liquor that alerted the sinuses and went down with a funky dirt mossy aftertaste, but somehow hit the spot. Looked like moonshine, but there was a lot going on in that tiny glass. "By-shu" he smiled and the truck washing man was happy to pour more, once he saw I appreciated the dessert shots. The evening closed down with Grandpa and I taking turns in the back of the house with his flavored tobacco, drawn out of what looked to be a classic long-stemmed opium pipe. Another great family I just happened to stumble into.

The next morning's mountains were beautiful, like the Sierras or high Rockies during spring runoff. A cold clear stream pounded down a rocky bed as I altered in and out of deep pine shadows and sunlight, through mountain villages. The slab sides of some giant river bound boulders had word characters chiseled in deep and painted red. It wasn't graffiti, it was faith. The roadway archways, the chiseled boulders, this was sacred land. So many single hut businesses sat behind wide cement apron areas, set up for multiple truck washing; other smaller hut collections seemed abandoned. A few times, somewhere out of sight, I could hear distinct voices in chant wafting from behind the pine curtain, not eerie; harmonious. Then the afternoon's ride gave way to a few fast descents and I tried holding the reins back, ever skittish that we were so close now, don't blow a turn. Soon enough, the freak was back and all admonishments of reining speed were gone. Zoom past the cautious cars...ease brakes to the apex and... release through the turns. Childlike blind faith in the slim tires.

I walked into a cafe in Shangluo to fill the bottles, and when I came out, one of the pumps at next door's gas station was literally covered in thousands upon thousands of bees. The queen must have parked her butt there and the huge colony followed, the air all around was full of buzz. As I stared transfixed, two of them landed on the back of my head and nestled into the hair, and I went back inside. A man jumped up to stop me from swatting and then lit a cigarette. He began blowing smoke at the insects, hoping they'd fly away peacefully as I became the center of the cafe's attention. People circled around and smiled and gave their own two cents at the predicament. With the bee storm outside keeping me put, and the hopes of avoiding the sting, I played along. I was quite humbled at everyone's concerns, or maybe they just loved every bee. A few minutes later, as the guy lights his second cigarette, the final bug took off and so did I. There was no telling how long this could last, so I took the chance of rolling a wide berth back up the road, then quickly pedaled past the station when the air cleared for a moment. The gas pump appeared to be breathing inside an ocean planet of insects wavering to and fro, it had three times as many as before, could have been a million.

In the town of Denfeng the day ended at a $7 no hassles motel. Here, the river valley ended, and the next morning would begin with a climb. Holed up in the tiny quiet room, alone with a few beers, the thoughts arose of how much has passed and how little remained. The intense fear of not making it wasn't relenting, it was growing. If something ended the ride now, everything I'd been through from the start would be a waste of time and serious money. The approaching return of real life was oppressing the philosophy of enjoying the moments, harboring with it a race day mentality. Make the finish, place well.

Not only today's risky descents, but the concerns of how I had become heedless of existing within elbow-inches of trucks and cars for thousands of miles, began to play up. These moments alone allowed the force field of self to drop, the daytime's lonely hours in the saddle too focused to dwell on the exposure. The reality was that no one back home, even the closest forever kind well-wishers, would see anything short of the goal as a failure. "Yeah that was great, but it would have been amazing if you'd have made it all the way." Why does the confidence stumble at times? Why do the conclusions of others mean so much one day and so little the next? A see-saw of never knowing how you really felt, where you stood.

The rash was spreading up my hands, and a tiny spot on the forehead was noticed. The itching helped on the long climbs, providing a point of discomfort to focus on rather than the burning legs, but every disparity takes a mental toll. I was using a diaper ointment to combat the spread, and changing shirts every day, rinsing the sweat out of them at night. Nothing seemed to help. You're just wearing down, it'll be fine til' you get home. Stay centered, make good choices, drink a beer. Pop that final Vike from Mom's stash. Do or do not. There is no try. I remember that guy.

The climbing began right out of town on a cool mountain morning. Head down, pace the gears, find a rhythm. The route and the natural lay of the ridges combined to cause the climbs and descents to seem tumbled about, like scattered tiles. Perhaps little engineering thought was paid to the pattern of the land, maybe the road follows an ancient route. Maybe the mind is making excuses, just wanting the ride to be done. The reality was a morning of substantial climbing that humped traversing ridge lines. While pumping uphill, about 18k's into the ride, the slow clattering of a loaded car carrier came up from behind. The truck was plodding the grade, just a touch faster than I was. I reached out to a passing rail, and gripped tight.

Pulled along slowly, while navigating the thin margin between the road's edge and the carriers frame, I leaned in with the left arm arched, and blessed every metre that the legs needn't move. The passenger's face in the side mirror seemed nonplussed at the new parasite and life was good, until about 2k's later when another dark tunnel appeared. I released and flashed thumbs up to the mirror's face, thankful for the lift. Then, just before the hole, the truck pulled over.

The two men were all smiles and handshakes, and motioning to a flat spot on the trailer tongue, big enough for a bicycle. A truck ride through the tunnel? Hell yes! We tossed the panniers into a trunk of one of the three Xi'an built BYD cars they were hauling, and lashed down the bike. Like an amusement park ride, the world went from light to dark as we entered the long dim tunnel. When we emerged a kilometre later, the basic hand signs and halting how-do-you-do's were just beginning. They were happy to have me along, the three of us trying to relate where we had started and how far to their favorite lunch diner and the beauty of Xi'an, all without a common word between us. The truck just kept rolling along, and I sat in the sun-warmed seat and did my best to tell the tale. Shamelessly, time rolled by.

As did the k's. After another noodle diner lunch, the boys dropped me off some 70 k's later at a crossroads, leading south towards Shiyan. Seventy k's of these crisscrossed mountain ridges was more than a day of pulling hard. The guilt of the ride crept in, but I wouldn't have traded it for gold. Seventy k's closer was all that mattered. The ride began again in the early afternoon on G209, through a truly placid valley following the river Qihe into Hubei Province. Farm fields, creeks and small villages were wound through a serpentine crevice of hillsides, covered in thick pines. In the late afternoon, in another village to mispronounce and forget, it was an $8 hotel and a quiet night of patching tubes. Thanks to the BYD boys, it had been a good day, the pin on the map moved. The

map showed the road south of Shiyan as small and winding, meaning steep, but it would drop me out on the mighty Yangtze river just above the Three Gorges Dam.

A human engineering marvel, an ecological and social nightmare, an economic machine. I'd read about the loss of ancient villages and temples, the government's cruel disregard of a million people, and their lands and homes affected. The draw was twenty plus of the largest generators ever created, churning out more power from a single point than anywhere else in history, all in a massive layout of modern cement architecture. I had to see it. As a child, the parents toured us through Nevada's Hoover Dam, I remembered the chill of standing in chambers enclosed by a wall of water on one side, and a deep void on the other; the temperatures dropping the deeper we descended. The Three Gorges was many times its size, and this time I would understand it.

But not before earning it. "Some of the hills very steep" noted in the journal. A day of incredible mountain scenery, with hours of serious climbs and zooming descents, but the mileage guesses were frustrating. The road map claimed Denfeng to Shiyan at 103k's, a distance well gone by, given the truck lift and a day and a half of riding. Along the route today, the land was jammed with stacked rock terraces, filled with corn crops. There were small villages every few k's, and dozens of creeks streaming into the Qihe river. Cars would slow to a crawl to stare, and a hundred "neehow" and "hallos" were blurted as the wheels passed by farmers and villagers. I tried to get a kilometre guess from them, only to be stared at, and every answer was different. Even here in Baisanguanzhen, the signs still put Shiyan at 75k's away. "Shee-an" versus "Zee-an." Maybe they thought, with my mangling of their language, I was asking for Xi'an, yet headed the wrong way? Baisanguanzhen, a 10y room! That's about a buck and a half! Cheapest yet! It wasn't the Ritz-Carlton, but once you close your eyes, they all look the same.

The push to the Yangtze motored on the next day, September the 4th, after the little gasoline stove heated up enough water for a salty ramen packet breakfast, and another whore's bath. Noodles were now reaching the disdain point of Russian vodka, and a soothing cup of morning joe was a memory. I pedaled straight into a rising G209 that labored on for hours, broken up by the fall and rise of a valley cut by the Han Shui River. An amazing Tomorrowland-esque bridge, with two wishbone towers anchored by hundreds of steel cables, spanned the Han. It was like riding into an unearthly-sized strung harp, a statement of the country's infrastructure resources. After another climb out of the river valley, the sight of Shiyan finally appeared.

Rolling in brought the strangest take on the city. A working man's industrial domain whose mechanizations were folded into a mountain town, set among deep green forested hills that are home to some of the country's oldest Taoist Tai chi temples. Shiyan is a national center of automotive production, namely the giant truck manufacturer Dongfeng, and a compliment of vehicle and engine parts producers. The dichotomy of major resource dependent enterprises, built far from supply lines and end markets, didn't make sense. Up front.

But Beijing doesn't just let things happen. A small town was turned into a major industrial center in the mountains, far from borders and coastlines. It was built up during the Cold War years when the threat of possible invasions still lingered on the leadership's memory. Perhaps a lesson from Stalin, who had to shift complex industrial factories from the Western front to the Urals, while on the fly, during the German invasion. But hey, the result for the locals in today's Shyan is a steady job in a beautiful place. Perhaps Henry Ford should have looked hard at Jackson Hole years ago.

It was midday, and with another climbing task ahead, I passed through Shiyan's central zone without stopping. Breaking away from the G209, the path started southbound, hiking up the narrow S235. The next few hours were spent climbing and rolling an incredibly narrow wooded rocky ridge line. Map wise, it was a direct cut south, but terrain and strategy wise, it was folly. The Yangtze was four, maybe five days away through deep mountain country. Knowing that China would soon relent into the tropical flats, the sadistic siren of humping the heavy bike up and down the steep hills, chalked with false summits, called out one last time. The burning legs, standing on the resistant pedals and earning every metre, satisfied a strange need for pain before it all panned out to the finish line.

Stopping at a rustic resort style hotel, the manager's first wavering reaction was that I couldn't stay there. Then I could. He asks for 30y, and when he couldn't make change for a 50, I indicated no problem. I'm going to unload, then come down for a meal, we can square up later. Not that succinct of course, but we were both smiling on the same page. While settling in, a knock at the door made my heart jump, I know what's next. But no, it was the happy-faced manager, bringing a clean towel and soap! After a shower and a nice outdoor dinner, I played a little ping pong with some other guests. Before retiring to the room, I went to the front desk for my due change.

Now my smiling innkeeper wasn't smiling. He now says he doesn't owe me 20y, the room is actually 80y, and the towel and soap an extra 10. With the language barrier suddenly in full force, I grab a pen and paper and plainly noted his bad math. And what's up with the towel and soap I never asked for? His story was that the 30y was for one hour, staying all night is 80. One hour, as if I was stopping by to get laid or what? The clown wanted 90y total, I'd already "paid" 50. He knew what he was doing. Outside, a dark night on a mountain road waited; of course, I gave him the extra 40. Reflecting, the total seemed in line with the place's status, but still. Ass.

Rested, but happy to leave the next morning, the road continued its climb for hours until a long 10k descent. Stopping at a small store to snack, three buses pulled in and unloaded. The groups split off into the store and the restrooms, some stood aside for a smoke. Three young men began asking about the bike ride. "Why are you out here?" "Well I'm cutting south, headed for the Yangtze and the Three Gorges Dam, really want to take the tour." They began talking between themselves, and then told me "this way is not possible."

The road between here and Fangxian goes through a military zone. "You're an American, you'll be cuffed and held, they'll ask for money." Others chimed in, backing up their tale. But as you now know, I had heard this worn out story line before...and yeah, that last time they were right.

I backtracked my way up the road a few k's to small shop I'd previously passed, and found a local village woman who taught English. She affirmed the warnings. "A pity you cannot go this way" she says. I still didn't want to believe it, but why would different parties say the same thing? So, do I go for it and see what happens, or hump back over the mountains a day and a half to Shiyan? Backtracking and routing around Fangxian would place me too far east of the Dam. I had to try, how else was I going to see it? What the hell did these people, people who had passed through that zone and actually lived in this area, know? They knew. They knew, and I didn't. With visions of my last detainment, the Three Gorges Dam plan began to melt.

But sure as hell I wasn't going to fight that mountain again. With my tail between my legs, I stuck out a thumb and was soon picked up by a trucker. We twisted and turned over the grades and he dropped me off back in Shiyan by late afternoon. From the trucker to others in Shiyan, I couldn't get anyone to pinpoint the military zone, they all just smiled a lot and pointed in the general area of Fangxian. Dumbstruck with cold acceptance, I'd lost a full day or more of progress. Turns out the Chinese Alternate Military Command Center Fangxian, something akin to a second tier NORAD facility (note to Jason Bourne: 31-57-48N / 110-38-26E) remained safe from my second spy mission of the trip.

Riding out east of Shiyan, I spotted a woman crouched over a creek on the side of a new office building, scrubbing her laundry with rocks. I wondered if any of the suits inside were embarrassed. Then again, they may be staring out the big windows wondering when their Brooks Brothers would be ready. After the day's disappointment, the rash spreading up the legs, stomach, and forehead; the trip money wearing thin, and now the sad reminder of an everyday person's life, the wonder of China was fading. Feeling weak, I found a 50y hotel with a hot shower and a washing machine. That revived the spirits somewhat, and when the next day dawned, it was met with a determination to try and put China behind in 100k chunks.

After some nominal morning climbs, the afternoon finally descended into the humid flatlands, leaving the big climbs and long dusty tunnels of the gorgeous Qinling and Wudang mountains behind for good. The final stage was beginning. The road passed by farmers wearing misspelled western T-shirts, spreading corn and wheat, peanuts and peppers out to dry in the highway margins; using beer bottles to mark the zone to alert cars. It recalled and made sense of the green peppers people out in the desert. Many small farmers here couldn't afford pouring a large cement drying slab, they used the roadway. The wind blew off an old man's coolie hat that I damn near grabbed for him on the fly, missing it by inches as I rolled past. The day ended in Laohekou on the lower banks of the Han Shui River. Lying in bed that night, knowing the hardest part of China's geography was now past, everything seemed post climatic. The hot wet air was making the skin crawl like a thousand red ants, the still flickering

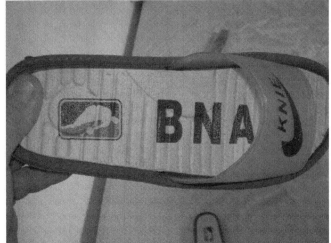

importance of the Three Gorges goal all but gone.

The Paralympics had just begun. The State TV's overtly pro-China propaganda robot offensive of the Games showed no relenting, as did the continuing of commercials that were just tourist ads about how great the provinces were. No laundry soap or aspirin or motor oil pitches here. Sour attitude, tired and tired of the journey, the mercy Vikes gone. Over a thousand k's to go to Hong Kong and the ache of a bug was coming on, plus I knew tomorrow's big to do was getting the visa extended. China's U.S. visa in 2008 was good for a year, but only for sixty days at a time, after which one would have to exit then reenter the country. Mine was expiring in six days. Almost two months ago at the Kazakhstan border, the station chief said to drop by any police station and they'll grant an extension of another thirty days, which would give plenty of breathing room to reach the finish line. For a State that is founded on the power of hierarchical authority, it was nice to know they made it that easy.

28. seven days

Out of the mountains and across the muggy flats. Accustomed to the high altitude, the legs and lungs motored like Lance across the G316's low rice paddies that were dotted by peasants and oxen working the fields. Driven by the momentum of putting China away and controlling the destiny of home, I put aside thoughts of discomfort and pedaled on; putting to good use the extra oxygen. Be the moose Brian, just buck up head down and go. Hong Kong ain't comin' to you boy! I rolled over sections of road where piles of rice stalks, almost two feet high, spanned across both lanes and were being shuffled about by farmers. They were cleverly using the cars and trucks and bicycle tires to thresh their crops. It looked like a common practice of necessity.

Turning south on G207 through Xiangyang, my wheels ambled through little villages with firecrackers going off everywhere. It was some sort of election day, and people sat about in groups drinking and eating, celebrating the vote all day.  Fifty k's later the day ended amid Yicheng's streets, also littered with piles of firecrackers. A few were still going off, it was like riding through popping corn.

307

It had been well over a 100k day in the new heat. With the guard dropped and feeling exhausted, all I wanted was a meal and a bed. It was now past 7pm, the police station visa visit could wait.

Waking up on the 8th of September, it was pouring outside. I hadn't had a day off since leaving Xi'an, and I felt like hell. Once the rest decision was made, the body gave in and the lingering bug hit hard with a fever, aching and squirts. Made it out around midday with the idea of re-upping the visa, but only managed to find a market, then realized I wasn't ready for food. Back at the room I wrapped myself in blankets and then spent hours surfing the excellent television programming of Kung Fu soap operas and the constant prep updates of China's upcoming spacewalk mission. Through the night and another morning, I was still in no condition to ride and as much as I hated to, went down to the front desk and paid for another day. Suddenly a light bulb came on. I remembered the kick ass Ukrainian pepto pills! After popping one and giving it a few hours to cook I pedaled across town to the police station, there were three visa days left. From that moment on, a carousel of events began to unravel, they would change the journey from here until Victoria Harbor.

The policemen outside the station stared as I walked up with the bike, they quickly opened the front door and a desk clerk cheerfully asked for the passport, and then left to fetch a translator. As the translator walked in he was checking the visa date, so I hardly had to explain my request. Behind my smile, all I could think was "let's just get this over with fellas, I need to back to the room and hide." The man looked confused, and polite as can be, he informed that the answer was "no." But that ain't all.

No police station, no town this small, has this authority. I had to go south to Jingmen and find the Public Security Bureau, something of a rung up on the government ladder. The officer was helpful enough to give an address in Jingmen, a day's ride away. He was also quick to add that I shouldn't make any stops, traveling in China with an expired visa was a serious matter. There was a concern in the air, my request here seemed odd to them, the gut felt a rift coming. "And the office hours of the PSB?" "I don't know when they open and I don't know when they close", two pieces of handy information. Drained and disappointed and sensing a trip through bureaucracy land, my only hope now was to charge off early the next day. I prayed that my plumbing would cooperate, as well as the Jingmen Public Security Bureau.

The risk of having the visa expire is of course some sort of temporary detention, and a fine, until things are sorted. I hadn't looked into the severity of each, but so far, anecdotes observed that China's punishment systems were rarely half measures. My main worry was the powers may decide "your game is over Mr. Tripp, thank you for playing, we shall kindly escort you to the nearest exit." Wanting to get home or not, it had to be on my terms. Rolling out of Yicheng the next day and mulling these thoughts, and the police officer's ambiguity on the Jingmen PSB's hours, made me push the red button. Let's not gamble with this. I flagged down a freight truck and later bummed a ride on a bus, pulling up to the Jingmen Bureau by noon. Safe! The sign said their afternoon hours began at 14:30; a police station with a long lunch? I had time to secure a 100y hotel and hit the ATM, and by 14:20 I was back on the stoop. 14:30 passed without any signs of life. The fruit stand lady next door pointed at my watch, gesturing that he comes to work at 15:00. Two and a half days to go on the visa clock.

At three o'clock, a stocky buzz cut uniformed chap in his late thirties arrived and unlocked the door, never acknowledging the smiling foreigner on his doorstep. Inside, I waited while he turned on lights and ruffled about a backroom. When he was good and ready, he asks in English "how can I help you?" He pages through the passport as I explain the urgency, clinging to the belief that all that is required is a few forms, some cash, and an official stamp. "I cannot give you a new visa." "Don't need a new visa, just an extension." "I cannot help you, go Changsha." What? Yicheng bumps me to Jingmen. The officer in charge of this referred office, in a large city, with an English sign reading "immigration and visitor affairs" bumps me to Changsha. His smirk conveyed that clearly, there was no wiggle room here. I was back on the stoop, looking at the map.

Changsha. Apparently, it was pretty damn big city and looked to be about 400k's away to the south. As I sat outside the office figuring my options, the guy came out and began locking the door behind him. I gave it one more go, pointing out my transportation, and he reemphasized that he cannot help. "Go to Changsha." So, I had to ask, how is it that a PSB in Changsha could grant an extension, but his could not. He replies "there is no reason. I do not want to give you a visa." Probably machismo speak for "I don't know how." He then walked away. And that was that, shut down and shut out in Jingman.

On the way back to the hotel I stopped at a McDonald's. I hadn't dared eaten for more than a day, and needed a burger and coke to center the mind. Changsha was a four to five-day ride away, a train trip was the only answer. Upon returning to the hotel, I inquired to the staff for information and they were very sympathetic; they offered to arrange a train ticket for the next day. I could be there by 11am, but would have to leave the hotel by 3am to catch the train. Let's do it. Turns out, Changsha was a city of five million, if it couldn't be accomplished there, then where? Failing in Changsha would leave me 24 hours to train to Shenzhen, to cross the border into the free zone of Hong Kong province. The ball had been dropped and was rolling downhill real fast. Was this really happening all of a sudden? Surely Changsha will save me, big city equals big authority, just get there and work the process. It will work out if I just jump through their hoops. Calm down, what could go wrong?

The answer came a couple of hours later. In the early evening the desk manager came to the door and told me the train won't accept the bicycle, "pity, there is only room for passengers." She also contacted the bus station, they said the same thing. "Perhaps an early bus will have the space, you can try." Oooh boy. A friend of hers was there and offered to help, Biyu took me to a nearby police station and explained to the officer in charge about the whole running-out-of-time problem. She made the case that if he cannot get the visa renewed here, and cannot get to a bureau that can help, he'll be in violation. But to no avail. They saw the American's problem in simple terms: he must leave the bike here and get to the PSB in Changsha. "Please do not wait."

They were right, that was the only way. The passport was demanded almost daily by police and requested at every hotel desk, and even by curious citizens. At every turn an expired visa meant at least some detainment where I'd lose dominion over the bike and more importantly the journal and the camera. As we sat outside the station, I relented to the idea of paying for another day or two at the hotel to store the bike. But what if Changsha throws a curve ball? If something went wrong there, then time would force me to head directly to Shenzhen and cross the border to Hong Kong. After re-entering back into Shenzhen, the two-month clock would reset. I'd then have to jump a train back to Jingman to fetch the bike. Then begin riding to Hong Kong again? Fuck that. I thanked Biyu for all her efforts but decided to roll the dice. Get up early, pedal across the city to the bus station and see if there was any way to catch an early bird, I wasn't leaving the bike without a last-ditch effort. And bless her heart, she offered to meet me at the city bus station in the early morning to translate, and help secure a ticket. These people.

After lugging the loaded bike down to the lobby at 3:30am I realized that I had left the formatted directions to the bus station on the bed stand. I received a quick rough-points surmise from the night clerk, hastily ball pointed on my left palm. Pedaling through the quiet streets, before the early morning jaoza and noodle vendors had even began to fire up their steaming sidewalk pots, I knew today was going to be monumental. Today could end with a new lease on the adventure or nightfall may find us straddling the Hong Kong province or...?

I was so torn between wanting the trip over versus keeping the experience alive that either outcome was welcomed, just gonna roll with the gamble at the Jingmen bus station. All this over a damned visa extension. The blame falls on the Kazakhstan-China border officers, or the many policemen that didn't mention the process during all those interviews. The Russian travel visa guys back in San Francisco, they should have emphasized the process from past experiences. No, no and no. The blame falls on moi'. My own lack of inquiry, concerning an important trip ending possibility.

Bah. Shake it off. Yesterday unfolded as it did, as did the days before that, today and tomorrow will unfold as they will. Nudging the journey, not directing it, has been the flow that has served so well so far. As I rolled into the early lights of the Jingmen bus station, I resolved that today would be good day, the only day that mattered.

When they saw the loaded touring bike pull up, I was immediately approached by several waiting passengers and station workers. Quickly, I brought my new best friends up to speed and they began chattering back and forth and asking the ticket agents and porters about times and luggage space, everyone was so helpful. The driver stepped off the idling Changsha bus. After hearing the plight, he expressed a "sorry, no", pointing at the bike and motioning at the coach. Clearly, he was claiming no room. He was looking at the laden mule and I wasn't making the selling point that, within moments, the bike could be broken down. I danced around charading how the bags and wheels and seat all come off, but it wasn't swaying him. More chatter ensued with the crowd and the driver, he then realized the goal wasn't Changsha, it was the visa. "Wuhan" he said. The collective solution of Wuhan circled about and emerged from the group. A teenage boy explained that the bus to Wuhan had room, "Wuhan can help, Wuhan is big." This is happening, this is bouncing, the day is flowing to Wuhan. Awesome...where's Wuhan?

Wuhan was a 250k ride east, and one of China's largest cities. Three giant population centers, Hankou, Hanyang and Wuchang melded into one metropolis at a confluence of the Yangtze, supporting over nine million people. Steel and textiles, electronics and agricultural industries; all centrally placed between Beijing and Hong Kong on a deep river that flowed straight to the ports of Shanghai. A mega city twice the size of Los Angeles, granted a 3500-year head start. I'd never heard of it, and bought a ticket. Just before departure, Biyu showed up at the station as I was taking the bike apart. She was happy the immediate problem was solved and I thanked her for her effort, and asked her to thank her friends back at the hotel. Another person who had stepped out of their lives and tried to help me out. I don't know why I worry so much.

The bus arrived in Wuhan around 11am, and on the ride over to their PSB I passed a bicycle shop. After a few hello's, I arranged for a cardboard bicycle box and told them that if the visa issue isn't solved today, I'll be back. The bike will be broken down and the whole kit and kaboodle mailed home to Patterson, I'll catch the next train to Hong Kong. With Plan B in place I felt empowered, I'll walk into that office and if the big hats don't want to do their job, they can kiss my butt, I've seen enough of their lovely country. This headstrong approach wilted a bit when I arrived at the office and of course, it wasn't open. Sign said 13:30, I knew what that meant. When it opened at 14:00, I was told the officer I needed to see wasn't in yet, "please wait here." Rather, I opted out the front door and hit up a soda vendor, then sat down on the curb. I plugged in the tunes and peacefully waited while watching Wuhan walk by. That warm sidewalk, a Coke and a smoke, a choice that gifted a beautiful stroke of fate.

All my troubles on this magical quest have been solved by luck and the graciousness of good people. Salvation rolled by on a mountain bike, the rider doing a double take at the sight of me and turning around. I sensed he was a Westerner before he opened his mouth to say "where are you from?" Jacky was a Chinese-American bloke from Seattle that had been living here for years, and owned a coffee house just down the street with his girlfriend Kat. After a quick run-down of why I was sitting on the curb, he offered that I wait at his place. He promised me the best cup of coffee I'd had in months, and off we went.

Jacky's place was a small cozy coffee bar. Downstairs, there were couches and a few tables with books spread out, and the essential hipster wall posters. Upstairs, a quiet loft to sip and read in, it was a peaceful getaway in the city center. His beautiful fiancée Kat greeted us, surprised at what her man just dragged in the door, and cheerfully began brewing as I told them how I'd routed into Wuhan. The two knew coffee and took it seriously, explaining to me the

importance of the texture and roast, the feel of the bean's oils and above all, only buying enough at a time to ensure freshness. I soon felt at home with them and knew, if it all panned out, I'd be staying a day. Born in Hong Kong and raised in Seattle, Jacky decided to follow his roots back to China where he met his love, here in her hometown. He had a sense that everything was going to work out, he knew the PSB could handle the request and offered to help in any way he could. Jacky was an anchor.

After a couple of delicious and composing cups of fresh dark, it was back to the PSB. The modern office had that customs processing appearance of thick glass and long stainless counters, spurring the confidence that I'd indeed found the right place at last. A special officer looked over the stamp filled passport and then brought in another opinion. They passed the booklet back and forth and came to an agreement. "Do you understand this privilege expires tomorrow?"

"Well officer I knew this should have been..."

"Why have you waited so long to request an extension?"

"Yeah see I was told at the Kazakhstan border that..."

"Traveling is forbidden on an expired visa Mr. Tripp, you cannot leave Wuhan. We must know your location and contact information during processing, seven days."

Huh? What's that last bit? Seven days? Seven fucking days? "No Mr. Tripp, five (fucking) days. Not including the weekend. Seven days." So, this was not simply a stamp, the passport would have to be processed for a new visa sticker. And that wasn't all. He handed me a form and a requirement sheet, then he explained I must provide proof of funds to support myself for thirty days in the form of an official bank readout. Processing required two passport photos, and proof of registration at an approved hotel that will issue an "Alien Residence Registration" form. Well, my buddy at the Jingman PSB was on the level after all, he really couldn't have done this. Looking at the list like some bad joke treasure hunt, I made the point that all of this might take some time to accomplish. I won't be able to get it all done in the next hour and a half before their office closed. "I would not wait until tomorrow Mr. Tripp."

Back at Jacky's the brain twirled. They had played ball but it was their game, one with no black and white yes or no; and seven days of waiting. Jacky was all ears, and it was so calming to have him there to bounce it all off. We sat out on the front steps with a beer and a smoke and I told him quite honestly, waiting around for seven days when I was so close to the finish line didn't seem worth it. I'd already seen vast swaths of China, more than many of its citizens may ever see. I missed my boys and Sheree so much, and had certainly reached the goal of pedaling to China; I wanted to go home more than I wanted to stay. A week's wait. If I called it a wrap, I could be walking through my front door in just a few days. I was pleased with what I'd done, but the Hong Kong niggle was still there. After listening to my little butt hurt whine for a while, Jacky laid it on the table: "You know how far you've gone and where we are, but no one in the States knows where Wuhan is at. If you don't end this ride in Hong Kong, everyone there will think you failed."

Shhhit. That was pretty much the crux of it. But what do I care what people think? No one knows what I've been through, the sights and vistas and people;

horizon-filled days for months on end. Nights filled with folks of different languages and cultures, sleeping in the dirt of nine countries and waking up in two-dollar hotel rooms. Tilting at windmills for nine thousand miles, I've ridden an old bicycle through the pages of a National Geographic magazine. They'll never know. My view of the world will never be the same, everyone else's views didn't matter. I stood up from the stoop. "I'm going for a walk."

Another smoke. This was it, the clock wasn't suffering long decisions. Ambling around a couple of city blocks, just taking in where I'm at, and everything that has happened. And more important, everything I've told myself. So many times, I envisioned riding across the bridge into Hong Kong and stopping to buy three beers. The first one is dumped back and forth all over the orange mule, god knows it deserves a drink. The second one, I'll dump all over myself and dance a giddy makeshift Irish jig in the street. I'd just sit on the curb sucking down the third bottle asking everyone who passed by "hey you wanna know how I got here?" Do not be denied that moment, it will never come again. Buck the fuck up and make this happen.

Back at Jacky's, the treasure hunt was launched. When I returned with the decision, he went online and mapped out an attack plan for a hotel, what bank to hit, where to get a passport photo; local indispensable knowledge. I took off on his slick shod mountain bike zipping through the streets. After riding the wobbly mule for so long, his modern precise agile disc brake ride felt like a powered dirt bike. Ripping through traffic against the business day clock, I had to hit up three banks before finding one that would let me use their internet, and to print out my debit and Master Charge card balances on their letterheads. Of course, I lost precious minutes having to have my passwords resent to an email. After so long away, I'd forgotten them. The photo shop fella had me in and out in minutes.

Returning to the coffee bar, Jacky's friend Luke was there with his bike, and we set off on a dashing Mad Hatter ride to check on a couple of hotel possibilities. Following Luke's lead, we took to the sidewalks putting the suspension to use hopping curbs, dodging citizens, riding up and down steps and defying intersections; jeez I gotta get me one of these. At last, an approved 100y hotel was found that knew all about the "Alien" form, and we left with a room receipt. By now, the PSB office was closed for the day. The man said "I would not wait until tomorrow Mr. Tripp." See ya in the mornin' Skipper.

That evening I met Tony, a Wuhan police officer, who was one of Jacky's best friends. They'd known each other for years and had been on some long bike tours together. Tony was very western, spoke flawless English, and he was angling his career goal toward serving on China's United Nations Police team, for deployment on worldwide peace missions. Two more friends arrived, and the five of us sat outside the coffee shop until 1:00 am drinking beer and telling stories, before I pedaled over to my digs for the night. Lying in bed in the humid early hours, the skin itched and crawled as I tried to deny that this rash was rapidly advancing. A whole week in Wuhan with a great group of people, there would be so much to see and do, but it was clear that the store ointments and talcum powder were not working. I was scratching the skin raw, I had to do something smart about it.

The next morning, good ol' Tony picked me up and we drove straight to the PSB on the visa's final day. With Tony in uniform doing the talking, and a different officer at the window, things went much friendlier. He seemed to like that the American had a local officer overseer. This must have loosened up the rules a touch, because when we were done, Tony said that I'd been ok'd to change residences. Jacky had remembered a youth hostel from his search yesterday. It was on the other side of the Yangtze, but less than half the cost of my stodgy downtown hotel. With a weeklong stay ahead, and remembering the great time at the Xi'an hostel, I was all in.

We dropped by the hotel to collect the bike and gear before Tony dropped me off for a few lazy hours of sippin' bean and discussing coffee with the local connoisseurs occasioning Jacky's shop. Later, along with Jacky and Kat, the four of us enjoyed a late lunch of fine dining back at that same hotel's well-appointed restaurant, before heading for the hostel. Having arrived from the northwest, I was now crossing the Yangtze for the first time. The longest river in all of Asia spanned at least a kilometre across, and the memorable mid-bridge view was jammed with the twilight city-scape, twinkling its shores from wing to wing.

The Wuhan Pathfinder youth hostel was set in an old long red brick factory building, and exuded a welcoming vibe. It was spacious and airy with a large lounging section, filled with comfy chairs and couches under the old factory skylights, that toned the big room just so. Imagine a hideaway art guild, it was going to be a nice place to spend the week. The front desk had the requisite local tour brochures and offers, some of them for river cruises and bus tours to the Three Gorges Dam. A light bulb came on

So, here was one more chance. I had time to kill, this is China, so the bus tours were reasonable enough; and if I was to book now there was a good chance for a seat the day after tomorrow. And then the bulb went dim. I didn't have the passport. I couldn't book a tour or leave Wuhan without it, and sure as hell wouldn't be let anywhere near their national treasure during a terrorist paranoid Olympic season without someone in a big hat asking for some ID. Circling about that night I was apprised of the final nail: there was no tour into the dam's depth, the bus and boat tours merely brought visitors to the site. Due to security concerns, no one but authorized personnel were allowed inside, eliminating the big draw of seeing the massive generators.

The hostel was a serene setting surrounded by a busy, bristling city; I could drop the guards and relax. The sensible side knew this forced down-time should be spent wisely, by combating this insane rash that had grown out the shoes and was advancing Kudzu like up the limbs and torso. It was now intolerable, and without the road to deviate the mind, the next six days would be hell. The next day, when Tony came by for a morning Starbucks run, I asked him if it was

possible to see a doctor. Oh, how things fall into place. That bag of Karma must be damn near empty.

Wouldn't you know, Tony's wife was a nurse at a large military hospital that also served the public. They lived in a flat provided to them by her work, just a stone's throw from the facility. After a quick phone call, we drove over to the huge medical center. Upon entering, it seemed like a giant train station. The warehouse style room had a bare cement floor and pillars, and was arranged in an L pattern, with windows and counters stacked deep with people. To one side was registration, the other for picking up prescriptions. Tony's wife Zhu Qin met us and walked me through the process, which started in the registration line, where she did all the talking. Then it was off to the patient's room, something of a combo doctor's office waiting room and emergency area. There must have been forty people of different cringes, crutches, and bandages lining the walls in wooden chairs, waiting their first-come-first-serve turn to see the single physician. With Zhu Qin in her nurse togs, we walked past them all and shuffled straight into the doctor's small office.

Everyone stared as if to say "who's this and what the hell." I couldn't blame them a bit, but then again, so thankful. The doctor rose from behind his worn wooden desk and greeted me in perfect English. With the door closed behind us, his little office was an island of calm amid a sea of ailing humanity. Pleasant and unhurried, he told of his delightful years spent in Southern California, while achieving his degree from UCLA. He then segued into the problem at hand. After a quick exam and a couple of questions, he scratched out a report and a prescription. We shook goodbye and shuffled back out through the stares of the waiting room, the entire visit was about five minutes.

Following Zhu Qin back to that cavernous central station zone, we joined the teeming crowds in the prescription line, and was eventually asked for some cash to cover the exam and the brown paper bag of antibiotics, calamine lotion and four vials of who knows what. The next stop was to what I'd call the Drip Room, it was filled with a hundred identical blue cushioned comfort chairs, set in a jungle thicket of IV racks. Check in at the front counter, hand over a single vial from your paper bag, the attendant nurse injects the vial into a saline bag and has you follow her to your seat. Speaking Mandarin, it appeared that she asked if I was comfortable, and if I could see one of the multiple TV screens that hung from the ceiling all around the room. The arm gets poked, the bag gets hung on a rack, and there you sit for 45 minutes as you're hydrated and medicated all at once. Aside from sitting in a room filled with people suffering from a variety of sicknesses, the system appeared quite efficient, ObaMaoCare. No individual doctor's office visits with their extra charges, treatments are centralized no matter your malady. And to beat all, the entire affair, the doctor's evaluation and prescriptions and three days of IV follow-ups ran about $62!

And so, began a week of respite. Each morning, Tony would come by and cart me off to the hospital for the drip, after a stop at Starbucks. At the hostel I met a wonderful old hippie named Butterfly hailing from the Puget Sound area who was here to finally spend time with a lovely Chinese woman he'd been flirting with online for more than a year. His un-hippie name was Rob, and the two were touring about and going on river cruises, generally having a perfect summer romance. But he was also mixing a little business in with the fun.

In simply beautiful free flowing luck, he'd bought a small patch of land on the Sound back in the 70's, only to find out his shore was a natural breeding ground for geoduck clams. When he first moved in and set up a small home, he'd never heard of "gooey ducks." Butterfly now made a very comfortable living farming and selling the mollusks, especially to the Chinese, who were paying over $100 per clam. He was a bright guy to talk to, and even let me use his Skype, only the second time I'd ever used it, the first back in Chelyabinsk, during the Rover chaos. I had my first experience of a visual phone call home, and hah, no one was there. Mom was contacted though and so was stepbrother Greg, it was amazing to see them after so long, Skype was tomorrow today.

Sunday was Autumn Moon Day, a harvest season festival. Tony's family invited me out for a day to visit a couple of temples, and then to a nice restaurant for the day's tradition of a long casual lunch. I was never able to thank him enough for his help, but one morning at Starbucks he confided that I had brought him recent good luck, in the form of the Chinese custom of 2nd milk. The accepted practice, whereby many middle-to-upper-class men enjoyed and supported a mistress, was the sign of a successful man. He laughed at the national scandal treatment of American politicians doing the same, for here it was normal. He also had a go at our version of capital punishment, that allowed convicted murderers to languish in prisons for many years, filing appeals. "You know how we do it? One bullet. We take them out to a field a few days after the trial and one bullet, it's so cheap!" I tried to explain to him that much of our country thought a few days and a bullet was a bit hasty, but he didn't see the grey area.

The days were spent for the most part relaxing at the hostel and taking in their good coffee, watching DVD movies and experiencing the limits of the Chinese internet. Through Baiku, virtually their Google, the experience seemed normal until it didn't. Trying to access any newer websites for example was not possible, one theory was that as new websites pop up, they go into a digital stack that must be vetted for content before being allowed; no matter how vile or benign they may be. The slow process screens western journalism, risqué sites, and anything critiquing their vision of Beijing politics. Censored websites included movie reviews and social or gender lifestyles. Social media and human rights websites need not apply. Since arriving in China, to update my briansride.net blog, the text was Gmailed to Cody who would then paste it to the website, which I wasn't allowed to access. Google has since bowed out, refusing to obey the censorship rules of The Great FireWall of China. Baiku, one could imagine, jumped for joy. The bed of a global economy hosts some kinky partners.

On Monday, we again arrived at the Drip room. Without seeing the doctor or having a second exam, my case had been flagged for additional treatment; and a new prescription. It added a very strong skin astringent and three more drip vials, hence three more days. When I questioned the nurses as to why, they didn't care. They had orders from the Doctor, sit down please. Suppose it couldn't hurt. Again, Tony was good enough to take time out of his days, enabling me to make use of a week that was necessary and pleasant, despite the burning skin. Still, it was a sigh of relief when he arrived Thursday morning with the news that the passport was ready. Six days after submitting the application, I checked out of the hostel and went for one final drip session. We then hit up the PSB before landing back at Jacky's coffee house, I felt like I'd just been released from jail, albeit a very cool jail.

I wanted to hit the road the next morning, but while enjoying the comings

and goings of Jacky's customers that day, it just didn't seem right to rush off. Everyone had been so good to me here, and a day of relaxed celebration was in order. At some point of the afternoon, chillin' with a coffee and a smoke, Jacky postured the idea of a new name for the coffee shop, something Western. Playing off the Robert Johnson-come-Clapton Delta blues tune "Walkin' Blues" I tossed out "Walkin' Brews" and that stuck. Jacky liked it so much he deemed it the new name from here on, just needed a new sign.

A musician friend of Jacky's named Lee, who owned a blues club, came by with a beautiful custom acoustic he had just taken delivery of, and asked us to drop by that evening. That I was deep in Red China never came to mind that day as we hung out at the coffee house, ordered out for Chinese, and made our way through the city's evening traffic commotion to the night club. We could have been in Paris, Boston or L.A, the routines and conveniences the same. Lee began by playing piano for his first set, then moved on to the new guitar for the second using two different singers along the way; rolling from blues to light rock and roaming through improvised jazz to connect it all. He was polished and deliberate, displaying a talent that came from years of being comfortable around the instruments and a small audience. Afterward, I was introduced to the table of a wealthy Wuhan man who had made his fortunes in the chemical industry. He was quite taken by the quick tale of the journey, as his radiant young date deftly translated. Her command of the language was too natural, I knew she'd had much more practice than just school studies.

Soon after returning to our table, she came over and sat down. Her businessman and his associates were busy talking shop, and she was eager to tell her story. Natalie was in her mid-twenties, and had spent five years attending university and working in New York. Taking part in an exchange program, she had arrived in the States with just her classroom English. She had managed to master the written and spoken and idioms of it, while obtaining a business degree on the fly. After one year of working in the Manhattan finance world, she missed her family and returned home.

It struck me, perhaps unfairly, that she was in essence playing 2nd milk to the old man that she claimed was a friend of her father. If so, I wondered how a girl of her bearing could play the role, and as we spoke the gut sense told me she wanted to explain; as if she had been caught doing something she shouldn't. With my clueless grasp of the layered Chinese social customs, any delve may have come off as judgmental, so I sailed the talk around it to stay positive. She was bright and outgoing and spoke fluid American slang, the two us yammered on for some time until one of the associates came over. Whatever he said, it meant "you have talked long enough, return now." Without debate she sheepishly excused herself. As she returned to the far corner, I caught the chemical man's glare of disappointment, surrounded by his little money men like a sounder of swine.

I slept horribly that night in the upstairs level of the coffee house. The a/c was off and the treatments had begun drying out the skin so much that falling asleep in the still, humid air was hopeless. The pins and needle itching, caused by the cure, was commanding all thought. I awoke at 11 am, having finally drifted off in the cool early hours, just in time for another Chinese take-out lunch. Jacky and I then spent some time checking in on a shop restoring his fifty-year-old Chang-Jiang sidecar outfit, a model of note with a lineage

spanning history. Its origins lay with a late 1930's BMW military model, before its plans were traded east during the short-lived German-Soviet Non-Aggression Pact of 1939, just after the invasion of Poland. The Russians desperately and quickly produced them en masse during the war, and they still are made today, fundamentally unchanged as the Ural. Same basic design and sidecar. After the war, the Soviets shared the plans and tooling with China, thus awarding Jacky decades later with a vintage bike closely rooted in a 1938 BMW R71 war machine; sans the Soviet artillery and Bavarian prazision qualitat. A rolling, wind-blown slice of history on a nice day.

The next stop was a thrift store for a shirt. Kat's cousin, Ocean, asked if I would donate my 2007 Little Polecat Enduro t-shirt as an Americana piece to the coffee shop's eclectic wall décor. After the sacrificial t-shirt emancipation moment in the Taklamakan, and now this wall decor donation, I was down to one. Signed it "Brian Tripp RTW 2008 San Francisco to Hong Kong-thanks Jacky and Kate." I was jazzed to see it hanging on the wall, it was a once in a lifetime moment. I imagined trying to convince my wife that, somewhere in the world, one of my old t-shirts was considered art.

My final evening in Wuhan was centered at the Cafe Brussels. Jacky's friend Dave, a happy, stocky and bearded Belgian. He established the beer hall a few years back and the place anchored a surprisingly large crowd of expats from Europe and Russia; all enjoying the themes and atmosphere of home. The excellent tenderloin dinner, washed down with a proper choice of Continental beers, made for a great night of clumsily translated jokes and embellished stories. I made some wonderful, if temporary, international friends. And all the while, imagining I was sitting at a bistro table in the middle of Flanders.

29. breaching

W e're now sitting in a Shaoguan hotel room five days later, half guilt ridden and half can't care about feeling guilt. Tony, with his wife and son Steven, picked me up from the Walkin' Brews the morning after the Cafe Brussels. We dropped by Jacky and Kat's for final goodbyes and then drove out to the city's edge. Tony made a phone call and damned if we weren't soon following a police escort with lights flashing, zooming past traffic all the way out. As we unloaded the bike, Tony's fellow officers were laughing at the caper and introducing themselves, plus wishing me well, all at the same time. Good people are everywhere. Saying goodbye to

Tony's family and Jacky and Kat was like saying goodbye to people I'd known for years, wonderful friends who were a mountain of help to me. I could never thank them enough.

Expectedly, the 20th day of August on the northern cusp of South China, was morbidly hot and humid. The legs were nonstarters, like hollow logs with no synapse, and the crawling skin was so dried out by the astringent and treatments that they flamed. In the warm wet air, intense prickling was so much worse than the ailment. Sweat was pouring off the forehead, constantly salting the eyes; after forty k's I gave up. The week off the wheels had spawned a slug who had left his legs and will in Wuhan. I found a cheap boarding room in a village, Anshanzhen I think. 60y and a forgetful meal, I just wanted to eat and get back to the room. Arriving back at the hotel two young ladies, one I recognized from the check in desk, were there wanting to pose for pics. They were very interested in the story and wanted to arrange a lunch with their friends the next day. They were so pretty and polite but I just had to apologize out... I just couldn't. The rash was all over, the spirit was sagging, the fact that faltering any day now was delaying the flight home. They were so good about it, I just wanted to go home.

The next day the empty bag pedaled on, dawdling back and forth on the question of why am I doing this? I took a white towel from the room and tied it to the bars to constantly wipe the sweat out of the eyes, meanwhile the overwhelming rational played in the background whispering "hey, this game has already been won." This improbable venture started in Northern California seven months and three weeks ago, skipped past a slew of trek ending circumstances all the way to Eastern China and I'm pooped. Traversing Xianning, just forty k's along, once again I threw in the towel upon sighting a reasonable place that had air conditioning. I berated myself with scolds of weakness, having been near this mindset before, but knowing it's okay if you can come up with one more rally. Push through the woes, buck up cowboy. Somehow, just one more time.

Holed up in the cool room feeling like mud slush, wishing the road outside would lead back to the good folks of Wuhan. An early night didn't help as the next morning dawned and I just didn't want to go. But cha' can't stay here. The thoughts rolled that, given even a pressing pace, there's still two more weeks of one town after another. Two weeks in this swelter; two weeks in this skin. These kinds of compromising thoughts were like enemies finally breaching the gate, undermining the long journey's tenet: Don't stop! Just as a remorseful junkie or boozer knows as they reached for that sweetness for just a little, just a little to get over that hump, knowing what everybody who ever believed in them will think if they ever found out... I unfolded the tattered map, and my eyes settled on Ganzhou.

Ganzhou looked to be about 370 miles south. The idea of a train lift removing a week of riding just seemed so relieving. It would leave another 300 miles to Hong Kong, just to keep some shred of integrity. Once I found myself doing the time and mileage math it felt so right, the mind was made up. The integrity question, the failing discipline, weighed heavily. I had pedaled all this way, the trains and buses to this point were easy for me to rationalize. Going with Gennadi to Donetsk. Escaping the Russian border patrol or making up for a two-week transmission caper in Chelyabinsk. Then there's the last few days before Wuhan, scrambling to beat the visa clock. Today's stumble had no outside encouragement, no rational but for the skin excuse, and that wouldn't stand as adequate to others. I'd just seen enough. No one will understand but fuck'm. I just won't tell anyone.

As I pottered through Xianning trying to suss out the train station, that moment I'd been expecting for thousands of miles arrived. Riding along the right-hand edge of a main road, a city bus approached from a side street on the right and stopped. Rather than passing in front of it, I looped behind it. As I rounded the right side of the bus, a two-up motorcycle going the wrong way on the bus's inside right, hit me. Smack! The bike whacked my front wheel and handlebar, upending me as I fell to my left. It motored on and disappeared, the throttle's song never wavering, like nothing happened. The wow of it, the surprising point, was a bicyclist being struck square by a zooming motorcycle running the wrong way and no one near was fazed, no one even looked interested. I spent a few minutes to fetch an Allen wrench and straighten the handlebars and wondered, how different would the crowd's reaction to this be had it happened in one of the desert villages? Out there, I was always surrounded by friendly and helpful people. Here, re-approaching the masses, you ain't so special.

My Western mind map had always felt that once out of Western Europe, a feeling of dropping off the Earth began. Language, communication, familiarity. The notion that no one knew where I was. Months of running the gauntlet of the unknown had turned out good, the people were very sincere, bearing their faults and their life with resilience, decency and compassion. I was now nearing the centers of finance, industry and populace. The cities that play Asia's conduits to the global business and consumer world via China's East coast, I could feel the Western Earth returning. Humanity was all along the trail, but the mule and I were coming back into the humanity that played the game hard and fast, the higher pace palpable.

Brushing off the dust I wondered if this was an omen for the train decision? Was this a wake-up call that starting now, the increased masses carried increased travel dangers? Would dropping the guard with the finish in sight allow an error that skewers the moment of victory in Hong Kong? Was the pit in my stomach portending a disaster, a spiritual punishment for riding towards a train station for no other reason than you just don't want to play anymore? Shut up. Come on. This was just a couple of assholes on a motorcycle.

It took some collective help, but it was soon clear that there was no train to Ganzhou. When I was told the only way to connect was to take the train southwest to Changsha, I almost balked; that's the wrong direction. Don't make this hard China, I'm tryin' to throw in the towel here... alright, give me a ticket. It was a four-hour ordeal, standing in a packed aisle in a packed car keeping an eye on the four panniers, hoping the bike made it to the freight car and scratching the flaming skin. Like a crowded subway car sweating and jostling for hours, it was only as good as one could make it. "Yes, I'm American...California...oh yes, I love China", ambassador mode all the way. Dreaming of the empty days in the desert. Upon arriving in Changsha, the shipping window lady broke the bad news. "Very sorry, the bike never left Xianning." What? I froze, no... not this.

This is adding to my conspiracy, fate has slapped me for a moment of weakness. I've taken the path of least resistance and Karma has taken my dear orange mule away. I played it cool and smiled on the outside, assuring my captors that I was confident they will come through for me; a ruse in a tight spot, as well as my only hope. Sitting on a bench outside the office with the four red bags and a cigarette; a freight worker in a ding-ding cart rolled by staring at my sad state. As he jumped out, he was smiling, and saying something, it seemed good. He went inside and came out with the shipping lady. "This man has seen your bicycle." Wahoo! It had made the leg after all, "the reports of my death are greatly exaggerated."

And the hits kept coming. Very sorry Mister Slacker, no tickets available tonight or tomorrow for Ganzhou. Quite honestly, it was just a dart tossed at the map. So, what's behind door number two? A ticket is open for tonight to Shaoguan, a ticket to stand in the aisle all night. Or, wait until 11 pm tomorrow night for a seat. Well then, where's Shaoguan? A map check saw Shaoguan south of Ganzhou, towards Hong Kong. It shaved off about 80 miles from the original plan, giving me a 240-mile ride to the beer shower moment, and dipping my feet into Victoria Harbor. After this detour to Changsha and no lift to Ganzhou, there was no choice to make except for one; to sit or stand? I went for the 24 hours wait. I then grabbed a nice room just outside the train station and another

hamburger at McDonalds. And besides, when will I ever get to see Changsha again?

Beginning on the major north-south waterway of the Xiang River over three thousand years ago, this city of millions was almost the size of Wuhan. Three thousand years; it's not even comprehensible.

There is no short tale that could touch upon the rises and falls and moments in history of any place that was three thousand years old, much less a metropolis. Ancient dynasties had formed and faded and rose again into its status as a major city. It had been attacked by Mongols, suffered through civil wars; fended off invading Japanese during WWII. It was the formative college town of Chairman

Mao's introduction to Communism. Today, it was the highest of prefecture level cities, a province capital.

August 23rd was an all-day wait, spent riding around the city yet never finding a moment to relax. People and traffic swarmed. In one section, a swath of brick buildings that were identical down to their doorways and windows and railings, contained block after block of streets that were dedicated to clothing, others for tools, others for large home safes and car tires. The humanity wasn't just any major downtown crowding, there was also the wheels of havoc. Try to imagine this, commute crush-hour Manhattan crowds where the auto-jammed streets had drivers giving up and then pulling up onto the sidewalk and constantly hitting the horn... we were in their way! And people, yes annoyed people; never the less gave way and closed back in behind, garnering only a "oh another one of these jerks" look on their faces. I was agog that a driver had such audacity, but more so that it was treated as a normal stunt, and we gripe about skateboarders.

How could this be normal? A car driving on a crowded sidewalk? This place had too many people, in too small an area, for too long. For example, in Western cultures at an ATM line, we give the customary two or three metres of space from the machine. Not here. Here, you learn in short time to stand on the heels of the machine's customer, or else never get your chance. People just walk up and stick their card in; clueless. China had metamorphosed from the emptiest vista imaginable short of Mars into this chaos of human concentration, all within the past few weeks. And it would only become denser as I approached Hong Kong. I began to feel lighter about the train choice, this place was nuts.

You'd a thought the Rolling Stones had hit town and had announced a surprise show by the crowd outside the Changsha Rail Terminal ticket windows later that evening. I waded in, happy to have spent the $9 the night before. Again, the bike had to be loaded. The dear sweet older woman working security at the freight window was trying to help, but the language barrier was too tall. In a feat of graceful kindness to a stranger, she calls up her daughter in Beijing. The girl on the phone spoke perfect English, with nary an accent. Between the three of us, the bike was seen to. I was so grateful to the two of them for helping me with a task so simple, yet such a struggle without their teamwork.

Waiting near the freight docks for departure, the time was spent people watching. While there are a large number of people in China that owned cars, the volumes at the country's train stations signaled that a hell of a lot of folks didn't. Coming and going lugging their life's belongings; vast numbers were energized by a mouthful of areca nut and betel leaves, spitting out the slime when needed, amid a smoker's paradise. And the habit of nose picking, at best a discreet act anywhere else, was a public art form. I'd seen it a few times throughout the western half of the country but here, among large crowds, I realized it wasn't an odd aberration. It was the norm. Putting two and two together dawned that men often had a pinky finger nail grown to over an inch. And now I knew why, it was a scoop. I can't remember seeing women dig in but the men were definitely enjoying themselves and breathin' free. C'mon, admit it, we're all just waiting for that trend.

Just as the night before, the train aisles filled up to standing room only. I took my seat and began the six-hour ride, then managed to get a little sleep as we rocked eastward through the night. The concept of packing a long-distance train as if it were the morning commuter crush from Hayward to Embarcadero harkened of the numbers, the bulk of the country's 1.4 billion lived on this eastern half. Imagine our lower forty-eight and its 300-odd million. Then double it. Then double it again. Then shove roughly 95 percent of them into everything east of Kansas. You think New Yorkers are loud and cranky now.

Shaoguan station was dark, dark like everyone had gone home dark. Before stepping off, I had to check and double check that this was the place, then I prayed with blind faith that the bike had been unloaded. There was certainly no one at the baggage office until morning; 8:00 the sign said. I hadn't slept solid enough to ride, so after walking up and down the awakening street for a bit and being hounded by two and four-wheel taxi drivers, I found a nearby hotel for 100y. After a shower it was off to the market for some bread and fruit to hole up for the day. Then, back to the station to fetch the bike, which went pretty smooth.

And so here we were, the bike and I, taking refuge in a Shaoguan hotel room. The door is locked and I haven't any curiosity to see the streets. I slept most of the day, on and off, took a couple of cool showers to calm the skin pins. It was nice and quiet and peaceful, China was clamoring and honking outside that door, don't open it.

Awoke to a blissfully overcast and cool morning, I got underway early and enjoyed the day over a lush jungle mountain road broken up by pines that turned into bamboo and sugar canes nearing Wengyuan. Once clear of the city, it was like traveling back in time a hundred years. Farmers, husband and wife, trudging behind black wide-horned oxen in their sandaled feet. An oxen's head peered out of a rain-filled roadside ditch as he hung out in his happy place, beating the heat on his downtime. The best guess was Wengyuan marked 110k's for the day but who really knows? A serious half hour afternoon rain storm was actually enjoyable for reasons beyond explanation, anything to calm the pingles I suppose. Another 60y hotel, another boiled water noodle bowl in the room, another day closer to Patterson.

The next day the swelter returned, but it's been worse. Spent nearly all day climbing on a wide white fresh cement road, rewarded by a seven k downhill near day's end heading for Xinfeng. I could almost set the watch by the 3 pm torrential half hour rain blast, taking refuge under the eaves of a well-placed roadside shop and home. The lady of the house never spoke, and paid little attention once she saw the stranger was just gaining shelter. I sat silent in a plastic chair as she gossiped with a friend while preparing the evening meals. Without looking or missing a beat, she'd reach into a short barrel. She'd twist the chicken's neck, chop off its head, then hold it upside down over a plastic bucket and drained the bird like it was a quart of oil.

Twist chop drain pluck. Repeat. As the rain passed, I pedaled away with a hankering for a pot pie dinner. Riding over the clean wet road was a slick experience but everything seemed so fresh, for a spell the lanes were all mine and sucking in the new ions, I made hay. Another good day of progress ended even better when I spied a dirt mound in the corner of a vacant field. Just dusk, the coast was clear, so I shot over and hid behind it. It was one of the few places I'd seen in east China at the end of my day where there weren't people about. The wallet enjoyed the trip's final night of stealth camping. We were getting close.

After a few k's in the morning, it was breakfast time in a small village. The bowl of jouza and chili powder from a sidewalk steamer was actually becoming an anticipated meal. Sitting on the curb, unfazed now by the passing stares, I knew I had to address a broken rear spoke. The heavy duty tandem-grade wheels that went on at Mike's house in Gulf Breeze, had finally gone from an occasional broken spoke to a common delay. I didn't mind the chore, but I knew it would attract a crowd. And it did.

After chow the panniers come off, and the bike is flipped upside down. A few people slow their walk and some stop. The rear wheel pops off and a sprocket holder wraps around the cogs, breaking the gear cluster loose. There's a noticeable interest as more folks stop to see what's the attraction. The tire's deflated and pulled off the rim, along with the tube and puncture liner. Then the camera phones begin to click. The old spoke is fished out and the new one is angled in and secured. The laughing and pointing and chattering surround me. I smile and try to explain and demonstrate as the wheel goes back on and the pumping session begins. These people, they scurry undeterred, appearing oblivious through their daily routines with no animation, difficult to read them by their faces. But when they're happy they light up. They took simple sunshine in stopping to watch

the ten-minute spoke show and then expressed, all in their own ways, a sound of good luck and a wave goodbye. These people.

I'm noticing a change in the rising and falling tones of their voices and words, the Cantonese style is growing stronger as the road continues south. I feel I'm adapting well, since I had no problem not understanding Mandarin, and now I'm having no problem not understanding Cantonese. But of course, I'm a world traveler. Today's heat wasn't so bad and the terrain put up no serious climbs, the only trouble was having to pitch another rear tire that had a chronic slow leak, those damned steel slivers still the bitch. With the journey's final fresh tire and tube mounted, I rolled past classic pagoda palaces set upon cultured properties, perhaps weekend homes for the business crowd that dwell in the megalopolis expanse that crowds up against the free world portal of Hong Kong Province.

The thoughts of another free night in the sticks faded the closer I approached Huizhou. A true big city aura was beginning, like riding into the New Jersey coast. The road traffic increased as the lanes were tightening up, and the feeling that this was a bad place to be on a bicycle welled up when I passed a city bus stop. Lying spread out on the cement bench, was a filthy and haggard looking long haired young man; without a stitch on. He looked dangerous and homeless, and he set the tone. As the urburbia intensified, I knew attempting to cross Huizhou at dusk was a bad idea. When a deteriorated boarding hovel appeared on the frontage road, I pulled in. The room was only 40y, about six bucks, but it featured a cot and a door that locked.

We were not just entering another big city, we were entering the planet's largest commerce and port zone, the confluences extrapolated. Of the top ten busiest shipping ports on earth, seven of them lay on China's east coast, and three of those now surround me. The bulk of the world's consumer goods were created in this region, then came through here. Every product and business and huckster and ambition teeming at the golden border of Hong Kong and its market gateway. I knew come morning the tourist was done and the bicycle soldier began. Pilot the wheels the final few k's and deliver this campaign through potholes, underpasses and... puddles. I fetal-ed deep in the sleeping bag on the dirty cot as the hard rain began, and ran hours into the night.

And yet, Shenzhen and its border were still a ninety-k day away. It was August 27th, and for a spell after clearing Huizhou in the morning, the rolling terrain opened up a bit and I steadfastly motored on, making good time across some small hills before the expected chaos ensued. The first volley came with rude drivers giving zero margin, and then deeper into areas of motorcycles, scooters and pedestrians who seemed to move with little peripheral awareness; poker faces never revealing acknowledgment. Approaching Shenzen there was no sense of order at the intersections. Large trucks would just swing into the oncoming lanes, damn the torpedo's, forcing lesser autos to pull aside. Truly dangerous traffic, in the journal I described the day as "humanity unchecked, with cars." Nearing the inner city, the rains returned for their afternoon appointment, and at first, the natural move was to take a time out to avoid the inherent hazards. But I was within reach of Red China's border.

The giant puddles on the narrowing busy streets couldn't be avoided, and a dowsing splash after splash was showered upon me by the passing traffic. The bath was road dirt grimy, but warm, and the inner bicycle warrior taunted "bring it on China, it's only water." At the same time, I was praying a hidden grate or chunk of road heave didn't lurk as I forged the swamped low points. At one crossing, while trying to dodge another clueless Mom and Pop who were stepping into the street, I hit the curb and slammed down, tumbling onto the sidewalk. I jumped up, soaking warm and filthy wet, laughing, crazed by the moment. For today we slay the dragon!

And more animal people! I'd passed a shat spot in the road earlier that I swear looked human, and later, sure enough I came upon a buck-naked son of a bitch squatting monkey style on the roadway taking a dump! Why? Why in the busy road you deranged bastard? Lord oh Lord this place is crazy. If the trip all the way into Hong Kong after crossing the border tomorrow is like this, then I hope like hell there's still something left in that Karma bag. It's gotta be down to stems and seeds by now.

The warm rain finally let up as the border neared. It was no problem finding a hotel just a short roll from Shenzhen's Lo Wu crossing. It wasn't cheap, my goodness, I must have paid over $23! It was only about twice the size of a walk-in coat closet, but it was clean and cool and comfortable, a grateful reward after one of the wildest cycling days in memory. The hot shower ran on til' cold that night, washing off the dregs. I tried in vain to dry the shoes out by stuffing them with newspaper. The right one, already bound sole to upper with duct tape since Wuhan, was ready to toss.

30. checkers

The Lo Wu station crossing awaited. When my eyes opened the next morning, I couldn't wait. It was August the 28th. The control point was no simple thruway, after clearing the passport checks, the building was laid out so a poor sap would have to hump a loaded bike on his shoulders up and down a series of stairs and across different levels. Yet, it was no trouble. I was filled with a sense of grand exit, of leaving the Kingdom. The gauntlet had thrown a few final hazards yesterday and the task of heaving the 90-pound mule through the multi-level maze was like climbing a victor's podium. As I stood on the sidewalk on the free side of the border, the final stone was tossed: No pedestrians or vehicles may leave the control station without a special permit, one must take the train...and bicycles are not allowed on the train. It sounded ridiculous, smacking of blind-order bureaucracy. Or, a misunderstanding. But all that can wait. Over there... I see a Starbucks.

With my hands wrapped around a slow, peaceful exhale cup of tall black, I struck up a chat with some train station workers. They clarified that due to immigration risks, the train trip was a final guard to control the gates into the Hong Kong region. We were now inside the "frontier border restricted area." I'd have to consign the bike to a cargo car but, "if you want to ride just get off at the first stop." The train ticket office took a bit over ten bucks for bike and rider to go about 7k's, and to beat all there was no cargo car. The porter just had me follow him to the final car, he opened the door and wished me a nice day. It was all worth the trouble when I exited the train at the first stop.

There was a definite bent, hints of Europe. The streets were clean and tree lined, the buildings were orderly and void of the mish mash of misspelled signs, there were no squalid storefronts or makeshift repairs filling the view. Toto, we're back in Kansas. Level, unbuckled, sidewalks. Calm and obedient traffic, morning people sat at sidewalk tables drinking tea. I was in the Sheung Shui suburb and the British had left their mark. From there it was a pleasant, yet confusing, thirty-odd k journey along their winding, beautiful bicycle path system. The path leading to Kowloon passed through canyons of skyscraping apartment buildings, built among ample parks. The day's goal was to glide across the bridge over Victoria Harbor and into Hong Kong. Twice I stopped for directions and I must have appeared as a scruffy Chatty Kathy, bubbling over at the question "how far are you going?" "Oh, not far at all! I'm here!"

But alas, despite being so close to the finish line, I just couldn't stand the horrid clacket the chain and sprockets were making. The splashy warm deluge of yesterday had washed them clean of any lubricants and, initially, who cared? Hong Kong was almost in view, and it ain't like the chain's gonna break. But soon, it felt like mistreatment, and I had to act. Spool down excitable boy, take a few minutes and make this right. With the bike inverted, I was carefully drip-drip-dripping the tiny oil bottle on each link. A couple of folks on bikes stopped to talk.

K.S and Aubrey lived in Kowloon, they were avid cyclist and wide-eyed at the story. They were kind enough to let me use their phone, and their dialing help, to call Serini's Dutch friend Letty, who lived in Hong Kong...but no answer. No problem, I also had the contact number of Avis, a good friend of Demetri's from the Chelyabinsk adventure. But again, no one home. As the phone rang and rang, the two of them could clearly see the need. My plan was to reach the City and post up for a day, to ship the bike home and then catch a flight. "You're welcome to stay at our place."

The mind raced. I was on a mission. That mission was to fulfill those months of the three-beer bottle daydream. The dowsing of the mule, the jig in the street...the vision required the ceremony to take place on the streets of Hong Kong Island, not three miles away in Kowloon. And yet once again, I'd met compassionate people who were offering to take a stranger in to their home and meet their kids and then assist me with the task of shipping the bike. And then K.S. added "and I have to go into Hong Kong tomorrow for an insurance seminar, you'll have plenty of time to see the center".

That pushed me over the hump, the good fortune of meeting them, and honoring their goodwill, was so much bigger than a planned foolish moment. The Bicycle Ride, Briansride, dear readers; ended at that moment. A squeeze bottle of chain oil in one hand, a rag in the other; wheels in the air and the sunshine of the greatest accomplishment of my life beaming on my face. It didn't feel like the checkered flag, but it was. Over.

Their Kowloon home was a small five story apartment building. Theirs encompassed two floors and a rooftop storage area, one floor was the kitchen and dining rooms, the other floor contained the family and bedrooms. Their two sons Raymond and Simon, and daughter Grace, welcomed me and proudly showed off their home as Aubrey made supper. Bicycles and guitars, horns and a keyboard, a nice stereo system. The family appeared very talented and active, they had a happy rapport and all spoke wonderful English. Sitting with them around the dinner table, telling the tale and hearing about their lives and their schools and their own bike adventures, made me so glad I accepted their hospitality. It turned out that the route I was heading for to cross onto the Island was a tunnel, the other way was a bridge, just to the east of Kowloon. They both required that a bike to transported across, by rail or bus. Oh, and I had to stop calling it Hong Kong Province. They informed me that it was an autonomous Special Administrative Region of China. China had provinces, Hong Kong was an SAR. I'm still calling it a province, it sounds better.

The kids set me up on the home computer to email Cody, so that he could contact Tyler, an old friend from work. I had been on inactive leave status for so long I was no longer eligible for space available airline flights, I'd actually lost three months company seniority. Tyler had to issue me one of his buddy-passes  for the flight home. The best part of the session was when it came to updating the blog. I finally had the chance to tell all those at home: "Bang a gong! I'm in Hong Kong!"

Later that night K.S. took me up to the rooftop. He had been a bicycle dealer for a while and had just what I needed, a pile of empty bicycle boxes. We went to work breaking down the mule and condensing the bags and their contents into two packages, spare the few items I'd be needing. It would all be mailed off tomorrow afternoon. A couple of tire and tube sets were left over, a gift to my gracious host.

In the morning I jumped on the back of his scooter and we zipped over the motorway bridge into the city, onto Hong Kong Island. For several hours, as K.S. attended the seminar, I speed-wandered the busy shopping and commercial area of Wan Chai, our meeting place set for the Golden Bauhinia Square. Centered by a giant gold Bauhinia, a flower native to Hong Kong, it stood outside the Hong Kong Exhibition Centre; where Britain handed over Hong Kong to China, in 1997.

Despite meandering about the downtown in one of the world's most commercial districts, I didn't buy a thing. I wasn't there for that. I was there to feel it, to see it. Not long before my host picked me up, I walked down a cement stairway that disappeared into the vast waters of Victoria Harbor. The shoes and socks came off, and I sat there for a few minutes. The gentle waves splashed at my shorts, the submerged feet felt good. The thought that these waters eventually connect to San Francisco Bay really did occur. I was on the Pacific. I had crossed the finish. I could go home now.

360.   Epilogue

Clank...Slam...Ding...oowwwhee... A five-year-old child's earliest memories recall the parent's strict warning of to not go near big sister's bike "without one of us." Alone in the backyard at our house on Cullen street, in L.A.'s Whittier, where we lived before moving up to Carson City, I was tired of waiting.

Starting at the top of the driveway, that led to the setback detached garage, I pushed the two-wheeler up to speed. After several tumbling goofs, I managed to swing a short leg over and leapt on the seat, then curved to the right and into the backyard. White knuckles, wide eyed, feet dangling out, my first sensations of balance could only end smashing into the cinder block wall we shared with the Ruffalos next door. Time and again that day, the bike was pushed back across the yard and up the driveway for another try. Soon my PF Flyers caught the pedals, and discovered acceleration, the wall only hurt more. Then, slamming them back caused braking, easing them back brought control. By day's end, I could leap, pedal, brake, and steer the bike around the swing set and tree; then back up the driveway. As much as a scatter-brained child's gut could grasp an emotion, my belly knew that life forward would forever chase this sensation.

A childhood spent crayoning motorcycle pictures out of magazines, absorbing their stories of the racing world, heroes. Didn't care for the sports world, spare schoolyard football; that world was Joe Namath and Wilt Chamberlain, didn't feel it. Dick Mann and Gary Nixon, Evel Knievel and Then Came Bronson, I was one of them. My bicycle an imaginary Sportster, before moving on to an orange Sears mini bike, after moving to Nevada at the end of the fifth grade. Dear Dad, even when he was around, didn't have a mechanical mind, and early on it was clear; fixing a broken bike was the only way to ride again, and riding was the elusive dragon's tail. Compelled to chase that moment, the all-in of a fast turn, the airborne seconds, the downhill rush; or just being able to go. Independence. Two wheels defined my life.

Riding and maintaining them led to adventure, and the confidence in the pivotal post high school era to choose the next step, of becoming a jet mechanic with the Air Force; and its associated enduring illumination of experiencing

335

Europe. There, I met my wife; and in turn, the blessing of our two boys. Then, onto a good day job, working on passenger planes, and weekends filled with engines and spokes. And it all began with my sister's red bicycle, and a solid cinder block wall. I had now ridden a bicycle across the world from California to Hong Kong, my grandest adventure, my greatest enlightenment, and an accomplishment that made me whole.

It has been ten years since the journey ended; ever collating the journal and writing it all down. At times it was an obsession, other times a hobby. Other times, like moments in the odyssey itself, it didn't seem important. But I just kept coming back to the obligation that, this was crazy, and someone had to hear it.

As time passed by, the world kept changing. Notable to most of course, was in Ukraine, when the burgeoning Euro-leaning movement prompted Russia to annex the Crimea region and invade Eastern Ukraine in 2014, Gennadi's hometown of Donets'k becoming the center of the war zone. I managed to contact him at one point. Antony and Natasha had moved to his parents flat in Kiev, he stayed on to protect his home and business. Many of the small towns I had passed through in that area have since had their names changed; and in the layered grey convulsion of loyalties and Moscow chess moves, the act is labeled "de-communism." The regions administrative status is still murky as of 2018. G man told me not to worry, I expected that.

Less covered is the vicious crackdown on the Uyghur people of Xinjiang Province, in Western China. In mid-2009, a riot occurred between Han and Uyghur workers in a sweatshop toy factory in Shaoguan. Ironically, that's the city where I departed the train and began my final push towards Hong Kong. At least two Uyghurs died, a hundred more injured. Four thousand kilometres away, in the dominant Uyghur populated Xinjiang Province, peaceful protests over their deaths turned deadly, as thousands of Uyghur and Hans rioted for days. The crackdown by Beijing has been draconian. Dozens of Uyghur death sentences, hundreds of arrests and expulsions. Internment, or "re-education" camps have been established, with Amnesty International reporting over one million Muslims confined and forced to vow loyalty to President Xi Jinping. The border I crossed at Tacheng, was closed to all in 2009. China's response? What camps?

Since the story ended, my step brother Greg passed. Sheree's brother Glenn, who was so much help while I was away, suffered an untimely death at the age of fifty. Months later, on the day after Christmas in 2017, her dear mother Pam left us. The precious home on Woodland Park, in the little English village of Girton, sold away; ending an era for all of us. Life is so temporal, good memories of laughs and smiles, is all we leave behind.

But hey, look up! Jacky and Katt of Wuhan had a beautiful little boy together, and Jacky came to visit us a few years back. He was here on business and dropped by for a few fun days. I had a chance to show him around my world. I met up with Semey's Aleek and his daughter Diana for an afternoon in San

Francisco, just a couple of years ago. So many important and pivotal people had an effect on the trek, but our lives only touched for a moment. Maybe someday, this book will connect us, somehow.

The day after dipping my feet in Victoria Harbor, I caught a bus just outside of K.S. and Aubrey's place. It zipped me across three islands to Hong Kong International. I'll never forget asking to be signed up for a business class seat at my airline's counter. The smiling, chirpy agent typed in all of my info, and then handed me a ticket for economy. When I tried to correct the ticket, she said the reason I couldn't fly first or business was due to the policy of requiring space available passengers to wear leather shoes.

"But Ma'am, these are leather shoes" looking down on my tattered and taped mountain bike clogs.

"I know, but they look awful." She was right, but hey, it's a thirteen-hour flight.

"Ma'am, these are the only shoes I have."

"You're not getting upgraded, I'm sorry."

Time to impress her. Time to pull out the big gun. Stand back.

"Ma'am, you have no idea how I got here. I didn't fly in, I rode a bicycle here from San Francisco, it's taken me eight months."

"That doesn't matter to me sir, you're not getting into first or business with those shoes." Yeah. Welcome back to the machine.

In all, and in time, I came to understand it as my life's pivotal journey. A mid-life crisis, the idea sounds so foreign. A weakness, an excuse. A guy just wants to stop playing the same game. He really does want a red Corvette, a twenty-five-year-old girlfriend; but hopes to stay in good with the kids. That's all. He's not having a mid-life. Other, weaker men have those.

Everyone is different, and I thought I was too. I didn't want the car, although my sister suggested that. I didn't want the girl, no one suggested that; but I wanted out of the game. I couldn't stay plugged in and keep going, the hamster wheel routine, the stress of holding my personal life together. I needed a bicycle ride.

And in my case, it worked. Ever since it ended, everything remained the same, but it became completely easier. My job? I really don't care anymore what the corporation says or does, I just dig working on the planes, and enjoy my friends and workmates. Anything above my position isn't worth fretting; that's all truly out of my hands.

Above all, the priceless re-born comprehension of the blessings of home. Long before the trip ended, the yearning to just see them, to just sit with them again, drove me on. To once again feel, and not just say, life is truly about them, not me. A luck of the draw, that I had almost thrown away. I'm a happier person deep inside. The prey had been caught, the demons released, I made it.

The Code picked me up at SFO. We had time to kill before Sheree came home so I had him stop in at a pizza joint, it tasted so amazing after so long. Pulling into our driveway was the sobering moment, with the thought that the greatest thing I'll ever do, and my entire past life, was now behind me. A one-shot pilgrimage to visit our fellow travelers in space, fellow residents on this tiny rock, I needed to meet them.

A hot shower, a change of clothes, and time to just lay on my own couch; and think. A short while later the car pulled up. The driver door clapped closed, and the front knob creaked. My dear Sheree, walked through the door.

THAT'S ALL FOLKS !

27695665R00193

Made in the USA
San Bernardino, CA
02 March 2019